PROPERTY C
TRENTON PUBLIC S

D1014541

UNIVERSITY OF
AGRICULTURE

HIGH SCHOOL
JOURNALISM

HIGH SCHOOL
JOURNALISM

Third Revised Edition

HAROLD SPEARS

Superintendent of
Public Schools
San Francisco

THE MACMILLAN COMPANY, New York

© THE MACMILLAN COMPANY 1964

All rights reserved

Previous editions by Harold Spears and C. H. Lawshe
Copyright © by The Macmillan Company 1939, 1949, 1956

3 H

All rights reserved. No part of this book may be reproduced or utilized in any form or by any means, electronic or mechanical, including photocopying, recording or by any information storage and retrieval system, without permission in writing from the Publisher.

The Macmillan Company, New York
Collier-Macmillan Canada, Ltd., Toronto, Ontario

PRINTED IN THE UNITED STATES OF AMERICA

CONTENTS

v

PART ONE

THE FUNDAMENTALS OF NEWSWRITING

"Were it left to me to decide
whether we should have a
government without newspapers, or
newspapers without a government,
I should not hesitate
a moment to prefer the latter."
—THOMAS JEFFERSON

THE CHALLENGE OF JOURNALISM

Reporting is one of the most exciting of all forms of written composition. It throws the reporter into the center of civic affairs, chases him after the news that may or may not be, and slows him down to determine the significance of the latest scientific development.

He cannot retreat to his study, for his creation is not from his imagination but from the lives of others—their daily affairs, interests, plans, conflicts, successes.

The great fascination and value of journalism reflect its exacting nature and its demand for keen observation. Writing stories that are good enough to print, selling advertising that brings returns to the merchant as well as to the paper, and coordinating staff effort to get the paper out on time—these are the drives that make school publications so stimulating and rewarding to both student and school.

Like the city daily, the school newspaper must balance good reporting with good editing. It too carries the obligation of accuracy, reliability, and good taste. For both the reporter and the editor, student journalism presents an advantage over the daily press. They live in, and experience firsthand, the entire field of coverage—the school.

There'll be ads to sell and copy to read and subscriptions to get and proofreading to do and papers to circulate. Somebody will draw the cartoons and somebody will plan the make-up and somebody will take the photographs. But the heart of every newspaper is its writing.

Newswriting has its peculiarities. The student who can write a good composition is not necessarily ready to write a news story—for the news story is upside-down. In the composition the climax is usually found somewhere between the middle and the end of the account. In a news story the important facts are told in a short first paragraph, and the details are dropped in later, the most trivial appearing last.

Journalism has its peculiar terminology. It is the language of editors, reporters, and printers. For instance, do you know—

Where the staff keeps the *grapevine*?
That you can't *editorialize* in a news story?
What a *by-line* is?
Why many newspapers use *column* rules?
When a story meets the *cutoff test*?
That many newspapers have *ears,* and that they often box them?
That most newspapers use the *down style*?
What *families of type* appear in your school paper?
Who has the responsibility for *killing* stories?
That pages two and three of the four-page paper are usually *put to bed* before pages one and four?
Which comes first—*proofreading or copyreading*?
What's above the *fold* of the front page?
A *sig-cut* when you see it?
Why a *morgue* is a necessary part of any live newspaper office?
That every newspaper has a *flag,* but that it doesn't wave?

As you read this book and work on your school newspaper, you will pick up the vocabulary of journalists and use it to help you in the work of reporting and editing. (A glossary of such terms may be found at the back of the book.) Example 1 is a story picked at random from a high school newspaper. Notice the terms, listed at the side of the story, that label the parts and the characteristics of the account.

Yes, there's a lot to learn, but there's fun ahead, too. The chapters of this book will guide your learning about the many types of stories that appear in print and assist you in writing them and in publishing them. The fun is in the doing, and journalism is a "doing" course.

Summer Bicycler Relates Adventures

By ANDREA GORDON

← A *one-deck head*

← The *by-line*

← The *lead*

EXAMPLE

1

Spending a summer on a bicycle doesn't sound like fun at first, but many teenagers throughout the country have discovered that "American Youth Hosteling" isn't all hard bicycling.

Hosteling is an international movement which enables people, especially youths, to tour the countryside by bike or foot. It was started in this country more than a century ago and is quickly growing in popularity.

In the United States it is under the sponsorship of the nonprofit-making American Youth Hostels.

> Information about all American Youth Hostel trips may be obtained by writing to that organization at 14 West 8 St., New York 11, New York.

← A *box*

Covered Entire Country

← A *subhead*

The Transcontinental Trip that I took this summer was aptly named. By bike and train, I confess, we traveled through the whole country.

After a short orientation period in the Pennsylvania Dutch area, we headed west. We were a closely knit group and had as our leader a fascinating Norwegian exchange student.

The most beautiful scenes of our adventures were the Grand Teton and Yellowstone National Parks. Our week in San Francisco was spent on the cable cars. We saw Golden Gate Park and some of the highest hills in the country. No bikes here!

The Te-Hi News
Teaneck High School
Teaneck, New Jersey

4

THE EMERGENCE OF THE NEWSPAPER

Although printing was invented before the middle of the fifteenth century, newspapers did not come into existence for almost two centuries, for governments were aware of the threat of the printed word and closely controlled it. Furthermore few people could read.

The long wait for newspapers was bridged by two forerunners, the newsbook and the newsletter. The newsbook, appearing first in Germany, was the account of an event, issued by governmental instigation or clearance. The defeat of the Spanish Armada, published by Queen Elizabeth's staff, was covered in an early English newsbook. Newsletters were numerous in Europe in the seventeenth century. Bankers, for instance, depending upon international news, were avid consumers.

First English newspaper. In September 1621, the first English newspaper bearing a true London imprint came from the press. It was the *Corante or Newes from Italy, Germany, Hungarie, Spaine, and France.* These early news sheets specialized in subjects from abroad and avoided comment on local public affairs, which might antagonize the government. This era inaugurates a long period of interplay between publisher and government to determine the rights of the press.

Interest in public affairs is not easily controlled, and as time passed, editorial comment became the business of more and more papers; for instance, Daniel Defoe's *Review* and *Mercurius Politicus,* Jonathan Swift's *Examiner,* Richard Steele's *Tatler,* and the *Spectator* of Steele and Addison. Defoe, in fact, spent a year in jail for his printed comments on religious tolerance. John Wilkes was expelled from the House of Commons for his paper's remarks about the king. John Milton, in protesting Parliament's suppression of editorial opinion, wrote in 1643: "Give me the freedom to know, to utter, and to argue freely, according to conscience, above all liberties."

The first American attempt. On September 25, 1690, America's first newspaper, the four-page, six by nine inch, *Publick Occurrences Both Foreign and Domestick,* appeared. The publisher, Benjamin Harris, was an escapee from censorship in England, but his venture in public information was suppressed less than a week after the circulation of the first and only issue of the paper. The charges included printing without authority, publishing gossip about the King of

5

France, and criticizing the government's handling of the French and Indian war.

The Boston News-Letter. The first effective American newspaper was the famous Boston *News-Letter,* a single sheet, printed on both sides, which made its appearance on April 24, 1704, to be published for seventy-two years. Its publisher, John Campbell, was the Boston postmaster, a position which gave him full access to the news (in that day of unsealed mail) and the means of delivering it. Even so the newspaper was not a great success.

The Boston *News-Letter* was joined by two more newspapers in 1719—*The American Weekly Mercury* and the Boston *Gazette* (which combined with The New-England *Weekly Journal* in 1741).

In 1721 Benjamin Franklin's brother James first published the New England *Courant.* His weekly was the first to bring human interest and personal items to American journalism, and to establish criticism of public affairs as a newspaper's business. It was this paper to which Benjamin Franklin made his first editorial contributions. James was imprisoned for his criticism of the colonial government, and Benjamin, at the age of sixteen, assumed the publishing duties in his absence. In 1726 the *Courant* ceased publication, but in 1729 Franklin began his association with the Pennsylvania *Gazette,* which he developed into one of the most influential colonial newspapers.

Significance of early journalism. Perhaps the most famous name in the history of journalism is that of John Peter Zenger, editor of the New York ·*Weekly Journal,* a newspaper at odds with royal authority. Zenger, brought to trial in the first famous case testing libel and the freedom of the press, was acquitted of the charge of seditious libel in 1734—a milestone in American freedom of the press.

The newspaper is intertwined with the threads of American history. Consider the significant role in the progress of the nation played by James Gordon Bennett's New York *Herald* (1835), Horace Greeley's New York *Tribune* (1841), and the New York *Times* (1851).

Two hundred years ago Thomas Jefferson said, "Were it left to me to decide whether we should have a government without newspapers, or newspapers without government, I should not hesitate to' prefer the latter."

6

EARLY SCHOOL PAPERS

School journalism before 1900 is a spotted account with little significance other than the birth of the school publication. The few school publications were a combination of literary effort, news, and historical record; the impulse behind them was the literary essay. In short time the account of the athletic contest, the notice of the school society, the personal.item, and the various other copy now accepted as the school paper followed. This expansion was natural, for any student publication must respond to reader interest. Thus, the principle was established that *where there is a student body there is need for a news organ.*

By 1920 the literary essay had given way to the feature story. Poetry abdicated its position to the column; the news story suggested interpretation, and the editorial entered the paper. The growing enthusiasm of student editors called for larger sheets; in turn, formal notices of local business houses were added as a means of support. And the movement as well as the papers grew.

Nor was this all; four distinct types of publications emerged: (1) the newspaper, (2) the annual, now called the yearbook, (3) the magazine, and (4) the handbook. Their major functions are to cover the news, to record the history of a class or of the school, to act as a literary outlet, and to supply ready information about the school. Because of financial limitations, few schools, however, support all four publications.

By 1920, the time was ripe. Fully half of the school papers that are published today began between 1920 and 1940.

THE STUDENT PRESS TODAY

Today high school journalism is big business, financially as well as educationally. The enormous financial investment by advertisers, students, and school districts reflects the extent of the undertaking. One of the national press associations, Quill and Scroll, reports that virtually all of the high schools in the country support school newspapers.

The growth in number of publications has been phenomenal, but just as significant has been the advancement in professional standards. This advancement may be attributed to the leadership of national school press associations, the publication of good journalism texts, and the inclusion of journalism courses in the high school. The advancement continues today. Student journalism is never stationary; it is always responding to student ingenuity and changing times, and the present period is an exceptionally active one, with significant trends.

A modern high school does not exist in a vacuum. Its life and its program are geared into the local community and into the national and international scene. And the school newspaper reflects the student's awareness of the world about him. Note the following examples from high school newspapers (See Example 2).

The school paper's sphere of news coverage today is noticeably broader than a decade ago. Today's student editors are not willing to limit their news beats to school affairs alone. This indicates reader interest and demand, for in the beginning and in the end *news is what people want to read*. The paper that does not keep pace with the enthusiasms of its student body deserves its fate—extinction. By meeting this challenge of breadth and depth of coverage, today's student newspaper holds a significant place in the student's life. Newspapers in schools all over the country carry as part of their expanded coverage stories on curriculum changes, foreign travel, local, national, and foreign affairs, the future of the student after graduation—his life as a student and as a citizen.

The editorial column has become the platform of the significant issues of the day—in the school itself and in the community, state, and nation. Today's student editors are thinking more profoundly in both the selection and treatment of topics. The prosaic, "preachy" topic—such as school spirit—enjoys fewer and fewer column inches. The columnists, too, are shifting their attention from the trivial to the more serious.

But who is to say what the content of the school paper should be? To what extent should it be limited to the school itself, and to what extent should it draw upon the out-of-school world? These are matters to be decided by the school. The local staff, with the leadership of the faculty adviser and the administration, develops the paper's policy. Truly *a school newspaper is a matter of time and place*.

8

EXAMPLE 2

Sharon Reports From Moscow

By SHARON ROBINSON

MOSCOW, USSR — Red Square, the yellow buildings of the Kremlin enclosed by a high, red wall, and the glistening, gold, onion domed cathedrals — symbols of Moscow — have become a reality for me for 10 days.

The Kremlin Described

The Kremlin, the seat of the Supreme Soviet, the Council of Ministers, and the Congresses of the Communist Party, also contains the cathedrals and palaces of the czars. At the side of

The presence of an American in the village soon became common knowledge. One day, walking in the village square, I found the local youngsters playing soccer. When I kicked their stray ball back to them, I was shocked to hear the unanimous response:
"Tonk yooo!"
In perfect form, I replied, "Il n'y a pas de quoi."

HERE'S HOW—Foreign student Margaret Green learns about IHS from hosts Charla and Ken Greenman.

EMERALD ISLE COLLEEN

Meet Foreign Exchange Student

By Gail Hayes

...aces this year's Foreign Exchange of Belfast, Ireland, to the Student classes are easy, but in Ireland

Material things are all so "magnified," she said. People are the same where ever you

Postmark: Europe

Many Scienceites spent the past summer touring different parts of the world. Two of these write of the European scene.

Far from the Champs-Élysées, the home of the 50-cent Coca-Cola, I spent six weeks in Touraine, the area the French have named the "Garden of France." There, from a big manor in a little village, I toured the country of Rabelais, Balzac, and Vigny.

To the average French student at Science the phrase "châteaux

London.
Just seven and one-half weeks ago we landed here to begin a

Touraine.

Language Dept. Adds New Russian Course

By Martin Zatz

Into the language of the Czars, into the realm of set theory, into the secrets of the "perceptoscope," was written by Dr. Irving A. Dodes, chairman of the Mathematics Department.

Creative Writing & Humanities Courses Offered For Students

Shoreline has added two seventh period classes; Creative Writing and the Humanities, to give the students the best possible background for college and to add variety to Shoreline's curriculum.
The Creative Writing class is open to any students interested

Honor Society Stiffens Entrance Requirements

A new, tougher set of Arista entrance requirements and a new

Team Teaching Begins at SHS

Team teaching, one of the newest and most valued educational trends, is being tried out at Shoreline.

Advanced Curriculum Opens Four Classes

Southwest, one of the South's largest comprehensive high schools, offers its students an outstanding selection of courses in many fields.

High Schoolers to Profit From Foundation Courses

A summer science training program is offered by the National Science Foundation and is designed to provide the superior high school student with educational experiences in science and mathematics beyond that normally available in high school courses.

UN Educators Visit Sc...

Iceland and Ec... Bronx. nations of 10 e... the wor... September The ... week S...

Language ... **Grade E** working un... Mr. Fred C... son, Mr. Le... Keyes.
Two clas... one large...

H. S. Senior Goes

Agui Here from ...

With the arrival of Agui P... and the departure of T.H.S. seni... Teaneck High School for the fir... both aspects of the American Fi... gram.

Do You Have Mental Heal... It Depends upon Many Thing...

By DIANE HAMPSON

Do you tackle responsibilities and do the best you can? Are ...

things, lack of faith in oneself, lack of outside interests, fits of temper, avoidance of people, and ...

trying to find out whether people can be saved from developing schizophrenia by protecting ... n from harmful experiences childhood.

Another type of mental ill..., neurosis (or psychoneuro... is that which interferes n a person's happiness and

Fifth Model UN Assembly Meets In Bethlehem YWCA

The Fifth Annual Model United Nations Assembly met on October 24 in the new YWCA Youth Center. Students from all area schools were present.
The purpose of this model U.N. was to acquaint high school students with the workings of the real United Na...

Auditorium Decor...

The auditorium ...ated with large fl... by the Internation... Machines Corp. St... supplied by the B... Lumber Co.
All resolutions ...

APPROACH TO SCIENCE

Willy Ley Interviewed

MICHAEL ZURAWIN

"I was surprised that the Russians didn't launch ...

African Exchange Student Visits Clinton; Gets First-Hand View of U.S. Education

During the recent session of the U.N. General Assembly, ambassadors and diplomats from all over the world worked toward one goal: an enduring peace among nations.

André Carl Minnaar, an eighteen year old exchange student from Pretoria, South Africa, is

be an interesting experience to see not one, but two American high schools in action.

Thus, a few days later, André found himself the guest of Arthur Haymes, Arista president. He ob-

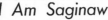

I Am Saginaw

I am a city. My name is Saginaw. If you live within the area of my influence, you are one of my people.

I am Opportunity. I escort people down the roads of success. I strengthen men's power and help them seek their goals.

I am Progress. I develop fine educational and cultural programs. My factories teem with action and split the air with noise. I strive for power an...

Japanese Guest—

Foreign Principal Visits Here

—Compares Schools

PURPOSES OF STUDENT JOURNALISM

While the student in a typical English class writes his story for an audience of one—the teacher—the student reporter writes his story for all the students and faculty. The quality of his effort is public knowledge, and the public responsibility he carries is greater than if he were meeting only a personal class assignment.

Although some of you who work on school newspapers will enter journalism as a profession, high school journalism is not usually taught with the idea of making newspapermen and women out of those who come in contact with it. Nonetheless, the journalism course and the school newspaper provide important objectives for you, the student reporter. The study and the application of journalism will train you:

1. To practice clear, concise, and accurate written expression.
2. To apply your skills in composition to functional purposes.
3. To organize your thinking.
4. To distinguish fact from propaganda, truth from hearsay.
5. To exercise initiative, ingenuity, and good judgment.
6. To increase your poise, tact, and self-confidence.
7. To utilize your talent through a worthy outlet.
8. To develop an understanding of the true significance of journalism and a free press.
9. To explore journalism as a possible career.

Student publications pay dividends to the school as well. Such benefits may be summarized as follows:

1. To educate the community in the work of the school.
2. To publish school news.
3. To create and express school opinion.
4. To capitalize the achievements of the school.
5. To act as a means of unifying the school.
6. To express the idealism and reflect the spirit of the school.
7. To encourage and stimulate worthwhile activities.
8. To aid in developing right standards of conduct.
9. To promote understanding of other schools.
10. To provide an outlet for student suggestions for the betterment of the school.

11. To develop better interschool relationships.
12. To increase school spirit.
13. To promote cooperation between parents and school.

The editorial purposes of one student newspaper are set forth in Example 3. They illustrate the determination of student editors in student newspapers throughout the nation to work for the benefit of their schools, their communities, and their country.

PRIDE IN ACHIEVEMENT . . .

EXAMPLE

3

Pride in achievement is a tangible quality which can be seen and felt by anyone who puts forth his best efforts in whatever area he is most likely to make the worthiest contribution—the dedication of himself to his work.

This feeling of personal warmth for a job well done is a reward whatever the outcome of a specific mission. Pride belongs to those who have done their best, though the end result be victory or defeat, preservation or destruction, in the red or in the black.

The athlete who contributes his most useful talents and strength to his team feels this pride—this satisfaction of having given his best. In the bleachers, the fan who has cheered the team throughout the sports season and has given his wholehearted support also knows this pride in achievement.

Outstanding ability is not a necessary requirement for those who would feel this personal pride. The end accomplishment is more important than the special talents needed to perform a task. The average student who does his best work can be as proud of the final results as the excellent student whose grades may be higher. Determination to do a thing the best way you know how and sticking to it until it is done are the only requirements needed to feel proud.

The boy who dedicates himself to turning out a fine piece of woodwork in his shop class earns this self-esteem. His sister who devotes her efforts to baking pies in her home economics class can also feel pride in achievement.

Such satisfaction comes with a devotion to helping others, adhering to good grooming habits, striving for top mental and physical health, active participation in clubs and organizations, accomplishments in athletic and academic areas. Homes, schools, churches, and sports arenas are places where pride in achievement can be born in each person who wants to do and enjoys doing a good job.

Why should a school publication emphasize pride in achievement? Because on these same pages you read the stories of those who have cause to feel such pride, because the school itself provides an impetus for this satisfaction which comes from giving time, effort, and energy to worthwhile work.

Too often reports of delinquency place juveniles in a bad light. We of the *Cardinal* editorial board feel that the student body and the general public must be better informed about the good which teenagers do. An emphasis placed upon pride in achievement should challenge today's teenager to accomplish even better things.

The following is how we plan to make pride in achievement and school spirit synonymous. Will you do your part?

STATEMENT OF *CARDINAL* POLICY

The proposed campaign of this year's newspaper is to develop and enhance "Pride in Achievement."

We shall endeavor to accomplish this by:

1. Whenever possible, publicizing people and projects on all grade levels and in all subject areas.
2. Promoting P.A. announcements of existing projects—displays, exhibits, etc.
3. Promoting more display areas in the building.
4. Intensifying reports on club activities—using as many names as possible.
5. Publicizing individual accomplishments in all areas (wood shop, athletics, music, academics, metal).
6. Providing information and suggesting a wider range of intramural sports.
7. Developing student-teacher rapport through information.

The Cardinal
Kenmore High School
Akron, Ohio

THE ELEMENTS OF A NEWSPAPER

What goes into a newspaper? Part of it is the art, photographs and drawings, and the advertising. The great bulk is stories or written matter of various kinds. This copy may be classified in the following ways:

The news story. This is the pillar of the paper, the account of something that has happened or is about to happen. The front page is full of news stories, and they are found throughout the paper. To inform the people of the news is the basic purpose of a newspaper.

There are various types of news stories, such as the report of an election, the report of a speech, the interview with an important person, or the sports account.

The editorial. This is the editor's opinion of something important in the news. The account of the event is found elsewhere in the paper. Editorial opinion may also be expressed in by-lined columns written by the paper's regular columnists. Such columns express the opinion of the person writing the column rather than that of the newspaper— although the two may be the same.

The readers' opinions appear in the form of letters to the editor— letters written to the paper by its readers on subjects about which they feel strongly.

Features. There are many entertaining, educational, informational, and other interesting items carried in a newspaper that are not actual news or interpretation of it. For example, the daily paper carries bridge lessons, schedules of television and radio programs, weather reports, fashion news, contests, horoscopes, crossword puzzles, and other such copy.

Feature stories. The feature story is a story rather than a feature, but it is not a straight news story. It is the reporter's treatment of a news item or a fragment of an event in a personal manner. He may emphasize something humorous or something sad. He may play upon one element of a news event and pass by the others.

Columns. The column has raised itself above the feature field as a distinctive element of a newspaper. It is the most personal of writing, for the reporter conducts his own column, carrying his name, from day to day or from week to week along a particular line—sports, news, fashion, and many more.

Reviews. The reviewing of stage and television plays, motion pictures, musical events, books, and records is a cross between news and feature, editorial and column. The account represents the judgment of the writer, who should have a substantial knowledge of the subject.

The distinctions found among types of writing in a paper demand study and practice by the beginning reporter. The study will be provided by the chapters that follow in this book, as will suggestions for practice. But the actual practice, your apprenticeship as a school reporter, must find its place in the classroom and the newsroom, where student reporters work at their trade.

THE CANONS OF JOURNALISM

Every profession has developed a code of ethics that stands as a guide for its members. Journalism is no exception. In 1923 the American Society of Newspaper Editors adopted such a code under the title *Canons of Journalism*. This seven-point directive has meaning for school journalists as well. It reads as follows:

I

Responsibility. The right of a newspaper to attract and hold readers is restricted by nothing but considerations of public welfare. The use a newspaper makes of the share of public attention it gains serves to determine its sense of responsibility, which it shares with every member of its staff. A journalist who uses his power for any selfish or otherwise unworthy purpose is faithless to a high trust.

II

Freedom of the press. Freedom of the press is to be guarded as a vital right of mankind. It is the unquestionable right to discuss whatever is not explicitly forbidden by law, including the wisdom of any restrictive statute.

III

Independence. Freedom from all obligations except that of fidelity to the public interest is vital.

1. Promotion of any private interest contrary to the general welfare for whatever reason, is not compatible with honest journalism. So-called news communications from private sources should not be published without public notice of their source or else substantiation of their claims to value as news, both in form and substance.

2. Partisanship in editorial comment which knowingly departs from the truth does violence to the best spirit of American journalism; in the news columns it is subversive of a fundamental principle of the profession.

14

IV

Sincerity, truthfulness, accuracy. Good faith with the reader is the foundation of all journalism worthy of the name.

1. By every consideration of good faith a newspaper is constrained to be truthful. It is not to be excused for lack of thoroughness or accuracy within its control or failure to obtain command of these essential qualities.

2. Headlines should be fully warranted by the contents of the articles which they surmount.

V

Impartiality. Sound practice makes clear distinction between news reports and expressions of opinion. News reports should be free from opinion or bias of any kind.

This rule does not apply to so-called special articles unmistakably devoted to advocacy or characterized by a signature authorizing the writer's own conclusions and interpretations.

VI

Fair play. A newspaper should not publish unofficial charges affecting reputation or moral character without opportunity given to the accused to be heard; right practice demands the giving of such opportunity in all cases of serious accusation outside judicial proceedings.

1. A newspaper should not invade private rights or feelings without sure warrant of public right as distinguished from public curiosity.

2. It is the privilege, as it is the duty, of a newspaper to make prompt and complete correction of its own serious mistakes of fact or opinion.

VII

Decency. A newspaper cannot escape conviction of insincerity if while professing high moral purpose it supplies incentives to base conduct, such as are to be found in details of crime and vice, publication of which is not demonstrably for the general good. Lacking authority to enforce its canons, the journalism here represented can but express the hope that deliberate pandering to vicious instincts will encounter effective public disapproval or yield to the influence of a preponderant professional condemnation.

15

CHAPTER LABORATORY

1. From both a daily newspaper and a school newspaper, clip an example of each of the elements of a newspaper (see pages 12 and 13.) Discuss your selections in class.

> SUGGESTION: Throughout the course you will be expected to clip various types of examples from daily papers. These should be presented in some organized form. For example, mount the clippings on the left side of a sheet of paper, and down the right side place any necessary explanation.

2. Choose one of these newspaper leaders for a report to the class: Charles A. Dana, Gordon Bennett, William Randolph Hearst, Joseph Pulitzer, Roy Howard, the Scripps.

3. Freedom of the press protects the public by providing news and editorial interpretation. Does the public need protection against abuse of such freedom by a newspaper? Discuss.

4. Write a 200-word account of your own specific interests in student journalism.

5. Most school papers exchange copies with other school papers. From an examination of your school's exchanges, select a paper you think not up to the standard of your school paper and one that is in some respects better. Discuss them in class.

6. To what extent should a newspaper choose its copy on the basis of reader interest? Consider how this method may lead to conflict with good editorial standards.

7. Examine two issues of your school paper. Which stories exemplify the trends mentioned in "The Student Press Today"?

8. Compare your school paper's published list of purposes with the list in this chapter. If there is no list, prepare one as a group exercise.

9. How are staff members selected for your school paper? How does a student prepare to meet requirements for membership?

10. Summarize the history of student publications in your school. If there is no such account, write one as a class project.

11. Using the glossary (pages 460-466), answer the questions on page 3.

12. The "Canons of Journalism" (pages 14 and 15) are significant for student journalists. From them, draw up eight one-sentence principles that would guide student journalism.

2 RECOGNIZING NEWS

A newspaper's primary purpose is to report the news—the events of the day, the experiences of people. This purpose has not changed since the first printed newspaper was issued in China more than thirteen centuries ago. Even though the modern paper brings to its readers much of interest and entertainment that cannot qualify as news, its chief characteristic and justification for being is still its reporting of the events that directly or indirectly affect the lives of its readers.

WHAT IS NEWS?

News is what interests the reader. If you were to ask a group of newspaper editors "What is news?" perhaps most of them would say that news is what interests the greatest number of readers. Editors must study their readers as much as they study events, for only if the editors hold the interest of the readers can they sell their newspapers. And, after all, journalism is a business.

Although there are a number of distinguishing characteristics of news, no two editors will fully agree upon the selection of copy for their papers. In a large city the readers of one newspaper make up a distinct set of news consumers, quite different from the readers of another newspaper. The readers of any metropolitan paper act as a

17

great influence upon the policy of that paper. It is just as important for the student editor to know his readers. It should be constantly remembered, however, that although news is what interests the reader, it does not necessarily follow that the news which interests or excites the greatest number is the most important event being reported.

News is what has just happened. News is what has just been announced for the first time and what is timely.

News is fact, not fiction. The basic feature of a newspaper, as distinguished from a magazine, is the factual reporting of things that are happening right now—since yesterday's paper was issued. The reporter or editor needs to report them honestly and accurately. Now and then a newspaper "colors" the news—that is, a story may be partially factual, but other facts important to the story have been intentionally left out in order to give a distorted, or "colored," picture of the news. The integrity of a paper is judged by its honest approach to its job.

News is what is significant. A good editor can begin with the basic facts and project his own good thoughts and practices beyond them. If he is a good editor, he will not be content to give his readers just what interests them at the moment. He will want to go beyond and think of the public welfare. He has the obligation to arouse interest in significant news even if it is apparent in the beginning that the average reader lacks such concern.

Yes, the responsibility of the newspaper goes beyond reader interest, on over into the area of social good. The influence of a good newspaper means much in the progress of a community. The influence of the school paper for good, for right action, for school improvement, for pupil progress and achievement, is demonstrated year after year in school after school throughout the country.

Two variables. An editor comes to realize that in every newspaper situation there exist two variables that make that newspaper unique. They are the reporter and the reader.

The reporter: Many of the events that find their way into the paper are so interesting, significant, or timely that they ask very little of the

18

reporter in recognizing their news value—just accuracy and speed. But a great percentage of the stories that appear in print do so because of the reporter's ability to make commonplace events take on significance and interest through good reporting.

The reader: The interests of one newspaper's reader may vary greatly from those of another. A comparison of the different papers published in a large city reveals these differences, as does the comparison of a village weekly with a city daily. Just as a good daily paper reflects its public, so does a good school paper.

WHAT MAKES NEWS?

News then, after all, is perhaps not the event itself, but rather the report of that event. Something may have happened long ago, but an alert reporter can make timely news of it today if it is particularly pertinent or has never before been reported. Furthermore, the thing that is timely may be news for some papers, yet not for others.

To say that news is the report of an event is a sound generality. Certain major factors or elements, however, stand out as earmarks of news. By the following "makers of news" school editors should also be guided.

Conflict. Any event that denotes a fight, a struggle, a difference of opinion, or a significant change is news.

Recency, newness, discovery. News is perishable and demands immediate attention. There is nothing deader than yesterday's newspaper.

Timeliness. A story about Christmas usually bears no interest in May, nor one about kites when kites are not in season.

Prominence, recognition. Prominent people in the school or the community are often the source of news—as much because of their positions as the event with which they are associated.

Nearness, proximity. Of first concern to the reader is the event of which he is a part; next, the events of which his friends are a part;

then the events of which his acquaintances are a part. Most of us are interested in our school before another, our city before another, our country before another.

Significance. The important event is of news value and must not be ignored by the editor.

The unusual. The strange is ever new and appealing to almost everyone's curiosity.

Adventure. As in literature, the movies, and television, the adventure found in the lives of students and teachers interests the reader.

Names. Names are always news—the more names, the newsier the paper.

Numbers. Numbers play a great part in the life of the community and the school, and, properly selected and presented, statistics often make interesting reading.

Amusement. One feature of the modern paper is its obligation to amuse. The possibilities are endless.

Animals. High in the list of reader interests is the animal story—often accompanied by pictures.

TYPES OF NEWSPAPER STORIES

Spot and anticipated. With regard to their genesis, newspaper stories are of two types—spot and anticipated. The first represents the unexpected happening, the second the expected. The first calls for rapid handling; the second usually assures a more deliberate approach. Both types of stories are on the front page of this morning's paper. Let's classify them:

Spot stories	*Anticipated stories*
A train wreck	The marriage of a nationally known figure
A prison escape	
A surprise change in the President's cabinet	Further negotiations in the local industrial strike

The overthrow of the government of a South American republic	The previously announced television speech of a senator
The death of a prominent citizen in an automobile accident	The death of a fireman reported in a previous story to have been injured
The discovery of gold in an Illinois river	The opening of the Community Fund drive

News and feature. With regard to coverage, newspaper stories are again of two types—news and feature. The former treats the event in a factual manner, emphasizing the facts as they can best be determined. In the feature, some particular aspect of the story or some unusual approach to it seems to the reporter to promise far more reader interest than the straight news facts themselves. Feature writing takes liberties with the traditional handling of the news, deviating from straight coverage for the sake of greater effect; the feature story, however, is good journalism and does not present faked news. Good feature stories grow out of human affairs just as do news stories.

Interview and speech report. The interview is a distinct type of newspaper story, an account of a discussion or question-and-answer period the reporter has had with one or more people. The prominence of the person or the topic on which he speaks is usually the justification for the story. As for style of writing, the interview story often resembles the report of a speech. In either, the reporter has the problem of alternating direct quotations, indirect quotations, summarizing statements, and some descriptive phrases.

Interpretation of the news. Newspapers are responsible for interpreting the news as well as reporting it, and journalism provides definite instruments for the purpose. The *editorial,* the *column,* and the *review* are the chief types of newspaper writing that permit the writer's opinion to come into play. The contributor's column—the voice of the people—must be added to these opinion stories.

The by-line on a news story gives the reporter some liberty in interpreting the news that he is reporting. It is a line at the beginning of the story that carries the name of the writer.

BEING A GOOD REPORTER

What makes news depends greatly upon good reporting. Every reporter begins as a *cub,* and his development thereafter is dependent upon his understanding of the job and his ability and desire to practice the principles involved. His progress can be measured along three lines—(1) attitude toward the work, (2) gathering the news, and (3) writing the story. Certain guideposts stand out boldly in each of these areas for the reporter who is seeking to improve himself. The first two areas are discussed below; the third has a chapter to itself. (See Chapter 3.)

Attitude toward the work. Being a reporter is not an individual enterprise; it is a team operation calling for close working relationships with the other members of the newspaper staff. Consequently, the following suggestions cover the reporter's activities within this setting.

1. Reliability is the first quality of a good reporter. He is depended upon to carry out his task promptly and efficiently.

2. Accuracy is a fundamental law of journalism. Nothing condemns the reporter and in turn his paper more than slipshod reporting.

3. Enthusiasm means the difference between dull copy and a quality newspaper. Great papers are built on the reporter's love for his work—reporting and writing.

4. Loyalty to the paper is essential. The staff member must feel free to criticize freely in staff meetings, but he should carry his criticism no further than the newspaper office.

5. To be a top reporter or editor, the staff member must place the newspaper foremost among his activities. School life is varied and interesting today, and many activities make great demands upon a student's time. Therefore the staff member should usually not assume other very time-consuming responsibilities that would interfere with his work on the paper.

6. A reporter must not confine his consideration of the paper to the period scheduled for the work. The star reporter is the one who thinks of everything in terms of news. It is that valuable person who keeps the paper timely, interesting, and a leader among the papers of the country.

7. He must respect authority on the staff—taking any assignments without hesitation. A school paper is no place for snobbishness, cliques, and petty jealousies.

8. The reporter's particular position on the staff is a trust that must not be separated from the total operation. Any weakness in the paper invites his interest and consideration.

9. A reporter must place himself in the position of the other fellow on the staff. Can the typist read his copy? Can the copy desk rely on his facts? Can the page editor expect the story by deadline? Can the compositor set the head he has written?

10. In turn, he must demand respect for his own position. If the typist is willing to labor over poor scribbling, she is encouraging staff inefficiency. If the business manager is content with poor circulation, he is doing the same. If the page editor peacefully accepts late copy, he is helping to wreck staff efficiency.

11. The reporter who complains that the assignment editors never give him any assignments indicts himself. Unsatisfactory or late copy makes the assignment editor hesitate to assign stories to certain reporters. The resourceful staff member can always find unassigned stories that will boost the total number of inches he has published.

12. In covering the news, the reporter's courteous and businesslike approach will produce more news and engender a respect for the paper that will bring further returns to the enterprise as a whole.

13. Close observation is a quality essential to good reporting. This trait can be developed even in the newsroom itself. Each time the reporter enters the room he should glance at the bulletin board for assignments and announcements. Spare moments in the newsroom may well be spent in looking over exchange papers, both school and daily. Needless to say, loafing has no place in the newspaper office.

14. A reporter must at all times be impersonal. Membership in a particular class or organization must not influence his selection and treatment of news. The staff member must see that the paper is not made a publicity organ for the staff personnel, but on the other hand he must never hesitate to cover such a story if the news is there.

15. A reporter's job is never finished. There is always something more he can do to improve himself and the paper.

Gathering the news. News is wherever you see it. The reporter's stories fall into two classifications: assignments given him by an editor and stories that he sees and covers on his own. The latter test his news sense and make the difference between satisfactory and star reporters. The suggestions that follow reflect the importance of both routine assignments and resourceful discoveries.

1. The coverage of a routine assignment should not blind the reporter to another story that wigwags for attention on the way.

2. Before starting out to cover an assignment, the good reporter jots down the possible sources of his information and considers the approach to be taken.

3. The reporter must be enthusiastic about each assignment, no matter how trivial it may seem on the surface.

4. The editor is never interested in why the reporter did not get the story for which he was sent. (There is a stock newspaper yarn about the cub reporter who came back to his editor with no copy on the wedding he was to cover. Asked why, he said that the groom did not show up for the ceremony.)

5. The reporter should never be satisfied with half a story.

6. He must be fair to all sides—get all the facts—not jump to conclusions. There are proper authorities for all facts. Let no person speak for another, if the other person is available.

7. News is not gathered solely from people. A story may require research in the newspaper files, school bulletins, and the library.

8. "Do you have any news for the paper?" usually brings a negative response. Students and teachers seldom see their experiences as news. Through casual conversation the reporter finds out what his prospect has been doing, what he has heard, what he expects to do, what he considers of importance at the moment—and then translates these experiences into news items for the paper.

9. A reporter can be a channel for news only by having many contacts with teachers and students. He soon knows which are his most promising sources of news.

10. The reporter asks himself of everything, "Is this news?" His mind is always at work on the theme.

24

11. As he develops his sense of observation, he must also develop that news sense which automatically sifts the chaff from the grain. He must distinguish truth from rumor, interest from monotony.

12. The successful reporter realizes that he must never break a confidence. No piece of news is worth it.

13. In interviewing people, it is now considered preferable for the reporter to concentrate upon the thought rather than the words, and thus to grasp the meaning of the discussion before any notes are taken. A question here and there clears up the account, and he can then ask the person being interviewed to repeat certain significant facts, such as names and figures, for him. By interviewing in this fashion and writing the story immediately afterward, the reporter produces a much more human story.

It is also desirable to ask the person being interviewed to write out a statement to insure accurate coverage of anything too technical for the reporter.

14. Only through practice can the reporter develop his nose for news. There are no common formulas for perfecting the coverage of the news, but one ingredient of all good reporting is concentration.

The day of an outstanding reporter. Now and then there appears that exceptional reporter who seems to have mastered the technique of gathering news as if he had been born with it. To identify him, look for the following characteristics—or something quite similar—but look fast, for he may soon be the editor of the paper.

1. He lingers with his friends in the halls as he enters school in the morning. He jots down notes and possibly follows up with pertinent questions.

2. On the way to his homeroom, he drops in to see a teacher who is one of his best sources of news. A ten-minute conversation results in a couple of stories.

3. He enters his homeroom and his classes with his eyes and ears open for a conflict story—nothing better than a good conflict story. A certain class has a unique procedure, or discussion, which he follows closely.

4. He notices a new student in one of his classes, and talks with him after class—good for a few inches of copy, maybe a picture.

5. All the while he observes everything in terms of news. He notices that study-hall conditions are better than usual; freshman study hall is under student control while the teacher is out.

6. He is concerned about two friends who are in trouble in the office. He wonders what some pupils are really getting out of school. Is it worth the taxpayer's money and the pupil's time?

7. Lunch time comes. He makes it a point to eat with two or three of the school's leaders. The conversation may lead to a good story.

8. After school he goes up to the basketball floor. Can he write a story about the practice session different from those in the files?

9. As he goes back to the newsroom, he passes the janitor and talks a while with him. The office is just dismissing some students kept in for tardiness. He asks the principal how many are tardy each day. The average is ten, an increase over last year.

10. He passes through the newsroom and glances at the bulletin board for late announcements.

11. At dinner he discusses the unusual class procedure with his mother and grandmother. He listens to their reactions, their own school days. Such a contrast—such conflict of the new and the old.

12. He checks his list of possible stories and finds that he has tips for half a dozen good stories and a couple of editorials. He writes two of them and goes to class the next day with information on the rest. Two of his stories have already been regularly assigned to other students. As he works away on the others he overhears a staff member complaining to the editor about not being assigned any stories.

THE REPORTER AT WORK

It is common for a newspaper, in assuring complete coverage of the news, to assign specific reporters to the continued coverage of given news sources. Such assignments are called *news runs* or *beats*. On the daily newspaper, such beats are the city hall, the police station, the emergency hospital, the school board, etc. On the school paper, typical beats are the principal's office, the athletic office, the music director, the student body officers, and so forth.

In the following examples (Examples 4 through 7), note the sources to which the reporters went for each story. The story reproduced in Example 4 was probably obtained on visits to the head counselor, the principal, and the school registrar.

Unexpected B-10 Hoard
Stuns WHS Counselors

EXAMPLE

4

Dismayed seniors and tired counselors seemed to be the rule rather than the exception on the first day of school. Seniors could be found walking around in a daze almost everywhere when they found that 804 new B-10's had invaded the hallowed halls of Westchester, and the already overworked counselors speedily reorganized plans when more B-10's turned up than they had expected. Actually the situation wasn't quite as hectic as it sounds, but everybody was a little surprised when the enrollment rose to 2,618 students.

Strays Increase

One of the most startling increases in students came from the group which the Attendance Office calls "strays." These are students that come from outside the Los Angeles City School District. Right now there are 241 "strays" among the new students. Head Counselor Mrs. Joan Nikirk attributes the rise in "strays" to the growing migration to California and to the increasing opportunities in the missile industries in Los Angeles.

Because of the tremendous influx of new students this semester, two problems have arisen. The first concerns classroom space and the second a lack of teachers.

The average B-10 academic classroom now holds about 40 students instead of the desired number of 35. To ease this problem two new buildings are being erected near the Girls' Gym.

Seven New Teachers

To help plug the hole made by the increased enrollment, seven new teachers have been added to the heretofore undermanned staff.

Trends other than size seem to be present in the B-10 class this semester. One of the trends is an unusual interest in the science languages (Latin and German). Head Counselor Joan Nikirk says that this is probably due to the increasing interest in the sciences. A greater sports spirit among the boys comprises the other trend.

The Comet
Westchester High School
Los Angeles, California

For the school newspaper, a reporter may very well cover more than one beat. In fact, the good reporter not only covers his assigned beats with dedication but looks for news wherever it may be.

In Example 5 the best source was probably the teacher sponsoring the event, but a student participant was also interviewed. The only possible source of information for Example 6 was the librarian, while the story in Example 7 was gathered by the reporter's moving among the students in a favorite gathering place.

Students To Participate In Model U.N. Assembly

EXAMPLE 5

The model United Nations General Assembly sponsored by the U.N. Association of Akron will be held April 8 at the University of Akron.

Delegates attending the Assembly will be high school seniors from area schools. Each school is permitted to enter up to four delegations composed of four students each. A total of 45 to 50 delegations will be present, representing many of the member nations in the U.N.

The primary purpose of this assembly is to help students gain a clearer understanding of the U.N. with its capabilities and its limitations. The delegates will study problems, present their views to the General Assembly, and discuss with member nations controversial world political problems.

Attending the convention will be twelve seniors selected by Mrs. Violet Hartney. The following students will represent France: Kenny Rhoades, Pat Kinney, Leonard Schlup, and Bonnie Rucker; Nigeria: Ken Smith, Mary McCarthy, Larry Harris, and Alyce Mills; Australia: Ken Reichart, Nancy King, Eloise Bumgardner, and Mike Davidson.

Bonnie Rucker, who also was chosen as Kenmore's one delegate to the U.N. Council, feels that "this will be a rewarding experience, for we will gain a better understanding of the world and learn how the U.N operates."

The Cardinal
Kenmore High School
Akron, Ohio

In Our Library

EXAMPLE 6

Africa is a continent in turmoil as it makes the transition from ages of servitude, feudalism, and colonization to freedom, independence, and modernity. This movement has created increased interest in Africa. For this reason, our library has added many new books on this continent. Some of these are as follows:

Hughes, Langston, ed.	*An African Treasury*
Rutherford, Peggy, ed.	*African Voices*
Carter, Gwendolen	*Independence for Africa*
Gatti, Ellen	*The New Africa*
Gunther, John	*Meet the Congo and Its Neighbors*
Hatch, John	*Africa Today — and Tomorrow*
Harrabin, James	*An Atlas of Africa*
Hunter, John	*Tales of the African Frontier*
Kittler, Glenn	*Equatorial Africa*
Lomas, Louis	*The Reluctant African*
Moorehead, Alan	*No Room in the Ark*
Nevins, Albert	*Away to East Africa*
Paton, Alan	*Hope for South Africa*

The Thor
Miami Norland High School
Miami, Florida

Foyer frequenters justify daily visits

By CAROLYN HANTAK

EXAMPLE

7

Between 7:40 and 8:13 A.M. every weekday morning, bits of conversation echo through the second floor corridors. By following the sound, any curious Bloomite can detect that the source is no place other than the foyer.

As the average Bloomite stands there, he wonders why everyone congregates in the foyer. Perhaps there is a mysterious force that draws the students there.

In an effort to solve the mystery, this reporter spent a few mornings in the foyer trying to unveil its drawing force.

Finds Solutions

Various solutions were discovered; for instance, Commissioner Dwight Dunn claims that he "discusses world problems and shares mental enlightenment with his friends," while Bob Strong, senior, gets down to earth and states that "there are more girls here than anywhere else."

Ron Harris, junior class president, explains that the morning foyer sessions help one to get into the swing of the school day and the liveliness of school work. Once again there is a contrasting view of Eddie Ueeck, junior, who comes "to see the girls in their short skirts."

Comes to Flirt

Bill Swartz, football player, stands in the foyer because he "wants to," while the Swedish exchange student, Olav Randsalu, asks, "Why should I go anywhere else?"

Maurice Myers, senior, claims that he "hears the latest gossip and other news," but Dickie Connors, senior, comes "to flirt with the girls."

"To see all the good-looking teachers," is the reason Ray Stabile gives for his morning visits. However Preston Bouler, student council parliamentarian, "looks at all the young ladies that go by and tries to be sociable."

Watches Special View

Sharon Petrarca and Diane Ribeca, seniors, "meet all their friends and everyone" as Elvis Roberts, football star, watches his "special view," whatever that may be.

After hearing Dave Rubley and Danny Fazzini, juniors, say "there isn't anywhere else to go before homeroom," one would get the impression that BTHS is a rather small place.

Meets His Girl

Although Larry Baer, senior, stands in the foyer "to meet his girl," he certainly can't miss seeing one half of the female enrollment as they strut by.

Nevertheless, whatever excuses the foyer frequenters may offer, the basic fact remains that students like to loiter before beginning a tough day, and the foyer is the best place to do it.

The Broadcaster
Bloom Township High School
Chicago Heights, Illinois

CHAPTER LABORATORY

1. List four news items that should be covered in the next issue of the school paper. Indicate which of these would be most obvious for news value, and which least.
2. Bring to class notes from which a story could be written for one of the items in Exercise 1.
3. Check the stories in the last issue of the school paper by this scale: (1) interesting to most readers, (2) interesting to some readers, (3) of doubtful interest. Use this check as the basis of a class discussion.
4. Look at the first page of today's daily newspaper. Indicate in one sentence why each of the stories merits its place on the front page. Discuss in class.
5. List in the order of news importance the *makers of news* found on pages 19 and 20. Discuss in class.
6. Bring in a list of the regular beats to which reporters on the school paper are assigned. If possible, suggest improvements.
7. Choose the beat that you would enjoy most and explain in 200 words its value as a source of news.
8. Clip from the daily paper stories that depend upon each of the following for their interest: (1) conflict, (2) discovery, (3) prominence, (4) proximity, (5) adventure, (6) amusement, and (7) the unusual.
9. Interview a teacher who has many interests and secure one or more suggestions for stories.
10. How much of the news on the front page of the daily newspaper represents local coverage, and how much comes from outside the community through press services? Check two different issues.
11. Examine the stories in the last issue of the school paper. Mark all those written from news sources obvious to any reporter. For each of the others, cite the element that made the story newsworthy.
12. Some stories are not covered by watching an event or interviewing someone. The source of such stories may be a printed source such as a school bulletin or the newspaper files or some other type of coverage. Find such a story in the daily or school newspaper and briefly describe the reporter's coverage.

3 WRITING THE NEWS STORY

Writing the straight news story is the most impersonal of all newspaper writing. The reporter's task is (1) to find out what actually happened, and (2) to write the story based on these facts. Even though he forms an opinion on the matter, he cannot give it in his story; he must write impartially, as a disinterested party. The news story gives the reader the facts—he forms his own opinion.

The reporter does not write in the first person. He keeps himself out of the picture and writes in an unbiased style, using the third person and giving the facts as accurately as he can determine them. He writes not for himself, but for the reader, assuming that the reader knows nothing about the incident being reported.

There are two major related elements in writing a news story—(1) the newswriting style itself and (2) the patterns of constructing a story. In both cases there are certain guiding principles to be followed. It is often difficult for the beginning journalist to master straight news style, for in writing English themes he personalizes his productions, expressing himself freely. This chapter presents the basic principles of newswriting and story construction and is perhaps the most important chapter of the book, for their creative application means the difference between good and poor school newspapers.

WRITING THE STORY

Once the reporter has collected the information, he is ready to write the story. Experienced writers have developed their own techniques for moving from the first to the second stage of news coverage, hardly distinguishing one from the other. But in general all reporters use the following guideposts:

1. The reporter should take pride in every item he writes.

2. He assumes that the reader is ignorant of the subject, and he knows that the first function of a story is to inform. He respects the reader, attempting to anticipate his questions and his interests.

3. It is as important to know what to leave out of a story as it is to know what to include.

4. He never misses the opportunity to include a name.

5. A close study of newspapers has revealed to him that newspaper paragraphs average six or seven lines. Long paragraphs are alternated with shorter ones. Since newspaper columns are narrow, there are only four or five words in a line. Consequently, paragraphs seldom exceed thirty words, and often carry no more than ten or fifteen.

6. He jots down his major points in outline form before he begins.

7. He opens his story with the most important information. In one paragraph, the lead, he gives the reader a digest of the story.

8. He writes his story as soon as the facts are gathered, while all the implications are still fresh in his mind. He knows that it is best to write the sections for which he has gathered material, even though there are still some further developments to come. It is good newspaper practice to piece new material into a story already begun. On a daily paper as many as six reporters may report different phases of a story—the whole thing being pieced together by a rewrite man.

9. Before he begins to write, the reporter sees a dominant point in his material that he wants to carry through his story. It may be the way the team overcame odds, the unusual nature of an assembly, or the phenomenal increase in one department's enrollment. In other words, although the reporter is obliged to report as a disinterested spectator, if his story is to carry any life he must look beyond the bare facts he has collected to broad meanings and implications. This

is done in every fine news story that goes into a big metropolitan daily. He can present his facts in such a way as to accentuate these meanings and in no way deviate from the straight news style. This is called "playing up" a particular point in a story.

10. The reporter whose stories never see print should take the hint that they may have been dropped because of dullness, poor construction, padding, or the disregard of facts.

11. The reporter cannot write without reading. There is a difference between reading and reading for a purpose. A constant study of the construction of stories in a good daily paper has no substitute for improvement of one's style in newswriting.

12. If in gathering data for a news story the reporter is so moved by some factor or other that he wishes to write his opinion on the matter, he should ask permission either to write an editorial in addition or to write his story under a by-line.

13. The reporter guards against misleading statements that may unintentionally come into the story.

14. The better he understands an event the clearer his story.

15. He tells the story in clear English with short sentences. The good reporter knows the value of every word he uses.

16. The length of his story is determined by its value in reader interest.

17. Fact and not fancy is his guide. He has used his fancy or imagination to conceive the story in the first place. Once conceived, the story then depends upon facts.

The by-line. When a reporter's name appears on a story, it is called the *by-line*. It gives the reporter some liberty in interpreting the news he is reporting but does not grant him liberties with the canons of good journalism. The by-line indicates special respect, in part to the reporter, in part to the news being covered.

The decision to include a by-line is the prerogative of the news editor, the editor who controls the copy as it is checked through the copy desk for final reading on its way to the presses. The by-line comes at the beginning of a story, between the headline and the lead.

A regularly-published column always carries the name of its author, placing the complete credit and responsibility with him. By-lines, however, originated with news stories. Since news coverage is an impersonal gathering and recording of the facts, a by-line is journalistic recognition.

Identification of names. One of the first rules of journalism is to identify the names that appear in a story. The reporter must assume that the reader will not know the person in question, regardless of his prominence. Following are examples:

Miss Esther Lehmann, music instructor, is in charge.
Principal J. A. Perino opened the assembly.
Jack Evans, program director and an engineer for KGO, will be present at each broadcast.
Seniors who applied were Wilson Horne and Dave Fowler.

THINK FIRST—THEN WRITE

Each news story in the current issue of the school paper tells much more than the subject it treats. Above all it reveals the thinking of the reporter who covered it. Once in print, the story is a mirror of the thinking machinery behind it.

In turn, the writer who learns the art of effectively organizing a news story improves immeasurably the art of organizing his own thinking.

The case of an athletic controversy in a given school is a good example. A week before an important basketball game two varsity players are suspended from the team. Their absence may determine victory or defeat, and the students are highly agitated.

The suspension is the major topic of discussion around the school, and student comments are running wild. Despite the principal's support of the coach and his explanation, rumor and suspicion are rife.

Of all the students, one person alone can put his thoughts down in black and white. He is the reporter for the school paper. He carries the responsibility for reporting the truth, a result he cannot achieve without thinking his way through the maze of possibilities.

His situation does not deny him the right to be emotionally involved and make preliminary snap judgments just like all the other students—he is not an outsider. But of all the group, he must make his comments stand the test of publication. They are the printed record. Consequently, he gears his mind to the foundation principles of reporting—reliability, accuracy, fairness, and thoroughness.

In other words, he cannot just talk on the subject. He must think about it, and his printed story will indicate his success. Journalism demands the development of thought through written expression, but it provides no lazy way to the goal.

CONSTRUCTION OF THE NEWS STORY

Behind every news story there is a framework, a pattern, on which the facts of the particular story are hung. There are three main patterns, used over and over and over again. In order of importance as testified to by usage, they are: (1) the inverted pyramid; (2) the chronological-order story; and (3) the composite, or many-angle, story. Once you have mastered the mechanics of writing the news story, you will recognize these skeletons in the stories that appear in the daily press.

Type 1: The inverted-pyramid story. In the lead the reporter usually gives the major points of the story. This opening paragraph is extremely short, but the reader could stop at this point and have the story, shorn of details. As the account proceeds, the details are presented in order of diminishing importance. Called the inverted-order or inverted-pyramid story, it is the most common and yet distinctive feature of journalistic writing.

The last few statements are so insignificant to the account that they could be left out without being missed by the reader. This enables the make-up man, in fitting his type into the page forms, to drop lines from the end of a story too long for the space. If a story is so written that it can be cut without harm to the account, then it is said to meet the *cut-off test*. This is good journalistic writing.

Examples 8 and 9 are good representatives of the inverted-pyramid structure. In Example 8 the skeleton is carried at the side to emphasize the decreasing importance of the information carried.

In Example 8:

1. The lead is only twenty-two words and one sentence long, yet it gives the gist of the entire story.
2. The significance of the event is emphasized in the second paragraph.
3. The specific junior high schools to be honored are named.
4. Less important details are carried in the other four paragraphs. The reporter recognized that short paragraphs were needed because newspaper columns are so narrow, and wrote only one sentence for three of the four paragraphs.
5. The last paragraph meets the cut-off test.

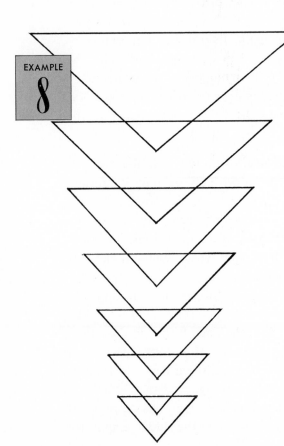

PTA LAST DANCE SET

The last dance of the year, "Good-Luck Capers," will be held tonight from 8 till 11 o'clock in the boys' gym.

Lincoln students are encouraged to attend, as they will help to make next year's sophomores feel welcome. Only owners of activity tickets will be admitted. They will be charged 50 cents as will ninth graders.

Each junior high school will be honored at the dance. The gym is to be decorated with the colors of Gault, Stewart, and Baker.

One fourth of it will be blue and gray, one fourth green and black, one fourth gold and brown, and one fourth gold and black, representing Lincoln.

The dance will give the ninth graders an opportunity to meet this year's and next year's student-body officers.

They will all be introduced during the intermission of the dance.

Refreshments are to be sold by the PTA. Lincoln High's dance band will provide music.

The Lincoln News
Lincoln High School
Tacoma, Washington

In Example 9:

1. The opening paragraph, the lead, gives the important news—that twelve students have received scholarships.
2. The names are given in the second paragraph; the limitations of a lead deny the inclusion of so many names in the beginning.
3. Paragraphs three and four bring out the qualifications for and the importance of the awards, this information being secondary to the names of the winners.
4. The last paragraph is the least essential to the story.

Students Receive Scholarships

EXAMPLE 9

Scholarships are being presented to twelve Moline students who qualified in the Illinois State Scholarship test taken November 7.

Out of the 2,673 high school seniors who are receiving this honor, Moline students are Sharon Blackburn, George Chase, Earl Davis, Linda Ewert, Jack Gellerstedt, Kenneth Hepfer, Sandee Huntoon, Jody Marquis, Barb Reuter, Hunt Sharp, Anne Starkey, and Karen Tracy.

Both monetary and honorary awards are granted winning contestants, the latter for those not in financial need. The applicant must rank academically in the top half of his class and be an Illinois resident of high character planning to attend an Illinois school.

The honorary award not only provides recognition for outstanding scholastic achievement, but would make assistance available should the holder encounter unfortunate circumstances.

Other MHS students who took the test should remain alert as some of the winners may choose to accept another scholarship or attend an out-of-state school.

The Line O'Type
Moline High School
Moline, Illinois

At times the lead gives but one significant fact or statement, instead of summarizing the whole story. In this case, the construction of the body varies slightly. A story that quotes a person freely often opens with a significant quotation which in itself in no way summarizes the whole account. However, the writer can still follow the inverted order. He may follow the lead with a summary paragraph and then proceed with the details; or he may move directly from the lead to the details.

A story may be built entirely around one incident, making all details an elaboration of the opening summary; or it may consist of facts more remotely related to the subject. The arrangement calls for careful planning before writing, a thing the beginner must do on paper.

37

Type 2: The chronological-order story. In the inverted form of writing just treated, the relative significance of the various facts and nothing more is the key to their arrangement in the story. At times, however, in reporting an event the reporter finds that the order in which the various incidents took place stands out as the natural arrangement. Thus he resorts to the second main pattern of writing new stories, the *chronological order*.

For the lead he writes a summary paragraph, or picks from his facts the most outstanding, important, timely, or startling. He then tells the complete story in chronological order, that is, just as it happened. Since the movement of events is emphasized, this type of story is also called the action story. The inverted-order story, in contrast, is called the fact story.

Example 10 is an excellent illustration of this form of construction. It covers a complete day and night of homecoming events in the order of their occurrence. The account includes: (1) a summary lead, (2) the morning assembly, (3) the afternoon assembly, (4) the selection of the queen and an interview with her, (5) the late afternoon parade, (6) the homecoming game, (7) half-time events, (8) the dance following the game, and (9) the cut-off paragraph.

Innovations Change Homecoming Procedure

EXAMPLE

10

Separate assemblies, a trophy for winning the game, and the junior high school not participating in the selection of the Queen were some of the changes made for Homecoming at Owatonna High School this year.

Because of the large enrollment at OHS, two assemblies were presented this year. Chuck Loberg mc'd both groups. At the junior high assembly, three skits were given and pep talks made by game co-captains Dennis Johnson and Jon Schwestka. John Haigh, seventh grade in-

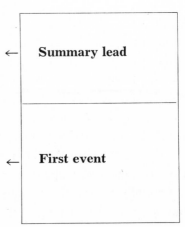

← **Summary lead**

← **First event**

structor, spoke for the faculty. At this time the five queen candidates, **Judy Evans, Joyce Hamren, Bonnie Jensen, Pam Lindberg, and Linda Schroeder, were introduced.**

At the afternoon senior high assembly the skits were judged, the sophomores winning first prize, the juniors second. Coach Neal Davis, Charles Herrmann of Josten's, and math teacher Victor Greier gave the pep talks.

Highlight of the afternoon assembly was the selection of the queen. Shouts of approval were heard when Dennis Johnson named Bonnie Jensen the winner. **Interviewed later Queen Bonnie commented, "It's the most wonderful day of my life."**

A parade, featuring floats made by school organizations, climaxed the afternoon activities.

Highlight of the day was the game against Winona, won by the Indians, 19-7. An innovation was the trophy presented by Josten's to our winning team. This trophy will be presented annually to the Indians if they win the homecoming game.

During half-time the prize-winning floats and the queen's float, designed and made by Robert Bzoskie, paraded around the field. The freshmen won first prize for their float. The club division was won by the FHA and specialties by the biology club.

After the game students and alumni were off to the dance sponsored by the junior class. The Troubadours from Mankato provided the music.

This day of festivities was the result of the combined labor of the junior and senior high schools, and required much of the fall for preparation.

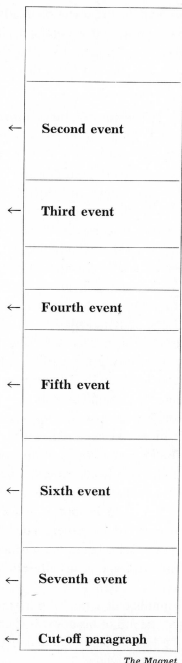

← **Second event**

← **Third event**

← **Fourth event**

← **Fifth event**

← **Sixth event**

← **Seventh event**

← **Cut-off paragraph**

The Magnet
Owatonna High School
Owatonna, Minnesota

39

This plan of organization lends itself well to the coverage of an athletic contest, and is commonly used in sports stories. As shown in Example 113, Chapter 13, such a coverage story begins with a paragraph or two summarizing the game and then gives the account in order of play.

Type 3: The composite or many-angle story. Most of the routine news stories found in school newspapers are relatively simple in style. One reporter can usually handle the assignment, getting most, if not all, of his material from one source.

But in many news tips there is the invitation for the reporter to go beyond the single-incident coverage, to follow his nose for news, to find the new and related angles among more or less hidden possibilities. This story, combining a number of incidents or facts held together by a common thread of interest, is known as the composite story, or the many-incident, many-angle, or string story (from the idea of stringing many incidents together into one story).

With the daily newspaper, composite stories are relatively common. For instance, a murder may lead the city editor to set three or four reporters following the various angles. As the reporters secure their contributions, they send them into the office where a desk man pieces them into one complete story.

Through press associations, such as the Associated Press (AP) and United Press International (UPI), a story that breaks out simultaneously in different sections of the country is brought out as a composite story under one head. Always good for a composite is that first real cold wave of the season when the thermometer takes a nose dive. This type of story can be put to work by the school staff to extend the news interest of its paper. The assignment editor who sees such a story may want to give the various angles to different reporters, but since the coverage is usually all within the school one reporter can often very well handle it.

If a number of school reporters are assigned to such a story, each writes at the top of his copy the general topic, as well as the particular angle he has covered. These short accounts are then turned back to the assignment editor. The job of combining them into one story may be delegated to a reporter who has had an important angle.

Whether the facts have been gathered by one reporter or many, the story will take practically the same form. In writing the lead the reporter may (1) feature all the important angles in a summary lead, (2) pick out the big point of the story and play it up in the lead, (3) combine the two methods when one point barely stands out above a number of others, or (4) place the latest news first. The sections are then added in order of diminishing interest or importance. The story must move smoothly from one section to another, with no sharp break noticeable to the reader.

The staff member most likely to see the possible source of this type of story is the assignment editor. It is part of his job to seek new stories. He has the task of getting the reporter to see the same possibilities in a source that he saw, a task that must not be underestimated.

The topic for the story is not unusual: it is the coverage and treatment that make news by bringing out unusual angles. Notice the various angles of the assignment that follows, each of which might be covered by a different reporter. Note that in each angle the editor saw a possibility for news, and that some of these angles will develop nicely while others may result in nothing significant. Again the reporter's resourcefulness may be pointed out as the guiding factor.

Big Game Assignment

Westside's homecoming game with Central. Story may reach eight hundred words, depending upon coverage.

Angles:

1. Westside's record this season and Central's, game for game.
2. Record of all past football games played between the two schools. How did the rivalry develop?
3. Treat high points of last year's contest.
4. Condition of the two teams, man for man. Consideration of possible participation by those now injured.
5. See faculty business manager, Arad Riggs, about additional bleachers and other arrangements.
6. Plans for the pre-game assembly and booster bonfire.
7. Talk to coaches and players for comments, human-interest stuff.
8. Check cheerleaders' plans.
9. Try Claude Smith for anything unusual about the band.
10. Get starting line-ups.

The assignment editor, in this case the sports editor, takes no chances on full coverage of the story; he spells out the possibilities. He divides the angles among two or three reporters and will then assemble the final story himself, adding other information he has secured.

Opening-of-school example. The opening of a new school year is invariably front-page news for a school newspaper. There are always many leads to follow—new teachers, school enrollment, new building facilities, changes in course offerings, and many others. Often these are treated as separate stories. At times they are assembled into a lead story, a composite story that brings the reader into his changing school.

Example 11 is such a story. An unexpectedly heavy enrollment commands first attention, as noted in the headline and the lead. How does a school meet the problem? In this case, new courses, new teachers, and triple sessions. It seemed natural to this student editor to handle all the news in one composite story.

The detailed information presented in the story would indicate that a number of reporters were assigned to cover it. In unusually good reporting, the new teachers step out of the page as personalities.

2946 ON TRIPLE SESSIONS
6 New Courses, 28 New Faculty Spark Active Top Enrollment

EXAMPLE
11

Bewildered sophomores, determined juniors, and assured seniors were confronted with revolutionary changes as a new year began at Southwest. A leap in enrollment, six new courses in the curriculum, 28 new faculty members, and three sessions greeted students the first day.

An increase of approximately 600 students brought early enrollment figures of 2,946, largest in the history of the school.

NEW COURSES OPEN

Two new television courses, English 10, taught by Mr. Bain Lightfoot, and English 11, by Mr. Joseph Shaw, will reach 850 students. The language laboratory will pioneer in the use of special devices in second year studies, under the direction of Mr. Alfonso Alonso.

Experimental advanced classes will be offered in biology and physics under the watchful eyes

of Mr. Edward Staniski and Mr. Michael Kambour. Mythology studies, directed by Mrs. Sue Addington, and Latin American History, taught by Mr. Joseph Ward, are two new courses that are being offered for the first time at Southwest.

Students, who are used to going to school together, find things different this year. Seniors begin classes at 7:30, juniors 8:30, and sophomores 9:30. At 9:30 homerooms are held for all sections.

NEW TEACHERS ADDED

New teachers, who will try to open the eyes and sharpen the minds of the students, come from various places and have varied backgrounds.

John D. Ramey, guidance, formerly taught business courses to paraplegics and patients with tuberculosis, while William D. Nagle, art, taught "Creative Crafts" on Channel 2 this past summer. Foreign affairs, anthropology, and sociology interest William Altmann, French teacher, while Gerald Bennett, Latin, is interested in photography and wood carving.

Language teachers Miss Ruth Meltzer, Robert D. Lowenthal, and Miss Margery Ann Jenkins were all born in the North, although Miss Jenkins lived in Cuba for 17 years. Mrs. Flora Mamakos and Mrs. Dorothy Roeth will teach business education. Mrs. Mamakas has two young children, while Mrs. Roeth holds a private pilot's license and a real estate license.

Four new social studies teachers joined Southwest's faculty. Jesse D. Wilson belongs to civic and fraternal organizations and works with youth groups; Joab L. Blackmon, Jr., was written up in "Who's Who in the South and Southwest" in 1961; Mrs. Nancy Davis received the Valley Forge Freedoms Foundation Classroom Teacher's Medal, and John D. Sheridan spent several years as personnel manager of Hayes Aircraft Company.

For the past two years Miss Susan Winter, biology, has been doing research in hematology, and she holds a bachelor of science degree in zoology. Boating, water-skiing and dancing are hobbies of Mrs. Marcia Plager, science teacher. Jay Werner, another new science instructor, holds the 1961 National Y.M.C.A. All-Around Gymnast Title.

FORMER UMPIRE TEACHES

Mathematics teacher Thomas J. Smith was a minor league baseball umpire and athletic director; W. J. Schmeisser, a development engineer; Edward Stafford flew faster than sound; Mrs. Deborah K. Forer graduated from the University of Florida; Jay Rudolph has two married sons, and Sam Lastinger, Jr., spent 16 months in Germany.

The English Department has added three new men. Roy French was a member of the University of Miami's undefeated debate team; Calvin L. Hussey has traveled throughout the United States; David Van Duren taught public speaking in New Jersey.

The new teachers who belong to the physical education department are Miss Sadie Presnell, cheerleader sponsor, who travels every summer, and Miss Roberta Ann Boyce, G.A.A. sponsor, who was in the F.S.U. Hall of Fame.

The Southwest Lancer
Southwest High School
Miami, Florida

43

News briefs. A school is full of small news items not large enough to stand as significant stories but with enough reader interest to command editorial attention. They are covered in two ways: (1) as small individual items used at the end of columns to fill out an otherwise short column, and (2) as a combination column with a blanket head. In the latter case, the head runs uniformly from issue to issue, and the story usually holds one position in the paper.

The following titles are representative: *News Briefs, What's New?, Covering the Corners, News in Capsule,* and *What's Happening?* (See Example 12.)

What's Happening?

EXAMPLE

12

The newly founded Writers' club, under the supervision of Miss Ruth Render, English teacher, has elected officers. They are Ray Hatchett, Dave Hippensteel, Kathleen Mis, and Diane Schmidt.

* * *

Thirty-eight students from the chemistry classes of the Community college visited the Dresden Nuclear power station near Morris, October 23.

* * *

A social studies seminar will have its first of six sessions, December 5. Contact Mr. Emmett Richards or Mr. Richard Sherman for details.

* * *

Bloom Proudly Presents, now being broadcast at 3:30 on WCGO, will have a program on the band.

* * *

Linda Trotier, Richard Bushno Paulette LoBue, and Bill Stokes, accompanied by Miss Amy Applegate, science-department chairman, will attend a bio-medical career conference at the University of Chicago on Saturday, November 18.

* * *

The Amateur Radio club has installed a new directional antenna on top of the building. It is a Mosely, three element, tri-band beam antenna.

* * *

"Origin of Life," a project by Gerald Levy, and another boy, is published in the NABT magazine.

* * *

The Debate club heard a debate by Richard township high school in Room M-163, November 9.

The Broadcaster
Bloom Township High School
Chicago Heights, Illinois

This same method of treatment is used regularly by school papers in reporting news about school clubs. (See Example 13, and Example 103 in Chapter 12.) A newsy headline is often used to advantage in covering a large number of clubs.

44

State Meets Top FTA, Latin Club Plans

By VELVIA BISHOP

EXAMPLE

13

Five **FTA** members are in Denton today for a state future teachers' meeting at Northwest Texas State College. Carolyn Hill, club president and state recording secretary, made the trip along with Marilyn Billington, Barry Simmons, Shirley Waggoner, and Beverly Mitchell.

Group activities will include a Western barbecue supper and officer elections, relates Marilyn Billington, vice president.

Barry Simmons has been elected FTA president for 1961–62, and Shirley Waggoner is vice president-elect. Other officers will be named later this year.

Miss Frances Wilson, secretary for Mr. Nat Williams, spoke to club members recently on high school preparation for teaching and college entrance.

* * *

Twelve **Gens Togata** delegates will travel to Austin by chartered bus next Friday for a state Junior Classical League meet.

Attending will be Sylva Telford, Parks Turner, SuEarl Bullock, Cecil Puryer, Terry Myers, Keith Billingsley, Jane Roberts, Sue Taylor, Carole Stanley, Susan Sanders, Kathy Ashdown, and Donna Heath.

* * *

Maureen Malley, sophomore, was named February Clubber-of-the-Month, an award based on outstanding club work.

* * *

Development of a person from infancy to old age through portraits was demonstrated by Mrs. Connie Martin, local artist, to **Splash or Splatter** members Wednesday, reports Roger Gore, vice-president.

Making water-color designs and viewing films have highlighted other recent meetings. Also, Mr. Don Kittrell, architect, showed slides of Greece and Italy recently.

* * *

A membership drive is on the agenda for **Band Boys** next week. It will be climaxed by a party at Mr. Paul Branom's house, reports Tommy Nichols, president.

* * *

Making short work of a world tour, Mrs. Marie Allen, Wilson Junior High School teacher, will discuss "Around the World in 60 Days" at the **NHS** Banquet at 9 P.M. Tuesday at the Lubbock Women's Club, reveals Cecile Camp, president.

Mrs. Allen's talk, based on her world trip last summer, will deal primarily with her three-week stop in Siam.

Later, a prize will be awarded the person who has accumulated the most club service points, Cecile says. Committee heads for the event are Dora Riddel, program; Barry Simmons, menu; Sylva Telford, decorations; Shirley Waggoner, theme; and Ann Miller, phoning chairman.

The Western World
Lubbock High School
Lubbock, Texas

TYPES AND SOURCES OF NEWS

News falls into two classes—the anticipated, as an assembly scheduled in advance, and spot news, as an explosion in the chemistry laboratory. A game is anticipated news, but the collapse of the bleachers is spot news. The bulk of school stories are anticipated.

A reporter may gather the facts for his story (1) as an eyewitness, (2) by interviewing one or more people, or (3) from written or printed sources. All three of these means are revealed in a study of a good daily newspaper. Any one, or even all three, may be used for one story. The object is to get the truth, using the natural means of doing so.

For every story there are authorities from whom to secure the information. The reader's opinion of the paper will depend upon how accurately it gives the facts over a period of time. Accuracy, even to the spelling of each name, must be the reporter's constant guide.

A beginning reporter, in checking his story to determine if it is complete, may ask himself—does it tell who, and what, and when, and where, and why, and how? The experienced reporter automatically answers them as he writes.

THE MORAL TAG

For the beginning newswriter, often the most difficult thing to learn is the art of withdrawing himself from the story he is covering. The temptation to inject his opinion usually comes in closing the story.

These tail-end personalized comments on student stories are so common that they have come to have a name, the *moral tag*. The following are some examples taken from the front-page news stories of one school newspaper:

Central will be indeed sorry to lose such a fine teacher.

Central students and faculty want to extend to you, Mr. Olsen, their hearty congratulations for this honor that has come to you.

For this splendid program the class all extended thanks to the committee. They have spent hours of their own time to prepare it.

The assembly should prove to be entertaining.

46

The members of 238 have been very enthusiastic about the drive, contributing from their lunch money. Why don't you?

If you have any suggestions about noontime activities, why don't you contact Mr. Sproll.

As indicated earlier, the reporter gives the reader the facts and lets him form his own opinion. Some of the same points in error above could have been handled with good journalistic approach. For instance,

Jim Knoll, president of homeroom 238, has pointed out that other rooms could follow its example of contributing to the fund.

Mr. Sproll, dean of boys, has asked that suggestions for noontime activities be handed to him.

The basic style of newswriting is that of the straight news story. The reporter cannot learn that style too well. Once mastered, the liberties extended him by other types of coverage can be learned, and the variations that characterize these forms of writing will come readily.

Three more examples of good, straight news stories follow (Examples 14 through 16). They are all relatively short, showing the reporters' ability to go straight to the point in carrying the news. Excessive length in any story may be a threat to the adequate coverage of all the news. The number of stories carried and the relative length of each are conditioned by the size of the school paper.

JOURNALISTS RECEIVE AWARD

EXAMPLE 14

Ten members of the *Southerner* staff have been selected for the Quill and Scroll International Honorary Society for High School Journalists. In order to be a member of Quill and Scroll, students applying must meet certain requirements.

All students must be in the senior or junior classification; they must be in the upper third of their class, have done superior work in some phase of journalism or school publication work.

They must be recommended by the supervisor, and, before being accepted, all students must be approved by the Executive Secretary of the Society.

The ten new members are: Arlene Quickstrom, Joan Feldstein, Jo Anne Rootes, Helen Ksiezarek, Sharon Cribb, Charles Becker, Dan Mason, Dave Norman, Marilyn Hanson, and Karen Waller.

On Awards Day, June 13, these students will receive gold pins, a certificate, and a one-year subscription to Quill and Scroll magazine.

The Southerner
South High School
Minneapolis, Minnesota

47

Adams' Dress Code Abolishes
Fashions Unsuitable for School

EXAMPLE

15

Heavy make-up, especially heavy eye make-up, extreme hair-dos, sweat shirts, culottes, and short skirts are taboo at John Adams.

"Abolishing fads unsuitable for school and promoting better dress" is the current project of the Student Congress.

These principles of better dress the Student Congress hopes to attain by endorsing the enforcement of the present dress code.

A special committee, comprised of Virginia Koneval, 12B, chairman, Randy Adams, 11A, Ronald Amigo, 12A, Shirley Collier, 11B, and David Netzband, 12A, has been designated by the Student Congress to suggest new rules for the dress code.

The present dress code of John Adams is based on the ideal that the dress habits of students influence their study habits. It consists of 10 compulsory rules which must be obeyed by all Adamites.

Boys are to wear T-shirts only if they have another shirt over them. Levis are not to be worn in school. Belts must be worn with slacks. Gum chewing is not allowed.

Extreme and improper hair styles will not be permitted. Girls are not to wear sheer blouses. Tight sweaters are prohibited.

Heavy make-up should not be worn. Conspicuous or excessive jewelry cannot be worn. Outdoor jackets are not to be worn by any pupil to classes or study halls. (This does not include suit coats, school sweaters, or blazers.)

"With the support of the entire student body, the dress code will be re-established and retained," remarked Virginia Koneval.

Students violating the Adams' dress code will be sent to the office.

John Adams Journal
John Adams High School
Cleveland, Ohio

Jefferds Gets Grouse Limit

EXAMPLE

16

Although the weather was perfect for the opening of the small game hunting season on Saturday, Kane High hunters report light kills.

Von Stanley of Room 25 is the only nimrod to report a turkey, but Dave Jefferds of Room 27 brought down two ruffed grouse.

Those with other successful kills were Larry Starner who got a grouse; Don Walter, a rabbit; and Harry Whittemore, one grouse and two squirrels.

Paul Swanson got a grouse; Dan Gullifer two grouse; Dan Koza, a gray squirrel; and Tom McCormack, a rabbit and a ring-necked pheasant.

Bob Mix reported one "gray squirrel and two sore feet"; while Herb Engman got a black squirrel and Dan Cappello, a chipmunk.

Marshall Miller shot a rabbit and three squirrels while his dad got four squirrels.

Hi-Life
Kane Area High School
Kane, Pennsylvania

SUGGESTIONS FOR PREPARING COPY

Since all copy for the school paper must be read by one or more staff members and since the printer must read it before it can be set up in type, it must be prepared in a form which can be read *quickly, easily,* and *accurately.* For this reason the standards below are usually followed in the preparation of newspaper copy:

1. Always typewrite all copy. This rule should never be broken unless there is no possible way for students to have access to typewriters. In this case, large free handwriting, with a soft, black pencil, may be substituted.

2. Always use full sheets of 8½ by 11 inch unruled paper. Regular rough copy paper, either white or yellow, is preferred.

3. Always begin the story from one third to one half the way down the page. This allows the copyreader to write headlines on top when necessary.

4. Leave a one-inch margin at the sides and bottom of all sheets. When more than one sheet is used, begin two inches from the top on all but the first.

5. In the upper left-hand corner of the sheet, type the name of the story. Condense the name as much as possible. *Example:* Hi-Y assembly, Bicknell-Central game.

6. Under the title of the story, place your name.

7. Under your name, indicate the exact number of words in the story. This enables the editor to determine the amount of space it will occupy in print.

8. Triple space all copy. When wide spaces are left between the lines, changes and additions can be made more readily.

9. After each paragraph, indicate in a circle the number of words in that paragraph.

10. At the bottom of each page except the last, write the word "more" and draw a circle around it.

11. At the bottom of the last paragraph, use the end signs "#" or "30."

CHAPTER LABORATORY

1. From the following facts, develop a news story using inverted order. Be prepared to discuss your story in class.

   American Legion Post 151 sponsors two Central students at Boys State.

   June 17-24, State Fair Grounds, Sacramento.

   It is a citizenship program supplementing classroom teaching.

   Ronnie Davis and Charles Spencer will attend. They won the tryouts over 15 others.

   The boys are divided into 12 cities, six counties, and two parties—Nationalists and Federalists.

   Wilson Schwartz is alternate.

   There will be 718 delegates from the state.

   They set up and conduct city, county, and state elections.

2. From both school and daily papers, clip examples of all three forms of news stories discussed in the chapter. Discuss in class.

3. Clip a violation of the cut-off test in your school newspaper. Mount it and correct the close of the story.

4. From your school newspaper, clip a news story that does not properly identify its subjects. Mount the story and at the right indicate the identifications that should have been included.

5. For your school paper, write a column of five news items and provide a column head.

6. From the following facts, write a news story with a summary lead, followed by a chronological-order story.

   Series of election crises hit Johnson District High School.

   April 19—election day—voting machine breaks down.

   April 15—two out of three candidates for junior secretary announce their fathers have been transferred and they are moving from state, Henry Gilbert and Joyce Lockerwood.

   April 6—student council questions school by-laws on nominations. Are fifty names on nominating petitions too much? What would fair number be to admit all qualified applicants who may not yet be well known around school?

   April 19—Voting machine repaired fourth period—election held fifth period.

April 9—Mr. Jeffers, adviser of French club and International Student League, questions whether Harold Leach, president of French club, can manage activities if elected President of Senior Class.

April 16—Council nominations committee meets to discuss vacant candidacies for junior secretary.

April 19—John Greenwall elected.

7. Clip and mount a story that carries a moral tag. Correct by rewriting the close.

8. Present a subject for a school story suitable for composite treatment, and list four angles that could be covered.

9. Rewrite the following story in better news style. Use many more paragraphs, and eliminate personal opinion and other violations of straight news writing.

> Wednesday, Sept. 14, the Boosters Club will sponsor their annual Bar-B-Q. Besides the Bar-B-Q there will be a huge bonfire, pep rally, and all kinds of entertainment. The run will start at 5:00 and the food will be served until 8:00. Last year over 3500 attended this affair, and this year we expect at least 5000. Not only Central students, but parents, friends, and people who just plain like good Bar-B-Q are invited.
>
> The proceeds go to the Boosters Club fund. This worthy group takes that money and does great things for Central with it. One of the improvements they have brought about is the new athletic field built this summer. The only ways the Boosters Club has of raising money are membership fees, football programs, and the Bar-B-Q. So come on, Bears! Have a good time and support your school. Eat Bar-B-Q Wednesday night!

10. Consider Examples 14 through 16, all straight news stories. Using the following points as the basis, discuss in class the good reporting found in these stories. Make your notes ahead of time. (1) the use of a quotation to show news significance, since the reporter cannot give his own opinion; (2) use of a paragraph that could have been dropped—the cut-off test; (3) identification of persons; (4) use of background information on the assumption that the reader may know nothing about the subject; (5) the limitation of coverage to basic facts to hold interest; (6) summarization of the story in the lead paragraph; (7) the use of short paragraphs; (8) the use of short sentences and simple constructions.

4 THE LEAD

Charles Dickens opened his famous *Christmas Carol* with only six words, "Marly was dead: to begin with." He needed only three words—a total of twelve letters—to give the facts, then added three more short words to invite the reader to go further.

In journalism, particularly, with something to say, the reporter goes directly to it.

Every story has a beginning, but a newspaper story has a special one—the most important paragraph of the entire account. We call this opening paragraph the *lead* (pronounced *leed*).

A reporter is not interested in constructing a smooth ending to a news story. When the last fact is told, usually in order of decreasing importance, the story stops abruptly. Because newspapers are read quickly, the opening section of a story receives most attention from both reader and writer. The reader samples it, and may remain to read more or may jump to another story to try it. Thus the lead has also become the most important part of the news story to the reporter. Even the leads of such other types of stories as the interview, the feature, and the critical review, are the most polished paragraphs of the accounts.

For convenience in study, leads are generally divided into two broad classifications: (1) the conventional, often called summary, lead; and

(2) the unconventional or unorthodox lead. It is usually, but not always, true that news stories use the former, and feature stories the latter. The conventional lead tells the facts in a natural, straightforward manner, while the unconventional lead is an intentional effort on the writer's part to introduce his story in a novel way. The conventional is most common. These two classifications are not overlapping, and the division is based entirely upon the purpose of the lead.

CONVENTIONAL LEADS

Conventional leads may be classified by content (who, what, when, where, why, and how leads) and by structure (the grammatical beginning lead). The first is analyzed by determining which of the natural reader questions the opener answers, the second by determining the grammatical form of the opener, that is, *noun, participle,* etc.

Who-what-when-where-why-and-how leads. This classification of leads is the oldest known to journalists. Kipling, in reference to his own newspaper experience, once wrote:

> I have six honest serving men;
>   They taught me all I knew;
> Their names are Where and What and When
>   And How and Why and Who.

Into the first paragraph of the conventional lead, the reporter packs the feature of his story, answering as he does so the reader's natural questions—who? what? when? where? why? and how? Whichever of these is answered first—and that depends entirely upon what the reporter considers most important—determines the name of the lead. A lead beginning with the name Hugh Forster would be a *who* lead. The *who* and *what* are usually the most important elements of a news event, the *when* and *where* the least.

Who?	Where?
Marjorie Collins, freshman, was injured Monday, November 4, in an automobile accident in front of school.	In the front hall on Friday, November 15, the Withrow-Hughes football booklet will go on sale for fifteen cents.

EXAMPLE
17

What?

Radio Station WLW of Cincinnati is sponsoring a United Nations Essay Contest in the interest of better service to the nation.

When?

Monday, November 4, as the clock struck nine-thirty, four Withrow seniors, Rosemary Garn, Alice Saar, Nancy Simons, and Helen Pascal, strode excitedly into the office of Mr. Rayburn Cadwallader, principal of Western Hills High School.

Why?

To earn money for their various plans in the coming year, several clubs have been selling food and soft drinks at recent football games.

How?

After protecting a slim six-point lead through two quarters, the freshman squad hit their stride in the fourth period and pushed across two touchdowns to unhorse the fighting Cavalier freshmen from Purcell 19-0.

Withrow Tower News
Withrow High School
Cincinnati, Ohio

Seldom does a lead answer all of these questions, for it must achieve a fast start for the story. In the leads that follow, some natural questions were left unanswered:

The class Gay Nineties Night will be presented twice tomorrow.	**When?** (At what hours?) **Where?**
The final meeting of the Book Club will be held today, period 9, in room 219.	**What** is planned?
Astoria's 4-H Club boasts a grand champion winner in last week's state contest in Madison.	**Who** is the champion?
The greatly anticipated event—graduation—to which seniors have been looking forward so long, is just around the corner.	**When** is it? **How** many seniors are there?
Two new musical organizations have been added to Central's music groups this fall.	**What** are they? **Why** were they formed?

The good reporter tries to place the big feature of his story in the opening five to eight words of the lead, usually the first line of type. This is especially true of the conventional news lead. It is natural, therefore, that the articles *a, an,* and *the* are considered poor words to open the lead; their frequent use robs the writing of individuality and marks the page as generally monotonous.

54

In most instances it is well to hold leads to three lines, which means about fifteen to twenty-five words. *The well-written summary lead has only one sentence, certainly no more than two.* One idea, one main point is sound advice for the opening paragraph. The lead should say something definite, making every word a useful part of the statement. Capital letters, titles of organizations, and difficult ideas may hinder the smooth beginning needed.

In a news story, the reporter goes directly to the point, especially in the lead. In the sentences below, note the direct approach of the statements in the second column as contrasted with those in the first.

The president of the debating society called for order last night so as to open the meeting and discuss debating schedules with the teams of other schools.	Jim Robbins, president of the debating society, last night opened the first meeting of the semester with a call for student participation in inter-school debates.
As soon as the bell rang on Monday, the opening of New Webster's first driving class began.	When the 9 A.M. bell sounded, Monday, September 23, New Webster's first driving class began.
Emphasis was put upon the point of lowering the legal voting age to eighteen by Henry Jensen, president of the student council, in the parent-student assembly in the Western High auditorium on Tuesday night.	"Let's Lower the Voting Age" was the title of an address by Henry Jensen, president of the student council, to the parent-student assembly held Tuesday evening in the Western High auditorium.

Study the leads below, and analyze the characteristics that have made the second in each pair the stronger of the two. In each case, name the who-what-when-where-why-how elements in order of appearance.

Weak Leads	*Stronger Leads*
All students who plan to compete in the annual All-City Oratorical contest met Tuesday in room 206 with Central's speech director.	Three boys and one girl will represent Central in the annual All-City Oratorical contest, March 7, it was announced yesterday by Carl Shrode, speech director.

55

Members of the Microscope Club met Monday, November 7, in room 34 for the purpose of electing officers.

The first paper collected in the homerooms was turned in Monday at the Boys' Federation council meeting.

In meeting Wednesday, the Senior class voted upon dates for Class Night and Varsity Show.

Mrs. William Koenig, president of the Parent Teacher Association, told the students yesterday in assembly that the Benson district may not have a teen-age club.

The electric and radio classes of Arthur Turner's shops repair many motors each week.

Henry Bass, new president of the Microscope Club, upon being elected to office Monday, immediately called for a constitutional revision.

Over two tons of paper was the record contribution of East High's homerooms, in their first collection of the year for Boys' Federation.

June 12 and 15 are the dates to remember for Senior Class Night and the annual Varsity Show.

Because of lagging interest among student leaders, Benson district may lose its teen-age club this year, stated Mrs. William Koenig, Parent Teacher President, in assembly yesterday.

Electric motors of all descriptions are being reclaimed from the scrap pile by the boys of Arthur Turner's electric and radio classes.

Grammatical-beginning lead. Leads may also be studied by their grammatical beginnings: noun, participial phrase, adverbial clause, noun clause, infinitive, and so forth; for instance:

EXAMPLE
18

Noun
Plans for the installation of a permanent public address system in the Northeast High School auditorium were announced recently by Principal R. S. Mickle.

Participle
Encouraged by a total of $31 profit from the Lincoln High concession, the Rockettes this week begin the sale of Rocket reflectors.

Noun clause
That the Monocle is the mouthpiece of the school was maintained by Miss Florence Ryland, as her homeroom 115 subscribed 100 per cent.

Conditional clause
If the local Red Cross drive continues at the pace set during the first two days, John Marshall will have reached its goal by the time this story is in print.

Prepositional phrase

With the annual physical check of the seventh- and tenth-grade boys and girls completed, the girls' examiner, Doctor Ruth Warner, revealed that she had found few students at Northeast to be examples of perfect posture.

Infinitive

To prepare to help during the Christmas rush, 29 E.H.S. pupils received credit in the classes in pre-employment taught by Miss Fern Hubbard, supervisor of secondary distributive education in the public schools.

The Northeastern
Northeast High School
Lincoln, Nebraska

The Monocle
John Marshall High School
Richmond, Virginia

UNORTHODOX LEADS

There are unorthodox or freak leads of all kinds created to attract attention or to communicate the purpose of the story. (See the following examples.) The reporter's individuality stands out in this type of lead. A clever editor of a daily newspaper soon learns to detect the writers of feature stories by their leads. Blanketed as unconventional leads, and found generally on feature stories (occasionally on news stories), unorthodox leaders are defined as follows:

Astonisher is an exclamation.
Contrast describes two extremes or opposites.
Epigram opens by quoting a common expression or verse.
One-word consists of a single key word.
Punch crowds a dramatic statement or much action into the lead.
Question opens with a question.
Sequence reports the events in the order in which they happened.
Suspended interest carries the big point late in the lead.

Astonisher

Better look your prettiest this week!

Contrast

Capitalism versus socialism will be the discussion topic at the meeting of the Forum, November 27.

Epigram

Like father, like son! So goes the old axiom. And rightly so in the cases of Pat Wieland, cheerleader, and Mary Sue Holland, Pepper. Right that is, except for the "son" part.

EXAMPLE
19

57

One word

Pictures!

The Camera Club continues to bring them in by the score each month in its all-school contest.

Punch

Dust off your monocles, fellow students, and take a good look at the contents of the six show cases that line the walls of Northeast.

Question

Why be a wallflower? By following a few simple rules of femininity, you too can be the "belle of the ball."

Sequence

On Thursday of last week, the proposed Pep Club group met at the encouragement of Principal Mardis. Just one week later the Student Affairs committee approved the Club. Tomorrow Pep Club meets officially.

Suspended interest

By some trick of fate the first period newswriting class in 203 didn't rate the usual semi-weekly news broadcast last week.

The Advocate
Lincoln High School
Lincoln, Nebraska

The Northeastern
Northeast High School
Lincoln, Nebraska

PRECAUTIONS

The who-what-when-where-why-how mold is a treacherous thing. It tempts the beginner to keep pouring facts into his lead until it is a bulky, unwieldy paragraph that exhausts the person who tries to read it. The lead must be short and inviting, not long and discouraging. The grammatical classification may also be treacherous to the high school reporter. He may play around with variations just for the sake of change, and present perfectly phrased leads that sound unnatural to the reader. The experienced newspaperman does not think in terms of who and what leads, sequence and epigram leads, or noun clause and preposition leads. From his facts he hastily grasps the most startling, the most important, the most picturesque, or the most unnatural element, and begins with it. Through experience he has learned to vary his beginnings.

The beginning high school reporter should look upon this approach to lead writing in the same manner. The rules he is asked to follow here are not sacred within themselves; they are steps to automatic lead writing. At first the reporter will be conscious of the rules as he constructs his leads; gradually the rules will fall away as an old shell that has served its purpose, and his ability to write leads almost automatically will emerge.

58

CHAPTER LABORATORY

1. Examine the front pages of the daily papers, and clip an example of each of the following types of leads: (a) who, (b) what, (c) when, (d) where, (e) why, and (f) how. In each case, list the elements in the order in which they appear in the lead, e.g., why-when-who, or what-when-who-how.

2. Suppose that you attended an assembly program yesterday as a reporter for your school paper and collected the following facts.

> An assembly was held yesterday morning in the auditorium. Miss Maude Lewis spoke. The assembly was in charge of the local chapter of the Junior Red Cross. The title of the speech was "How You Can Help." The speaker is a national Junior Red Cross representative. Miss Lewis discussed American youth and today's world. Miss Loraine Zuelly is sponsor of the local group.

Before you write the lead for this story, you will want to organize your facts. Write the elements of the lead (who, what, when, etc.) in a column on the left side of a sheet of paper. Then opposite each of these words, write the particular fact that answers the question asked. For example, after "who" you will write "Miss Maud Lewis," and so on. All elements are not always found in each news story.

Next, assuming that "who" or "Miss Maude Lewis" is most important, place *1* after this element. Place a *2* after the one you believe to rank next in importance. Continue until you have numbered all the elements.

Now write your *who* lead in one sentence, using all of the elements in the order that you have planned. Note: Remember that you are writing only the lead and not the whole news story. You will not need all of the facts listed above for your lead.

3. Below are facts for a news story with a *what* lead. Select and number the various elements for this lead as you did above, numbering the *what* element first. Now write your *what* lead.

> Miss Jane Woods of the English department has been compiling the honor roll record for the past quarter. One hundred and six students were included in the list. This represents an increase over last quarter's list, which consisted of seventy-one. The 12B's held first place with nineteen members receiving the rating.

59

4. Using the facts presented below, write a *why* lead. Generally *why* leads start with *because, because of, in order to,* or *due to.* Again, arrange your elements in order of importance.

The third week of the next quarter has been designated "Museum Week." Plans are being formulated by the Archeology Club. A committee has been appointed to plan an open house. An assembly program is being planned and students will be permitted to visit the museum during lunch periods. According to L. T. Buck, sponsor of the club, members expect to create interest in the school's collection of relics.

5. Following the same plan, write a *how* lead from the facts below.

Dale Phares will participate in the district oratorical contest at Princeton next June. Dale won the right to take part by defeating Central and Western Hills representatives in the all-city contest yesterday. He spoke on "The Motives of Russia."

6. *When* leads, that is, leads with the *when* or time element at the beginning, are rare. From actual occurrences in your school, choose some event in which time is important and write a *when* lead.

7. From the front pages of daily papers, clip examples of five different grammatical leads. Mount and label each.

8. Using the following facts, write a single-sentence summary lead, beginning with a noun.

The first basketball game of the season was played between Central and Bicknell last Friday. The Central Bears were victorious by a 40-17 score. Mark Wakefield is Central's coach.

9. Write a single-sentence summary lead with the preceding facts, using a prepositional phrase at the beginning.

10. Write the lead prepared in Exercise 9 using a participle at the beginning. Present participles end in *–ing* while past participles end in *–ed.*

11. Rewrite the same lead, beginning with an infinitive.

12. Clip from the front pages of daily papers samples of five different types of unorthodox leads. Mount and label each.

13. Use the following leads as the basis of a class discussion. Classify each lead in as many ways as you can.

1

Under an agreement between the Minneapolis Retail Association and the Minneapolis School Board, high school students will be excused from classes to work December 16 to 20, the week preceding Christmas vacation.

2

Have you future botanists signed up for the **Botany Club** yet?

3

An article on Costa Rica translated by Janie Ericson, 11A, 230, appeared in the November issue of *Jaycee,* published by the Minneapolis Junior Chamber of Commerce.

4

WHAT: Thanksgiving Day.
WHEN: November 28.
WHERE: In homes all over America.
WHY: To give thanks for the blessings of life.

5

Each Thursday, Blue Tri sponsors a candy sale in the front hall. Dolores Fritz planned the October 31 sale, Ruth Elliff the November 7 sale, and Joan Grife the one on November 21.

6

Do you avoid walking under ladders? Do you wear a horseshoe around your neck? Do you carry a salt shaker in your pocket? The "A" Seniors' advice is "Why Worry?" Come to the class play, **Friday,** December **13.**

7

Two scholarships of $150 each will be given by the Apollo Club, the oldest male singing organization in the United States, to a boy and a girl in the vocal finals in March.

8

"Raw brain power is the most serious wastage in America today!"

9

Thanksgiving vacation this year will bring an added thrill to five West High students, when they attend the National Scholastic Press Association convention in Milwaukee, Wisconsin, November 28–30.

West High Times
West High School
Minneapolis, Minnesota

14. Use the following leads as the basis of a class discussion. Diagnose each lead carefully.

AS NEW SOPHOMORES enter B-CC each year, they must become accustomed to the environment of a senior high school for the first time. The road is rough at first.

TWENTY STUDENTS will represent B-CC in the Maryland All-State Orchestra Wednesday, Thursday, and Friday in Annapolis.

TO DIRECT the work of the senior class, chairmen of special committees have been chosen by the Executive Committee, announces Miss Margaret Cooke, adviser.

B-CC WELCOMED 2,199 students and 104 teachers September 5, according to the official report of Mr. Ray O. Zimmerman, vice principal.

61

ROME WASN'T BUILT in a day, nor was the Bethesda-Chevy Chase high school stadium.

REPLACING the old Bi-County League, of which B-CC was a member, are the newly formed Montgomery County, and Prince George's County Leagues.

MR. LEROY JONES, Mr. Robert Foster, and Mr. Harry Botsford have assumed responsibility for the fate of the Baron football squad.

"RETARD THEM, RETARD THEM, make them relinquish the ball."

This and other "intellectual" cheers have been heard at recent B-CC football games.

SPONSORED by the National Honor Society, a tutoring service is being offered to those students who have difficulty with their subjects.

WHILE PRACTICING offensive plays and working on fundamentals, the B-CC soccer team looks ahead to a return match with Suitland.

The Tattler
Bethesda-Chevy Chase High School
Bethesda, Maryland

15. *Group activity.* Using a section of your bulletin board or a large piece of wallboard, lay out a chart similar to the one below. Clip leads from daily papers and locate them on the chart with thumbtacks. For example, a *who* lead that is also a noun lead will be placed in the upper left space. A *why* lead might begin with a prepositional phrase and would be located in the second space from the top of the fifth column. Can all spaces be filled?

Grammatical Beginnings	*Who*	*What*	*When*	*Where*	*Why*	*How*
Noun	x					
Prepositional phrase					x	
Infinitive						
Participle						
Noun clause						
Concession clause						
Conditional clause						

16. From your school newspaper, select five leads you think could be improved. Mount them on a sheet of paper and at the side of each write an improved lead.

5 THE ADVANCE AND FOLLOW-UP

Seldom is a news story on a significant subject complete within itself in the daily press. The paper goes to press carrying the developments up to the deadline. The next day another story brings the reader up to date, and so on as long as reader interest is sustained.

If a popular event is to be held, such as a concert or a public address, stories about the affair are published before it takes place. Such a story is known as the *advance*.

In the case of an important or interesting trial, the proceedings are covered each day. After the first report, the succeeding accounts are known as *follow-up* stories. They can be compared to installments in a magazine or chapters in a book.

Thus the *advance* and the *follow-up* are news stories, links in a chain of news coverage on a given subject. Their presence, and their number, depend primarily upon reader interest. Two examples of such sequences might be:

1	Advance	Advance	The event	Follow-up
2	The event	Follow-up	Follow-up	

THE ADVANCE STORY

For reader interest and lively journalism, the school newspaper depends heavily upon the event that has not yet taken place—the advance story.

The great news value of the advance is in revealing the unknown. Since students generally know important school events in advance, the news value of such a story rests upon the coverage of angles that are new to the reader. It might be called reporting "the unknown of the known." News is not necessarily that which has just happened, but often that which has not been reported.

Types of news. As you have learned, news is of two types, *spot* and *anticipated*. While spot news—the unexpected happening—is the daily paper's chief interest-bearing commodity, it means little to the school press. The things that happen around the school have been expected, with few exceptions.

Occasionally the unexpected will occur—a sport's upset, a fire, a major accident. But by the time it is reported in the next issue of the school paper, it is no longer spot news, merely the accurate recording of something that is already history. The story of the game not yet played can be much more exciting than the account of one the students saw last week.

Thus the advance offers the staff a chance to pack into the paper reader interest built upon facts hitherto unknown to the student. More than half the coverage of high school newspapers concerns the future rather than the past.

The future book. The responsibility of keeping the paper alive through advance coverage is centered on the assignment editor, whose job it is to anticipate news. To do a thorough job he keeps a *future book*—a calendar of possibilities. Its effectiveness reflects his thoroughness in listing scheduled school affairs and his ingenuity in seeing related news possibilities. A glance into such a book early in October might reveal the following:

October 10. Host to Bay Area press conference.
       11. Washington game.

13. School drive for live specimens for biology lab. Question of need—editorial as well as news story.
14. Proposed council changes to be treated in homerooms. Get opinions.
14. Coach King's birthday.
15. Home economics classes to judge all lunch trays. Feature by Stemper.
17. Annual spelling-bee assembly.
18. Lincoln game.
20. Printing classes on field trip to *Chronicle*. Check other field trips.
21. First issue of the paper published in 1924. Photos, comparisons, interviews.
22. Last day to enter oratorical contest.
23. Tryouts for one-act plays. Feature.
24. Assembly for Mission game.
24. Term open house, new biochem lab.
25. Mission game.
28. Official school enrollment report due. Compare with last year.
29. Work-experience assembly. Important civic leaders as speakers.
31. Halloween.

Typical advance. Example 20 is a typical advance story. It covers the subject in straight news style, presenting the major points early in the account with successive facts arranged in decreasing order of importance.

Running this story two or three weeks before the event makes it possible for the editor to schedule a second advance, bringing out interesting angles or new developments not treated in the first account. The coverage of the actual concert, the story following the performance, would deserve less space unless something unanticipated and highly newsworthy took place. It might be well, however, to present material for a review, of course under the reviewer's by-line. (See Chapter 11.)

Other examples of advance stories indicate the possible range of coverage in this form of newswriting (Examples 21 and 22.) Note that although they all concern school events, the advance can be adapted to community and national stories.

Band and Orchestra Plan Spring Concert

EXAMPLE

20

The place: Parcells Auditorium. The date: Wednesday, May 18. The time: 8:15 P.M.

Those present will hear the Grosse Pointe High School Concert Band and Concert Orchestra present their annual spring concert.

The reputation of these groups is widespread. As a result, scattered in the audience will be band and orchestra conductors from all over the state. Several members of the Detroit Symphony are also expected.

Guest soloist at this concert will be Mr. William Bell, tuba virtuoso of the New York Philharmonic Orchestra, conducted by Mr. Leonard Bernstein. Mr. Bell was once hailed by the great conductor Arturo Toscannini as "the greatest tuba player in the world."

Mr. Bell has been acclaimed by critics all over the world. Recently, he accompanied the New York Philharmonic on its history-making tour of Russia.

He will play four popular numbers with the concert band: his own arrangement of "The Carni-

val of Venice," "The Elephants' Tango," the famous Mozart aria "Isis and Osiris," and finally the tune he made a hit, "When Yuma Plays the Rhumba on the Tuba."

The orchestra will open the first half of the program with the rollicking "Il Re Pastore" overture, by Mozart.

Violinists James Taugner, Larry Engelhart, and cellist Francis Guice will be featured in the Vivaldi *Concerto Grosso in A Minor.*

The concert band will present three of their numbers from the state festival competition. The unusual and little-known Sousa march "Nobles of the Mystic Shrine" will open the second half. The contemporary American composer Robert Ward will be represented by his Gershwin-like "Jubilation, An Overture."

The program will close with excerpts from the Lerner and Loewe musical *Gigi.*

Tickets are 25 cents with an S.A. ticket, 50 cents without, and $1 for adults.

Tickets may be purchased from any student in the instrumental music department, or at the door.

The Tower
Grosse Point High School
Grosse Point, Michigan

Become Citizens on Hoover Stage

EXAMPLE

21

For a brief span of an hour and a half, the Hoover auditorium will become a "legal courtroom." A special court session will be witnessed by most of the students, Thursday morning, November 9, when the naturalization of 140 persons will take place. Judges Fred Kunzel and Jacob J. Weinberger will preside at the hearing.

The granting of citizenship outside the District Court is not an unusual procedure, according to Mr. Melvin C. Anderson, naturalization examiner, United States Immigration and Naturalization office, who will also participate in the program. The ceremony has been held, on occasion, in other school auditoriums. The ceremony at Hoover will be one of the highlights of American Education Week.

Naturalization, the procedure aliens must complete before becoming citizens of the United States, requires much basic knowledge. This includes a knowledge of English, both written and oral, and a familiarity with United States' history and government. Judge Weinberger says that one of the most valuable qualifications is that all aliens must be "attached to the principles of the Constitution."

After completing and meeting all qualifications, the applicant for citizenship prepares for the naturalization ceremony. This ceremony is usually conducted in group form, usually at the United States District Court House. It may, however, be performed individually in any place. Judge Kunzel said the last ceremony held out of the office was held aboard the carrier *U.S.S. Kearsarge,* two miles at sea. The next group ceremony will be held at Hoover.

Following the hearing will be a reception in the clubroom for the "new" citizens, Judges Kunzel and Weinberger, guests, and various members of the faculty.

The Cardinal
Herbert Hoover High School
San Diego, California

Boys', Girls' Leagues Present Assemblies

Slippery When Wet, a surfing film, will be presented and narrated by Bruce Brown, well-known surfer and photographer, during the Boys' League portion of the assembly today.

Brown, appearing in person, has won many surfing championships. He also has made several surfing films, such as *Surf Crazy* and *Barefoot Adventure.*

Slippery When Wet shows hilarious exploits of surfing in Hawaii. It tells about five boys on a record-breaking, low-budget, stay in the fiftieth state.

Plan Program

Gary Anslyn, Boys' League president, was assisted in planning the program by John Marshall, vice-president; Tom Fry, secretary; George Davis, treasurer; and Mr. Max Shelley, sponsor.

"I Enjoy Being a Girl" will be presented by the Girls' League today in their part of the assembly. It will feature Girls' Glee, Drama, Modern Dance, a quartet, and a fashion show.

The models were picked on the basis of their good grooming and were selected from those who do not usually participate in assemblies. They were chosen a few days before the show and were asked to wear exactly what they were wearing.

Cheryl Hesser, Girls' League president, was aided by Wanda Raab, vice-president; Elaine Jones, secretary; Roselyn Garibay, treasurer; Linda Ferandell, social chairman; cheerleaders Erika Noll and Haydee Neri; and Mrs. Verjean Avila and Mrs. Hope Jeter, co-sponsors.

Franklin Press
Franklin High School
Los Angeles, California

EXAMPLE
22

The advance as publicity. The advance story is most often used by school papers to develop interest in coming school events, the basketball game to be attended, the school paper to be subscribed to, the student activities ticket to be purchased. Interest and enthusiasm can be incorporated in the treatment without violating the principles of good journalism.

The *moral tag,* the personalized tail-end comment added by an eager or inexperienced reporter, may easily creep into the beginning reporter's advance stories, in the form of such statements as these:

Come on out, students, and support your team this Saturday.
The play will certainly be worth the fifty cents.
In their behavior, students must show their appreciation of these lunch-hour dances in this first trial that is coming up.

To bring about student action in a school event, the reporter writes an interesting and factual account; he does not resort to direct editorial appeal. The advance story is a form of news story and must be governed by news principles.

The school paper often carries a series of two, three, or even more advance stories leading up to an important event and creating interest in it. Such a series must be planned from the beginning, all possible angles being determined and then divided among the accounts. Proper handling of coming events calls for a sound and balanced news policy, a comprehensive method of determining those events that deserve extra publicity, and a thorough gathering of the facts by the reporters. Example 20 presents the first of a series of advance stories written for the annual spring concert. Notice these points:

1. The writer writes a news account, an announcement giving the reader only the facts; he keeps his feature angles to build up interest in future accounts.

2. He gives the facts but does not appeal for student attendance.

THE FOLLOW-UP STORY

The daily press. A daily paper transmits to its readers the news that has occurred or become known since yesterday's paper was issued.

68

It cuts a twenty-four hour swath through the intertangled, continuous affairs of men, assuring the reader the continuation of these stories in tomorrow's issue.

In any one issue there are a number of stories in the middle of coverage, others being concluded, others beginning a series of accounts, and some that were not there yesterday and will not be there tomorrow. And so should it be with a good school newspaper.

Early in the working day the desk man of the daily paper runs through earlier issues in his own and other newspapers to determine which stories deserve further attention. His sense of news values coupled with his knowledge of his readers' interests and the policies of the paper will tell him which stories should be treated.

If another paper has run the first account, the desk man either (1) turns the clipping over to a rewrite man who rewrites the story for their paper, or (2) he puts a reporter on it to follow it for new developments as if the story had first appeared in his paper. In either case accuracy must be assured. The first approach results in a *rewrite* story, and the second in a *follow-up* story, sometimes called a *follow*.

The school paper. The editor of the school paper, however, faces an entirely different situation. The infrequent issue of his paper lessens the use of the follow-up. Consequently, it tests the creative ability and the journalistic ingenuity of the student reporter to find new angles that justify further treatment of a subject. Just as soon as the paper is off the press, the alert assignment editor will search the issue for possible follows, and will assign them at once. Usually the reporter who handled the previous story is the logical one to follow up the new angles. The good reporter assumes this responsibility without being told. His news sense leads him to new facts that will answer questions the preceding story has raised in the minds of its readers.

Thus the follow-up is distinguished not by its style but by its chronology. It simply is not the first story that the paper has carried on the subject. Consequently the reporter must take into account all previous coverage. If two advance stories are carried on a coming game, the second is a follow-up as well as an advance. The follow-up is nothing more than good journalism.

Example 23 includes two stories on a subject, the advance and the follow-up. At the end of the first account, it is quite apparent that another story can be expected, for the first leaves the student council seeking solutions to two problems. Although the writer of the follow-up has not included a true tie-in paragraph, he links his new developments so closely with what has gone before that the reader has all the information he needs. A tie-in could have mentioned previously suggested solutions, the length of time the council has struggled with the two questions, and committee members mentioned in the first account.

Smoking Now Problem, Says S. C. President

EXAMPLE
23

"Two of the greatest problems now facing the Student Council are those of smoking and parking," states Arthur Chavez, Student Council President.

"Perhaps the largest problem is that of smoking," he continues. "The number of boys who stand out in the street in front of 'A' building are giving the school an unfavorable atmosphere."

Mr. Micah Ruggles, Council sponsor, suggests that some place be provided for the smokers— using Tech High's seventh floor smoking room as an example, or possibly something on the order of the army day room.

At the last Student Council meeting, a report was made by the committee for investigating smoking. Suggestions were that smoking be permitted only during lunch hour and in lavatories exclusively.

Committee members are Jerre Brigham, Charles Steers, and T. C. Slack.

"Parking and driving of cars is the other problem, and many high school Harrys are driving in a way which endangers the lives of students and teachers, in fact, of anyone who walks,"Ruggles says.

"The situation has gotten entirely out of hand, and the Student Council may call in the Highway Patrol to take over," he concludes.

Although both questions have been before the Council for several meetings, no definite steps have been taken on either as yet.

Council to Permit Smoking at Lunch

"There will be no smoking on or across the street from the school grounds or between classes; only during lunch hour will smoking be permitted, and then on the road that leads north from the gym." So reads the new regulation in force since Monday.

70

Co-operating with Mr. H. N. Rath, principal, and Mr. Micah Ruggles, Student Council sponsor, the council appointed a committee which in less than two weeks submitted this plan.

Vote Improvement

Smoking has diminished considerably—there are almost no cigarettes in evidence now—but a detention study hall will be held for any who do not obey the regulation. An "F" in conduct will also be entered on the permanent record.

Parking, the other problem before the council, has been investigated by a committee chaired by Mario Alfonso. It is reported by this committee that, under existing rules, parking is permitted ACROSS THE STREET FROM "B" BUILDING, ON BOTH SIDES OF THE STREET OPPOSITE "C" BUILDING, AND DOWN BY THE GYM.

No Parking "A" Building

The space in front of and across the street from the "A" building is reserved for school busses and patrons of the school, while the parking space in front of "B" building is for faculty parking. Motor scooters, like last year, are to be parked in the space between band and shop portables. Bikes, as usual, should be placed in the space provided by the agricultural portable.

Although there had been some controversy as to whether students were to be permitted to go to South Miami for lunch, it was discovered that anyone may go who secures written permission from parents.

The Ponce Tribune
Ponce de Leon High School
Coral Gables, Florida

Construction. In the daily press, the reporter places in his follow-up lead the new angle that seems to be most significant or timely. He follows this with the tie-in, one or more paragraphs that briefly summarize what has appeared before. This satisfies the reader who has not followed the story up to this time, and it is brief enough not to disturb the reader who has.

With the lead and the tie-in out of the way, the reporter continues as in any good news reporting, using chronological or inverted treatment of the other facts. Some follow-ups have at least three or four paragraphs of new developments before the tie-in appears. At times the new development fills the first half of the story, while the last half summarizes what went before.

Since the school paper deals more with anticipated than spot news, the true form of the follow-up story is usually lost. Although Example 24 illustrates this form of writing, most follow-up stories in the school press give little indication of previous coverage. The subjects treated often do not require the tie-in.

Links Board
Members Chosen

EXAMPLE
24

Members of the new *Links* board are announced today by Miss Sarah T. Muir, faculty chairman. They are as follows: editor, Kathleen Schreiber; managing editor, Warren Wise; business manager, Dean Haupt; biography editor, Keith Van Arsdol; and photography editor, Norma Chubbuck. All five of these are seniors, and three are former *Advocate* members. The staff is to be chosen later.

Sixty-three students applied for the positions, and were interviewed Tuesday, Wednesday and Thursday, October 29, 30, and 31. Fifteen of these were recalled for second interviews on Friday, November 1.

Applicants were asked to fill out questionnaires in which they indicated the position desired, high school organizations belonged to, outside work, and school activities.

The new board will hold its first meeting, Wednesday, November 13.

Students were judged on fitness for their particular choice of position. Some were rejected because of too heavy schedules and too much outside work.

Judges were Miss Elizabeth Grone, Miss Sarah T. Muir, and Frank Kane, the faculty board.

The *Links* is the Lincoln High yearbook and is published in the second semester.

The Lead
Contains the latest, most important development—the announcement of the five students elected to edit the school annual, the *Links*.

The Tie-In
These paragraphs go back to pick up information carried in a previous story but needed here to complete the account.

Additional Facts
The tie-in is now followed by new developments that are less important than those treated in the lead, in order of decreasing significance.

The Advocate
Lincoln High School
Lincoln, Nebraska

CHAPTER LABORATORY

1. Using a copy of your last school paper, mark all the advance stories on page one.
2. Clip and mount an advance story you consider a brief announcement. Do the same for a more detailed story, one that was written as advance publicity.
3. From the last issue of the school paper, select one story that deserves more attention. In 200 words, .indicate your ideas for additional coverage.
4. List five events that you think should be included in the future book of your paper.
5. Select one of these events and write a timely advance story of 250 words.
6. List five good rules to be followed in covering advance stories. In class discussion these ideas should be combined into one selected list for class use.
7. Examine three consecutive issues of a daily paper, and clip the continuing coverage of a news item that has appeared in all three issues.
8. Using a copy of your last school paper, mark all the follow-ups.
9. From the school paper, select a story that deserves a follow-up and write one 200 words in length.
10. Write a third and final story for Example 23, about 300 words, from your imagination.
11. List ten big news stories that have received continuing coverage by means of follow-ups in your daily paper during the past year or two. Compare the lists in class discussion.
12. From the next-to-the-last issue of your school paper, select a story that merited a follow-up but did not receive it in the last issue. List the new developments or angles that might have been covered.

6 REPORTING A SPEECH

The report of a speech is a distinct type of straight news story, and an important one. Who reads speech reports? Naturally, two types of readers—those who were present at the address and those who were not. The former are interested because they were part of the occasion, the latter, because of the appeal of the person, the subject, or possibly the reporter's presentation.

The reporter's main task in covering a speech is that of reproducing for his readers the original message of the speaker. Since news space for such coverage is limited by both reader interest and the pressure of other news, speech reporting usually is a process of condensing. In this the reporter must not only be accurate, he must also be faithful to the speaker's intentions. Although the reporter follows the principles of straight news reporting, he depends largely upon his ability to retain the original spirit and substance of a speech no matter how much he must condense it.

COVERING A SPEECH

In addition to reporting what was said, the reporter must accurately search out and utilize important supplementary information. This includes the following points:

74

1. The complete name of the speaker or speakers, accurately spelled
2. The identity of the person, including his significant position
3. The reason or the occasion for his appearance here
4. The exact title of his talk
5. The time and the place
6. The nature of the audience

He collects much of this before the talk, seldom any information from the speaker himself. At times professional reporters are able to secure a copy of the speech in advance of delivery, although they must still be present to cover any last-minute changes. School reporters cannot expect this convenience, for seldom does the school assembly speaker duplicate his speech for the press. The most effective way to cover a speech is actually to be present.

The reporter does not attempt to take down everything the speaker says. He takes down the important statements verbatim, which means he must retain a statement in his mind long enough to get it on paper, and at the same time follow the speaker's next remark. If he expects to quote a statement directly, he makes sure he has it word for word. No speaker likes to see himself misquoted. It may mean embarrassment, or even libel, to the paper.

The reporter takes his notes in longhand; seldom is shorthand used in speech reporting. He condenses long statements while taking notes, thus saving himself work then as well as later when he writes the story. Except for direct quotations, he can handle most points with summary notes. While covering the story, he notices the reactions of the audience, its size, and any other significant details.

As in all straight news reporting, the reporter keeps himself and his feelings out of the account. He may not agree with what is being said—in fact he may not even be interested—but he takes it down as accurately as possible.

It is usually possible to get something further from the speaker through an interview either before or after his regular address. A few questions, properly selected and handled, can make the speech given in the school assembly interesting and vital to the student reader.

WRITING THE REPORT

The reporter writes the report immediately after he has covered the speech, while the speech and the surroundings are fresh in his mind.

The news and interest value determine the length. The order, however, is determined by the reporter, who finds a purpose behind his report and organizes his material to best carry out that purpose, regardless of the speaker's order. The speaker usually begins with minor elements, leading up to the important points late in his talk—the reverse of new-story order. After selecting his lead, the reporter can hastily skim his notes and number the parts in order of their use.

Statements in themselves mean nothing unless the writer has a clear understanding of the speaker's general point, which is why it is unsatisfactory for one student to take notes on a speech and another to write the account. The writer must transmit the speaker's point. Even exact quotation does not guarantee fair coverage. The story must retain the tone and the significance of the speech and the occasion.

The lead follows the style of a news lead. It may summarize the general text or topic; it may open with a striking statement; it may even begin with the speaker, the audience, or the occasion if any of these seems to be the significant point. Additional material secured through an interview may suggest a lead. Naturally, the speaker's name and identification will come in the first or second paragraph.

The occasion or circumstances, the time, the place, and any other points in the setting will follow the lead, unless included in it.

In dealing with the speech itself, the writer should avoid monotony by varying the style with (1) direct quotations, (2) indirect quotations, and (3) summaries of sections of the speech, enabling him to condense a long speech into a convenient story. He should avoid including both direct and indirect quotations in the same paragraph.

Securing variety in the story. One way of maintaining variety in the story is by the judicious use of synonyms—both for the speaker's name and for the word *said*. It is important that the reporter not repeat the speaker's full name from paragraph to paragraph. Principal Jonathan Smith might be referred to as *the principal, Principal Smith, he, the speaker,* or *Mr. Smith.*

Many words (see the following list) may be substituted for the relatively colorless *said*. They should be selected with care, however, for such synonyms have two effects: (1) some words are direct synonyms, substitutions carrying no significance—such as *he talked, he noted, he expressed, he declared, he went on;* (2) others can be cleverly used to help summarize and communicate the speaker's attitude as well as his remarks—for instance, *he insisted, he reassured, he protested, he urged, he warned,* etc. These must, however, summarize the speaker's attitude, not the reporter's.

he warned	he urged	he pointed out	he favored
he proposed	he questioned	he expressed	he described
he commented on	he advised	he answered	he asserted
he reviewed	he added	he admitted	he compared
he predicted	he declared	he mused	he upbraided
he alleged	he avowed	he assured	he announced
he appealed	he held	he went on	he protested
he noted	he charged	he talked	he reaffirmed
he insisted	he conceded	he attested	he reassured

Verbatim quotations are the spice in the report of any speech—if they are carefully selected and not so commonly used that they lose their significance. One part direct discourse, one part indirect discourse, and one part summarizing statement is a good formula to follow when in doubt. Remember that quotation marks must be used with every direct quotation. When the quotation is more than one paragraph long, quotation marks begin each paragraph, but follow only the last one.

Select your style. Remember that news stories can be written in an inverted-pyramid style or in a chronological style. In writing the report of a speech, a form of news story, the reporter can list the speaker's points in the order of diminishing significance, or he can give them just as they were given by the speaker. The former method is often the more effective.

The diagrams of two stories follow. They analyze how the reporters secured variety by alternating direct and indirect restatements of the speaker's views. Stories from daily papers can be analyzed the same way. An actual story is accompanied by a diagram in Example 25.

DIAGRAMS OF TWO ACCOUNTS OF SPEECHES

First Story	Second Story
Lead gives speaker's name, his subject, and the time and place of the talk.	Summary lead, including in order—what, when, who, how.
Second paragraph reviews main point of the talk.	Second paragraph identifies the panel of speakers.
Direct quotation.	Indirect quotation.
Indirect quotation.	Direct quotation.
Direct quotation.	Indirect quotation.
Indirect quotation.	Direct quotation.
Indirect summary of less important points.	Indirect quotation.
Last paragraph tells main facts about next school assembly.	

Journalists Hear Editor at Ann Arbor

"Don't say we have no new frontiers. The buffalo is gone; the Indian sits by the railroad tracks weaving blankets and selling jewelry. That frontier is gone. But a thousand frontiers of the mind await us," Mr. Allan Keller, editor of the *New York World Telegram and Sun,* told a meeting of the Michigan Interscholastic Press Association.

The meeting, held in Ann Arbor at the University of Michigan, was attended by 46 journalism students and *Tower* writers from Grosse Pointe High.

Mr. Keller emphasized the need for men and women who can translate the complex world of the scientist and technician to the average man. . . . He said that the great intellects would be working in a vacuum without the writer there to tell the world.

"The poorly informed newspaperman is about the most useless thing there is," the speaker commented. In this connection he emphasized the need for a college education in newspaper work.

"The good writer," Mr. Keller said, "is always walking a tightrope between dullness on one side and purple prose on the other."

By controlling his skill with words, his style, and his capacity for interpretation, Mr. Keller said a newspaperman could "take an idea, hone it to a sharp edge, and use it." He said that when craft and aims or ideals are combined, the result is good writing.

Mr. Keller, a newspaperman for over twenty years, is the assistant city editor of the *New York World Telegram and Sun,* and adjunct professor of journalism at Columbia University.

EXAMPLE

25

Lead opens with a quote from the speaker, includes his full name, identification, and the occasion.

Second paragraph gives the place and identifies the participants.

Indirect quotation.

Direct followed by indirect quotation.

Direct quotation.

Indirect quotation incorporating direct quotation.

Report ends with more details about speaker.

The Tower
Grosse Point High School
Grosse Point, Michigan

1. Diagram Examples 26 and 27. The paragraphs are numbered for easy reference.

Health Class Learns of Court Cases

EXAMPLE
26

1   "Tacoma's Family Court tries to reconcile couples who are getting a divorce," said Theodore Marchesini, Family Court Commissioner, to Miss Helen Clark's health classes in a talk this week.

2   Mr. Marchesini said that the court saved about 25 per cent of the marriages brought before it. Not all these couples remained together after the court had reconciled them, nor did all the ones that they did not help go through with divorce proceedings.

3   The court can only help those marriages in which one of the members wishes to stay married, he said. A petition of reconciliation has to be signed, he added.

Men Come to Court

4   Generally the agency sees those who have children, he said. Then, if it has time, it takes those marriages without children.

5   It is usually the man who comes to the family court, he revealed.

6   Most divorce actions, he said, were filed by the women, although this trend is rapidly changing.

7   The biggest reason a man divorces his wife is because he lacks respect for her, he added.

8   "Divorce does not solve all problems," he cautioned.

9   The divorced woman now has the problem of her support confronting her, he said. "She will have a harder time remarrying."

Everyone Needs Love

10   "Every human being needs to love and be loved," he stated.

11   People should not go into marriage with the idea that if the marriage does not work out a divorce can be secured, he said.

12   Marriage, warned Mr. Marchesini, is not a solution to unhappiness in the former home.

13   "Take a good look at the person and make sure he is what you want," he said. "The marriage ceremony is not a ritual that changes people."

Love Will Not Disappear

14   "If it is love, it will not disappear in a year or two," he said. "So don't rush into marriage—be sure."

15   People, he said, think less about getting married than about lending money.

16   "If you have to prove to a boy that you love him, then he does not love you," he concluded.

17   "We want to show people what goes on in their lives so that they can be happy," Mr. Marchesini said. "Sometimes we have to hurt them a little bit to show them."

18   According to Mr. Marchesini, rich, poor, old, and young come to the family court for help.

The Lincoln News
Lincoln High School
Tacoma, Washington

Show Biz Hopefuls Should
Stay Home, Says Tony Karloff

By DICK STOCKER

EXAMPLE

27

"The best chance for young hopeful entertainers looking for success in show biz is to stay in their home towns and not to go to a big metropolis like New York or Hollywood."

This advice was given by Tony and Gloria Karloff, professional entertainers, in a talk to the second-period journalism class recently.

Discover Home Town

"If you are a good entertainer performing in your own home town," Karloff said, "your town will discover you and push you."

Mr. Karloff, whose headquarters are in Akron, Ohio, has been in show business for 23 years. His act consists of humor sketches, mimicry, and impersonations. Another part of the act is his wife, Gloria, who dances and takes part in the sketches. She has been in the act four years.

According to Mr. Karloff, the preparation for becoming a good entertainer should include acting in a home town little theater organization. Also, college courses in radio broadcasting and dramatics should definitely be encouraged.

Need Diploma

Karloff, born in Tacoma, attended Bellarmine High School and also began his career as a youthful entertainer here. He entertained at the Elks and Eagles lodges. Then he realized that the theatrical agents were in Seattle and not in Tacoma, so he moved there.

"I never finished high school and I regret it to this day," said Karloff, "because a person needs a high school diploma and some college under his belt to round out his background as a person."

"It's a good idea to line up another specialized field for security," said Gloria, who holds a teacher's certificate for the state of Ohio.

The Lincoln News
Lincoln High School
Tacoma, Washington

2. Diagnose Examples 25, 26, and 27, using the following study questions:

   a. What kind of lead does the story have? Why did the reporter decide upon such an opening? Would you suggest a different opening statement?

   b. When does the speaker's name first appear?

   c. Is the speaker adequately identified? When?

   d. Is the occasion fully explained?

   e. When is the setting presented?

      f. Does the story leave the reader with one definite impression of the message the speaker gave, of what he was trying to say?

      g. Does the reporter leave out his own opinions?

3. Clip a report of a speech from a daily paper and mount it. Estimate the percentage of space given to (1) summarization, (2) direct quotations, and (3) indirect quotations. In class, compare your analysis with those of the other students.

4. Clip the leads of three speech stories from the daily papers— one opening with a summary, one opening with a direct quotation, and one opening with an indirect quotation.

5. From the daily paper, clip a speech story with several direct quotations. Mount it and at the side rewrite each quote in indirect style.

6. From the *Reader's Digest* or a comparable magazine, select a short article that might serve as an address. Pretending that the author had spoken in assembly the morning before, write a 200-word story for the next issue of your paper.

7. Have a speaker talk to your class on an interesting topic and write a 250-word report of the talk. Discuss the reports in class.

8. As a class, agree upon a specific speech to be carried on radio or television during the week. Write a 200-word report of it. After the stories are written, discuss them in class, using the questions in Exercise 2 as an outline.

9. Find and diagram one speech story written in the inverted-pyramid style, and another in the sequential order of the speech.

10. Write three different leads for a speech story based on the following paragraph. Classify each lead in accordance with the classifications in Chapter 4, and indicate your preference.

    Dr. Harold Jones spoke to the students in assembly yesterday, third period. His subject was "Teaching, a Chosen Profession." He said that too few high school graduates go to college. He told of his own experiences as a boy. He is president of State Teachers College. He said more good students should go into teaching, a profession offering many opportunities for community service as well as great personal satisfaction. After the assembly many students came up to him to discuss how they could get into teachers colleges.

7 THE INTERVIEW

On July 13, 1859, Horace Greeley, editor of the *New York Tribune,* stopped at Salt Lake City on his way to the Pacific Coast and interviewed Brigham Young, president of the Mormon church. This is the first real interview known in the history of journalism.

Three months later, the elder James Gordon Bennett, editor of the *New York Herald,* published an interview obtained by one of his reporters in connection with the John Brown raid at Harpers Ferry.

The interview has grown in importance until today it is one of the primary techniques in the handling of news events. Although its use has broadened, the basic purpose of the interview is still to obtain information. Greeley's interview, in the files of the *Weekly Oregonian* of Portland, shows that for information about the Mormon church he went directly to Brigham Young as the highest authority on the subject. His story reveals that he went quickly to his subject, with the intention of getting definite, factual information across to the reader.

The Harpers Ferry interview, available in the files of the Congressional Library, also shows the interview to have been used to obtain a direct, authoritative statement. A reporter was sent to Syracuse to see one Gerrit Smith, a rich and influential Quaker, to ask if the reports that he had secretly supported John Brown's raid were true. This interview was carried out and reported in a direct manner, and the story quoted Mr. Smith freely.

THE ROUTINE INTERVIEW

Reporting is primarily collecting the news. As the reporter gathers the facts for his routine stories, he talks with many people. He knows, just as did the editors of 1859, that authoritative data are obtained from the proper sources. Personal contacts made on the regular rounds are but one of the three classes of interviews—the routine interview. This informal discussion is more precisely called a tool of reporting, however, than a true interview.

THE SYMPOSIUM INTERVIEW

Out of the regular news of the day has come the symposium interview, sometimes called the group or composite interview, in which a number of people are asked to express their opinions on a timely topic. (See Examples 28 and 29.)

Students Talk on Meaning of Education

EXAMPLE

28

Editor's note: This is American Education Week. During this week we honor the administrators and sources of our education. The following are ideas expressed by numerous students when asked "What does education mean to you?"

* * *

"Education to me is being capable of thinking and expressing new thoughts more intelligently and interestingly," is how Peter Hollbert answered the question "What does education mean to you?" in this, our salute to the educators of H.H.S. and those the world over.

Lurlene Gallagher summarizes her feelings for education as "The media of education is the road to a better life—by thinking and doing what, through experience, men before me have gathered in history."

Other students evaluated the importance of education as:

"... education means freedom. People who are ignorant of their environment are not capable of improving it or maintaining it." —Mary Ellen Fletcher.

Celia Navarro commented on what an American education means to her as a Cuban.

"If you have never studied out

of your country, probably you do not understand all the advantages of the American education.

"Here you have more dignity as a person, a chance to develop your own ideas, electing the courses you have some facility with, and not taking just what your teacher thinks is best for you to know.

"You do not have to be under a strict and old system where the boys and girls are separate.

"Here your teachers tend to be your friends and not your dictators. Here you find the natural way to think and live. Because you have more opportunity to think and live on your own. This seems more democratic to me. In a democracy the schools should be democratic, but many American children do not know this because they can not compare their schools with the schools under dictatorship."

Hialeah High Record
Hialeah High School
Hialeah, Florida

EXAMPLE

OPINION POLL

Which shopping night do you prefer?

Herb Johnson, Senior

I think stores should be open on Monday nights. Friday night is the best night for a date and who wants to go shopping on a date? School activities are also in conflict with Friday night shopping. With my shopping done on Monday, I have the rest of the week open for other activities.

Karon Summer, Senior

I prefer Fridays. I like weekend shopping the best. You can go wherever you like and you don't have to think about getting up the next morning to go to school. It has been an old tradition for the stores to stay open on either Friday or Saturday. So the good old fashioned way is good enough for me!

Bob Moe, Junior

I would rather have the stores open on Friday because it gives me a chance to stay out late that night without having to get up the next morning for school. Also people get paid at the end of the week and so have money on hand to buy things.

Sandra Pace, Junior

Let's keep our stores open Monday nights! That way those people who have to shop at night can still come to the games and support our team. Also then the guys and girls who work downtown can come to games and play in the pep band.

Mary Hanson, Sophomore

The stores should be open on Monday nights so store employees can attend the football games and watch our team win another victory. All students who have shopping would probably have plans for Friday night with the games and mixers. But most important, on Monday I still have some money left over from my allowance.

Mike McCord, Sophomore

I would rather see the stores open on Monday nights. There are usually athletic events on Friday nights, and anything people need can probably wait until Saturday morning.

85

Such a story must be built around a good question, one that provokes thought and interest. The question may concern the important or the minor news of the day. It may be profound or entertaining, but it must always be interesting. If the topic is significant to the student— whether on a school, community, state, or national level, or on the personal level of books, music, television, and such—the reporter is showing good news sense.

Since this type of interview consists of the opinions of many people, each response is generally limited to a sentence or a short paragraph. It is generally effective to include the question in the lead, which, in fact, sometimes summarizes the entire interview. The opinions then follow, each in a separate paragraph introduced by the name and sometimes the picture of the person being interviewed. Indirect quotes rather than direct quotes are often used to speed the flow of the article, but not always! (See Example 28.)

It is usually better for one reporter to conduct the entire symposium, especially on school papers. He may be more successful if he draws out his subjects indirectly, rather than asking a direct question. This, however, depends upon the situation and is not an excuse for prying.

On both school and daily papers, an *Inquiring Reporter* column published at regular intervals often attracts the continuing attention of readers. In the school paper, students, at times teachers, and occasionally even parents or interested bystanders may be asked for their opinions. Reader interest, however, lasts only as long as the column warrants it.

THE CONVENTIONAL INTERVIEW

Today the story devoted to one prominent or interesting person is considered the true interview. It is really a member of the feature-story family, a first cousin of the personality sketch.

There are four types of interview subjects popular with the student journalist:

1. The celebrity or the prominent person, often in town just for a day to appear in a stage show, campaign for public office, speak at graduation exercises or give a public lecture (Example 30).

2. The student who promises to be good copy because of something unusual he has done, is doing, or is about to do. The exchange student, the student who has traveled or who has a responsible position in the school, the student with an unusual hobby, are among the favorites in this classification (Example 31).

3. The faculty member or any adult connected with the school who is a source of interesting information (Example 32).

4. The outsider who is not a celebrity but who is truly interesting because of something newsworthy in his life (Example 33).

A story built around a person depends upon the writer's ability to bring his subject to the reader as an animated personality, with the reporter in the background. The emphasis is upon the person's remarks, for this is an interview and not a personality sketch. In routine interviewing it is the story that leads the reporter to the person; in the true interview it is the person who leads the reporter to the story.

'Madwoman' Meets 'Wonderful Levenson'

By JOY OPPENHEIM

EXAMPLE

30

He thought that I was a madwoman, and I thought that he was wonderful, but, of course, you can't trust snap judgments at 7 o'clock in the morning.

"He" was Sam Levenson and "I" was sleepy. After somehow running into each other at a prearranged spot, we proceeded to the airport coffee shop.

The waitress showed us to a table for two and asked if we would please sit there. Mr. Levenson said that we would try.

I took out a pencil and began to ask questions. After a while, I no longer needed to ask questions; I just wrote as fast as I could.

Knowing that Mr. Levenson had been a teacher in New York City for some ten years, I decided to ask him for his opinions on certain phases of education.

"A good teacher is a person who possesses a love of scholarship, a joy in transmitting ideas, and an outside job," he said. "A good student possesses much the same qualities. His IQ is not important, but, rather, his desire to know.

"A teacher must love his pupils and try to see them as greater tomorrow than they are this morning," he continued between sips of orange juice and coffee.

On the question of the importance of a college education, Mr. Levenson commented, "It's not important for everybody. Everybody needs education but not necessarily a college education."

He went on to say that if he were in charge, everyone who had the desire or the interest to go to college would be given more of an opportunity to do so, even if his grades weren't "up to par," and those who had neither the desire nor the interest would not be allowed to attend.

"Ridiculous!" was Mr. Levenson's only answer to my last question, his opinion of interviews at 7 o'clock in the morning.

I still thought that he was wonderful, and I don't think he still thought that I was a madwoman —or maybe he did, at that!

The Surveyor
George Washington High School
Denver, Colorado

Press Conference: Constable Seeks Representation for All Groups

EXAMPLE

31

John Constable, senior class president, claims that the three social groups at Cody High School will be adequately represented on his new General Activities Committee.

Star reporters pounced on Constable and demanded that he define his term "social group."

"These groups have already been typed, not only by me, but by many students. First, there are the academics who stick their noses in books and leave them there. Second, there are casual types who concentrate on their cars. Finally, there are the sharp dressers who might be members of social clubs."

Reporters asked Constable how he would represent seniors who do not seem to fall into any of these three groups.

"Each group or type of student will be represented in the best way possible," Constable replied.

Constable has given the old Steering Committee a new look by giving it a new name, the General Activities Committee.

The committee will be composed of approximately twenty members, two or three seniors from each study hall.

Constable said that he is the main go-between of the class and the faculty advisers.

The class gives Constable suggestions, he tells the teachers, the teachers tell him, and he tells the class.

Constable said that there is a lot of prestige connected with being class president but there is also a great deal of work.

This remark caused reporters to wonder about Constable's being both class president and being in so many other activities such as ROTC and the fall play.

Constable admitted that he does devote a considerable amount of time to ROTC.

"I was City Commander up until June. I am now officially retired."

Constable said that being City Commander is a lot of glory but holds little power.

The only new proposal for the senior class so far is to have a senior-faculty basketball game during the fall semester as well as during the spring semester.

The Cody Star
Frank Cody High School
Detroit, Michigan

88

Counselor Whalen Explains Scholarship Applications

By LYNNE WALTERS

Does college occupy a prominent place in your future? If your reply is "yes," undoubtedly you are interested in scholarships.

Scholarship eligibility is based upon need, the quality of your high school record, and the results of your college aptitude tests, according to Counselor Annabelle Whalen.

"Usually students with greater financial need possess a better chance of obtaining scholarships than those with higher scholastic records but lesser monetary want," states Miss Whalen.

To determine the need for scholarship aid, parents must fill out the Parents Confidential Financial Statement. This is a searching investigation of a family's annual income, expenses, assets, and liabilities, she relates.

Parents Forward Statement

Parents then forward this report to the College Scholarship Service at Princeton, New Jersey, an independent organization which carefully analyzes the statements and determines the exact amount of assistance needed.

This proposed figure is sent to the colleges of your choice, where the final decision regarding the granting of a scholarship is made on the basis of your high school record, the counselor points out.

There are several sources of scholarships besides the colleges.

"Seniors who plan to enter an independent college — especially those who hope to enter a specialized field—should consult the *Directory of Scholarship Resources in Greater Cleveland,* states the counselor.

Rhodes Review
J. F. Rhodes High School
Cleveland, Ohio

EXAMPLE

32

Feiffer Addresses Editors

By JEFFREY KATZ

"Life, Times, and the Funny Papers" was the title of Mr. Jules Feiffer's talk to the New York City High School Press Council at its first meeting of the school year yesterday afternoon.

The address given by Mr. Feiffer, nationally syndicated cartoonist, was largely a question and answer session which opened with a discourse on the problems of satire and the difficulties of being a satirist.

Mr. Feiffer is a native New Yorker who graduated from James Monroe High School in 1946.

In a personal interview, he described his four years of high school, in which he served as cartoonist for his school paper, as a miserable time when he did not know where to fit in.

Today, however, he is quite happy in his field of cartooning. His cartoons are syndicated in forty periodicals throughout the country including the *Village Voice,* a Greenwich Village newspaper.

EXAMPLE

33

89

The best of these are collected at certain intervals and put into book form. These anthologies have included a number of popular works, such as *Sick, Sick, Sick, Passionela and Other Stories,* and *The Explainers.*

Mr. Feiffer was the first of a number of speakers who will address the Press Council at its forthcoming meetings.

The council is an organization founded by the High School Division of the Board of Education in order to promote a more favorable public opinion toward teenagers, and to serve as a center for ideas which will advance the standards of high school journalism.

Clinton News
De Witt Clinton High School
New York, New York

Preparing the interview. Good interviews do not come by chance. Once a good subject has been selected, the reporter still has much to do. Following are fifteen good rules which may help:

1. Arrange in advance for the interview if possible. Few prominent people will give an audience without a definite engagement.

2. Know everything possible about the person before the interview.

3. Guided by the situation and the person, choose one or more topics for the interview. Tie the person to the thing that marked him as a good subject. If the person strays from the original topic, let the importance of his remarks and your original plan determine the advisability of leading him back to the main channel.

4. In your mind, outline a few definite guide questions.

5. Meet the person courteously. Make yourself, your paper, and your mission known, and go directly into your topic.

6. Do not use a notebook. Have copy paper and pencil available.

7. Concentrate closely on the speaker's remarks.

8. Write the interview while your impressions are still fresh.

9. Put the big feature of the interview in the lead, if possible, or immediately after it. The setting—no later than the second paragraph.

10. Everything a person says is not worth quoting. Sift the interview into direct quotations, indirect quotations, and summary statements, possibly ignoring some things completely.

11. Alternate direct and indirect quotations for variety, but not too obviously. Do not include the two in the same paragraph. Use summary paragraphs here and there for less important material.

12. Use a question occasionally, either directly or indirectly.

13. Use the question-answer treatment if it can be done with verve. In this treatment the story opens with a lead and one or two other paragraphs that furnish summary and setting. The account then continues with the questions and their answers.

14. Give some attention to the subject's personality unless the sole purpose of the interview is information. Stop short of the personality sketch, however.

15. Use the telephone, but not at the expense of good coverage.

CHAPTER LABORATORY

1. From the daily paper, clip a story composed of facts gathered by interviewing those in a position to know. Discuss the stories selected in class.

2. Choose a subject of particular interest to your school, develop a thought-provoking question about it, interview eight or ten students, and write a symposium story.

3. Clip an interview story from the school paper, and study it carefully. Then discuss in class any other approaches that might have been taken.

4. Chapter 6 contains a list of possible substitutions for the word *said*. Select and list those words that would also be effective in an interview.

5. Review the four types of subjects for the conventional interview (page 86). Add any other classifications you can think of; then list one person under each who might be interviewed for your school paper, and give the topic.

6. List eight questions to guide you in one of these interviews. Obtain the interview and write a 300-word account, using what you have learned about the conventional interview.

7. Interview an interesting student in front of the class. Each student should take notes and write a 200-word story to be discussed during the following class period.

8. List students and teachers who might be good subjects for interviews. After each name, indicate the area of news interest.

8 PRINTED SOURCES

A reporter secures the facts for his story (1) as an eyewitness, (2) through interviews, or (3) from printed sources. Printed sources include not only materials actually printed but also ready-to-handle records such as mimeographed bulletins and letters. The actual presence of the reporter at an event or an interview is often the best source of news. At times, however, the most expedient, the most accurate, or the *only* source, is a printed one.

PRINTED SOURCES IN THE SCHOOL

Printed sources of news appear periodically within the school itself, for example, (1) the honor roll, (2) athletic schedules, (3) new student-government regulations, (4) minutes of meetings, such as those of the student council, (5) the morning notices, (6) the list of subjects to be offered next term, and (7) financial statements of school activities. In every school newspaper office these are handled as routine materials. The variety of subjects and approaches is limited only by the reporter's ingenuity. Example 34 shows how an enterprising reporter put his news sense to work with a set of dry-looking daily attendance reports. Every school office issues a daily list of absentee students, but only one school in a thousand has sensed news value in them. The school office may be an unexplored source of your school's news.

Absentee Lists Show Varied School Trends

By ARTHUR HANSON

EXAMPLE

34

Every morning during the first period, a girl from the office brings around a sheet of paper to each teacher. Anxiously awaited by the instructor, this is simply a list of the students who have been reported absent by their homeroom teachers.

Most teachers probably throw these sheets away, but if the lists are saved, as a few teachers have saved them, they provide an unusual record. Simply glancing at one of the absence listings, sometimes long, sometimes short, does not show much, but if the names are counted and the totals put down in table form opposite the dates concerned, a number of interesting facts can be gleaned from them.

For instance, as most of you will remember, we had a heavy snowfall, our first of the year, Wednesday, December 5, after we had already arrived at school for the day. Although the snow had begun to fall early in the morning, there was still not enough to keep students from getting to school. The absence that day was 114.

Snow Affects Absences

All through Wednesday and most of the night, the snow continued to fall, and by Thursday enough students were snowed in to bring the absence total up to 141, the highest it had been all year. As the snow began to melt and the weather cleared up, the rising temperatures brought 32 of those students back to school Friday to reduce the number of absentees to 109.

Another interesting fact is noted as one glances at the absence sheet for October 17. What happened on October 17? That was the day of the big entertainment show of the year, the Jackson Jollities. The show was advertised for many weeks previously, and on that day only 29 pupils were absent from classes, the lowest number since the first week of school. Perhaps it pays to advertise.

School was dismissed at 3 p. m., Wednesday, November 21, for Thanksgiving vacation. This was followed by at least two solid days of feasting and forgetting (mainly school). The effects were drastic and quite obvious. Monday's absentee list had swelled to a total of 121, the highest figure reached until that time. Maybe it was too much turkey.

Compare Weekly Averages

Weekly averages also provide comparisons of absentee lists.

Naturally students began the first week of school in good style, the average for the first full week being only 42. Monotony began to set in and a few more students decided to take a short rest, bringing the second week's average up to 60.

Next week's average improved slightly and the record stood at 48 for two consecutive weeks. Then as football season drew into full swing the average went down to only 41, even better than the first week's record.

During the next four weeks the list became fairly consistent in the high fifties, but the total sprang up to 75 in the week of November 13. From there it rapidly ascended near the one-hundred mark and rose to a high of 117 during the week of November 26.

Such attendance records as these would warrant investigation and study by persons trained in statistics and their relation to sociological problems. But through the few facts shown above, it has been pointed out that our daily attendance at school is affected by such matters as snow, an abundance of turkey, a football game, or even an assembly.

The Jackson Journal
Jackson High School
Charleston, West Virginia

Financial and statistical stories. Daily papers make wide use of the financial story, realizing that money is news. Most schools abound with financial reports; for example, budgets for student activities; proceeds from drives, such as activities-ticket campaigns; proceeds from a season of sports, such as football; bookstore receipts and expenditures; financial statements from a dramatics production; interesting features of the school-district budget.

The school newspaper should publish annually a simplified financial statement of its own operation and explore the possibilities of other financial reports. Example 35 is representative of financial reporting successfully carried in the school paper.

Death Takes a Holiday Yields Profit of $778.54

EXAMPLE 35

Miss Mary Henderson releases the following financial statement covering the Senior Class Play, *Death Takes a Holiday*, which was produced on Saturday, November 20.

The production netted a profit of $778.54, which will be divided equally between the senior class and the Home and School Association. Ticket sales amounted to $685; patrons and patronesses, advertising and commercial pa-patrons contributed $920.98, of which half, $460.49, is presented to the junior class to subsidize its Junior Night production and half supports the Senior Play. When expenses, amounting to $366.95, have been deducted from box office receipts and contributions, totaling $1,145.49, the production realizes a profit of $778.54 for the class.

The senior class contributes its share of profits to the Henry W. Foster Scholarship Fund, while the Home and School Association further endows its own scholarship aid fund.

Recapitulation

Patrons, Patronesses, Advertising and Commercial Patrons	$ 920.98
	$ 460.49
Ticket Sales	685.00
Total	$1,145.49
EXPENDITURES	366.95
PROFIT	$ 778.54

The Columbian
Columbia High School
South Orange, New Jersey

Letters. Letters can be the basis of interesting, stimulating stories; for example, Example 36 in which a letter to a popular author sparks a delighted response. Sometimes a principal receives an entertaining letter from a teacher or pupil who has moved to another town—more source material.

Student Corresponds with Authoress

By HALETTE MASLER

Many of us have probably wondered about what we read in fiction, and whether or not the event really happened. Theodora Elias, 1-1, wondered about this same thing while reading Maureen Daly's famous *Seventeenth Summer.*

At the suggestion of Mrs. Marguerite Young, the teacher of her reading clinic, class RC6, Theodora wrote a letter to Miss Daly, asking her whether the events were true.

"The story intrigued me, and I wondered whether Miss Daly had really gone through the same experiences that Angie did in the book," says Theodora.

On October third, Theodora got her answer. Miss Daly was delighted to learn that Theodora had enjoyed *Seventeenth Summer,* and answered her question this way:

"Yes, it is essentially a true story, based on a particular summer in my life. Of course the town Fond du Lac, Wisconsin, is a real place, and the town in which I was raised. Most of the characters were friends from high school."

Theodora was delighted when she received the response. "It was the first time I ever wrote to an authoress—or an author either, and I was just thrilled."

EXAMPLE

36

95

She says she loved *Seventeenth Summer,* as she does all teenage romance stories, and wants to read more of Maureen Daly's books. She can choose from such books as *Spanish Roundabout, Smarter and Smoother,* and a collection of Miss Daly's favorite stories, all in our school library.

There is a bulletin board in the library with a display concerning Theodora's correspondence with Miss Daly. There you will find Theodora's letter as well as Miss Daly's answer, both part of an interesting display mounted by Theodora, Gail Gibson, also of 1-1, and Mr. Stephen Parris, librarian.

Theodora now has the beginning of a valuable collection of authors' autographs.

The Walton Log
Walton High School
Bronx, New York

Most newspapers, school and daily, solicit correspondence from their readers. These letters are published on the editoral page, sometimes in a "Letter to the Editor" column. No anonymous letters should ever be considered for publication, and it is good policy to publish the names on the letters. Contributors should not be permitted to hide behind anonymity, for anonymity encourages irresponsibility.

NON-SCHOOL SOURCES

Printed sources from outside the school include statistical reports, charts, bulletins, circulars, proclamations, articles in magazines and newspapers, and similar materials. One school reporter wrote an instructive and interesting story from a post-office circular giving directions for mailing Christmas packages.

An Ohio school ran a weekly series treating the colleges and universities most popular with the students. The publicity bureaus of the colleges willingly supplied printed material from which the reporters developed their stories. (See Example 37.)

In Example 38 the reporter worked from a bulletin on the services of the Institute of International Education, a good printed source.

College Corner

By CAROLE SLATSKY

Now that the seniors are practically settled as far as college plans are concerned, this column will assist eleventh graders.

Short sketches of study courses and various types of colleges will be presented to aid juniors in their search for the proper college.

96

It is advisable first to become acquainted with the six state colleges in Ohio. They are Ohio State University, Ohio University, Bowling Green, Kent State, Central State, and Miami University.

Tuition, room, and board to each college comes to approximately $1100 a year. This does not include books, club dues, and any extras students wish to indulge in.

Each college must accept all graduates of accredited high schools. It is recommended that applicants take the American College Test.

Degrees are offered in elementary and secondary teacher training, art, agriculture, business, engineering, home economics, industrial arts, music, physical education, liberal arts and sciences, pharmacy, and nursing.

All are coed. Each is a large college with an enrollment of over 5,000.

Further information can be obtained from the latest issue of the booklet "Toward College in Ohio." The booklet is available in the Guidance Center.

John Adams Journal
John Adams High School
Cleveland, Ohio

EXAMPLE
37

FOREIGN EXCHANGE . . . STUDY, TRAVEL, FUN

By WORTH KITSON
Panther Staff Writer.

Have you ever dreamed of going to Paris? or to Japan? or anywhere out of the United States? There are a great many exchange opportunities available to the young adults of America.

Summer study abroad offers a great deal. The Institute of International Education, 800 Second Ave., New York, New York, handles summer courses in 26 different countries.

The cost of these courses varies greatly, but tuition is generally lower than in America, and there are some scholarships available.

An increasing number of colleges and universities are sponsoring the "Junior Year Abroad" program. Under this system, a student may do semi-independent study in the country best fitted to his course of study.

The International Educational Exchange Program offers many exchanges to graduate students. Grants and scholarships in this program fall into five fields: graduate study, elementary and secondary school teaching, lecturing and university teaching, research, and public lecturing.

The program provides for citizens of other countries that want to come to America under similar conditions. Now is the time to start investigating opportunities for study and travel abroad. Know what you are eligible for, prepare yourself by careful study in your field, and then apply for an exchange program.

Palmetto Panther
Palmetto High School
Miami, Florida

EXAMPLE
38

School newspapers exchanged with other schools relate interesting and unusual curricular and extracurricular school practices. When rewritten, these can appear as separate short stories or in column form. A few papers run regular exchange columns in each issue, relating in short-item form the practices of other schools. Some papers pick up the stock jokes published in the exchanges. A good reporter can create a good story from his careful examination of the papers of other schools, but it is not an assignment for a beginner. See Example 39 and Example 98 in Chapter 12. Nothing is duller than the routine coverage of the warmed-over life of other students. In Example 40, however, the writer went back twenty years to the files of his own school paper and produced an entertaining story.

Across The Potomac

EXAMPLE 39

(Editor's note: This information was collected from various newspapers obtained through the *Surveyor's* extensive exchange program in the United States.)

Students at Rishel Junior High who become lazy are required to count all holes in the ceiling. The only complaint of this disciplinary action is stiff necks.

* * *

Teachers at a Denver school are wondering if spittoons are the answer to the problem of gum-chewing students.

* * *

At Lane High School, Brooklyn, New York, the students have George Washington's birthday off.

* * *

In Belmont, New York, the student council makes money by auctioning off incoming freshmen as "slaves" to the upper classmen. For five days "slaves" have to bow to their "masters," carry books, shine shoes, and dress as commanded. Everyone has fun, and at the same time, the student council makes itself a tidy bundle.

The Surveyor
George Washington High School
Denver, Colorado

Back Then . . . "C" Spirit Unaltered During War Years

By BARBARA BUMFORD

EXAMPLE 40

October 9, 1941—the Cardinal headlined "Castellan Price Rise Looms." This increase in price meant that Cooleyites would probably have to pay 70 cents for their yearbook—18 cents more than they paid the previous semester.

98

Also sharing the front page was the 12B class play story. That year, the seniors were to present a cast of 48.

During the war-torn era, Cooley was doing its part to boost the sale of United States Defense Stamps. Broadcasting over the study hall loud speakers, Cooley's Radio Players inaugurated an advertising campaign. Detroit schools set the pace which made Michigan the leading state in stamp sales and the model for the entire nation.

JOBS SOUGHT

As the holiday season was fast approaching, 175 girls in CHS's business department were being trained for clerking jobs. The potentials were eying jobs at Sears Roebuck, Montgomery Ward, and the five-and-ten for the Christmas rush period.

Making the social scene in 1941 were such organizations as the Forensic Senate, Chess Club, Stamp Club, and the Library Club.

On the light side, ancient portraits of counselors, faculty members, and students of renown comprised the "Who's Who" exhibit of the Theodore Roosevelt Hall on display in the office show cases. The childhood snaps were reported to be most entertaining.

ATHLETES EXCEL

The sports page revealed that the golf team copped the city crown, the cross-country boys looked unbeatable, and the gridmen had not yet been knocked out of the title race.

All this—the teen world of October 1941.

The Cardinal
Cooley High School
Detroit, Michigan

Books and periodicals. A book, too, may be the source of a story that is definitely not a book report. In Example 41 a resourceful reporter noted the interest inherent in some historical facts and fallacies found in a book and built a skillful composite out of them.

Magazines are an excellent source of school news. Example 42 reports the results of a survey by *Scholastic* Magazines on a timely topic—curriculum preference. Magazine coverage provided greater scope than the staff could have secured from only its own students.

U.S. History Is Proved Wrong: Fallacy or Fact?

Did you know that Lief Ericson discovered America?

Many people believe it was Christopher Columbus. Almost five centuries before Columbus landed in the Caribbean, the Viking explorer landed on the New England coast.

EXAMPLE

41

99

This is just one of the common fallacies that have occurred in United States history, according to a book written by Mr. O. A. Lindquist. The following are a few of these:

Fallacy: Many witches were burned at the stake in Salem.

Fact: The people of Salem saw 19 witches hanged but not one burned at the stake. At one time the practice of burning witches was common in Europe, which may account for the idea that Salem did also.

Fallacy: George Washington wore a wig.

Fact: Washington never wore a wig. He powdered his own reddish-brown hair and tied it in a queue.

Fallacy: Daniel Boone wore a coonskin cap.

Fact: Boone despised coonskin caps and refused to wear anything but a hat.

Fallacy: Mrs. Bixby had five of her sons die in battle.

Fact: After Lincoln wrote Mrs. Bixby a letter when he was informed that she had lost five sons in the war, research proved that only two had died in battle. One was taken prisoner, one deserted to the enemy, and as for the fifth and youngest, many excuses were made—he was insane, too young, and was in the army against his mother's will. He was to be discharged, but they found that he had already deserted and gone to sea.

The Cody Star
Frank Cody High School
Detroit, Michigan

High School Students Request Tougher Courses, More Work

EXAMPLE
42

Ten thousand American teenagers last month wrote out a "report card" on United States high schools. Taking part in an Institute of Student Opinion poll which covered 192 secondary schools in 45 states, the teenagers rated 11 different subjects.

"Should American high schools," the poll asked each student, "place more, less, or the same emphasis on the following subjects: agriculture, commercial courses, English, foreign languages, home economics, mathematics, music and visual arts, physical education, science, shop, and social studies?"

Results indicate that the vast majority of students want more work in the so-called tough academic courses rather than less work in other courses. For example a majority of boys and girls combined want more science, math, foreign languages, English, and social studies. Only one in five wants less music, shop, or home economics—but this is balanced by the one in five who wants more music, shop, and home economics.

The Institute of Student Opinion, an independent activity sponsored by Scholastic Magazines, Inc., has been conducting nation-wide surveys of teenagers since 1943. This scientifically-drawn sample of nearly 10,000 students covered grades seven through twelve in schools of all sizes, public and private, throughout the country.

100

Students' Report Card on School Curriculum

Subject	More Emphasis			Less Emphasis		
	Boys (%)	Girls (%)	Both (%)	Boys (%)	Girls (%)	Both (%)
Agriculture	35	27	31	9	9	9
Commercial courses	24	41	33	9	5	7
English	51	61	56	10	4	7
Foreign languages	62	68	65	8	6	7
Home economics	17	26	22	20	16	18
Mathematics	73	60	66	4	6	5
Music and visual arts	19	25	22	26	18	22
Physical education	51	32	41	9	18	14
Science	75	65	70	3	4	4
Shop	34	15	23	24	19	21
Social studies	51	55	53	8	7	7

The Polaris
North High School
Minneapolis, Minnesota

STYLE OF WRITING

It is well to remember that *the printed source is not a form of writing, but rather just a source of news.* A printed source of news may suggest straight news coverage or feature coverage or perhaps an editorial. It may even lend itself to none of these, but rather to the reprinting of the material as it originally appeared.

In some cases, the reporter goes to the printed material for the information he needs in a routine assignment; but often a printed bulletin or a letter is actually the impetus of the story.

CHAPTER LABORATORY

1. From the daily papers, clip several examples of stories that have been written from printed sources and mount them. Indicate the source in each case.
2. From the daily paper, clip a story of student interest. Mount it and rewrite it for your school paper.
3. Secure at school one of the routine pieces of printed material such as the morning bulletin or the honor roll. Prepare a news story from it.
4. Choose some printed source not directly connected with school and yet related to the students, and write a news story from it. A report of a new driver's license law or a city bicycle ordinance might be examples.
5. Using a letter which some student or teacher in your class has received, write a news story. Letters from former students, foreign students, or people who have visited the school might be used.
6. From *The Reader's Digest* or a similar magazine, take a story that you think worthy of mentioning in your school paper and rewrite it—150 words.
7. From the school newspaper exchanges that come to your school, develop an exchange column of eight or ten interesting items.
8. Examine four issues of your school paper, mark all the stories written from printed sources, and then suggest the types of sources not being used.
9. Compile a list of eight principles or suggestions to be followed by a reporter in handling a story derived from a printed source.
10. List five timely subjects for stories from printed sources to appear in the next two or three issues of your school paper.

PART TWO

STORIES
WITH A PERSONAL
TOUCH

" 'The Press!—What is the Press?' I cried
When thus a wondrous voice replied:
'In me all human knowledge dwells;
The oracle of oracles,
Past, present, future, I reveal,
Or in oblivion's silence seal;
What I preserve can perish never,
What I forego is lost forever.' "
                    —JAMES MONTGOMERY

⑨ THE EDITORIAL

The editorial is the voice of the newspaper. It is the paper's means of discussing the significance of the news. It is the interpretive and influential arm—the means by which it makes its position clear and attempts to influence its readers.

The writer of the editorial speaks not for himself but for his paper. Consequently, his name is not carried on the story. To carry a student's name on an editorial violates the principles of good journalism and weakens the editorial, which should transmit the opinion of the paper. Now and then the "editorial we" is used to denote the newspaper, but by and large the editorial is written in the third person.

STRUCTURE OF THE EDITORIAL

The writer of an editorial sets out to interpret a news event, a situation or condition, or an occasion. He may wish to clarify a situation, suggest several possibilities of interpretation, stress the newspaper's interpretation, influence the reader's thinking, or lead him to take particular action. Within the limits of journalistic good taste, the editorial is the personal voice of the newspaper. The construction of such an editorial is a challenge, and the writer must follow certain principles:

1. The subject of the editorial must be interesting, and the writing must be clear and brief.

2. The reasoning must be sound, with every point supporting and leading logically to the conclusions.

3. The writer must be content to put one idea across; in so doing he must move directly into the task without unnecessary words, presenting facts in support of his thesis rather than preaching to or scolding the reader.

Although there is no limit to the variety of forms the editorial may take, generally it has three parts—a beginning that acquaints the reader with the topic, the body of the editorial, in which a case is built through a logical sequence, and finally the conclusion, which either summarizes or drives home the point.

Each year one of the Pulitzer journalism prizes is given for the best editorial. The points on which the editorials are judged indicate *the criteria of a good editorial—(1) clearness of style, (2) moral purpose, (3) sound reasoning, and (4) power to influence public opinion.*

THE QUALITY OF THE EDITORIAL

Editorials must compete for attention with all the news and feature material in the newspaper. They must be interesting, thought-provoking, and timely. To what extent are editorials actually read? Doubting editors of dailies have been asking this question for years. It is important that school editors also consider it. Fairly accurate interview-surveys reveal that one out of every five readers of the daily paper reads at least one editorial.

The school paper is small, however, and a vital part of school life; if its editorials are not read, they evidently do not merit reading. Editorials must touch school life, as well as students' other interests.

The school editor will pick out of the many events of the week perhaps two that most deserve editorial comment. Between these editorials he might well publish an entertaining or lighter editorial that may also have grown out of a news event.

No two of these three should be written by the same reporter, and the total space given editorials should be reasonably balanced with the total copy in the paper. The total wordage of the three should seldom exceed 750 words; it must be an exceptionally fine editorial to run above 300 words. By policy some school papers carry only one editorial topic per issue, its complete coverage making it an outstanding element of the issue. The determination of editorial subjects for the week may rest with an editorial board.

WHOSE OPINION

This moral purpose behind the editorial often leads the high school writer astray, and he loses his reader by preaching forcefully and earnestly for some cause such as better hall order. He must remember that he speaks for his paper, and that his paper speaks for the students. Naturally, the emphasis in editorial writing must be away from personal opinion toward group opinion, away from convincing toward explaining.

A case in point. The school paper's platform pledges support to the student council. The student council has passed some strict hall-traffic regulations that displease 75 per cent of the students. The school paper cannot ignore the case in its editorial columns, but before speaking it must carefully consider the entire school situation. The editorial writer must reserve personal opinion and build his case on facts free from exaggeration and feeling. Facts are always more convincing than dictatorial and opinionated statements. The high school student of today reserves the right to think for himself.

TOPICS FOR EDITORIALS

Two things make up a stimulating editorial: an interesting topic and good writing. The editorial lacking either of these is dull and will not be read to the end. *Pick an important, pertinent subject; then be per-*

suasive, not argumentative. If the subject is stimulating, good writing is easier.

Pressing issues, the true significance of events, thoughtful interpretations of new policy, considerations of changes in the make-up of the school (or the lack of such changes), constructive proposals toward the solution of recognized school problems, consideration of community and national problems—these are the materials of which stimulating editorial pages are composed.

The following thought-provoking editorial subjects were found in an examination of one hundred honors-winning school papers. Some of these subjects point beyond the campus, reflecting the current trend to broader and deeper school coverage.

> Should the school year be extended?
> Voters must pick leaders
> A mandatory course in politics
> Automatic vendors and litterbugs
> Time to forget campaign opinions
> New idea—year 'round colleges
> Atomic shelters—be prepared!
> Is freedom the school's goal?
> Are you standing in the shadow of the crowd?
> What I can do about communism
> Confusion in parking lot
> Remember—vote November 8
> Can we choose the very best?
> Respect for teachers
> International lingo necessary in world
> Execution is barbaric custom
> Teachers should stay in own field
> Crisis in Congo
> The new class schedule, good or bad?
> Nuclear testing gives United States toil, trouble
> County parks need support
> Presidential campaign concerns youth
> Are seniors treated like first graders?
> Traffic mishaps produce killers
> Mutual understanding with elders
> Clever youth required to unite chaotic globe
> School loafers cost taxpayers four hundred dollars each

TYPES OF EDITORIALS

There is almost no limit to the variety of forms the editorial may take. One need only scan the daily papers to become aware of these many variations. The freedom given the writer of the editorial, in comparison for instance with that given the news writer, accounts in part for this situation.

The more apparent characteristics of the seven most common types are indicated below. The overlapping reveals the difficulty of classifying an editorial.

1. Editorial of interpretation. Explanation and information are the ingredients of this common type of editorial. The subject is usually so significant that the editor wants the reader to understand the situation fully. The facts are there, but the writer goes beyond information to give the paper's view of the situation. (See Examples 43 and 44.)

These Are Important to You

Four important rules were introduced to the student body by Mr. Robert Wuflestad, vice-principal, at the recent orientation assembly.

1. Students are not to occupy their cars during school time, including lunchtime. The administration feels a responsibility for the students during their attendance at school. The rule was set up for the safety of students as well as for younger children in the neighborhood who may be going home for lunch. Also, some students do not return to school on time for their next classes.
2. Students are not to eat in their cars. "Since the enforcement of this regulation, a great lessening in litter out by the cars has been seen," stated Mr. Wuflestad. Some students still do not use the litter cans put there for their use while eating outside.
3. Trays should be put back; stools should be put up; trash should be thrown in the convenient trash cans. Some students are still leaving these tasks undone.
4. Smoking is not permitted in a block radius. Since this rule, complaints have been received from people two and three blocks away who find cigarette butts on their front stairs. Respect for other people's property is lacking.

Following these few simple rules could do a lot to improve Lincoln and its neighborhood.

The Lincoln Totem
Lincoln High School
Seattle, Washington

A NOTICED PRIVILEGE

EXAMPLE

44

Students at LHS are lucky. We truly have freedom of the press. Perhaps this can be best illustrated by a discouraging incident.

At a Redlands University Student Government Conference attended by Lynwood students several weeks ago, there were different discussion groups, one of which dealt with the student paper in the school.

Three fourths of the delegates participating in this discussion claimed that their school papers play no important role in school affairs because they are constantly subjected to adult domination and censorship. Editorials have to be approved by school administrators, and papers may campaign only for unimportant or uncontroversial matters like school colors.

This is not at all the situation at our school. No stories or editorials written by journalists have to be submitted for approval to any teacher or administrator. But naturally, we do depend on guidance from our adviser. Our school paper can criticize or comment on any phase of school life as long as the facts are straight and the commentary reflects a reasonable approach.

How did this come about? It came about because the students of LHS have sensibly tackled problems through their paper without abusing the privilege.

All views expressed in this paper are initiated and developed by students. No story or editorial is a cover-up for a faculty idea or belief. Truly we can consider ourselves extremely fortunate as long as we continue a level-headed and thorough approach to school matters.

There is no doubt that we have freedom of the press at LHS. And there is no doubt that students appreciate this and will strive to maintain this privilege.

Castle Courier
Lynwood High School
Lynwood, California

2. Editorial of information. The editorial of information limits itself to the review of certain facts; the mere handling of them in this manner emphasizes their importance and clears up some misunderstanding. It differs from the interpretive editorial by not drawing conclusions so obviously. (See Examples 45 and 46.)

Point System Limits Students

EXAMPLE

45

A great deal of discussion has been stirred up here by the recent announcement that the CHS extracurricular point system, long unenforced, is to be strictly carried out this year.

The substance of the system is that no student is to be allowed a total of more than twenty points at one time, points being given on the basis of the amount of time and work involved in any ac-

109

tivity. Thus *The Caldron* or *The Spotlight* major staff members, the leads of the senior class play, the varsity football team members, and those holding other positions considered of major importance are given fifteen points. Other point totals are given for duties involving varying degrees of time and effort.

Students with too many points have two roads open to them. They can drop some of their activities, or they can present a request in writing to the Extracurricular Point Committee, of which Mr. James McFadden is chairman. Students who do not do this may be asked to drop all their activities.

There are obviously two sides to this matter. One is presented by the majority of the faculty and those who are somewhat less active in school activities. They say that the point system is more democratic, a way to distribute school honors evenly, and that far too many people of real talent are overlooked in the mad scramble for the same person who got in the headlines last week. Further,

they claim that some students are so busy with extracurricular activities that their schoolwork suffers.

The others, a strong minority, are made up of the most active and so-called "big shots" of the school. They say that the system is undemocratic in that it limits personal liberty. They cite instances of past years when the editor of *The Spotlight* or *The Caldron* was a member of half a dozen other clubs and still came out valedictorian of his class. Further, they say that the number of students willing to work hard enough for three years to gain recognition in the fourth is limited; and that to limit anyone to one 15-point activity, a Boosters Club advisory councilship, and one other club is ridiculous.

At any rate, it seems probable that the success of the point system depends upon two things: first, the manner in which the Committee interprets the rules; and second, the participation of an increased number of Central students in extracurricular activities.

The Spotlight
Central High School
Fort Wayne, Indiana

What Does The TOTEM Cost?

EXAMPLE 46

Printing an eight page tabloid like the *Totem* costs $249.66 per issue, plus an additional cost of approximately $20 for film and engraving of pictures. The money received from activity-card sales supplies the paper with $100 per issue; this leaves at least $170 that must be paid through advertisements. To meet this cost, 220 inches of ads should run in each eight pages.

The special 16-page paper put out by last year's *Totem* staff cost $452 to print and required double the number of inches of ads.

It is obvious that advertisements are essential if the *Totem* is to be published every two weeks.

The importance of advertisements to the *Totem* is easy to understand; the degree of importance of advertising to the merchant is up

110

to the students who read the ads. Mentioning the ad to the advertiser, while shopping, lets him know that his money is being well spent. The life of the *Totem* depends on his money.

The Lincoln Totem
Lincoln High School
Seattle, Washington

3. Editorials of criticism and reform. The great bulk of the editorials that appear in the student press criticize existing conditions and suggest changes. Some writers have called this the editorial of argument and persuasion.

Such an editorial takes a definite stand and attempts to convince the reader. Although some editorials of this type are limited to influencing the reader's thinking, many call for definite action on the reader's part. Alert as school editors are to improving school conditions, it is not surprising that they favor the editorial of criticsm and reform.

In determining how far to go in taking issue with school policies, the judgment of the school editor in consultation with the adviser is often effective. (See Examples 47 and 48.)

OUR OPINION

THE LIMITATION OF ACTIVITIES SYSTEM in effect at B-CC assigns each extracurricular activity a certain number of points and permits each student six of these points.

EXAMPLE

47

The present system seems at least inaccurate and sometimes even unfair. Its advocates claim it distributes leadership and prevents a drop in grades due to excess activities. One can readily understand the reasoning behind the latter argument, but the former seems based on faulty suppositions. Leadership to many is the holding of an important office with an important name. But leadership is really assuming responsibility and, according to Webster, "guiding others." One need not be president of a club or editor of a publication to guide others; a club or committee member sometimes assumes more actual leadership and responsibility than the chairman. Therefore the opportunity for leadership in some form is available to almost anyone who wishes it. This leadership may not bring glory or a hero's badge, but it carries with it the responsibility that all should experience.

If maintaining a high scholastic average and not distributing leadership is the true goal of a point system, then our system needs a major revision. An SGA committee should be established to investigate the amount of time each extracurricular activity draws away from schoolwork. A more satisfactory system should be based on careful research and evaluation.

Many people will argue that any easing of current limitations will give a person a chance to assume too many important activities. Since all students have a chance to assume leadership in some form under any point system, this is irrelevant. And, more important, most positions of honor or leadership are chosen through some type of election or appointment; it is really in the hands of the students as to who will hold the post.

"In short, the perfect society would be that in which each class and each unit would be doing the work to which its nature and aptitude best adapted it to, and rule over such a society would be by the wisest and most qualified." So stated Plato over 2,000 years ago. This idea can be applied to the present point system, too.

The Tattler
Bethesda-Chevy Chase High School
Bethesda, Maryland

Improve or Kill Senate

EXAMPLE

48

Is each Mills student represented in student government by his senator? Do the senators really use the powers bestowed on them, or is the Senate a convenient way to get out of class?

Every two weeks approximately 75 students get out of one of their classes to attend a Senate meeting. At the meeting, usually held in the cafeteria, the senators congregate with their buddies and are half willing to devote all their attention to the matters at hand.

After five minutes, the meeting is called to order. An effort is made by all to hear, but a microphone would be appreciated. After the flag salute—if there is a flag—the senators listen to the old business. On the whole the senators do not participate in the discussion, and for a majority the information is boring. The same "steadies" carry on the discussion while others take notes, but all the senators should have an active part in the business.

After all, they are the ones who are supposed to guide the school.

Rarely at a Senate meeting is new business brought up from the floor. The senators could be bringing up new possibilities for rules or activities, but they are either shy, disinterested, or do not care. At the November 2 meeting, the majority of Senate time was spent trying to find the correct parliamentary procedure concerning an amendment or addition to the school constitution.

If this is what a typical Senate meeting is like, is the Senate necessary? It definitely is a necessary part of our student government, but the senators themselves should attend a preleadership course. If the senators were aware of parliamentary procedure, perhaps the officers would have to be on their toes more, and the efficiency of the senators as well as of the Senate leaders could be improved.

Thunderbolt
Mills High School
Millbrae, California

112

4. Editorial of tribute, appreciation, or commendation. This editorial lauds somebody for worthy action, expresses appreciation for something, or acts as a tribute to the deceased. (See Example 49.)

To Our Friend and Teacher, Mr. Dewey

EXAMPLE
49

IT WAS A SIGHT, Elmer, the way you'd walk down the hall with that old bear coat hanging down to your ankles, carrying that old beat-up brown felt. It was absolutely "scandalous" the way you talked at times, but we loved it, and envied the way you got away with it. It was impossible for you to teach just commercial—you just couldn't help giving an informal education that the books didn't go into. Why, who ever heard of discussing juvenile delinquency in a bookkeeping class?

There was another side of you, too—the side that was so generous, so encouraging, so good. You always knew the answer to our problems; you always told us we could do something if we had just a little faith in ourselves; you always had time to do nothing but talk, if that's what we felt like doing.

School wouldn't have been school without you in 216 and your unusual sense of humor and your unending supply of nicknames, and—well, just your being here.

We'll miss you, Elmer.

East Highlights
East High School
Rockford, Illinois

5. Editorial of entertainment. Written in light vein, this editorial has as its purpose the entertainment of the reader. Student editors are so busy working for the betterment of the school that they do not often enough take time out to laugh or chuckle in the editorial column. (See Example 50.)

'You Look Very Pretty Today' *Means 'Yesterday You Didn't'*

EXAMPLE
50

Have you ever received a compliment that made you wonder whether to punch the giver in the nose or gratefully thank him? You probably have had this experience, since there are many of these two-faced praises in common usage.

They really may be innocent, well-meaning compliments—but don't bet on it! Here are just a few to beware of:
- "You look years younger with your new hairdo."
- "We were just talking about you."

113

- "I've heard so much about you."
- "I'm so glad to meet you. I've met so few students in this school."
- "I've been telling John how frightfully intelligent you are."
- "It was so nice to meet your sister. I didn't know you had a younger sister!"
- "I envy your happy-go-lucky attitude toward life."

Miami High Times
Miami High School
Miami, Florida

6. Editorial of special occasions. Thanksgiving, Christmas, Washington's Birthday, the annual United Fund Drive, and dozens of other significant occasions lend themselves to editorial treatment. In spite of the interpretive nature of many of these pieces, they are generally considered a type unto themselves. (See Examples 51 through 53.)

Lincoln — the Man

EXAMPLE
51

He wasn't a Caesar, a Roland, a Luther, a Cromwell, nor even a Washington but just—Abe Lincoln.

That is why (without a crown, a sword, a sermon) we love him as we do. Homely, gaunt, ungainly, yet cheerful, wise, and patient, he lived as "Honest Abe" and died his country's "savior."

Lincoln did not lead an army nor take a single fort; he joked, he hauled a pig from the mud, but he raised a drooping standard and won a people's heart.

Men write the name of Washington with a silent awe, but they tell Lincoln's stories as though he were only a departed friend.

The San Diego Russ
San Diego High School
San Diego, California

Is Santa Commercialized?

EXAMPLE
52

"Here comes Santa, Mommy, but what is he wearing?"

Yes, what is Santa wearing? He's all wrapped up in billboards, ad displays, and red tape! "Merry Christmas," says Santa, "buy Smoker cigarettes and elastic gum."

Maybe our parents have something when they talk about the "good old days." At least, in the time of the horse and buggy, peo-ple had a clear focus on Christmas and its meaning. At least families worried about how happy they could be instead of how big a bill they could run up at the local department store.

Why can't we have Christmases like the one pictured in the twin of this editorial? [next page].

Let's remember we can't buy Christmas spirit!

114

What Is a Real Holiday?

There are still many people in the world who know and experience the wonderful spirit of the Christmas season. These people paint the picture of the huge cedar tree placed in an imposing position before a window, of the many sparkling and tinkling ornaments which load its limbs, of the bright lights, and yes, of the strings of popcorn criss-crossed about the tree.

The picture would not be complete without stacks of presents piled about the base of the cedar. The gifts are simple, ones that should be given and that should be appreciated. These are not gifts bought because of scintillating window or newspaper displays or because "I must get Johnny a present; he gave me one last year."

Happy people pulling bright ribbons from packages add the finishing touch to the picture.

Isn't a real Christmas peaceful, like this?

The Holmespun
Holmes High School
Covington, Kentucky

Salute to Freedom: the Printed Word

EXAMPLE

53

"Were it left to me to decide whether we should have a government without newspapers or newspapers without a government, I should not hesitate a moment to prefer the latter."

Although Thomas Jefferson said this over 150 years ago, it is as true in the present space age as it was than. Perhaps it is even more meaningful now.

Unfortunately, we live in a world where people believe lies because propaganda is the only information available. These people are not free to have a press which prints facts. In countries such as Cuba and Red China the government checks the newspapers, while here, newspapers check the government.

The high school newspaper also has a responsibility to the school it serves. It must represent student ideas and uphold the honor of the school. A school paper must have freedom to discuss controversial subjects and question school policy. The principles of the free press begin with the scholastic press.

National Newspaper Week is a time to realize the responsibility we Americans have in preserving our basic freedom of communication for ourselves and for future generations. The principles of the free press, which we honor this week, are the core of our democracy, our contact with the changing world, and the protector of our American heritage.

John Adams Journal
John Adams High School
Cleveland, Ohio

7. Editorial liners. A liner is a short statement on a general or a specific subject, either serious or light, which depends upon cleverness or punch to make up for its brevity. These liners are dropped in at the end of editorial columns. Sometimes they are not original but are the sayings of great men. Liners are very popular with the daily papers, but school papers have not used them to any great extent. (See Example 54.)

EXAMPLE 54

SPEAKING in behalf of under-privileged children who often cause less concern than a mistreated animal, Judge Gilliam related, "The parents of a neglected waif purchased a thoroughbred piglet at a sale and took it home. That night, when the baby began to cry, the mother asked the father to go quiet it; she was too tired. The father replied that the baby would soon stop yowling, and then went back to sleep. Then the pig began to squeal and the man leaped out of bed, jerked on his overalls, and ran to its aid. The only difference between the baby and the pig was that the pig had a thoroughbred for a father."

The Orange and Black
Grand Junction High School
Grand Junction, Colorado

Guest Editorials

1—"Dost thou love life? Then do not squander time, for that is the stuff life is made of."

2—"Little strokes fell great oaks."

3—"Vessels large may venture more, but little boats should keep near the shore."

4—"It is hard for an empty sack to stand upright."

5—"Experience keeps a dear school, but fools will learn in no other."

6—"A man may, if he knows not how to save, keep his nose to the grindstone."

7—"There was never a good war nor a bad peace."

—Benjamin Franklin.
Born Jan. 7, 1706.

Hi Gasher
El Dorado High School
El Dorado, Arkansas

Editorial Shorts

Laughing gas has proved very useful when one is suffering great pain. Why don't they pass it out at report-card time?

"Home Ec Club Installs Cannon"—*High Times* headline. And we thought the way to a man's heart was through his stomach.

Girls High Times
Girls High School
Atlanta, Georgia

That offside penalty—The penalty for being offside in a football game is only the loss of five yards. The penalty of being offside crossing a street may be the loss of your life or a serious injury.

Poly Spotlight
Riverside High School
Riverside, California

116

Editorial cartoons. Growing in popularity with high school newspaper editors is the use of the editorial cartoon to emphasize the point of view advanced in the editorial. Executed by talented students, such cartoons add variety and graphic appeal to the paper.

Example 55 is a good example of an editorial cartoon well executed by the student artist and well chosen by the student editor to help promote a worthy school drive. (See also Chapter 19.)

EXAMPLE

55

Support the Teams by Buying a Button!

The Tattler
West Tech High School
Cleveland, Ohio

THE EDITORIAL PAGE

The editorial page may include the following types of copy: (1) two or three editorials, (2) the flag (mast) of the paper, (3) letters to the editor, (4) surveys of student opinion, (5) reviews of books, theater, concerts, movies, records, (6) personal columns, (7) educational features, (8) and editorial cartoons. Their arrangement is often a distinctive hallmark of the newspaper.

Both solicited and unsolicited letters from readers are presented on this page, for the editorial page is a platform for the readers' opinions as well as the paper's. At times the letters are grouped under a blanket head such as *Voice of the Student*. In no event are anonymous letters ever considered for publication, and those letters published should carry the name of the correspondent. Anonymity encourages irresponsibility. Contributions should be screened so that the responsible student finds voice in the school paper.

An editorial page devoted primarily to editorial opinion—the paper's and the readers'—is reproduced in Example 56. Another, Example 57, emphasizes the lead editorial with a cartoon and then shifts to other good editorial-page material.

EXAMPLE

56

Page 2   LINTON HI-LIGHTS   October 28, 1960

What Do You Think Of Discontinuing Regents?

Mr. Kroman: One of the things which has kept our state on top has been these exams. If they weren't given, teachers wouldn't have any incentive to cover the work, especially if the class was slow.

Larry Wasserman: Regents have become too important. Kids worry too much about learning just what is in them, rather than other information which may be more important.
—Camera Club photos by Bob Franciose

Benson King: I am in favor of Regents because they insure the fact that the necessary material in a course is covered. Without them a transferred student might run into trouble.

Dave Glater: Too many teachers teach just for the Regents. Kids sometimes learn the, mechanics, but get no understanding of the basic facts.

Mr. Harold Rowe: I want to make it clear that my remarks are only in connection with the Chemistry Regents, whose use I favor. I feel it is quite important that students take an examination not made up by teachers. The Chemistry Regents syllabus leaves plenty of time for teachers to enrich the course beyond the requirements and it doesn't tend to prevent the use of new materials.

Mr. Anthony Prindle: Regents are the traditional evaluative device at the end of any course. However, tradition in itself is no reason for maintaining them. If the Regents become the goal of a course, its entire effect is lost. But the merits of this well constructed instrument far outweigh its deficiencies. I feel that we truly owe a large part of the supremacy of our New York State Educational System to the Regents and that they should not be abolished.

We are devoting this page to a discussion of the pro's and con's of possible discontinuation of Regents examinations. You will find the views of students and teachers and of Dr. Robert Murray, superintendent of schools, and a brief history of Regents exams.

Your newspaper reflects your idea of excellence

Regents Exams Essential

We were pleased to hear that the State Board of Regents will keep its exams at least another year. Although they have many faults, they do play an extremely important role in the New York State Educational System. We feel that they are still an important means New York State has of controlling its quality of education. It is not difficult to see what would happen after several years without them, especially in schools with low standards.

Regents will have to be maintained until another more efficient system of uniform control is devised and used.

The Regents Question

Vital Arguments

For –

Regents provide a uniform control over what is taught in New York State Schools. Without them, teachers wouldn't have a specific goal in mind, and would tend to leave out important or difficult work, especially if the class happened to be slow. Consequently, New York's quality of education would go down. There would probably be the same problems as in many states where there is no uniform control.

Regents are not being replaced by the College Boards because both the exams serve different purposes. The latter are mainly designed to determine a person's outlook for college work, while regents test his act-

Against–

Regents' format inhibits creativity, self-direction, and problem-solving, and in effect results in mediocrity. It is not kept on a high enough level for today's secondary school student who wishes to go on to college. For this reason, many of the functions once served by the Regents are now being taken over by other exams.

Passing Regents exams becomes a maximum objective rather than the minimum standard which they are intended to be. This is true of both students and teachers. The syllabus discourages the use of modern teaching techniques, and often

Murray Expresses Opinion On Importance of Regents

Recently, we interviewed Dr. Robert Murray, Superintendent of Schenectady Public Schools, who will comment on the controversy of discontinuing Regents examinations.

Question: What effect do the Regents examinations have on Schenectady Schools?

Answer: Students in Schenectady public schools have been taking Regents examinations for many years and will continue to take them. Both of the high schools offer the Regents examinations. They are given in most college preparatory courses as well as in some commercial courses.

Question: Is the emphasis that has been placed on the Regents examinations still as apparent as it was before?

Answer: No, they still don't hold the same place they did in the past because of the introduction of many valuative procedures for examinations. A good example is the college entrance examination given by the College Board. Also, in Schenectady, Regents examinations no longer are offered on the lower grade level.

Question: What significance does a Regent diploma have today?

Answer: A Regents diploma does have a significance in that it indicates that a student has been able to satisfy standards set by the Regents. Regents examinations are carefully planned, well-prepared tests. In years past, they fell into bad repute because they weren't used properly. Students, teachers, and schools graded on Regents marks alone. However, if properly used Regents are very helpful.

Question: Are school final examinations better than the Regents?

Answer: Each has its own place. Regents can be advan-

The Fourth R----Regents

—Art by Mary Ann Gutowski

Preparation of Regents Exams Requires Much Planning, Talent

Regents are the most widely used exams of their kind in New York State, but of the millions of people who have taken them, there are probably very few who actually know very much of their history or how they are prepared. trict superintendents, five high

EXAMPLE

57

'Tram' 'Deals From Bottom'; Still Says Bus Won't Pay

DISREGARDING A POLL TAKEN from 1358 students, the Denver Tramway officials "will not extend the number four bus line under any present circumstances."

According to a Tramway official, it takes 75 students a day to come out even. He disregarded the fact that 109 Patriots ride the bus right now, with a promise of more to come. "It still won't pay."

Due to these officials, Jefferson students, who must walk further than we have to charter a bus for $42 a day. We can promise the "bus boys" $63 per day! How much does it take to fill their linings?

We hope that the D.T.C. will open their tightly closed eyes before some student is hurt because he had to walk to school on a treacherous highway where there isn't even a sidewalk.

"Face it," stated the official. "An extension just isn't in the cards."

No tears are shed by the D.T.C. for the 109 students who are being lost in the shuffle, and being dealt off the bottom of the deck.

* * *

DON'T THINK YOU CAN TAKE school much longer? Cheer up! There are only 43 school days until the end of this semester.

* * *

Learning Palace Still Clean

"DON'T SCRATCH ANYTHING THAT doesn't itch," one teacher recently wrote on his blackboard.

Very few hand prints, pencil marks, carvings and crayon drawings have appeared on the walls and desks at G.W. so far.

Our multi-million dollar palace of education is a very beautiful school. It would be a shame for a few thoughtless individuals to ruin it for the many students who are proud of their school.

The walls are clean. Let's keep them that way!

Is Freedom School's Goal?

ARE WE BEING EDUCATED for freedom or conformity, courage or security?

In the National Education association news release commemorating this week, Nov. 6-12, as American Education week, the purpose of the week was stated: "to make every American aware of the important role education plays in a democracy."

Our democracy was built on freedom and courage. Our educational system must have the same basis if it is to uphold its purpose.

We, as students, must then ask ourselves, "Am I forced to think and write a certain way to get a good grade in Mr. X's class?"

"Are grades so important that I feel it necessary to give up the exploration of an interesting subject to do numerous 'busy work' assignments, which should have been done during class time?"

If the answers to these questions are overwhelmingly affirmative, a drastic revision of grading scales should be considered.

Whatever the answer, one point is clear: Our freedoms will be secure only so long as we have the fortitude to fight for them through education.

Surveyor Staff

Vol. 1   November 9, 1960   No. 3

Published Every Other Thursday During the School Session by the Students
of
George Washington High School, Denver, Colo.

Editor-in-Chief .... Bob Birney
Business Manager .... Sue Willung
Sponsor .... Mr. Robert Rothstein
News Editor .... Nancy Gillett
Rewrite Editor .... Carole Katchen
Copy Editor .... Susan Collins
Page Editors ...... Ron Berenbeim, Nancy Berman, Joy Oppenheim, Susie Williams
Publicity Manager .... Barbara Rhodes
Supply Manager .... Madge Sonders
Exchange Editor .... Lyne Martin
Special Writers .... Fred Cohn, Alan Grossman, Doug Hart,
Karen Johnson, Bob Kippur, Sue Werthan
Art Editor .... Larry Aumiller
Photographer .... Mike Carson

Seniors Receive Recognition

Nineteen seniors at George Washington were honored for outstanding performance on the National Merit Scholarship Qualifying test given last spring. Each student received a formal Letter of Commendation signed by Sam Waldman, principal, and John Stalnaker, the president of the National Merit Scholarship corporation.

Letter Winners

Commended students are Richard Barton, Brent Brandenburg, Doug Clifford, Barbara Coombs,

Rowena Corbin, Michael Faith, Dennis Grogan, David Jonas, Carole Katchen, Douglas Kimmel, Sharon Marks, Gary McCool, Roberta Peterson, Jeffery Poole, Dennis Roark, Carol Segelstrom, Nancy Silverberg, Barry Smernoff and Susan Williams.

Mr. Stalnaker stated: "While these bright youngsters did not reach the status of semifinalists in the 1960-61 Merit program, they are so outstanding that we wish to single them out for special attention."

mended students together constitute.

"The semifinalists and comtute less than three per cent of all high school seniors, and this certainly signifies noteworthy achievement."

The National Merit Scholarship corporation gives recognition to two groups of students who achieve high scores on the N.M.S.Q.T. The semifinalists group is composed of the highest scoring students in each state and in United States territories. Some 10,000 semifinalists will take a second examination in December to establish further their eligibility to receive Merit Scholarships.

Several Objectives

"The Merit program has several objectives," Mr. Stalnaker continued. "One is the selection of Merit scholars from among the semi-finalists.

"However, we also strive to foster the pursuit of excellence among all highly able students. We urge the students honored to make every effort to attend college and to develop to the fullest their promise of achievement."

The commended students were among the high school juniors in more than 15,000 schools who took the N.M.S.Q.T. last spring.

Scholarship Program

This year's program will conclude about May 1, 1961 with the naming of students who will receive four-year Merit scholarships to the colleges of their choice.

Faculty Forum

by John T. Reeves

We Americans have weeks and days, to the point of absurdity, to commemorate or to recognize some one thing or another. Conscious of this absurdity, Will Rogers once spoke of "Don't Beat Your Wife Week" and "Be Kind to Man's Best Friend Week." It may be, however, that in the midst of all the groups and institutions to which a week or a day is devoted there are some institutions which do merit a week of special emphasis. American Education is one such institution.

One View

I have been asked to give one teacher's views during American Education Week, in the hope, perhaps, that these views may reflect the thoughts of other teachers about their part in American education.

What is the role of the teacher? Is he a disciplinarian? an assignment maker? a paper grader (lavish to the point of demoniac glee with his red pencil)? a giver of grades? All these? Yes, but not one nor all these together can give more than an inkling into the most important function of the teacher.

As a disciplinarian he merely provides a favorable climate for learning; assignments are important, but not the whole of teaching, despite the obvious fact (ask any student) that teachers fiendishly collaborate in length and frequency of assignments; paper and test grades are only a part; and, as for the role of gradegiver, I could wish that this role were seen in its proper light.

Role Is Guide

The real role of the teacher is that of a guide. He does not think for someone else, but he should guide his students to recognize good thinking and to learn how to think for themselves. He can-

not tell one what to read, but he should guide students to an appreciation of what is good literature. He does not solve all problems, either in algebra or in life, but he should guide students to the knowledge of how to find their own solutions.

Without apology, I take liberty to adapt an idea from T. H. Huxley. A teacher, like a master chess player, will not play the game for his students. His real function is to guide them in their efforts to learn the rules and the principles of play for themselves.

To most teachers, this is serious business, for we know that those who fail "will be checkmated, without haste and without remorse."

by Douglas Hart

Sophomores who want a pep assembly, beware!

For those of you who have just escaped from junior high, I will explain such an assembly.

You have already seen a milder variety early in the year. Wait until you see a big assembly. No, don't wait; I'll invent one for you.

This is a red letter day. Washington's girl varsity gossip team has captured the city title and will compete for the state championship Friday. As we file into the auditorium, an awe inspiring spectacle greets our eyes. The auditorium is dark except for a spotlight on the stage. The crowd is seated and the assembly begins.

The noise increases as people from the audience join in. Perhaps this could be expected in

the jungles of New Guinea, but certainly not in a modern high school of the U. S. and A. The madness reaches a peak and slowly dies.

When a girl on the stage approaches the microphone, people clap until their hands are raw. You have never seen her before, and you're afraid to ask who she is. A murmur runs through the crowd and your question is answered: "That's Betta Zetta, muscular, but modest captainess of the gossip team."

Betta begins to talk, "I think we might win tomorrow, maybe." The crowd goes wild. The roof falls in. The cheerleaders turn handsprings and pickpockets circulate freely through the crowd.

You try to sneak out the back of the screaming madhouse. You step over four or five people who are happily rolling in the aisles. After staggering to the door, you walk out, remembering too late that you're on the third floor.

That is a big pep assembly. Sophomores, beware!

CHAPTER LABORATORY

1. On a slip of paper, write what you consider to be the most interesting and important news subject around school. Compile the items suggested by the class into a list for group discussion; in class, select one news subject the group considers worthy of editorial coverage by the paper.

2. Of the seven types of editorials discussed on pages 108 to 116, choose the one you think appropriate for the subject agreed upon in Exercise 1 and write a 200-word editorial. Indicate the type of editorial in the upper left-hand corner of the first page.

3. Of all the examples in this chapter, how many use the "editorial we"? In each case, tell if it was justified or if the third person should have been used instead.

4. Study a set of school newspapers, and as a class determine the popularity of the seven types of editorials.

5. Write a 150-word editorial of occasion, using as your topic the nearest holiday.

6. Study the editorials that appear in your own school paper and judge their quality. What will you use as criteria?

7. Write an editorial of interpretation, treating a school club or some other extracurricular activity about which you know a good deal.

8. Study the editorial pages of daily and school newspapers, and list the types of copy that appear there in addition to editorials.

9. From the daily paper, clip an example of each of the seven types of editorials you have studied in this chapter. Mount them and discuss their classifications in class.

10. Choose an editorial from the last issue of the school paper, and determine which of the seven types it was; then rewrite it as one of the other seven.

10 FEATURE STORIES

The feature story is the spice of a school paper. A student paper can easily become nothing more than a chronicle of the things that happened yesterday and an announcement of those that will happen tomorrow, but the feature story seasons news coverage and makes it palatable.

Roughly speaking, the articles that appear in newspapers can be classified as (1) news stories, (2) editorials, and (3) features. The news story is the news as it happens, with no opinion or other embellishments. The editorial is the interpretation of these events by the paper. In every newspaper, however, there is a great mass of material that is neither of these. This material may supplement the news, it may entertain, it may explain, it may amuse, it may invoke sympathy, or it may even inform. This is the feature story.

CHARACTERISTICS OF THE FEATURE STORY

There is no formula for writing the feature story, but its main characteristics are distinguishable.

121

Timeliness. The good feature story is usually dependent upon "something that is going on." But a good feature that ignores the current always bobs up and thus prevents this general statement from becoming a rule. Some of the best feature stories are timely, tied into the news background in some way or other, but some find their place in the reader's interest with no timeliness whatsoever. Events that have little news value are often the basis of good human-interest stories.

Literary qualities. The feature story is not an essay, nor a theme or a composition as conceived in a course in English composition. But many feature stories do have a certain literary quality. Although the feature story often springs from something of current interest, it seldom derives its appeal from the significance of that news but rather from the reporter's treatment of the story.

The reporter has a long line of forebears distinguished in both literature and journalism. The feature story is perhaps the closest link between these two fields. The American lineage includes among others, Alexander Hamilton, Benjamin Franklin, William Cullen Bryant, Harriet Beecher Stowe, Mark Twain, Eugene Field, Ernest Hemingway, and John Steinbeck.

The reporter can look back in the roster of English authors to associate himself with Daniel Defoe, Joseph Addison, Richard Steele, Jonathan Swift, Rudyard Kipling, James M. Barrie, Arnold Bennett, John Galsworthy, G. K. Chesterton, St. John Ervine, H. G. Wells, George Bernard Shaw, and Rebecca West.

Direct quotations and dialogue have a preferred position in the account, for they provide a human touch. If a reporter overhears or witnesses an event that would be entertaining to his readers, it is up to him to reconstruct it if possible. Therefore, quotations and statements of fact are paramount in the feature. It is often a mistake for the reporter to try to explain the incident in his own words. Let the reader enjoy that first-hand sensation.

Length. A feature story has no "approved" length, for the length is determined by reader interest. The instructional or informative feature is more inclined to be consistently long. Unlike the news story, however, the feature should not be cut by the make-up man. It is a story with each part in a specific place for a specific purpose, supposedly with no extra words that could be cut. Since school papers are limited in space, assignment editors must control the length of features as well as news stories. Reporters should think accordingly as they plan and write.

The third person. As in the news story, the good school feature story shows a maximum use of the third person. However, there is always the exception that prevents the formulation of an air-tight set of principles.

The lead. Seldom does the feature story open with the summary lead of the typical news story. The liberty allowed the reporter is utilized from the beginning—the effective feature usually has an unorthodox lead. Note the examples included in this chapter.

Freedom of expression. Freedom from straight news limitations does not permit the reporter to be rude, unkind, flippant, silly, or sloppy, nor does it permit him to reveal confidences or transmit gossip. Rather it gives him the freedom to exercise ingenuity in locating a good subject and in writing his story.

TYPES OF FEATURES

Feature stories can be roughly divided into five general classes, although overlapping prevents strict classification: (1) features that inform; (2) features that entertain; (3) human-interest stories; (4) personality sketches; and (5) news-features.

Features that inform. The daily papers are full of supporting material for the news stories of the day. There are unlimited possibilities in the school for creating stories by relating generally unknown factual information.

Examples 58 through 60 are excellent illustrations of the feature that informs. Few subjects hold greater interest for the high school student than beauty, military service, and college; what is more, all of these features are well written and hold the initial interest through the reading.

Ohio University Combines Athletics, Year-Round Study

By LARRY ASTRAUSKAS

EXAMPLE

58

Ohio University, situated in Athens, is a coeducational institution. It was established by an act of the Ohio Legislature in 1804.

Those who planned its founding were members of the original Ohio Company of Associates. They came from New England and understood thoroughly the supreme importance of higher education.

Through more than 150 years the university has grown into a complex organization of seven colleges, five schools, and other major divisions.

Year-round study opportunities are provided, and programs leading to undergraduate and graduate degrees, including the doctorate, are available.

The costs of attending Ohio University are lower than most universities of similar high standards because it is supported by the state.

This college offers an extensive program of recreational activities and intramural sports for all students. In intercollegiate competition its varsity teams constantly rank high in the Mid-American conference.

Ohio University has a friendly campus atmosphere. The faculty and administration strive to give students an education and to make life as pleasant for them as possible while they are obtaining a college education.

With nearly 8000 students on its campus and residential area, the university is large enough to sustain a true college atmosphere, but not so large as to endanger the personal relationship that should exist between student and administration.

Ohio University welcomes consideration of all serious-minded youths who are giving much thought to the preparation they need to live a more effective life.

Blue and Gold
East High School
Cleveland, Ohio

Specialized Hair Styles Flatter Face Shapes, Sizes

EXAMPLE

59

Are you a square? Or is your face round or triangular? A good way to find out is by outlining your face on a mirror with a bar of soap or an old lipstick and examining it critically.

After you have done this, you can compliment your face shape by adjusting your hair style. Perhaps these hints will be helpful.

Square Shape

A bubble is the coif for you! Keep your hair fluffed out softly and away from your face line. To achieve this, use medium or jumbo size

124

rollers. After the set, a vigorous all-over brush-out will not destroy its shape. In fact, this helps push the hair into form. Curls or soft bangs at the forehead will detract from the squareness.

Round Shape

Using a combination of clips and rollers will produce the hairdo that best suits you. Large clip-curls at the sides will help lengthen your face shape. Slimmer hairdos cropped close to the head are perfect for this shape.

Oval Shape

Experiment! Your facial shape is the goal of every girl. Bouffants, vamps, pageboys—choose what you wish. Wear what your mood suggests, changing your "dos" often. Try some of the smart accessories which are so popular, such as bows and bands.

Triangular Shape

Keep your hair full at the crown but no bangs. Wear hair off the forehead, using wide swept waves which fan in and hug temples, thus making them seem closer together.

Downward Triangular Shape

The popular pageboy will fit your needs. To give jawline more width, set hair to fit around cheekbones and flare out at bottom. Too much fluffiness on top will exaggerate the width there.

Diamond Shape

Your main objective is to widen the forehead and jawline. You may achieve this effect by wearing your hair back at the top and full at the temples. Also, you should set hair so that it is full at the jawlines. A pageboy would be good for you, but keep the top light and high.

The Western Breeze
Western Hills High School
Cleveland, Ohio

All 18-year-old Males Liable to Draft

By JUDY PADUR

EXAMPLE
60

Every male American must register for the draft when he reaches 18. He is then not liable to call for another six months. But in practice (as of now) he will not be called until he is 26 —unless he has formally applied for deferment, in which case he remains nominally liable until he is 35.

A draftee is liable for two years of active duty, two more years in the Ready Reserve, which means attending classes once a week and spending two weeks a year in camp, and two more years in the Standby Reserve. In this case there is no choice of service; it's the army.

An alternative to the draft is volunteering for induction. This involves telling the draft board of one's immediate availability. It does not mean that he will be immediately accepted. In this case also there is no choice of the branch of the service.

A person may, as early as 17, enlist in the branch of his choice. This usually means a longer

125

period of obligation, meeting higher mental and physical standards, and finding a waiting list ahead.

One cannot volunteer for any service once he has received his draft-induction card.

Recently, the six-months programs have been the most popular. With slight variations, these programs call for only six months of active duty but with a longer period of reserve obligation, for a total of eight years instead of the draftees' six. Quotas for these programs are relatively small and frequently full.

For straight enlistment in the Army, the age range is from 17 to 34. This includes three years of active training, one year in the Ready Reserve, and two years in Standby Reserve.

The Navy age range is 17 to 31. The enlistment includes four years of active service, one year in the Ready Reserve and one year in the Standby Reserve.

The Air Force program, with a 17 to 34 age range, entails four years of active service, one year in the Ready Reserve, and one year in Standby Reserve.

Three years of active service, two years in Ready Reserve, and two years in Standby Reserve is included in the Marine Corps program, with an age limit of 17 to 28.

Last but not the least, the Coast Guard enlistment, with an age limit of 17 to 25, includes three years of active service, two years in the Ready Reserve, and two more years in the Standby Reserve.

The Lincoln News
Lincoln High School
Tacoma, Washington

Features that entertain. The public likes to be entertained in feature style. The story that treats the baseball game in feature style has a good chance of overshadowing the news account of it. Amusing incidents on hall monitoring may deserve more space than an editorial on hall order. Stories might well be built around proverbs or the unusual names of students.

Examples 61 through 64 barely indicate the scope of subjects possible for the feature that entertains. They illustrate clearly, however, that it is the treatment of the subject that determines the classification of the story.

EXAMPLE
61

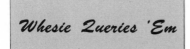

Whesie Queries 'Em

M. L. S.

Now what did Harry tell me to do? Oh, yeah—interview important students in our school.

Hi, Crone! Oh, lookie, there's Claiborne Pete; I'm going to interview him.

"Clai—borne! Yoo Hoo! I want to interview you and—You don't want an interview? But, Claiborne, you'll get your name in the paper and everything! So you don't want your name in the pa-

126

per, eh?" These problem children!

There's Jabie Heyward, but he's not important so I won't waste my precious time messing with him!

"Hello, Katherine Seymour; what's the lowdown on Gertrude Parker? She's going to Tennessee? Isn't that grand? When? Oh, she isn't going to Tennessee, she's going WITH 'Tennessee.'" Pardon my quick getaway!

Now let's swing and sway with Urwell-Bay, 'cause here he comes, he's gonna play! My, that horn makes pretty music! "Say, Ted, how about giving me an interview? Ted, I'm talking to you! Stop playing on that thing! Stop it! Be quiet! Hush! Quit now! Grrrrrr!" I wish these people wouldn't be so undignified. How can I interview them when they won't even listen to me? You'd think I was a member of the family!

Now if I could just find the janitor. He sure is important. But, fish, he ain't no stewdant! "Hello, Ham. Oh, fine!"

Who is that I see now, trucking down the hall, she's going to town oh boy and how, Ouch! She bumped into the wall!

"Don't cry, 'Cassie,' it couldn't have hurt you, *much!* Oh, I didn't mean it that way, honest I didn't. Come on, old gal, give me an interview. Please, I just gotta have this story by this afternoon." So you won't, huh? See if I help you up.

Gee, I'm an hour late and I haven't got an interview yet. Well, come to think about it my story was supposed to be on activities!

Knock me down with a feather!

Goldsboro Hi News
Goldsboro High School
Goldsboro, North Carolina

Cass Status Seekers

In an era when most of one's material possessions have become indicators of one's social status, the *Technician* thought it apropos to print this handy guide to Cass status symbols. We note that this guide is subject to exceptions and changes due to phenomena more or less beyond the control of man or the *Technician*.

Auto students—(Status Symbol)—A car in the process of being taken apart . . . traces of grease under traces of fingernails . . . a girl friend who looks like Tuesday Weld—(Non-status Symbol)—an A in English . . . drivers training . . . a Volkswagen.

Art students (female—Status Symbol)—Eyes lined with India ink and shadowed with water color . . . an egg beater instead of a comb . . . an A from Mr. Johnson—(Non-status Symbol)—an art-comp. design stolen from a 1949 copy of "Graphics" . . . lipstick . . . shoes resembling those worn by American teenagers.

Science students—(Status Symbol)—The structure (skeleton) of a lab coat autographed and cartooned by all other science students . . . a home lab fully supplied with Cass equipment . . . a leather slide rule case that looks as though it served in both world wars—(Non-status Symbol)—an unknown . . . a breakage card . . . friends who chickened out of the curriculum.

EXAMPLE

62

127

Science & Arts students—(Status Symbol)—Friends who chickened out of the curriculum . . . a fraternity sweatshirt . . . pleated skirts worn above the knee — (Non-status Symbol) — good hours . . . a 3.00 average.

Teachers — (Status Symbol) — An ulcer . . . a reputation of being sadistic . . . being taller than any one of his students—(Non-status Symbol)—A fan club . . . having to ride to school on the bus . . . a cowlick.

Technician
Cass Technical High School
Detroit, Michigan

As It's Done in the N. B. C. Club

EXAMPLE
63

CHAIRMAN: In the name of the N. B. C. of Franklin K. Lane High School, I hereby open and call this meeting to order.

FIRST MEMBER: I object.

CHAIRMAN: To what?

FIRST MEMBER: To calling the meeting to order.

CHAIRMAN: Will the secretary please read the minutes?

SECRETARY: At the last meeting of the N. B. C., we had as speaker Mr. Abbidacabrasky.

SECOND MEMBER: How do you spell it?

SECRETARY: I object.

SECOND MEMBER: I object.

(Everybody begins to argue about the spelling of Mr. Abbidacabrasky's name.)

CHAIRMAN: Quiet! Quiet! The minutes are accepted. The club now proceeds to the business of electing the officers. Nominations for president are now open.

THIRD MEMEER: I nominate—

SECOND MEMBER: I second it.

THIRD MEMEER: I withdraw that nomination.

SECOND MEMBER: I protest.

THIRD MEMBER: I withdraw that

FIFTH MEMBER: I *PRO*test.

SIXTH MEMBER: I pro*TEST*.

FIRST MEMBER: I object. This isn't parliamentary procedure.

(After a long, drawn-out argument, three candidates are finally nominated.)

THIRD MEMBER: I make a motion that nominations be closed.

(Nobody wants to second it. THIRD MEMBER seconds the motion himself.)

CHAIRMAN: Nominations are closed. We will now proceed to the voting. Z——, you be teller.

(Vote is taken accompanied by much discussion. Nearly everybody votes two or three times.)

CHAIRMAN: Very well, A. has it.

FIRST MEMBER: I protest. I demand a recount.

(Vote is retaken this time, with everybody voting three or four times, and this time B. gets a majority.)

CHAIRMAN: Very well, B. has it.

SECOND MEMBER: I demand a recount. It's undemocratic.

(CHAIRMAN starts to take another vote; the bell rings.)

FACULTY ADVISER: We will have to postpone the elections until the next meeting.

FIRST, SECOND, and THIRD MEMBERS in unison: This is undemocratic. My candidate is the new president.

CHAIRMAN: In the name of the N. B. C. of Franklin K. Lane High School, I hereby close this meeting.

The Lane Reporter
Lane High School
Brooklyn, N. Y.

128

Frosh Complete Evolution To Attain Senior Status

EXAMPLE

64

Four years of high school life bring about many changes. You can usually tell whether someone is an upper-lower classman, or a lower-upper, just by the way he expresses himself.

Do any of these comments sound familiar?

FRESHMAN: Mother, could I please have my 25 cents allowance for this week?
SOPHOMORE: That's right. A raise!
JUNIOR: Where's your purse?
SENIOR: There's only one ten in here. Holding out on me?

FRESHMAN: C-could I-I please s-speak to Margaret, p-please?
SOPHOMORE: Is Meg there?
JUNIOR: It's me again. Mags still speaking?
SENIOR: Hi, Mom. How's Dad? Your beautiful daughter in?

FRESHMAN: I'll really have to hurry to get all my homework done before the bell rings.
SOPHOMORE: Why isn't everyone studying?
JUNIOR: I'll just do the assignment in class.
SENIOR: Homework! I should wash your mouth out with soap!

FRESHMAN: Somehow these tennis shoes just don't seem right for the prom.
SOPHOMORE: Well, would French heels be all right?
JUNIOR: Yes, it's a basic wardrobe necessity.
SENIOR: Where's the charge-a-plate?

Benson High News
Benson High School
Omaha, Nebraska

Features that have human interest. No event is too insignificant to attract reader attention if there is human interest in it. What are the students thinking and talking about?

The type of feature called the human-interest story is written from small incidents packed full of human appeal. This type of feature is usually short and gives the reader a chance to suffer and sympathize or smile and laugh with the characters of the story. Although these characters are usually people, they may be animals as well.

There is great human interest in dogs and horses, man's two closest animal friends. So valuable are they as news sources that one daily maintains two men who devote their time exclusively to reporting and editing news about these animals. Dog shows, horse shows, and hunt meets have great reader following.

Examples 65 through 68 illustrate the attraction of short anecdotes about people and animals. Such anecdotes have a universal appeal; those about people bring to the reader the feeling of the subject; those about animals bring to the reader pleasure and a smile. Unlike the gossip column, the human-interest anecdote never relates malicious prattle, insinuations, rumors. No reputations are ever hurt; in fact, nothing is included which would not be enjoyed as much by the subject as by the reader.

Motovich Rings Own Bell, As Coniff Circulates Suit

EXAMPLE 65

MR. ESAU MOTOVICH started to talk about the art department. "I don't mean to ring my own bell . . . " he said modestly.

Then the bell rang.

MRS. VIRGINIA L. CONIFF was explaining to her third period economic geography class about the quality of Harris Tweed.

"Today I have worn a Harris Tweed suit to show you the fine weave of the material," she said, "and now I shall pass it around."

IS ANYONE ALLERGIC to cats?" Mr. Ralph P. Iacangelo asked his Biology 2 class. "You know you'll have to dissect them later in the year."

"I am allergic to oak trees," replied J. D. Eveland. "So if the cats were in contact with such trees, I would probably have a reaction."

MR. KENNETH FRISBIE'S third period United States history class was discussing polygamy practiced by the Mormons in the nineteenth century.

"Well, Solomon had 700 wives," said Mr. Frisbie. "There's safety in numbers!"

AS A TARDY GIRL tripped into class, Mr. Donald Williamson remarked, "Oh, it's so good of you to come."

"WHICH WEIGHS MORE, a pound of feathers or a pound of lead?" asked Mrs. Matrina Howe.

"They weigh the same," responded Peggy Dirks.

"I'm glad you got that so quickly," said Mrs. Howe.

"We had it in second grade," Peggy replied.

MR. PAUL MAGEE announced to his students that it wouldn't benefit them to acquire test answers from students he had had previously. "I keep the same tests every year, but the answers are different."

The Tattler
Bethesda-Chevy Chase High School
Bethesda, Maryland

130

Jumping Mouse Joins Zoo 29

Bill Cook once promised the biology department that he would provide a "jumping mouse" for them. Months passed, but Bill was not able to make good on his promise, until last Monday when he rescued a captured but unharmed jumping mouse from a cat's mouth.

These animals have a three-inch body and a five-inch tail and are able to jump ten or more feet at a time. They are equipped with cheek pouches for carrying food.

Jumping mice are true jerboas, related to the jerboas of Europe and China. Their nightly, deathlike hibernation is another of the strange habits of these small, interesting animals.

The celebrated jumping mouse may be seen in 29.

Hi-Life
Kane Area High School
Kane, Pennsylvania

EXAMPLE
66

Police Chief Nabs Own Dog

This is a tale that friends of Police Chief Miles Norton should enjoy.

The other day a school official phoned the police station. "Send an officer at once to take care of a bunch of dogs that insist on running in and out of the building," was the request.

Chief Norton's house is situated next door to the school. He also owns a bulldog named "Skippy." The dog is never allowed out of the yard. That day he escaped, however.

The officer came but caught only one dog. Triumphantly he had it jailed. An hour later Chief Norton inspected the catch. It was "Skippy."

The Ah La Ha Sa
Albert Lea High School
Albert Lea, Minnesota

EXAMPLE
67

IN THE HALLS OF HENRY MANY GIRLS TRAP BOYS

In the halls of Henry today, the girls are finishing their long chase. Tonight, February 3, the girls will get their chance to marry the boys they have trapped at the annual Sadie Hawkins Dance.

When asked how she trapped her boy, **Rita Dorr** said, "I got him in physics, and if he had said no I would have turned on the water and dunked his head."

When **Karen Hoel** was asked what was in the large burlap bag she was dragging behind her, she just smiled.

Michele Harris refused to go to the show until her date said yes. It took **Nancy Sundholm** three days to decide the method to use on **Bob Schmidt**. **Linda Rarick** casually stuck out her foot while **Jim Jones** was at work in Shopper's City. **Carol Charlie**, running down the hall, quickly asked **Larry Kreuter**.

EXAMPLE
68

131

Next the boys gave their views on how they were trapped. **Dick Odette** said, "It was so early in the morning I didn't know what I was doing."

Bob Waite, with chattering teeth, said, "I was outside, and it was so cold I had to say yes to get back into the house."

Rick Lund, with a puzzled look still on his face, said, "I was just standing innocently by my locker, and she got me."

Rick Fors, for a switch, paid his girl with a picture to ask him.

The Patriot
Patrick Henry High School
Minneapolis, Minnesota

Personality sketches. The personality sketch, the story that treats an interesting or outstanding person, is a favorite type of feature story with student journalists. Most of the subjects for such stories are prominent students and teachers, but reporters often go outside the school for material. The personality or biographical sketch usually emphasizes the present activities of the subject; in fact, it is quite often necessary for the reporter to interview him. Thus the interview can act as the basis of both news and feature stories; all depends upon the subject, purpose, and treatment. (See Examples 69 and 70.) In Example 69 the subject is anybody's parent.

Ideas Not from Computer, Just Parents' Decisions

EXAMPLE

69

In the home of every teenager we find a very complex, compound, supernatural machine. You might think it a "501 computer" when you learn that with it the odds are always changing.

But the machine isn't a "501 computer," and the odds aren't based on the election returns. The machine is the everyday, ordinary-type parent. The odds, as everyone well knows, are whether you get the car for the big dance or the new dress for the big party next weekend.

However, Dads and Moms are really almost "ordinary" people. They have problems, too. No lie —once in a while they have to even make a decision. The men, being "superior," make the big ones. Dad as head-of-the-house chooses who pays the newsboy, while Mom is busy contemplating the last United Nations crisis.

But every teen must realize that his folks have just entered into the toughest period they have ever experienced. They have just begun to enter into that process of continual worry. They wonder if their "little darlings are growing up too fast."

On the edge of a complete mental panic, they begin the well-known lectures which begin, "Now when I was your age . . ." This statement soon grows

132

into a picture of their always perfect life. But we must remember that they are actually concealing their doubtful feelings of their own teen years.

When Moms talk about those "ridiculous skirts" we wear, they are trying to hide the memory of their own favorite Charleston dresses. **And all that scream over Avalon and Fabian makes them remember Valentino and Vallee.**

Actually parents really are people, and we should be nice to them. After all, where would we be without them?

The North Star
North High School
Omaha, Nebraska

Sedlecky, Prize-Winning Scientist

By RICHARD RHEDER

A Nobel prize winner from ND? Well, not yet, but Robert Sedlecky, 4B, is headed there.

Always working on science projects, Robert is now "remaking the periodic table of the elements."

In layman's language, Robert is taking the conventional periodic table, which is constructed on a systematic building block pattern, and copying it on a circular chart, which by spiraling out keeps all the elements of a chemical family together. He hopes that he is simplifying it.

"By using this chart, I can finish my chemistry homework in about half the time," he says.

Robert is studying to become a virology-biochemist. As such, he will deal with the relation of viruses to heredity.

Since his father, Alex Sedlecky, is employed as a civilian attorney for the United States Air Force, the family has moved around the country quite a bit.

ND's young scientist served as master of ceremonies on a weekly television program in Mobile, Alabama, entitled "Dr. Marshall Presents," while Dr. Marshall, author of the scientific show, vacationed. Robert was chosen because at the time he was president of the Mobile Region of the Alabama Junior Academy of Science. He also was chairman of the Science Club of McGill Institute.

In his sophomore year, Robert won the medical prize in the Mobile Regional Science Fair, for his work on tissue cultures. He kept living tissues in an artificial solution similar to human-body fluids; his prize: three months of experience as a paid assistant in the pathology lab of Immaculate Conception Hospital.

Last spring Sedlecky took first prize in the science division of the Dallas Arts and Crafts Fair for his model of the Deoxyribonucleic acid (DNA) molecule.

Robert is not all work and no play. He played fullback on the Junior Varsity League in Mobile for two years, and was chosen as a member of the all-state second string team at Chaminade High School in Dayton, Ohio.

Robert would have found a place in the Bulldog line-up if he had not broken a foot in Ohio.

Robert regrets that he will not be able to get his diploma from North Dallas, since the Sedleckys must move to Florida, in December.

The Compass
North Dallas High School
Dallas, Texas

EXAMPLE

70

133

News-feature story. A term sometimes used by school newspaper advisers is "news-feature." It has apparently risen out of the difficulty of classifying borderline stories as distinctly news or feature. In many features the news treated could have stood as straight news had not the reporter added the feature touch. (See Examples 71 through 73.)

Methods, Sequence Changing in Math

By ARDEANE DAVIS

EXAMPLE

71

Parents of math students have found that the methods they learned in high school are of very little help in solving a son's or daughter's math problems.

Many new ideas have come into use, and old ones have been discarded. Mrs. Marjorie Adams and Mr. Barry Moore found this to be true when they were taught some of the new approaches in classes they attended last summer at the University of Nebraska.

Math instructors have a very difficult time teaching the new methods as most teachers are still used to the older methods. "To understand this new approach to an old subject, teachers often must be retrained," Mrs. Adams pointed out.

Many math professors believe that students should be taught more of the basic facts earlier in school. In grades one through five, the concepts of sets, the decimal system, uses of different laws, and a few other fundamentals are being taught with a new approach. Prime numbers, factoring, numbers with a base other than ten, solutions of equations, and other new devices are being given a try in grades six through eight.

In algebra classes there is a much greater emphasis placed on graphs. Teachers are using more symbols in their teaching, and many students have been solving equations and learning about inequalities. Properties of functions, trigonometry functions, and expotential functions are more ideas taught.

Some math professors also believe that a little geometry, such as construction of figures and a few theorems, should be taught in the eighth grade since math must be taught gradually. This would help students taking a full course in geometry later.

A few of the new concepts seem to be confusing at first but appear much easier after one gets used to them. Math student Phil Lyons insists that his favorite new theorem is "the area of a square is measured by his height, weight, and Robert Hall suit size." No comment could be obtained from Mrs. Adams, Miss Clark, or Mr. Moore.

The Northeastern
Northeast High School
Lincoln, Nebraska

134

Pen Pals

By SHARON BELCHER

In all I have six pen pals: Erica, 18, lives in Australia; Friedirike, 16, lives in Canada; Suzanie, 15, and Carmelita, 16, live in a country of 7000 islands—the Philippines; and Miss Daw Hla Tin teaches school in Burma.

The sixth is Merle Cooper, 18, who lives with her parents and brothers Noel, 19, and Bob, 22, in Tauranga. This is a small but growing town on the North Island. Merle's sister, Lois, 24, is married. Merle is the smallest pen pal I have, standing only 4'10" and weighing 84 pounds. Her shoes are size 4.

This is her first year of nurses training. The complete course takes 18 months.

One of the reasons I enjoy writing to Merle is the difference in phrases we use. Examples: she calls her mother "Mum"; sometimes she signs her letters "Cheerio for now"; and once she wrote, "That picture was just smashing." They call elementary through high school "college."

We exchange ideas on clothes, dating records, and movies. We have traded magazines, maps, recipes, stamps, coins, photographs, and post cards. She likes the magazine *Seventeen* but is unable to buy it at her stores, so I have sent her some.

If you are interested in writing to a foreign friend, there are four organizations to help you: The English-Speaking Union, Pen Friends Division, 16 E. 69th Street, New York 21, N. Y., c/o Dept. A. V.; Pen Pals, University of Minnesota, Minneapolis 14, Minn. (include $.25 for postage and some very helpful information); Letter Abroad, Inc., 695 Park Ave., New York 21, N.Y.; International Friendship League Inc., 40 Mt. Vernon, Beacon Hill, Boston, Mass.

When requesting a pen pal, state your name, address, age, sex, and the language which you are able to write reasonably well. An extremely helpful book available for only $.35 is *The World of Pen Pals* by E. Max Paris. If you have any questions, you may consult the writer, at *The Arrow.*

The Arrow
Southwest High School
Minneapolis, Minnesota

EXAMPLE 72

Reading-Improvement Courses Recommended to CHS Students

One thousand words per minute by a modified egg timer tells the what and how of the reading improvement and skills classes at Claremont High.

"This class is designed for those students who would like to increase their reading skill and comprehension," says James Grove, reading improvement teacher. Sophomores are offered this course along with the regular English class.

Fred Turner, another teacher, has three classes in reading improvement.

The modified egg timer mentioned above is actually a rate-

EXAMPLE 73

ometer, which is used to "push the eyes along," thereby increasing the reading rate. Also used in the class is a tachistoscope, which flashes numbers and phrases on a screen.

This machine forces the student to increase his speed and comprehension by visually grasping these screen flashes. Students record their improvement on individual sheets.

By this method, students usually increase their reading rate by about 500 words, while improving their comprehension.

According to Mr. Grove, one of the most often asked questions is, "How can I study effectively?" The answer to this question can be found by using the SQ3R method.

Step One, Survey—Look over the material to be studied. Find out what you already know and what you do not know.

Step Two, Questions—Answer the questions at the end of the reading and answer those of your own.

Step Three, R1: Read Rapidly —Set the time you want to spend on the material according to its difficulty. Then read it at one time from beginning to end.

Step Four, R2: Recite—Do this by making an outline of the material.

Step Five, R3: Review—Look over the material again.

The Arrow
Claremont High School
San Diego, California

POSSIBLE ASSIGNMENTS

The following assignment list is included as an incentive for reporters and assignment editors rather than as suggested stories for them. It is a list to prime one's thinking about one's own school. Thinking through the sources indicated here should lead you, the reporter, to develop a list for your own school. Each item is phrased as an assignment that has been given the reporter to cover. No distinction has been made among types of stories, for often the type depends upon the source or the treatment of the material. The assignments have been worded as the assignment editor might word them.

1. Queer mistakes that have been made on recent examinations. Ask teachers if you may see papers. Don't use names. Write amusingly.

2. Review the basketball season. Use plenty of statistics. Determine significance of the season; use by-line but avoid too much opinion.

3. Basketball-letter winners will be announced next week. Can you determine now by the records who will receive them? Include requirements for earning a letter.

4. Basketball season has just closed. Write an advance story on next year's team. Determine who the first six or seven will be. Interview them. Announce tentative schedule.

136

5. In a lively manner, describe the tests the physical director puts boys through in his gym classes—rope climbing, chinning, etc. Use direct discourse and other techniques of good feature writing. Watch the classes.

6. Assume you're a travel editor. A week's spring vacation is coming soon for students. Suggest two-, three-, and six-day trips from your town. Include camping, automobile, bus trips, etc. Estimate costs, equipment. Be specific.

7. Rehearsals are taking place for Senior Distinction Day assembly. In a lively feature, describe the progress made. Use names, dialogue; make the reader want the day to arrive.

8. Write a story on how firms are subscribing to advertising in your school paper, how some run large ads weekly over a period of years, how others place ads unsolicited. Mention firms, quote officials on value of advertising, etc.

9. Check student and faculty opinion on the possibility of another war, weaving an interesting story into it all. Ask ten people for opinions.

10. An interview with the head custodian. *Suggestions:* number of brooms, brushes, fuses, paper towels, etc., used a year; long hours; unusual experiences on the job; human-interest stuff!

11. A feature on "chasing synonyms" for editorial page. It's good sport to get a good-sized dictionary, look up a word, trace its synonym to another, and so on, trying to shade away from the original meaning until it's completely gone. Contradict the geometry proposition that things equal to the same thing are equal to each other. Make account vivid, detailed.

12. Cover the school broadcast this week from inside the studio. Have a fellow reporter cover it from outside. Write your stories to be run side by side.

13. Instructional feature on how to protect one's "house" (locker). Cautions on "setting locks," leaving books in auditorium, cafeteria, etc. Mention lost-and-found bureau. Handle as an advice feature, not as editorial.

14. It's not too early to find out what colleges the seniors are considering. Give reasons for their choices.

15. Interview the head of the English department on changes in the method of teaching grammar.

16. With a tape measure, make a chest-expansion inspection of boys around school—athletes, scholars, etc. Weave in names, expansions, and humor.

17. Here's the old one: Is it a myth that redheads are fiery tempered, at times extremely so? Investigate—with names and opinions—examples. Ask biology teachers why redheads should be more fiery than blondes and brunettes.

18. That twenty-fifth hour! If you had an extra hour in your day, anywhere in the day, to use as you liked—what would you do with it? Interview all types of students. Drop in a couple of faculty answers. For Inquiring Reporter column—25 people.

19. An investigatory news-feature. Look into the new hall system this semester. Chat with monitors on duty; quote them. See the faculty sponsor. Draw conclusions after presenting facts.

20. Choose two families that are most represented in your school (four Lindseys, etc), and write good personality, human-interest story, stressing likes, dislikes, abilities, news, etc.

21. Ascertain how many twins there are in the school—interview—comparisons—contrasts—lively human-interest stuff. Arrange for picture. Avoid the prosaic treatment that the twin story usually gets in school papers.

22. Special feature on how students may earn their way through college if they only care to expend the effort. One of last year's graduates now works in a sorority house at a near-by university. Interview faculty members for ways in which they earned college expenses.

23. A Did-You-Know? feature gathered from homerooms, advisers, and pupils. Feature jobs boys and girls hold, distances covered in coming to school, attendance records, peculiar items, or where students once lived. One big feature with many names.

24. Investigating reporter looks over lost articles turned into lost-and-found bureau, commenting and describing.

25. Is left-handedness an asset or a liability? Bring out amusing advantages and disadvantages through interviews with any left-handers in the school. Quote. Can you account for left-handedness? Is it wise to try to change a left-hander to right-handedness when young?

26. What blackboards will tell. Make a tour of the building just at close of school. Take notes, include names—feature treatment.

27. Do colleges actually make inducements to high school athletes? Talk with coaches, ex-college stars in town, etc.

28. On their enrollment cards, the freshmen have to indicate what vocation they expect to follow in life. Write a lively feature with names.

29. Is dieting common among the girls in the school? Watch their trays as they leave the lunch line. Talk to them. What do boys think of all this?

138

30. How do the members of the basketball team rate scholastically? Are the eligibility cards readily signed? Are there any interesting yarns of various players who were pressed to keep eligible for a certain game? Why do they have to keep eligible? Quote the Association rules on this. Consider story carefully; names of players may not be suitable.

31. Our school is constantly training for leisure. How many of our past students are playing in church or in city orchestras? singing? in local dramatics? etc. Investigate fully. Use many names. What school classes, clubs, and other activities are training for leisure?

32. Arrange with lost-and-found department to get a weekly list of pupils who turn in lost articles to the office there. Secure this first list for the paper—write the introductory article of the series.

33. Prepare a feature on the opening of track season, giving the state records in all the events and the names of local athletes who will participate in each event.

34. School compared to Hollywood—students take the parts of about 20 or 30 movie or television stars.

35. The last five minutes before the dismissal bell at 3:00 P.M.

36. Begin a series on basketball rules, explaining them to the average student so that he may better appreciate the decisions of the officials. If properly handled these stories should make for better sportsmanship.

37. Prepare a short personality sketch of each of the eight members of the basketball team about to enter the tourneys (100 words to the player); lead to cover entire story.

38. Student assistants to teachers. Survey entire field to reveal regular assistants and what they do. Quotes here and there.

39. Some social-studies classrooms are now equipped with tables, and a laboratory-type procedure is followed. Investigate this method. Quotes.

40. Begin a series of articles about the people whose pictures are in the school Hall of Fame. Introduce them to the student body.

41. Begin a series of birthday stories. Secure information from the office files.

42. Shakespeare's vocabulary was 25,000 words, Milton's 17,000. What's the average student's?

43. Short feature on student forgetfulness, of keys especially.

44. Secure from the college scholarship committee a complete list of all scholarships available. Describe fully the method of applying for each—examinations, etc.

45. Imaginary story of the ghosts of former good track stars playing

around the school field at the sectional meet here next Saturday. Bring in their names, records, etc.

46. Positions various students assume when sitting. Use humor, but also bring in serious aspects of posture. Quote health teachers. Consider posture pictures taken in health classes.

47. Special feature on why pianos must be tuned. Consider the school's pianos. Why is it that a piano cannot be said to be in tune unless it is actually out of tune? Write for the average reader.

48. Describe the home of a certain teacher. Descriptive feature.

49. Effect of food on disposition. Interview authorities—teachers or authors. Do we really eat too much? What do we eat too much of?

50. Get exact latest office figures on the size of each class—seniors, etc. Any interesting points to note, such as the percentage of drop-outs as the students advance in school?

51. An essay on a trip through the country. Describe the autumn foliage. Tell why a person should get out in the country these fall days, etc.

52. The greenhouse is being prepared for frosty weather. A chatty, conversational article giving various observations about the green-house—quotes, facts, etc.

53. Get exact figures on the size of each department. Play up the unusual numbers—large and small. Are all large departments due to graduation requirements? Why are some departments so small? Interview authorities.

54. Food at football games. Actual facts and figures about the concessions—number of hot dogs, soft drinks, etc., sold. Who gets the profits? What are the profits?

55. Write the first article of a "Where to Go" series especially designed for freshmen. For instance, where would a student go in case of accident? In what rooms are first-aid cabinets located? Is the school responsible for accidents?

56. On the faculty there are teachers who once graduated from this school. Get a story of the school changes. What were the teachers' activities when they were in school? Who were their teachers?

CHAPTER LABORATORY

1. Clip and mount five feature stories; one that informs and one that entertains, a human-interest story, a personality sketch, and a news-feature. Discuss in class.
2. Clip and mount the best feature you have seen in your daily paper during the past week. Which of the five types is it? Write 100 words explaining what gives it this distinction.
3. Prepare a list of ten possible feature stories that you could write for the school paper during the next two weeks. How long should each be? Discuss in class.
4. On pages one, two, and three of the last issue of your school paper, indicate which stories are news and which are features. Discuss in class.
5. From your list of possible feature stories, select a subject for a feature that entertains; then write it.
6. Compare the feature stories in at least two different daily newspapers, and decide if newspapers have different policies concerning feature stories. Discuss in class.
7. Which of the feature stories in this chapter depend upon timeliness for reader interest? Which depend upon the style of writing? What do others depend upon?
8. Write a human-interest story of 100 words about an incident that occurred in school.
9. Compare for quality the personality sketches in your school paper with the four examples in this chapter.
10. From a recent issue of your school paper, clip and mount a news story upon which a feature story might be written. Outline such a story.
11. Write a 250-word feature story about an unusual procedure that some teacher is using in his classroom.
12. Write a 250-word feature built around a group of students. A homeroom, an athletic team, a cast for a play, a debate team are but a few of such groups around the school.

11 COVERING THE ARTS

There is little place in high school journalism for the critic as known in the daily paper. Covering music and dramatic events, art exhibits, and literary works for the school paper is, after all, but a form of news reporting—demanding an acute news sense. The reporter who possesses and exercises this lively news sense finds the step to critical reporting a natural one.

Critical reporting is divided into three main fields: (1) musical events and dramatic productions, (2) art exhibits, and (3) book reviews. All of these should periodically find a place in the school paper. The three types of reviews have much in common, and much that applies to one field may apply equally well to another. Practically all reviews appear under by-lines; such reporting places an additional challenge before the reporter who knows his name is going to appear with the story.

MUSIC AND DRAMA

All the world's a stage—according to Shakespeare—and all the school's a stage according to the student reporter. He records the events of the week, but now and then pauses to distinguish the make-believe.

If the reporter happens to cover the news for the *Linton Hi-Lights* of Linton High School, Schenectady, New York, his treatment of the school theater is carried on a special page devoted exclusively to dramatics. (See Example 74.) But no matter how presented, the story of the school play leads the field in coverage and interest.

EXAMPLE 74

LEFT: Richard Thornton receives last minute instructions from Mrs. Dorthea Hilbert, director of the play, "Seven Keys to Baldpate," which was presented in the auditorium Nov. 18 and 19. CENTER: Gail Byrnes (background), Richard Foreman, who had the lead, and Carol Robbins rehearse lines in preparation for the production. RIGHT: Miss Eleanor Cleland, this year's assistant director, checks the script as she gives actors their cues.
—Camera Club Photos by Bob Ales

Pupil Depicts Actor's Life
By Dick Foreman

You have just finished trying out for a part and are sitting backstage hoping against hope that you've gotten it. The director, wishing to see how the cast looks as a whole, is lining it up on stage. He calls the name of the character, and then the name of the person who he has selected to play that part.

The name of the character you auditioned for is called, and it seems an eternity before you hear your name announced.

So you got the part, did you? Well, that's swell, but as they say in the song, "You Ain't Heard Nothin' Yet!"

REHEARSALS BEGIN

You remain in a state of self-glorification until you find yourself leading through the script and noticing how many times your character's name appears. It's not until rehearsals start that you finally realize just how many lines you have and how quickly you must learn them.

Soon movements and props are added to the lines, and things reach a fever pitch. The director shouts that you have to learn your lines and fit the movements to them; the property committee tells you to stay away from the props; and the lighting crew pleads with the director not to move the set out from under the lights again. Of course, someone always drops a line or steps off with his downstage foot, or one of the props disappears, or a set moved. But who cares? The world doesn't end.

OPENING NIGHT

Now, it's opening night. All is confusion backstage—people in costume, people out of costume, people in between, people laughing, people almost in tears, people repeating their lines, people biting their fingernails, and people so calm they make you nervous.

Suddenly, you don't know how you got there, but you're on stage. The lights are glaring you. The palms of your hands are bathed in a cold sweat. You can barely distinguish a few blurred faces in the front row, but you're sure that everyone in the whole auditorium is just waiting for you to "goof".

Soon, you've finished the scene and you're off the stage, and you wonder how all those weeks of work and sweat could result in such a short end product.

After the last curtain call, there's confusion backstage. The same comparisons as above hold true, except that there is no nail biting. You've made it!

Applying Stage Make-Up Requires Time and Effort
By Eliana D'Jimas

Let's pretend that we are watching the rehearsal of "Seven Keys to Baldpate."

During this rehearsal, no make-up is being used. If we were sitting in the back row, we could see what the brilliant stage lights do to the faces of the actors. The natural colors are burned out. The features cannot be distinguished and most of the facial expression is lost. Make-up counteracts the effects produced by strong stage lights. It can also do a great deal to make a character part convincing.

Have you ever wondered what basic make-up an actor needs to wear? Actors require a great deal of basic make-up. First of all, a foundation of grease paint or pancake make-up is used. It is applied evenly and thinly over the face and neck.

EYE LINER USED

Eye make-up is next. A brown eye shadow is used on most brunettes and on boys. Girls with blonde hair and blue eyes wear blue eye shadow. Eye liner is used to accentuate the eyes by drawing thin lines close to the eyelashes. These lines are extended until they meet a short distance beyond the outer corners of the eyes.

Rouge comes next. There are four common shapes of faces: oval, round, long and thin, and square. The oval face is ideal and, therefore, all the other shapes are made to conform with it. A round face is made to look oval by placing the rouge farther from the nose and blending it in a horizontal direction. The rouge for a square face is applied like the rouge for a round face. The fullness of the jaw is lessened by lowlighting it with a powder several shades darker than the foundation. Rouge is applied to an already oval face by blending it away from the center, horizontally, and high on the cheek.

POWDER APPLIED

Finally, powder is applied. It should be patted on with a powder puff in a lighter color than the foundation. Any superfluous powder is removed with the puff or with a baby brush.

This is the basic make-up which an actor has to wear. When all the make-up is on, the actor will look his part. Now, let's go back to that rehearsal we were watching. Now the actors are wearing make-up. Don't they look wonderful? It was all well worth the time spent on it. Well, on with the play!

Students Become Expert Salesmen As Ticket Sellers

Approximately forty-five students sold tickets for the school play "Seven Keys to Baldpate."

The group, under direction of Mr. Charles Pitts, sold tickets each morning in homeroom before and after school.

Mr. Pitts said, "The cooperation given to this committee by the students and faculty was a significant factor in the success of our pledge to pack the house with capacity audiences both nights."

"Much of the credit for the success of the committee is due to Mr. Dawes and his trade printing class who printed tickets and posters, Miss Follett who prepared our special record forms, and to Mr. Holbrook, last year's ticket chairman, whose advice made my work much easier," Mr. Pitts added.

NEW FOOTLIGHTS were specially constructed for the play by the lighting crew. Left to right: Edward Bisner, Art Kline, George Sharpe, and Alan Shutz.
—Camera Club Photo, by Bob Ales

Lighting Crew Plays Big Role
By Dave Cohen

Stage Crew Has Variety of Duties
By Tom Forgette

The stage crew perhaps has more responsibilities in the production of a play than any other committee—at least it seems so.

Stage crew duties include placing on stage all equipment to be used in the play, moving equipment when necessary during the play, manipulating curtains, and supervising all other activities connected with the stage except lighting and sound.

"Stage crew played an important role in 'Seven Keys to Baldpate' as it does in any play. The stage crew is always on hand to help in the production of the play. Without the stage crew, there just wouldn't be any play," notes Mr. Christian.

For a person to understand fully how a play is constructed behind the scenes, he must start from the actual assembling and construction of the equipment.

The first thing the lighting crew of "Seven Keys to Baldpate" had to consider was the special footlights needed for the play. We found that we would have to send away for these footlights. While we waited, our school wood shop was hard at work constructing the sets for the lighting decks.

FOOTLIGHTS BUILT

When our consignment arrived, we began the work of assembling the lights and decks. The footlights were about thirty feet long, and, under direction of Mr. Kenneth Moran, our advisor, we wired them in such a way as to provide three separate circuits. Each of these circuits controlled one of the three primary stage lighting color—red, blue, or green. By manipulating these circuits we were able to produce almost any color we needed.

Every new prop for the play had to follow several steps of development before it could be used. The first step was to requisition all necessary parts. Then the requisition had to be approved. Next, we ordered the materials and upon their arrival, we fabricated the prop. A good example of this process was the construction of the footlights mentioned above.

In addition to the footlights, we were also responsible for setting all the spotlights into their proper positions for the play. This is particularly difficult due to the extreme height of the auditorium. A slip here could have been a serious injury.

SET LIGHTS

Finally, when all our lighting equipment was set up, we began to familiarize ourselves with the script. Setting lights for a play such as "Seven Keys to Baldpate" is a major factor in transmitting the mood of a play to the audience, and so we had to be very attentive to details and to our cues. Cues were given to us over the back stage phone which connects the projection booth with the lighting panel.

When the play was in progress we took our positions at a panel about fourteen feet above the stage and from there we controlled the lighting. This panel works on a scientific method of utilizing charts and color patterns based on each individual play, and greatly aided us with the lighting problems.

The advance story appears weeks before the date of production. The event may be important enough, in the opinion of the editor, to warrant a number of advance stories. Thus one school's play resulted in the coverage shown in Example 75, plus a follow-up article in the next issue devoted to a costume designed and made in the home-economics department and a photograph of the leading lady wearing it. Many aspects of the play or concert furnish material for the advance story: the history of the violinist, his orchestral affiliations and previous concerts, the history of violin concerts in the school or in the community. Some data can be obtained from the files of the school paper; for instance, *Why the Chimes Rang* is to be given as the Christmas play. How many times has the school given it before? Who were some of the former leads? Have any of them followed dramatics after graduation? As shown by Example 76, the account of what is to appear later on the stage can be treated in feature as well as straight news style.

Thespians Present Wilder's OUR TOWN

EXAMPLE

75

Just a few more days and the great day will be here. This is the day the play cast, the stage crew, the Thespian Club and many others have been eagerly and anxiously awaiting.

THIS IS IT

On Friday night of this week, the curtain will rise on the Thespian production of *Our Town*. There is still opportunity to buy a ticket, priced at sixty-five cents, so that you will not miss what many are prophesying will be the finest production Chadsey has seen.

The differences from past productions will be evident as soon as the audience walks into the auditorium. For the curtain will be up although not a member of the cast will be on the stage. The scenery, or rather the lack of it, will be in full view.

MORE SURPRISES

Another surprise will be offered to the audience. At 8:00 P.M. the stage manager will walk out on the stage and present the cast. He will then describe the town itself. All this is part of the play.

If you are not satisfied with a completely empty stage, you can still be happy. There will be two trellises which will serve as scenery.

As the stage manager, portrayed by Lawrence Jordan, describes the play, he will play havoc with time. He explains that automobiles will start showing up in *Our Town* in about five years.

DEATH AND FUNERALS

He tells you that the people you are soon to see will be dead in a few years. He then goes on to describe their funerals.

144

Larry himself has this to say:

"The cast in this play will have to work much harder than the casts of other plays. Much of this play is done in pantomime, and with no scenery, they will find it much harder to get across to the audience. However, I think this will be done successfully, and I am confident the play will be a great success."

SOUND EFFECTS

Many noises will be heard by the playgoers this Friday. Chickens and roosters will crow even though none of these are seen on the stage. These effects are part of the play.

There will be many such animal noises, and there will be no visible structure to support their credibility. The stage crew will be producing them.

The Thespian Club formally invites every Chadsey student and his parents to buy tickets to Chadsey's play. The time is 8:00 P.M. The place is Chadsey's auditorium. The play is *Our Town*.

The Explorer
Chadsey High School
Detroit, Michigan

Backstage Preparations Worth Twice Cost of Ticket

Oft times the behind-the-scenes action of a performance can top that part which an audience views. *The Little Dog Laughed*, LHS's Senior Class Play, was an excellent example.

If there had been a chance for the viewer to buy a ticket for that first make-up or dress rehearsal, a landslide ticket sale might have ensued. These two events are definitely the best part of any show.

For instance, cries of "more color!" "you're too old!" "not enough gray!" are commonly heard as make-up is initially checked. (It is surprising how many ancients are developed with one sweep of a shadow stick!)

First and second dress rehearsals are usually almost hysterical as anyone who has ever glimpsed one will attest. It is at this time that the actors do their best to show the director how things will appear on show night if done at the worst possible.

Lines are quite a joke, too, as the performers forget cues and whole speeches. At this crucial moment, someone cracks a joke.

This year the Senior Class had an "extra." Theirs was to be the first show in the remodeled auditorium. On show night, this fact was a decided honor, but during rehearsals the situation was a little more dubious.

Loud hammering, the clacking of ladders, and the occasional shouts of workmen made rehearsals a rare experience.

The wild backstage preparation plays an important role and will be remembered in the actors' minds, along with that initial thrill when the curtains opened to reveal the blazing footlights on opening night.

Liberty Life
Liberty High School
Bethlehem, Pennsylvania

EXAMPLE

76

145

Writing the review. In covering the performance, the school reporter does not pose as an expert. The critic on the daily newspaper is a professional who covers professional performances. The school reporter is an amateur covering amateur performances; his lack of professional qualifications means that he is not capable of critical judgment. He gathers his material by noting such things as the performers, staging, plot, direction, musical selections, and composers.

The reaction of the audience is most helpful to him. His job, in fact, is to cover the entire spectacle. It is a fact to say that a particular performer was best received by the audience; it is an opinion to say that this person did the best piece of acting. When speaking of such personal matters as performance and direction, comment limited to facts is most tactful for the school reporter. Even praise, unless bestowed upon all alike, is a most discriminating weapon. Material matters such as lighting and stage effects are more open to comment.

It is a challenge to cover a theatrical production, for the review must enlighten both those who saw the production and those who did not; beware, however, of telling the plot.

Example 77 is typical of the stories covering the arts for high school papers. Ordinarily such stories carry by-lines at the beginning of the account, however.

A PAGE FROM *PRIDE AND PREJUDICE*

EXAMPLE
77

Pride and Prejudice, presented on January 20, satirizes the old tradition of bringing up girls with one goal in life—to catch a husband! Centered around the Bennet family, which has five daughters of marriageable age, the play shows how Mrs. Bennet turns her attention to aiding her daughters in finding husbands.

Adding to the confusion, one daughter not only possesses the most terrible quality in women, intelligence, she allows it to show!

She actually refuses two suitors.

The set was directed in the manner of the 1880's while the costumes were modern. The combination was pleasing.

The cast of the play is to be congratulated for giving good performances in major and minor roles. SALLY STEWART, as the scheming, if not too brilliant mother, was a delight. Her squeaky voice and agitated actions added to her characterization. TERRY ANDERSON as the snobbish Mr. Darcy and JACK NELSON as the debonair clergyman, Mr. Collins, gave good performances, as did all down the line to DIANA STULL who added to the fun by just making a face and saying "Shh!"

More than acting goes into the making of a good show. Reversible flats were used cleverly to make the set change into three different rooms before one's eyes.

Good make-up helped make the characters believable, while JUDY PLACKNER'S piano playing made intermissions pleasant.

The skillful directing and producing of Mrs. Mary Hafner and Miss Zarm Keljik were evident in many clever devices throughout the play. It was a most enjoyable performance.

The Surveyor
George Washington High School
St. Paul, Minnesota

In Example 78 the real touch of the critic is felt from the headline on through the entire review. There is nothing unsportsmanlike about such a treatment, for the paper indicated the standards that have been expected in such productions.

Did You Feel Disappointed, Too?

By RICK FREEDMAN, East-124

EXAMPLE **78**

WHEN THE CURTAIN went up on Yamo, a show with a great potential was unveiled. This potential was never fully developed because of a general atmosphere of confusion.

Several of the show's acts suffered from a befuddled lighting crew which illuminated surprised bench carriers more often than performers. There were times when stage crews noisily covered lines to a point at which only a few in the audience were able to hear. But then, cast members did not always know their lines. Once a chorus boy apparently forgot to show up.

Despite these inadequacies, Yamo did offer some excellent performances. Among these was Steve Samler who displayed rare skill as he played the difficult "Ritual Fire Dance" in a scene entitled "The Practice Room";

the applause thundered long after Steve left the stage.

Barbara Radner, classical guitarist, and Barbara Power, who sang "The Sound of Music," won great acclaim from the audience. Miss Power suffered, however, by following a tedious slow-motion spoof of football.

Jazz was the word as the Windjammers, a Dixieland outfit, brought a beat into the show. The group included Ron Hockett, Mike Katz, Jack Howe, John Teising, and Jim Getzgoe.

For comedy there were Karen Johnson and her male cohort, Marc Levenberg. Together they brought roars from the audience with their rendition of "Honeybun." Separately they pleased, too; Karen as Miss Blue, the college nurse; and Marc as the campus character, a Don Martin cartoon come to life.

147

Both dance numbers were good, with "Love Is a Dance," choreographed by Ken Lee and Jane Van de Voorde, achieving brilliance. "Together," the second dance number, provided a light, gay interlude as interpreted by Bob Price, Dick Brown, John Brauer, Ercelle Kay, Sally Morier, and Nora Gaffin.

Of the four vocal groups, the barbershop quartet of Sherman Finger, Dick Brown, John Shuford, and Mike Katz was the best. Saturday's customers missed the impact of an Israeli folk song sung by Mary Wagner and Kathy Field who had a little trouble harmonizing. Friday was a different story, as their act was one of the best Yamo produced.

The level of the revue could have been far higher if tryouts had been held this fall rather than last summer.

Why not a spring Yamo?

The Evanstonian
Evanston Township High School
Evanston, Illinois

Occasionally school papers carry reviews of legitimate stage shows. This is especially true of the New York City school papers. A legitimate dramatic production may be critically reviewed, but the reviewer should bear in mind his lack of professional credentials.

A school musical production is part of the musical history of that particular school. Few musical or dramatic productions should be looked upon as isolated events, but rather as parts of all such productions that the school has ever had. Example 79 is noticeable for the care and understanding given to the coverage of the concert.

Seniors Present Recital by Kunce

By JAY FISCUS

EXAMPLE 79

The artistic performance of Robert William Kunce on January 14 at the Twentieth Century Club was received with sincere enthusiasm by a responsive audience. The promising student's ability to master selections by Purcell, Handel, Bach, and Mozart was confidently displayed in the first section of the program.

The first movement of Beethoven's "Sonata No. 21" was not altogether demonstrative of Robert's opening presentation of skill. However, his original "Prelude in G Minor," "Orchestral Rhapsody No. 1," and "Impromptu Suite" were unmistakably indicative of Robert's fine style and interpretation.

The last portion of the evening's program completely captivated the audience as the young musician, obviously enjoying the novel selection, romped through Shostakovich's "Polka."

Robert's poise and finesse enhanced the commendable performance and together with his talent marked an enjoyable evening. The senior class should receive thanks for sponsoring the successful affair.

The Red and Blue
Reno High School
Reno, Nevada

MOVIES AND TELEVISION

The movie review differs somewhat from the school-production review. The student who sees a motion picture witnesses a professional undertaking, and if he writes under a by-line he may use greater freedom.

Television reviews are finding more and more space in the columns of the school newspaper. Here, as well, the reporter must raise his critical standards, for he is judging professional performances. Futhermore, so much of the average person's time is spent watching television that the good television review attracts great reader interest while informing and educating the reader. (See Example 80.)

"Critic" Hurls Kudos, Barbs

By DENNIS ETCHISON

What's wrong with TV?

Now that summer reruns are upon us, let's consider some possible answers:

1. Excess of cheap filmed shows thrown together to get on the current bandwagon—like westerns, "private eyes," etc. Most are just cheap carbons of a successful original (like Gunsmoke).

2. **Several good filmed shows folded largely because of lack of concern for consistency in script quality, e.g., Johnny Staccato, Brenner.**

3. The ax has been taken to live dramas. Playhouse 90 and Sunday Showcase have been scratched. Remember Studio One? Kraft, Philco, Goodyear, Alcoa, Kaiser theaters? Even the *Play of the Week* series which just about

topped them all is gone.

4. **Instead of good drama, live TV budgets are spent on "specials" with big stars and production numbers, often superfluous and often poorly planned.**

5. The few good "specs" produced are not advertised or are put on so late or in such a wretched time slot that nobody sees them. So, no good rating. So, no more good specials.

Looks to this viewer as if pay TV, already well on its way in many cities, may hold within its coin-slotted brain at least some of the answers. When folks start paying, they'll demand something worth paying for. And the quality available for pay will force free TV to up its standards. I hope.

Castle Courier
Castle High School
Lynwood, California

EXAMPLE
80

THE BOOK REVIEW

A book review may summarize a book or criticize it, but it must adhere to the standards of informality, brightness, and conciseness. The first paragraph of the review must attract the reader just as does

149

the lead of a regular news story. It carries the punch of the story.

Unless the review is merely an announcement of publication or of the book's acquisition by the school library, the reviewer must read the book carefully, discover the author's purpose, and determine how well he has accomplished it. (A critical review always carries the reporter's by-line.) Nowhere, however, should too much of the plot be revealed. Remember that many reviews can be made more interesting by including personal angles about the author or the book itself.

Practically all school papers that carry book reviews carry them on the editorial page. However, from the standpoint of reader interest, a particular review might crowd material of less importance off page one. The book-review column provides an excellent opportunity to introduce a number of books to the reader and also to inform students of new books as they arrive in the library. (See Example 81.)

Book Babble

EXAMPLE
81

Leo Szilard, one of the world's leading nuclear scientists, has made his bid for a rational consideration of the danger of nuclear power in the form of a delightful collection of socially and politically satirical short stories entitled *The Voice of the Dolphins*.

The title story concerns a successful achievement of disarmament as suggested by a group of American and Russian scientists working in collaboration with a group of dolphins. This story succeeds in doing what negotiations and speeches have heretofore failed to do: impress the extreme complexity of solving the problem of the nuclear threat.

"My Trial as a War Criminal" is a story which makes one wonder where the line is drawn between vengeance and justice.

"Calling all Stars," is a radio message received from outer space expressing alarm at nuclear testing and war on earth. Reading it will make you think twice about the atomic dilemma. "Report on Grand Central Terminal" is the story of a visit to earth by scholars from outer space after World War III. They visit Grand Central Terminal, and from a close examination of the building, make some hilarious conclusions as to the nature of the human race.

These stories will, as the publisher puts it, make you laugh because they are funny but cry because they are true.

The collection is available in soft cover with an introduction by Stephen Vincent Benét entitled "A Nightmare for Future Reference." From the standpoint of writing skill as well as meaning and importance, *The Voice of the Dolphins* rates very high.

The Eagle
Washington High School
San Francisco, California

150

THE RECORD REVIEW

A type of review akin to the book review gains favor with high school newspapers. This is the record review. Like the book review, it deals with a professional product and may be reviewed critically. Like the review of a concert, however, it should be attempted only by someone who knows something about music. For the newspaper with no one of musical judgment on its staff, a periodic listing of new and interesting records will enliven the editorial page. (See Examples 82 and 101.)

Platter Chatter

EXAMPLE

82

Charming young Hayley Mills, despite her obvious lack of singing talent, has really rocketed to the top of the charts with "Let's Get Together." The number is from her picture *The Parent Trap* and is magically appealing.

"The Astronaut" by Jose Jimenez, is a very, very popular novelty record, both as a single and as an album. It's been around on the various surveys for about three months.

For those with more exotic tastes, there's always Dave Brubeck's "Take Five."

One to watch is "Without Your Love" by Wendy Hill on the Era label. Every gimmick in the book —chamber, banjo, chimes, etc.— has been used on it, but it will surely be a "goer" none the less. It just recently made its debut on the charts.

Dion's "Runaround Sue," the woeful tale of a fellow whose girl steps out on him, seems to be a real winner around Banning.

"Hit the Road Jack" by Ray Charles, on the ABC-Paramount label, was recently nudged out of the number one position by "Runaround Sue," but is still one of the sharpest discs around.

The Portlight
Banning High School
Wilmington, California

THE ART EXHIBIT

Reviewing an art exhibit calls for some knowledge of art. The reviewer should be able to distinguish among the mediums used—oil, water color, opaque, charcoal, pencil, pastel, engravings, wood blocks, and various others. The art teacher can supply information.

Such critical writing is subjective and calls for keen observation and discrimination. The unusual techniques called by such names as *abstract expressionism, surrealism,* or *impressionism* require recognition and familiarity.

The reporter must note color treatment, subjects chosen, and techniques used, and be ready to comment upon the unusual as well as the pleasing. He should follow student discussion of the exhibit carefully before he writes his article. Which pieces are causing the most comment, and why? He will secure further information and impressions from the art teacher, the artists themselves, and printed sources.

He will recognize and appreciate individualism. He will not neglect facts, such as the place and time of the exhibit, the occasion of it, the number of pieces exhibited, the artists represented, the winners, and the awards. Notice, after all, how much critical school reporting goes back to the straight news story for its basic features. Art exhibits that are not the work of students should be handled in the review style.

Since many students have practically no interest in art, the challenge is all the greater. Covering the art exhibit is perhaps the most difficult assignment treated in this chapter. (See Examples 83 and 84.)

EXAMPLE

83

They Call It Art
By Olivia Davis

"The Whirlwind," a mass of curved lines and varied tones, has proved to be the most popular piece of work in the art exhibit now on display in the lower halls.

The exhibit is circulated from the New York School of Fine and Applied Arts, and has come to Bosse through the courtesy of Miss Kaloolah Howe of the local Temple of Fine Arts. Thirty pictures are on display.

Some Whirlwind

A storm of criticism has arisen over the modernistic whirlwind, about half of Bosse's students looking at the composition and asking somebody to point out the whirlwind. On the other hand, the other six hundred have called it the best piece in the exhibit, attracted by the graceful lines and startling color.

Four Mediums

Four mediums can be detected in this group of pictures—wash, pen and ink, opaque, and water color. Practically all the pieces have a decided commercial touch, which can be expected since they represent the work of art students. One passes from rifles, through interior sets, and on to department stores.

A series of six drawings for children's magazines seem to lack some important lines, but we are told that modern art encourages such tricks.

Two of the most attractive works in the entire show are the group of four calendar plates and the costume illustration done in brush after the Japanese fashion —you know, hands in awkward positions, figures in unnatural poses, and color not evenly distributed. The former group pleasantly parades such things as beaches, dusky lifeguards, snow, masked balls, and new-fangled firecrackers.

The School Spirit
Bosse High School
Evansville, Indiana

152

Three Centuries of English Painting

By Victoria Forster

EXAMPLE

84

Currently being shown at the Milwaukee Art Institute is the "Three Centuries of British Painting" exhibition which will last until December 1. Through the constant efforts of Burton Cumming, director, this show includes paintings representing 32 artists ranging from the period of Charles I to Queen Victoria.

One superb portrait after another shows the dignity and grace of English beauties, from their satins and lace to their lifelike painted expressions. Among the portrait artists are Reynolds, Gainsborough, Lawrence, and Romney.

Reynolds' "Earl of Errol" is a huge oil canvas which is dramatic yet rich and warm.

In rivalry with Reynolds, Gainsborough paintings seem more gentle and poetic. His coloring is soft and cool as shown in his use of blues and greens in "The Cruttenden Sisters." These regal-looking women might be going to a dance of today, for the manner of dress seems very similar—upsweep hair-dos and low-cut necklines.

English artists paint landscapes well, perhaps because they seem to love the out-of-doors. There are a number of English landscape artists who prove that this runs true to form.

One of the popular landscapes is Constable's "Weymouth Bay." This picture suggests the sea coast of New England as it is painted from a cliff showing the wide expanse between the sea and the coast. It is not highly colored, but it gives the feeling of rain-washed wind ready to sweep down across the cliff.

As the story goes, Constable painted this landscape on his honeymoon. A minister lent him his home and added that the scene was worth painting. Many years later Constable went back still to find this splendid view which looks off toward Solent.

There are landscapes by Turner: "Hastings Beach," "Alpine Valley," and "Aosta." Of the three, the view of Aosta, done in splashy water colors, is the most modern-looking. Among the other dull-colored paintings, this adds that spark of light.

Marlow has a quiet, serene, yet old-world looking landscape "Castle on the Rhone," while Ruskin is represented by a water color of "Church and Vista on the Bay of Naples."

Horse lovers will enjoy the works of Morland and Bentley Ward; Marshall Ward's "Portrait of Smolensko, Winner of Derby 1813" is an oil of an English black beauty standing into the wind with an adventurous gleam in his eye. "Wellesley Gray" by Marshall is an oil portrait of a famous Arabian horse. Although the background isn't too authentic, Wellesley Gray is a graceful dynamic-looking horse.

Both Bentley and Morland are represented by the famous red coat hunting scenes. They recall the much-read-about hunting spirit of the past.

Shorewood Ripples
Shorewood High School
Milwaukee, Wisconsin

CHAPTER LABORATORY

1. Clip and mount two book reviews; in a few sentences, indicate the impressions the writers wished to communicate.
2. Clip from daily and school papers samples of as many other types of critical writing as you can find. Use for classroom discussion.
3. Write a 250-word critical review of a book you have recently read, remembering that your task is to interest the reader.
4. Make a list of past and coming events that suggest dramatic, music, or art reviews.
5. Write a critical review of a movie you have seen recently.
6. Write a 250-word review of a play you have read.
7. Write a column of six or eight paragraphs, each treating a different television program that you have seen.
8. As a class, agree upon a radio or television concert scheduled for some evening this week; listen to it, and write a review.
9. Examine the last three or four issues of your school paper, and make a list of all the books reviewed in those issues. Interview students to determine how widely these were read. Did any of those interviewed read the books after reading the reviews?
10. Interview your librarian on the effect of book reviews on library circulation. Write a news feature on the interview.
11. Most schools have paintings or prints hanging in the halls or elsewhere in their buildings. Treat these as an exhibit and write a critical review. If your school has no pictures, write an editorial pointing out the need for them. An interview with your art teacher might be helpful.
12. Attend a school musical production, and report it in 250 words.
13. Attend a school dramatic production, and report it in 300 words.
14. Write a review of an appropriate school assembly program.

12 CONDUCTING A COLUMN

Events of the day—the trivial as well as the significant—pass before the public eye and invite comment from clever newswriters known as columnists. A writer's comments, appearing each time under the same head, usually in the same place, form a feature known as the column.

Columnists form a picked group of commentators. Being a columnist is not a privilege to be given any reporter; it is an honor to be won through the demonstration of outstanding ability. Keen observation, good judgment, sound reasoning, a knowledge of human nature, wide acquaintanceship, an original style, tact, a wholesome sense of humor, a spirit of restraint, respect for the school, freedom from petty prejudices—these are the qualities that distinguish the prospective columnist. The privilege carries heavy responsibilities.

NATURE OF THE COLUMN

Column writers, being avid readers and observers, float their columns on the passing news of the day. A column must be timely, but it does not have to be heavy. These features, by-lined, may be editorial treatment of the day's news, satire, gentle burlesque, personal bits, pathetic

155

or amusing incidents, anecdotes, emotional appeals, pithy statements, witticisms, verse, or other varied and fresh forms.

The great majority of professional columnists handle editorial discussions of the news, usually devoting a day's column to one subject. On the other hand, the great majority of student columnists deal in light merchandise—the personal item, the quip, light verse, the short joke often borrowed from another paper, and personals about fellow students—usually a collection of short items.

To maintain a balanced newspaper with a proper proportion of all the various types of stories, a four-page paper seldom carries more than four columns. A larger paper, of course, permits greater coverage.

Dangers of column writing. Journalistic opinion finds an outlet in two different types of stories, the editorial and the column. The editorial speaks for the paper as a whole, the column for the writer only. The editorial bears no by-line and uses nothing more personal than the "editorial we." The column bears the name of the reporter, and makes full use of the pronoun *I*. The opinions expressed in a column are so much the columnist's own that occasionally a newspaper will attach an editor's note stating that the opinions presented in the column are not necessarily those of the paper.

Column-writing presents dangers as well as opportunities. It invites the misguided reporter to set himself up as an oracle. His great freedom may be his undoing. In the newspaper field today, columns have become big business. The columnist need not pose as an expert. Rather he must show considerable modesty in expressing his opinion, which should be based on careful study of the news and its background.

TYPES OF COLUMNS

A good column depends so much on the individual that the examples in this chapter are not to be taken as patterns. Rather, they are samples of what is now being published in the nation's school papers. The student editor, the staff, and the faculty adviser together determine the paper's policy with respect to columns, and the result should reflect staff ability at the moment as well as local conditions.

Some of the most common types of columns now appearing in school papers are these: (1) the variety or humor column, (2) the personals column, (3) the inquiring reporter, (4) the exchange column, (5) news briefs and commentary, (6) the music column, (7) the fashion column, (8) club notes (the preceding columns are treated in this chapter), (9) the editor's column, (10) who's who, (11) twenty-five years ago, (12) the sports column, and (13) alumni notes.

The variety or humor column. This entertaining feature made up of short items—philosophical comments, a play on names, local humor, light thrusts at school happenings, puns, and jokes—is the instrument of a particular individual who holds the position all year, and it reflects his particular sense of humor. The clever title may carry either the columnist's name or his nom de plume.

If contributions from the readers are used, the columnist must assure himself that they are original. The policy of using borrowed jokes must reflect the combined judgment of columnist and editor. Original expression makes the school newspaper, but nobody can deny the reader interest attracted by a clever joke column. *The Rhodes Review,* in Cleveland, has cleverly named its borrowed-jokes column "The Thief of Badgags." Regardless of the types of items used in a variety column, the columnist must have a keen sense of humor, sound judgment, and respect for the boundaries of wholesome fun.

Although it appears anywhere on the second or third pages of a four-page paper, the most popular position for this feature is the last column on the second (editorial) page.

Small cuts often help the appearance of a column, and type can be used in a number of ways to lend variety. Certain items in boldface, some set six point instead of the usual eight, some set ten, some in caps or small caps, and an occasional use of italics help a reporter display his stuff in an attractive manner and suggest the variety that he strives for in his text.

This type of column often disappears with the graduation of its conductor, and new staff members produce new features suited to their talents.

The cleverness of this hodge-podge column is in direct proportion to the cleverness of its master. Taken as a group, Examples 85 through 91 represent ingenuity at its best and indicate the variety of ways that student reporters can approach this type of writing successfully.

"KASPAR LE KAT"

EXAMPLE

85

if scientists
are interested in space
why don't they use
the x-ray machine
on each others'
heads

speaking of space
if they send a monkey
to the moon
with geiger counters
gauges
instruments
radios
rockets
flags
and
the one hundred and one
other things
i hope
they remember to include
a couple bananas

—kaspar le kat

**more thoughts
of kaspar**

The Rebel Review
South Dade High School
Homestead, Florida

Crazy Injun Confuses Names

EXAMPLE

86

Bill arm weak
Bill exercise arm
BILL ARMSTRONG

Ada happy
Ada laugh
ADA BEAHM

Edward can't see
Edward open eyes
EDWARD SEYMOUR

John page
John squire
JOHN KNIGHT

Barbara aim
Barbara shoot
BARBARA CANNON

Dave talkin'
Me yawnin'
DAVE BOREN

Lenard stuck out foot
Lenard tripped man
LENARD FELDMAN

Cathy planted
Cathy watered
CATHY BLOOM

Toby try out
Toby get part
TOBY CHODOFF

Mike lights match
Mike sets fire
MIKE WILBOURNE

Nancy has shoes
Nancy loses shoes
NANCY BAREFOOT

Richard cool
Richard chilly
RICHARD COLE

Betsy see show
Betsy like
BETSY CLAPP

Emily good kid
Emily swell
EMILY TRUEBLOOD

Michael stop work
Michael finished
MICHAEL DUNN

Jean at beach
Jean stay in sun
JEAN BROWNING

The Tattler
Bethesda-Chevy Chase High School
Bethesda, Maryland

—by Karen Olson

EXAMPLE
87

Now that school has started again, everyone is probably worried about what his new teachers will be like. *The Eastonian*, Easton, Maryland reminds us that teachers aren't perfect either:

Professor: "Your last paper was very difficult to read. Your work should be so written that even the most ignorant will be able to understand it."
Student: "Yes, sir. What part didn't you understand?"

Teacher: Tommy, translate "Rex fugit."
Tommy: The king flees.
Teacher: No, it has the perfect tense. Use "has."
Tommy: The king has flees.

A professor of biology addressed his class thus:
"I propose to show you a very fine specimen of a dissected frog which I have in this parcel."
Undoing the parcel he disclosed some sandwiches, a hard-boiled egg, and some fruit.
"But surely I ate my lunch!" he said.

"I shall now illustrate what I have in mind," said the professor as he erased the board.

Study hard!

The Orange
White Plains High School
White Plains, New York

Just Jade

EXAMPLE

88

Not That Bad a Deal

With all the couples who keep steady company at Q. A., one is bound to hear some pretty choice verbal exchanges in the halls. Recently, I overheard a girl condescendingly say to her fellow, "All right, we'll compromise—you admit you're wrong and I'll forgive you!"

Famous Grad

Alan Latham, former KUAY associate editor, who first proved his worth as an honors graduate of Harvey Mudd Men's College, is now in the Rockefeller Medical Research Center on a three-year scholarship.

Bureau of Worry-Warts Inc.

. . . an organization of which I am a member in good standing. Field Operations: For instance, someone asks a member if he ever worries about the world getting blown up, and he replies that it all depends on what day it is—say, Wednesday is his day for worrying about personality problems and Friday for worry-ing about the world getting blown up! The Creed: Behind every silver lining there's a dark cloud.

Happy Birthday?

Art Daughters was, to say the least, rather startled when he received five whole yards of pepperoni for his birthday!

A Suggestion

If you feel the irrepressible urge to tell your problems to someone, don't bore your friends with them—tell them to your enemies who will be delighted to hear about them!

Congratulations!

Five of our six Braille students here at Q. A. made the honor roll. And one student missed it by only 1/10th of a point.

Quotation of the Week

"Wear your learning, like your watch, in a private pocket; and do not pull it out, and strike it, merely to show that you have one."

—Lord Chesterfield.

Kuay Weekly
Queen Anne High School
Seattle, Washington

EXAMPLE

89

"My aunt is so absent-minded," remarked **Brian Bettendorf**, "that the other day, when she went to make tea, she put the kettle on the arm chair and sat on the stove! We didn't know she was getting hot until she started singing!"

Seymour Sez

Jane Solberg—"Darling, can you drive with one hand?" asked Jane, in the seat beside **Jack Martin**.

Jack—"Yes, my love."

Jane—"Then wave to Mamma; she's in the car following us."

160

Greg Schwalen was walking across a golf course and got hit on the head with a golf ball. "I'll sue you in court for five hundred dollars!" he yelled at the golfer. "I hollered 'Fore,'" alibied Don Kelsen.

"I'll take it," yelled Greg.

The Beacon
Harding High School
St. Paul, Minnesota

TONGUE OF THE TIGER
—by Bill Dobak

EXAMPLE
90

The other day, we sent someone over to Education House to interview a member of the Board of Education and find out what progress was being made on the new high school. The following conversation was taken from the reporter's notebook:

Q. I understand that the homeroom system will be abolished this year.

A. That's quite right. We're having teacher-counselors instead; each teacher-counselor will be responsible for the guidance of a number of students.

Q. I see. In breaking up the homerooms, have you followed any particular plan?

A. Yes, we have. I. B. M. machines were used in the reassortment, to ensure that each teacher-counselor got an equal number of students from each grade, and from each of the sending schools.

Q. I hear that this year everything, schedule changes, registration of schedule changes, registration of marks, etc., will be done mechanically.

A. Yes, each student will be processed individually, by I. B. M. machines, by means of a series of small holes punched in the student's forehead.

Q. I see. How many students can the new high school hold?

A. About 2300.

Q. How about over-crowding in, say, ten or fifteen years?

A. There is that danger, yes.

Q. What will you do then?

A. Drain the swimming pool and divide it into classrooms.

Q. I see. Well, I guess that's all, sir. Thank you very much.

The Orange
White Plains High School
White Plains, New York

who's who on the slough

By John Weil

THE IN-BETWEEN DAYS: football is fast becoming a memory (thank goodness!), and basketball fever has not really hit yet . . . things I won't soon forget:

Mr. (Pied Piper) Endriss' personal contribution to Spirit Week (the faculty probably won't forget it, either), the spirit at the Big Game (card stunts and Lincoln Continental and Susie Ross

EXAMPLE
91

and Dawn Urbais), **Twinka Thiebaud's tragi-comic performance at the Tam funeral, etcetera . . . But let's not dribble over the past. Basketball is upon us and, I can hardly wait for the celebrated wit of Coach Hart ("Do your folks have any kids?") and the thrill of overtimes and sudden deaths.**

CANDID CAMERA: Watch out, Redwoodites, you're going to be in the movies. The Red Cross Club plans to photograph you *when you're not looking* and show the results at the intermission of their upcoming dance. By the way this group is now just, and simply, and only, the RC Club.

QUESTION TIME: **Three guesses at what's the biggest selling item in the student store, life savers . . . least profitable item—the rooters' caps that are half ivy league, half beret.**

The Redwood Bark
Redwood High School
Larkspur, California

The personals column. Pick up a small-town weekly newspaper, and you will find the personals column carrying the name of Mrs. Joe Doakes, who has done nothing more significant than spend the week-end with her married daughter who now lives over in the next county. Important news? Yes, to Mrs. Doakes, who is never going to have her name in the paper because her jewels were stolen or because she has been elected to Congress.

Pick up a large metropolitan daily, and you will note on the society page that a third son has been born to Mr. and Mrs. Philip X. Stuart, in the Wightman Hospital, that Mrs. Stuart is the former Miss Joan Goddard, daughter of Mrs. J. Anthony Goddard of this city, and that the child will be named Philip Anthony. Significant news? Yes, to the Stuarts, the Goddards, and their circle of friends.

Pick up the modern high school newspaper, and you will find it filled with names of students and teachers. Significant news? Certainly, at least to the person named and to his close friends. School papers usually group their personal items into personal columns.

Such a column is conducted by the same student for a semester or for a year. This columnist keeps a record of the names he includes from issue to issue, seeking to extend his coverage to more students.

Notice the abundance of names in Examples 92 through 94. These columns are about people rather than events. Of course the people are doing things, as recognized in the accounts, but the events are incidental in news value and represent little more than supporting structure for the names. This is the distinctive feature of the personals column.

SEEN, HEARD CORNER . . . .

By Lynne Loving

STAN DOZIER should be careful when experimenting with science; you know frozen fish are fragile . . . . KURT LEMON wears good-looking socks . . . . LINDA McSTAY is coming back to Paschal . . . . CAROLYN MALICOAT, MAURE LUKAS, KATY KIRBY, and SHARON COOK do a nice snake dance.

NANCY FELT and C. L. TURNER throw paper sacks at each other . . . . DON GILLESPIE, SHELLY BLANKE, RONNY REA, and PAT BRYANT were a few Exes from last year at Paschal on Homecoming day . . . .

TOMMY MENDINA and SANDY CASSTEVENS draw and letter very well . . . . COLLEEN PATTON drives on the wrong side of Eighth Avenue . . . . COLLEEN BAKER is embarrassed to play the piano.

JAMES MOSES cooks some mighty good cookies . . . . BOBBY BETHEA is a part owner with SUSAN BETHEA of a new jeep. . . . MARY ANN ARTHUR has school spirit, but she also has a sore throat . . . . SIM LAKE is known as a master when it comes to making money . . . . SHEILA WRIGHT is going to Europe this summer.

The Pantherette
Paschal High School
Ft. Worth, Texas

EXAMPLE

92

Beach Breeze

By Suzi Epstein

A sweet sixteen luncheon will be given in honor of Carol Waldman on Sunday at the Algiers Hotel. Helping to celebrate will be Phyllis Frank, Susie Schneider, Lynda Labell, Carol Lee, Sharon Kruger, Sue Skirble, and Cheryl Baida.

ROUND 'N' ABOUT

Beach High's famous dance partners did it again! Shelly Finger and Izzy Diner recently won Tom Looney's PAL dance contest for the sixth consecutive time. Keep it up kids!

After the Beach-South Dade game, Leon Firtel held an open house. Among the guests were Sandi Mudrick and Harvey Swickle, Efrem Lieber and Judi Kross, Jimmy Hauser and Lynn Froman, Arlene Silver and Bob Payton, Mary Jo Marchand and Mickey Aaronson. Leon's date was Eunice Cohen.

An oriental theme set the background for Mike Gaines' party. Those who "made the scene" were Abby Morris and Ricky Perillo, Mike Safier and Pauline Popoff, Linda Shanbrun and Seth Werner, Alana King and Harold Klein.

The Beachcomber
Miami Beach High School
Miami Beach, Florida

EXAMPLE

93

163

The Eagle's Eye

By JOY CHERRY

EXAMPLE
94

The Eagle's bright eye has been busy flashing around Eagletown and has located a variety of tidbits here and there.

While out surfboarding on Westwood Lake during the recent hurricane, Pat Dallas and Jan Glidewell came close to a watery grave when their surfboard overturned.

Ginny Law has recently gone beatnik by way of Greenwich Village. This summer she visited many beatnik espressoes there and made a number of unusual friendships. She says living the life of a "beat" is "way out, daddy!"

Dancing her way to Nassau this summer was Crystal Hill, who performed on the *S. S. Florida*. Crystal has entertained quite often this year but was exceptionally excited with her latest job.

This year on September 9, Southwest doors were opened to many new faces from foreign places:

Timothy Kelley, a sports enthusiast, has transferred from Christopher Columbus. **Carolyn** and **Susan O'Malley**, who attended Our Lady of Mercy High School, Detroit, Michigan, say "It's so different."

Taking her annual trip, Baia Castle returned to Puerto Rico where she visited relatives and enjoyed the island recreation. Judy Madison, who comes to us from New York, is slowly getting used to the half-hour lunch schedule in contrast to her past one hour.

The Southwest Lancer
Southwest High School
Miami, Florida

If the emphasis is to be on social affairs, as in Example 93, the columnist must see that this coverage is as broad as possible, and that new names keep appearing in subsequent issues.

Notice the effectiveness of capitalizing in Example 92, and of using boldface type for variety in Example 94. As a point of interest, "The Eagle's Eye," Example 94, set two columns wide, often runs the length of the page; then the column often runs thirty column inches.

The gossip column—a species of the personals column—is the questionable member of the column family. By itself, it causes more controversy than all other newspaper features combined. The very possibility of including such a column in a school paper is a matter of editorial policy—how personal shall the personals column be? This is a question requiring most careful attention.

That this column carries reader interest cannot be denied. Newspapers are made up of the personal affairs of man. The extent to which the paper may go in reporting these affairs is the test of an editor; the extent to which the personals column shall cover the boy-girl relationships about the school is the best test of the editorial policy of the paper. Examples 95 and 96 show clearly the issues raised by this question.

NO GOSSIP— HERE'S WHY

EXAMPLE 95

The most frequent suggestion brought to the attention of the newspaper staff within the last few weeks has been, "Why doesn't the paper have a gossip column?"

The editors of the *Bengal Lancer* have agreed that a gossip column has no place in our school paper. The objection of the editors to "gossip," no matter how harmless it may seem, is justified. We strongly feel that certain kinds of gossip can only result in more harm to the student readers than good. What seems hysterically funny to one may hurt another. Also, gossip may give rise to insulting, and sometimes damaging, rumors.

Thus far, the *Bengal Lancer* has solidly upheld a policy of service to Bogan's students and faculty through responsible journalism. By omitting such a column as has been described, we will stand by this policy.

The Bengal Lancer
W. J. Bogan High School
Chicago, Illinois

Journalism Class Vetoes Carrying of Gossip Column in *The Triadelphian*

EXAMPLE 96

Following a two-day discussion of the gossip column and its place in a student publication, the journalism class decided, by a unanimous vote, not to include such a column in *The Triadelphian*.

Said Sarah McCulley, "Such a column tends to encourage dirt spreading that usually results in loss of friends. Why make a point of a mistake at the expense of another's embarrassment.

"Gossip isn't news," answered Lucille Kimpel. "It is talk, passed from one person to another, usually started from a very innocent source. Gossip hurts when it is directed to yourself."

"Someone is always hurt when a school paper resorts to gossip," responded Marie Hand. "I always think of putting my name in the space filled by someone else's name. I know how I'd feel."

"Gossip tends to beget gossip, and by the mere spreading of a rumor a student's name is often blackened by stories that are malicious and often untrue," commented Phoebe Yarling.

The Triadelphian
Triadelphia High School
Wheeling, West Virginia

165

Gossip is groundless rumor or mischievous tattle; naturally a responsible staff can do nothing else but adopt a policy of no gossip column as such. However, a staff can still be professionally sound in endorsing a personals column that follows high standards and has as its goal wholesome reader interest.

Many fine personals columns being published in pace-setting high school papers have been misnamed gossip columns. The objective treatment of the party life of the students, as seen in Example 93, is good journalism, for it does not treat rumor and the material is presented in good taste. It is when the columnist moves from the larger groups, from parties, to couples or individuals that he often takes liberties in his comments. In fact, he may be violating the journalistic restriction that forbids editorializing in news coverage.

The following three ways of handling an item for a personals column may be taken as an example of this distinction. Bill Ward will take Ruth Curry to the junior prom: (1) the columnist may report this in a list of other "twosomes" attending the prom; (2) he may take a bit more liberty by reporting it in his column as a separate item, not treating other dates for the party; or (3) he may not be satisfied to let it stands alone, but adds something like this: "Wonder who Sam Anderson will take?" Thus we have three steps in moving from the straight personals column toward the gossip column. Such movement should be carefully considered; the extent of it should represent carefully determined editorial policy.

An excellent guide to editorial policy may be summarized as follows:

> **Standards for personals columns stand out distinctly— no untruths, no rumors, no insinuations, no reflections upon character, nobody to be hurt mentally or morally, nothing malicious, no use of the paper to "get even," no friendships to be endangered, and no editorializing about boy-girl friendships.**

Common practice does not necessarily mark the way for the staff studying the problem of personals. Perhaps it will conclude that it is

166

good student journalism to cover the personals about the school, but that it is poor journalism to report them in a manner that violates good taste. The real enemy of the personals column is the student columnist of inmature judgment, who has taken advantage of his position, or has been permitted to run wild. The conductor of a personals column should be one of the best and most mature students, and his column should represent a well thought out policy.

The Inquiring Reporter. The old favorite, the Inquiring Reporter, is common to school newspapers. Columns may come and columns may go, but the old reporter goes on forever—armed each time with a new question. The appeal of this column is universal; its reward is reader interest. A number of students and teachers, usually from eight to fifteen, are asked a common question dealing with the current affairs of the school. Their answers are recorded, their names often carrying more news significance than their words. The columnist is challenged to select clever questions and always to include some new students who otherwise seldom get their names in the paper. The question must bring forth a variety of answers. This excludes such questions as "Who is going to win the game next Saturday?"

Example 97 presents a timely subject for the inquiring reporter. IBM machines have just taken over some of the clerical duties of the teachers, and the reporter queries the reactions of the students.

Are I. B. M. Cards Too Impersonal?

How did Marshallites like the new IBM report cards, introduced last Friday, October 20?

Did they feel there was any loss of personal relationship with the teachers? Here are a few of their post-grade-time views:

Carol Beetler, 11A: There is no loss of personal relationship. Even though you do get the report cards in homeroom, you can still ask your teacher about your grades individually.

William Hotz, business teacher:

In most cases the student knows what grade he is getting before he gets it. If a student thinks he is unfairly graded, he will seek out his teacher just as he did with the previous system.

Mike Sexton, 12A: I think there is a loss of personal relationship because when you get your report cards, the grade is already on them, and you don't have much time to discuss them with your teacher.

Lee B. Bauer, principal: Each

EXAMPLE

97

167

teacher must make out an individual grade for each student. The only difference is that the cards are made out previously and are turned over to IBM for processing. This gives us the opportunity for more periods of class work.

Bea Jonak, 12B: I like the cards because they are a lot easier on teacher and student alike. Most teachers explain their point systems, and there is no loss of personal contact.

Nancy Kopec, 10A: I think there is some loss because we don't get a chance to talk to the teachers about our grades right away. We have to go after school when the grade is not fresh in the teacher's mind or ours.

Joe Segedi, 12B: Whether you come up to the teacher to get your grades or whether they are handed to you makes no difference.

Kathy Norwood, 11A: If the student is really interested, he will go to see about his grades after school. Teachers are glad to talk with you about your grades. All teachers should let you know what you are getting ahead of time, though.

Donna Siebler, English teacher: I feel that IBM cards do not result in any loss of personal relationship between student and teacher. Teachers are very willing to discuss grades with students if students are willing to inquire about them.

The Interpreter
John Marshall High School
Cleveland, Ohio

The exchange column. Many student editors use other high school newspapers as the source of material for a regular feature commonly called the exchange column. This column consists of a number of short items, digests of events occurring in other schools that will interest local readers. Usually there is no relationship among the items, the columnist's sole guide being "What will interest my readers?" However, as indicated in Example 98, to a thinking reporter who cares to spend the time, a collection of miscellaneous school papers can present some interesting, one-subject features.

Another excellent illustration of the exchange column is Example 39 in Chapter 8.

Glimpses of Far-away Fashions

EXAMPLE

98

Adoption of fashion ideas from other schools by PBHS scholars might work a slight change in their all-over appearances, but on the whole fashion fads are much the same. It's debatable whether such a change would be for better or worse, but it would be entertaining. If anyone should take to the idea of stealing fads from other schools, the following may be purloined without compunction.

———

Bangs are back with a bang! The girls at DeWitt high school are sporting this old hair style, recently revived in the lower grades.

Hi-Times
DeWitt, Ark.

———

One pair of socks on top of another is the newest craze in Arkadelphia due to the cold weather. Types most worn are heavy football socks and soft angora ones.

The Badger
Arkadelphia, Ark.

———

Jeans and sweatshirts, jeans and T-shirts, jeans and dress shirts, jeans and sweaters, jeans and loafer jackets, jeans and suit coats, and jeans and wool shirts are featured in the boy's fashion parade at Central high in Muskogee, Oklahoma. The school paper hints that soon they'll be wearing jeans with a cutaway or tuxedo.

The Scout
Muskogee, Okla.

Big bows are adorning little girls in Pittsburg, California. The school paper suggests that they look like they just stepped out of *Seventeen*, and probably did.

The Galleon
Pittsburg, Calif.

———

Fancy fads may attract attention, but in Louisiana the emphasis is still on the fundamentals.

Interrupting a homeroom session, a group of students accompanied by a teacher enter a classroom and demand that the girls rise. After a thorough visual inspection they depart, leaving the puzzled girls with no explanation. All very mystifying. But the secret is disclosed when the next day's bulletin announces the best dressed girls in school. As part of their class work, a New Orleans sociology class judged the unknowing contestants on aspects of clothes, neat hair, clean shoes, and suitability of dress.

The Broadcaster
New Orleans, La.

————

The Pine Cone
Pine Bluff High School
Pine Bluff, Arkansas

News briefs and commentary. There are two types of news columns, one composed of comments on current events about the school and the other of short news items grouped for convenience in making up the paper. The latter, the news-brief column, is more common. Example 99 is representative of this type of popular column.

Appearing in perhaps less than 10 per cent of the high school newspapers is the news-commentary column, usually conducted by the editor, who ordinarily treats one subject an issue, limits himself to school affairs, and completes his task within about three hundred words. Occasionally, various short news comments comprise the column. (See Example 100.)

The preferred position for this column seems to be the left-hand column on the front page or following the editorials on the editorial page. In Example 100, notice how the commentator has chosen for discussion passing events of the school that seem to him to deserve such highlighting lest their significance be missed by the average student. These columns resemble the interpretive editorial, but they differ in that they carry by-lines, are regular weekly features, and are rewards to outstanding writers.

News In Capsule

EXAMPLE
99

Jeannie Anderson . . .

June grad Jeannie Anderson is currently representing the entire United States at a six-week International Youth meeting in Denmark. At Lowell, Jeannie was a song girl and president of the San Francisco Youth Association.

Peter Tamaras . . .

On November 7, former Lowellite Peter Tamaras was elected to a second term on the San Francisco Board of Supervisors. He received the largest total of votes among the 33 candidates and will probably be elected president of the board.

Student Store . . .

Students can now purchase bus tickets, decals, pennants, etc., at the new Student Association Store, located in the boys' yard at the window nearest the flag pole. It is open daily during third, fourth, and fifth periods.

New San Francisco Magazine . . .

The Lowell has inside information that a new magazine dealing with entertainment in San Francisco (along the line of the *New Yorker*) will be published next year. Publisher William Frohlich informs *The Lowell* that it will probably be called the *New Argonaut* and will come out monthly.

The Lowell
Lowell High School
San Francisco, California

a face in the crowd

By Bob Thiel

EXAMPLE
100

THERE HAS BEEN some mention of having students replace teachers to monitor the halls during school. If put into operation the plan would require fifty students to give up a period a day, with eight students a period in all periods except third and sixth. Such an idea needs and deserves serious consideration. Student Council's Steering Committee has taken the question under advisement and I am sure that Committee or any other member of Student Council would appreciate some opinions, both pro and con, about such a plan from both students and faculty.

170

As the football season comes to a bloody close tonight at Reitz Bowl, due credit goes to Mr. Johnson and the marching band for an excellent series of halftime shows this year. A great deal of hard work, including practices at all hours, in all weather, went into the productions of what can easily be considered the best high school band in this area.

If there aren't as many people out at the Coral these days, it is only because most seniors are spending their free time in a wonderful place known as Termpapersville. After reading two hundred magazines and books about "The Sociological and Psychological Effects of an Iconoclastic Dictator on the Human Mind in the Sixth Century, B.C." ("A little broad don't you think?"), such a visitor has the challenging opportunity to condense this information into 2500 of his own words or less.

The School Spirit
Bosse High School
Evansville, Indiana

The music column. The music column, which reports the emergence of new records, has sprung into prominence as more and more students and their families own phonographs. Sometimes this column is limited to popular music; occasionally it includes recordings of both popular and classical music. The popularity of recordings with high school students suggests that this type of column, if handled by a knowing conductor, would gain a great student following for the school paper. (See Example 101.)

The Spinning Disc

By KAREN MICHAELSON
News Editor

EXAMPLE

101

"The people, yes!" said poet Carl Sandburg, and yes, it is the people of whom Joan Baez sings on her albums *Joan Baez at Carnegie Hall, Volumes I and II.* Miss Baez, called the hottest woman folk singer since Odetta, sings out the songs of the common man with a solid dose of soul!

Speaking of Odetta, she now can be heard wailing on her own disc *At the Gate of Horn* as well as joining Harry Belafonte *At Carnegie Hall.*

Perhaps better known as the voice of the common people is the original Kingston Trio who are *Going Places.* Since their original three-man group broke up and a new banjo player joined the trio, they have crashed out on the record scene with another moving album, *Make Way.*

Adding to the hand-clapping, down-beat rhythms of the people, Josh White's wild *At Midnight* disc cuts loose with a sensational, vibrant "Jelly, Jelly" that sets the theme for the whole swinging album. Josh also wails away on spirituals and gives lament to a mournful "Chain Gang" cut.

Three more hot groups voice

171

the plaint of the common folk—
the Weavers' *Carnegie Hall, Volumes I and II, Rally 'Round,*
shouted by the Brothers Four,
and a different, new group, the
Clancy Brothers, with Tommy
Maken, on a cut titled *The
Laughing Irishmen*. On this platter the Clancy Brothers sing not
only of the people, but with them
as the audience chimes in on the
old, familiar folk ballads and Irish
rebel songs.

The soul of the people is brilliantly revealed in a bright cut of
Lookin' Up by the Jubilee Four,
while the Sensational Nightingales, led by the Reverend Julius
Cheeks, fly with "Standing at the
Judgment," cut on a 45 r.p.m.
disc. The greatest of devotion in
songs belongs to Mahalia Jackson, who sings "Every Time I
Feel the Spirit" straight from her
great spiritual-swinging heart.

Errol Garner joins the trend in
playing for the everyday, plain,
old, whistling, toe-tapping common man with his neatly executed *Concert by the Sea.*

The Beachcomber
Miami Beach High School
Miami Beach, Florida

The fashion column. The fashion column grows in popularity with
the school paper. The columnist usually comments about the usual
and the unusual in student dress and hair style, and in so doing links
practice with person where possible. Although most columns are limited to styles among girls, some papers give column space to boys'
dress. *The Handy Pep,* Handy High School, Bay City, Michigan, has
run a full page for girls, treating clothes, make-up, hair styles, and
other subjects of interest to girls. This is possible since *The Handy Pep*
is an eight-page tabloid paper. (See Example 102.)

PROPERTY OF
TRENTON PUBLIC SCHOOL

Shape of Face Is Main Factor for Hair Style

EXAMPLE
102

Before you choose a hair style,
there are many things you should
take into consideration. First of
all, choose a style that goes with
the shape of your face. Generally,
a hairdo should contribute to the
illusion that your face is oval
even if it isn't. The shape of your
face contributes to your personality.

When your face is long, you
can make it appear shorter with
hairdos that have a bit of top
height and width at the sides.

Hide Square Corners

When your face is square, it
can look rounded off with hairdos that hide the "corners."

If you have a round face, you
can make it longer by choosing a
hairdo that breaks up the roundness, one with s-shaped lines and
a bit of top height.

Suit Hairdo to Glasses

If you wear glasses, a hairdo
that will go well is one which
is smooth, uncluttered, and not
particularly fuzzy at the tem-

172

ples. If you like to wear bangs, comb them to the side, and have them trimmed neatly and regularly. Frames for glasses are now so attractive and so well designed, that it's a fine idea to choose one that flatters your face shape, your eyes, and eyebrow line. Shop for the most attractive ones you can find; then find a smooth hairdo to match.

Those girls who are over 5 feet 8 inches should avoid long, droopy hairdos. Something fairly short and bouffant will probably suit you better and balance your tall figure. For those under 5 feet 3 inches, wear your hair short and neat, also. Do not wear a long or fluffy arrangement which will overpower your tininess—and you.

The Handy Pep
J. L. Handy High School
Bay City, Michigan

Club column. The practice of treating club items in one column focuses attention on club programs as a whole. It is apparent, also, that the convenience of grouping these related items into one story facilitates make-up. (See Example 103.)

CLUBS ARE TRUMP

EXAMPLE
103

JRC to Make Gift Boxes

"BY SERVING they gain." This describes the workers of Junior Red Cross, who meet the first Thursday of every month.

Next month's meeting on Thursday, November 3, will be a workshop at which members will make boxes to send to hospital patients.

THE JRC performs local, national, and international services, which range from first aid to the overseas gift boxes.

French Club to Show Pics

TRAVEL TALKS and slides will highlight the next meeting of the French Club, Le Cercle Français. The talks will be given by ETHS students who have visited French-speaking countries.

The meeting, Tuesday, October 25, is open to all interested students. There will be no charge.

Star To Describe Lacrosse

MEMBERS OF THE Cosmopolitan club will have their third meeting of the year at 3:20 P.M. today in room 260.

Helen Griffith, the varsity lacrosse player from Great Britain, will speak to the group about Liverpool, England, her home.

Objections Change Name

BECAUSE MANY attach an unfavorable impression to the name USSR, the USSR Club has decided to change its name to the "Russian Club," according to Mrs. Valentina Dziubinsky, Russian teacher and sponsor of the club. The decision was made after the September 29 issue of *The Evanstonian* was published.

The Evanstonian
Evanston Township High School
Evanston, Illinois

Informational feature column. Some columns present service to the reader in various fields; they may be grouped under the title "informational feature column." For instance, Example 104 gives information on colleges, Example 105 guides the student on cultural field trips, and Example 106 assists young men in selecting presents for their girls. This type of column may change its subject from week to week, but its purpose is service.

The Halls of Ivy

EXAMPLE

104

Macalester College is a coeducational, Christian, liberal arts college in St. Paul.

With a relatively small student body of 1200, Macalester emphasizes its concern for the individual student. For example, during the summer preceding entrance as a freshman, each prospective student is assigned both a faculty adviser and an upperclassman counselor. Classes are small; the ratio of students to teachers is 12:1.

The "liberal arts" at Mac include history, literature, philosophy, and religion. A strong background in these courses is required for pre-professional training in medicine, law, or dentistry, because good citizenship, spirituality, and understanding are considered just as important as vocational training.

There are no sororities or fraternities at Mac. Extracurricular activities are open to everyone, and offer anything from choral reading to frog-jumping contests with real live frogs.

Tuition is $400 a semester, or $800 a year, with an additional "activity fee" of $25 per semester. The cost of board is estimated at $200 per semester, and room rental at about $130. There are scholarships, work contracts, and student loans.

Consideration for entrance is given to a student's high school record, with a statement from his principal, and to his personality and character as demonstrated both in and out of school. The College Board aptitude test is required.

A junior or senior wanting more information about Macalester is urged to visit the campus or write to the Director of Admissions, Macalester College, St. Paul.

The Murcurie
Murray High School
St. Paul, Minnesota

CULTURE VULTURE

By MIKE MORGALLA

EXAMPLE

105

The Adler Planetarium is one of the treasures of our city. Here visitors can sit in comfort while the pageant of the heavens moves majestically across the great dome and lecturers explain the mysteries of the universe. All through October, a show, "Beyond the Milky Way," will be presented. Admission to the

174

planetarium is free, and it is open daily from 9:30 A.M. to 5 P.M.

The featured exhibit for October at the Chicago Natural History Museum is "Hall of Gems and Jewels," besides a special temporary display, "Birds of Greenland." Four great fields of research, anthropology, geology, zoology, and botany, are represented in this museum, which is open daily from 9 A.M. to 4 P.M.

Through November 15, the University of Chicago will present the "Old Hyde Park One Hundredth Anniversary" celebration. Included are balloon ascensions, the Great Ferris Wheel, old trains, stations, schools, streets, houses, unusual views of the early days of the University of Chicago, a pictorial exhibition, and a Derby Day. The time will be from 9 A.M. to 12:30 P.M. daily.

On the brighter side, the impudent hit musical, *Bye Bye, Birdie* arrived in Chicago for an indefinite run at the Erlanger Theatre. "Birdie" revolves around a chain reaction set off when a rock 'n roll idol visits a small Midwest town before being drafted.

Another acclaimed musical, *My Fair Lady*, starring Michael Evans and Caroline Dixon, is currently playing at the Schubert Theatre.

"The Traditional Sculpture of Africa," an exhibition of works by artists from forty tribes in twenty of Africa's new nations, was opened in the East Wing Galleries, The Art Institute of Chicago, and will continue through Sunday, November 12.

The peoples of Africa have a long and complex history, much of which is expressed through the arts, according to Allen Wardwell, Assistant Curator of Primitive Art. The exhibition covers four hundred years, extending from the ancient Benin bronzes of Nigeria to the near-modern Dogon sculpture of Mali. The Republics of Cameroun, Chad, Dahomey, Gabon, Ghana, Guinea, Central Africa, and the Ivory Coast are represented.

Works from the Congo as well as the new republics of Malagasy, Mali, Mauritania, Niger, Senegal, Somalia, Sierra Leone, Togo, and the Upper Volta are also included.

The Farragut Scroll
Farragut High School
Chicago, Illinois

Getting Girlwise

with PATTY ASHTON

Many boys may be wondering what they can give girls for Christmas. This is often a problem, although not a very hard one to solve. There are four things, if kept in mind, that may help you when you shop for a girl's present:

1. Keep it simple.
2. Keep it inexpensive.
3. Choose something a girl would really like.

4. Buy something useful.

There is no need to go to extremes when buying a gift for anyone, particularly for a girl. Most girls prefer conservative things. Make your gift one that any girl would be proud to receive.

Make It Inexpensive

Likewise, there is no need to go to extremes on price. Expensive gifts such as watches, rings, necklaces, etc., usually embarrass a

EXAMPLE
106

girl if she doesn't have one similar to give to the boy. . . . Of course, most boys are hardly in a really good financial position at Christmas anyway. For the male with the usual amount to spend, a wallet is nice, and most girls wear them out frequently. If the girl is an intellectual, what about a book you think she'd particularly enjoy? A scarf, gloves (if you're sure of the size), perfume, or a compact might fill the bill.

Knowing what the girl might like to have comes in handy.

However, if even a canvass of her best friends produces a blank, try to choose something you feel she would choose for herself.

Your mother is a good person to consult before you go shopping, and an older or slightly younger sister would be ideal.

After all, its the thought that counts. If a girl really likes a boy, she will love anything that he gives her; so he's really batting 1000 before he starts! Happy shopping!

Wyandotte Pantograph
Wyandotte High School
Kansas City, Kansas

TITLING THE COLUMN

The names of columns are often cleverly tied to the name of the columnist, the school, or the paper itself. For instance, in a region full of Indian lore, *The Flathead Arrow* of Kalispell, Montana, carries these columns: "Tepee Talk," "Council Fires," "Arrow Pointers," and "War Whoops." The *North High Polaris* of North High School, Minneapolis, includes these columns: "Circling the North Star" and "Beneath the Northern Lights."

A particularly clever head is often built around the name of the columnist and sinks to oblivion with his graduation. Note particularly "Dee's Diary," "Bank Notes," and "Ken's Korner" in Examples 107 and 108. "Palmetto Hass-iendas" reflects the names of both the columnist and the school. The name of the school produced "Brave Talk" and "Up 'N Adams." At times the title of the column indicates its type; for instance, "Reading Our Mail"—an exchange column, "club sandwich"—a column of club notes.

These heads are usually one-column cuts, often with an appropriate design. At times the column head is a two-column cut, but the story itself may be either one or two columns, depending upon editorial taste or make-up requirements.

176

The Cheering Section
By Mike Hurvitz

 From the Horse's Mouth

 READING OUR MAIL

 BRAVE TALK

EXAMPLE
107

 sounding off

 DEE'S DIARY

 UP 'N ADAMS

 Palmetto Haas-ienda
by
Kirk Haas

EXAMPLE
108

 Horse's Opinion

 club sandwich

Column Right

 Whirling Discs by Caryl

 BANK NOTES
By Sheldon Bankier

 KEN'S KORNER

CHAPTER LABORATORY

1. Bring to class one column selected from a daily newspaper. In class, discuss the following points: type of column, merits, unique features, and the suitability of this type of column for the school paper.
2. Using the last issue of your school paper for material, write a 200-word news-commentary column.
3. Collect items for a personals column, and write up six for publication. Using the style of Examples 92 and 94, mark some of the copy boldface or capitals for effectiveness.
4. Write a fashion, music, or movie column, including only enough items (three or four) and only enough words to show that you are familiar with the style of such a column.
5. In class, discuss critically the columns in your school paper. Judge the total coverage in relationship to the paper's size. Examine each from the standpoint of good writing, reader interest, and value to the paper and the school.
6. "Who's Who" is a column that usually treats two school leaders per issue, a boy and a girl. Prepare a stimulating 150-word sketch of such a student for publication, avoiding information already well known.
7. List two good subjects for inquiring reporters. Assemble a composite list in class, and give it to the editor of your paper.
8. State in about one-hundred words the policy of your school paper on gossip columns. If such columns are published, judge them against the treatment of the subject in this chapter.
9. The humor column is successfully conducted by only a limited number of journalism students. Try your hand at a short humor column and then discuss in class.
10. In about 150 words per subject, give your opinion of possible reader interest in (1) a column of school news of twenty-five years ago, (2) a column treating alumni news, and (3) a know-your-teachers column.
11. Of the examples of variety and humor columns in this chapter (Examples 85 through 91), select the one that you think has the most reader appeal, and defend your selection before the class. Does your school paper carry a better one?
12. Does the "Culture Vulture" column, Example 105, suggest such a possibility for your school paper?

13 SPORTS COVERAGE

A good sports page in a school newspaper depends first upon a competent sports editor. He knows the field and is enthusiastic about his job; he is systematic about full coverage and can squeeze reader interest into every inch of the limited space allowed him. Just seeing that the events are routinely covered and the deadlines met is not nearly enough, for sports are an important part of American life.

PLAYING UP SPORTS

Athletics are prominent in the life of the American high school, and justly so. There are physical and character-building benefits to the participants and beneficial influences upon the spectator—*esprit de corps,* coordinated enthusiasm, and the development of good sportsmanship.

Newspaper coverage should be proportionate. Practically every high school paper devotes one full page to athletics; in four-page papers, usually the fourth page; in six-page papers, the fifth or sixth. In a few instances, a six- or eight-page, five-column tabloid paper will regularly devote two pages to sports.

The complete sports story requires many types of writing and a careful balance among the various events. This balance can be achieved by coordination in writing and make-up.

Sports writing in general. Sports reporting demands (1) knowledge of the sport, (2) good journalistic sense, (3) enthusiasm for athletics, (4) knowledge of the sports fan, and (5) the ability to write well.

Any newswriter writes for its reader, the sports writer more so. The fan is a funny fellow. He sits in the bleachers figuring out the next play, managing the team to his own satisfaction. Just as he feels free to criticize the substitution made by the coach or the decision made by the umpire, he is a critical reader of the stuff written about that game. Poor reporting is often detected more quickly in this field than in any other.

Unfortunately, sports writers on many school papers use the poorest English, bring in the latest copy, and cause the copy desk more headaches than most of the other reporters. There should be one good sports "grammarian" on the desk to read this copy—one who respects the fact that good sports reporters have the privilege of using journalistically accepted sports jargon.

Color is essential, but not a flowery and highly dramatic style. The reader wants information, and no amount of adjectives and adverbs can make up for the absence of informative nouns and active verbs. The good sports writer is a go-getter who appreciates the value of leg work as well as head work. He goes where the news is, and he gets it all. Then his treatment cements it.

TYPES OF SPORTS STORIES

The types of stories commonly used in handling school sports are (1) straight news coverage of the game as it takes place, commonly called the *coverage story*, (2) the advance story of the game not yet played, (3) feature stories, (4) the sports column, (5) the editorial, and (6) the season's review.

180

Now and then sports require front page attention, but not often. The front page reproduced in Example 109A is one of those cases in which the editor knew that the significance of the sports news had outgrown the sports page itself. Example 109B shows how the advance story for this same game was handled by the paper of the opposing school, this time on the last page. See also Example 109C for more first-page sports treatment.

The coverage story. Management of the sports page demands good judgment. There must be proper coverage of athletics, but the adult reader must not feel that sports are the only activities and interests of the school. Good sportsmanship must be apparent; the alibi has no place in the sports story. Everyone wants to be winner, and the school that has no winning team places an added responsibilty upon the sports writer and editor, who must remember that fair play is as admirable, and as essential, on the sports page as on the athletic field.

Covering a game is no easy matter. The daily paper carries its account the day after, while the school paper must resurrect interest in its coverage sometimes a week or more later. This cannot be done with a prosaic, lazily-covered account. In Indiana, where basketball is a life-and-death matter in high school circles, the fan just naturally expects his reporter to give him such fine details as the percentage of shots each team made from the floor. At the right is a paragraph of such data, taken from *The Centralian*, the Central High School paper, Evansville, Indiana.

> Both teams were scorching the nets above par, and between the two it took an adding machine to keep up with them. The Bulldogs swished through 17 tallies for 65 tries, to rack up an average of .262, but the Bruins, to make their fans happy, rolled in 25 two-pointers out of 71 attempts, for a record average of .352.

A boxed summary account that shows the exact progress of the game at every moment is another revealing method of covering the minute developments of a basketball game. In Example 110 note the care the reporter gives to recording his notes as he watched the game.

EXAMPLE
109

GO TEAM!

Miami Edison Herald
Miami Edison High School
Miami, Florida

b

Neil Valleau, Roy Jones, Joe De Valentine, Phil Murray, Bob Astley, Ronnie Buschbom, Bob Ashworth, Ronnie Wright, Steve Smith, Pete Kieran and Bob Chandler.

Offense, Defense Ready For Miami High

During the middle of August, Coach Haywood Fowle opened the field house to the boys who were going to represent Edison in the Orange Bowl and around the state on various gridirons.

They worked, at first without pads. Tackling drills, agility drills, sprints, crabbing, all the necessities that gets a team in shape.

Soon the pads were donned. Leather started popping, tempers were tormented, and familiar yells were heard: "Tighten up in there—Who were you supposed to block on that play?"

The Football Clinic gave Raider fans their first look at the team. New game jerseys were seen,

dummy plays were run, and the first look at this year's cheerleaders were in order.

Then on September 15, the Raiders took the field against the Pioneers of North Miami. This year Edison fans were a little bit cautious about what they did before the start of the season. The 4-1-4 record of 1960 made people think twice before saying something they could possibly not back up.

As the game progressed began to see that Edison ing to be tough this year game, the defense, with playing of Jim Camp Pasteris and Charlie held the Pioneers scor

almost yardless. The offense racked up 39 points, and the first Edison victory for 1961 was put in the books.

The following Coral Gables met the Raiders on the gridiron. The Gables this year was one of the teams that different poth ranked high in the state. No doubt they were, for Edison scored less points on the Cavaliers than any other team to date. The Raiders came

ricanes 35-0. Pete Kieran, Bob Ashworth, Ronnie Wright, and Bob Chandler proved what the offense could do if given the chance.

Color Day came and went, but gave the Edison stands some anxious moments as Miami Jackson proved tougher than expected. Jackson moved the ball well against the Raider Defense, but still did not reach pay dirt. Bob

weren't after. The "breaks" of the game helped Edison to victory in this contest after the determinations of the Raiders to capitalize of Lee's few mistakes. Lee didn't go home completely saddened, as they were the first team to sneak across our goal line. The Raiders won, though, and that's what counts!

In the first five games, Edison totaled 135 points, while only giving up 7. With the Le

Left to right: Sidney Pickard, Jim Ca
nandez, J. D. Pasteris, Gil Paleaz, John M

a

Miami High Times
Miami High School
Miami, Florida

Miami High Times

Vol. 38, No. 5   MIAMI, FLORIDA   NOVEMBER 16, 1961

BEAT EDISON

Miami Goes For State Crown In OB Competition With Edison

The Miami High Stingarees play their biggest game of the season next week against the number one high school power in the state, the undefeated Edison Red Raiders. An impressive victory may propel the Stings back into the coveted rank of number one.

The Raiders boast the best offense in the state and practically the best defense. The Edison goal was uncrossed through the first four games with Jacksonville Lee breaking the ice in the 6th. Jacksonville Jackson scored 12 points against the Raiders and Norland scored six.

Edison's standout stars are quarterback Pete Kieran and halfback Bob Ashworth. Kieran has averaged seven yards per carry, tops in the county. At the other half is Bob Chandler.

The Raider defensive wall is bolstered by Henry Hernandez, Charlie Gaussiran, Mickey De Brald, J. D. Pasteris and Jim Campbell. The offensive line is led by Bob Astley and Ronnie Buschbom.

The Miami backfield is led by

top scorer, rusher Pete Stroud. Quarterbacks Jim Bennett and Jerry Pearson direct the rest of the backfield, consisting of Mela Carbonell and fullback Robin Payan.

The Edison team also has two fine place-kickers in Barry Nickerson and Bob Chandler who consistently make the extra point after Raider touchdowns. The Stings have not had so much luck with conversions this year. Steve Schwabe and John Battle have not always completed the extra point and, until the Lakeland game, it was not necessary.

In 1953, at the first Homecoming game in the Orange Bowl, "Beat Jackson" was the cry of the cheering section. The Stings walked away with a victory.

A year later, the Junior Class and faculty sponsors of the Homecoming activities changed the Homecoming opponent to Miami Edison and designated the week of Thanksgiving for the gala festivities. The Stingarees greeted the new Homecoming fete with a 6-0 slap in the face.

An interesting fact about the Miami High-Edison series is that the Stings played Edison when the Red Raiders were called the Lemon City Aggies. Edison was once an agricultural high school.

Whatever the teams have done so far, the tradition of the Turkey Day Classic and Homecoming fun and will continue to make this one of the top games in high school football.

Quarterback Jerry Pearson

End Mike Fortier

Pan American Club Promotes Better Cultural Understandings

"To promote a cultural exchange between English and Spanish speaking students at Miami High is the purpose of the Pan American Cultural Society," announces Mrs. Natalie DeBerly, the club's founder and sponsor.

This organization, which had its first meeting Oct. 30, has approximately 100 members and is divided into five groups of activities: a drama group, a musical group, a newspaper, a debate group and a current events discussion group.

Mrs. Frieda Hoffman, Mrs. Lila Powers and Mrs. Olimpia Busada are in charge of the drama group whose presentations will be in Spanish. Miss Mary Morgan will lead the musical and current events discussion group, both of which will be in English.

The Spanish newspaper will have

Mr. Armando Garrido as its adviser. Mr. William Fuller conducts debates.

The membership, composed of Latin American students and students taking Spanish or Latin American history, held its first social affair, a dated dance, Nov. 3.

"Most people felt a need for this type of club," Mrs. DeBerly states, "because Spanish National Honor Society is just for those students who maintain an A average in Spanish for two semesters. Most Latin American students are not eligible for this and since they are not well known, membership in clubs would be difficult for them to obtain."

Test Calendar For December

Dec. 2—
College Entrance Examination Board Test
Time: Part I—three hours (morning session); Part 2—can be omitted or run to three hours.
Fee: Morning $5; afternoon $3 (optional).
This test is necessary for admittance to most colleges and universities.
Dec. 3—
Navy Reserve Officers Training Corps Test
Time: 3 hours.
Fee: Free.
Qualifying test for officers training college program.
Tests for 1962 will be outlined later in the TIMES.

Tag Day Collectors Earn Band $1,775

The "Million Dollar Band" collected $1,775 on Tag Day. The combined forces, worked one day and can now claim to be $1775 richer.

On Tag Day, Nov. 4, the band, majorettes and flagettes, wearing their respective uniforms, were scattered throughout the city to solicit funds for the band.

"With the money collected," says Mr. Gus Perry, band director, "purchase of lights for the marching field will become a reality."

Stoporian Club To Print Pulse, Coming Out Twice This Year

"We're very optimistic about the PULSE magazine this year because we have money enough to have it printed professionally," says Ronnie Rothbart editor.

The PULSE is published by Stoporians, the creative writing club. President Calerie Weissler says, "The club seems to be generating more and more interest, but in a school of this size there are probably many more students who are interested in writing than we have been able to find."

Anyone may submit his writing to the PULSE to room 310 Stories should be 500-2500 words, 25 lines the limit for poems; essays and stories should be 600-1400 words. Contributions should be typed, double spaced and identified by

name, homeroom and telephone number. Contributions which do not conform to these qualifications will not be accepted.

The PULSE will be published at the end of January and a second issue may come out during the second semester.

Other magazine staff members are Barbara Juskewitz, assistant editor; Jessica Hurvitz, poetry editor; Lester Repp, fiction editor; Andy Gray, art editor; Bob Clark, photo editor; Barbara Bivens, advertising manager; and Gloria Whitman, business manager.

Homecoming Plans Ready

By BARBARA COLLINS and PAULA CATALANO

Miami High will be a checkerboard of blue and gold when the Junior Class kicks off Homecoming Week Monday. On this day, juniors will wear blue and gold tags to emphasize the importance of Color Day.

Wednesday the student body will show its school spirit by wearing the school colors, blue and gold. "Color day is the most important project of the Junior Class, and we hope that all the student body will back this project," says Joe Farina, Junior Class president.

Other festivities for Homecoming Week, Nov. 20-23, will include a decorating contest, pep rally, crowning of Homecoming King and Queen, and the Thanksgiving assembly. The week will be climaxed by the Miami High vs. Edison football game.

KING AND QUEEN

Senior Class Secretary Barbara Rachlin and Bob McRae, Senior Class president, will crown the Homecoming King and Queen at the biggest pep rally of the year: Tuesday. This year for the first time the football players can't be nominated for Homecoming King because the coaches want the football players to be in uniform ready for the big game.

HOMEROOM CONTEST

Meanwhile, homerooms will participate in a decoration contest. Three rooms on each floor will receive prizes for the best blue and gold decorations.

First prize is $5; second, $2.50 and third, $1.

ASSEMBLY

The Thanksgiving assembly will end the week's activities before the game Thursday night. It will be given by the combined efforts of the drama department, orchestra and chorus.

"Homecoming has always been a great tradition at Miami High School. In order for it to be a great success each student at Miami High should back it fully," says Craig Logan, vice president of the Junior Class.

Parents To Relive Their School 'Daze'

"Where do we go now?"

"To the third floor! But we're in the gym!"

Such may be the comments as parents return to the halls of learning Nov. 16, for Back - to - School Night.

"Students" will report to their homerooms at 8 p.m., and then follow their children's daily schedule.

"This annual event gives parents an opportunity to become better acquainted with their young people's teachers in somewhat of a lifelike atmosphere," says Miss Isabel Back - er, activities director.

A Noiseless Pep Rally ?

Miami High recently made an unusual contribution to high school education—the noiseless pep rally. This gift is one of the fringe benefits obtained by the new auditorium improvements.

Now cheerleaders can jump all they like and not cause students in nearby classes to jump out of their seats from the noise. When the auditorium doors are closed, it is practically sound-proof.

Aluminum insulation was used to improve the acoustics. A switch panel has been installed to control the various stage lights, and electric motors have been placed in the overhead lights so that they may be lowered or raised by a switch.

West High To Meet Elder In Annual Rivalry

Game At Trechter Stadium To Start Another Tradition

THE WESTERN BREEZE

Vol. 26, No. 4   Western Hills High School, Cincinnati, Ohio   November 22, 1961

Health Scholarships Offered To Graduates Entering Field

Pow Wow Fires To Ignite Spirit

Songs, Baskets, Pep Talk In Thanksgiving Assembly

The Western Breeze
Western Hills High School
Cincinnati, Ohio

Statistics for a story may also be boxed and inserted within the account of the game, as was done in Example 111, clipped from a longer account in *The Chatterbox,* Walnut Hill High School, Cincinnati.

Placing the statistical summary of a game at the end of the story speeds up the running account of the story. The paper will want its reporters to follow a uniform style in reporting these statistics. If one basketball account carries the name of each player, number of field goals, number of free throws attempted, and the number of free throws made, then the other accounts should do the same. Most readers appreciate the care shown in the type of statistical summary illustrated by Example 112.

Besides the coverage of the game itself, it is often effective to cover the entire competitive situation in which the local team finds itself at the moment; the reporter must be up-to-date on the sport he is covering. He cannot properly handle a particular basketball game, for instance, unless he has followed the season up to that game and knows its significance and implications.

A number of reporters should be assigned to handle each game, each covering one phase. One may take the baskets attempted and made from the field, another the human interest of the occasion, and another the body of the story. The story itself modifies the laws of the

183

news story. The lead brings out the climax, but the remainder of the account is often unconventional. By-lines are often carried on sports stories.

```
                  SUMMARY
                First Quarter
                                        Cen-
                               East    tral
Perkins—shot from side... 2 ..
Boetticher—Perkins' foul. 2 .. 1
Steiner—long shot........ 4 .. 1

                Second Quarter
Perkins—Boetticher's foul. 5 .. 1
Maglaris—side .......... 5 .. 3
Perkins—under basket.... 7 .. 3

                Third Quarter
Steiner—long shot........ 9 .. 3
Main—long shot ......... 9 .. 5
B. Lomax—Main's foul ...10 .. 5
Boetticher—Lomax's foul.10 .. 6
B. Lomax—under basket..12 .. 6

                Fourth Quarter
Barr—under basket ......14 .. 6
Perkins—under basket....16 .. 6
Perkins—Boetticher's foul.17 .. 6
Maglaris—one hand, side..17 .. 8
```

Again the Eagles took to the air. Sullivan tossed an aerial to Melzer for the second Eagle tally of the game. Sully plunged over for the extra point. Score: W. H.—13, Wyoming—0.

Walnut Hills		Wyoming
91	Yds. gd. passing	19
128	Yds. gd. rushing	174
7	1st downs	2
22	Passes attempted	14
10	Passes completed	3
3	Fumbles	3
60	Yds. penalties	20
31	Punts (aver. yds.)	19

Before the second half was two minutes old, Cecil recovered a Wyoming fumble. A pass to Paul Seigel put the ball on the Wyoming 22-yard line. Seigel then caught a Sullivan pass on the one-yard line and crossed the goal.

PLAYER	SHOTS TAKEN	MADE	FREE THROWS	MADE	P.F.
Coomes	8	2	1	0	2
Bohm	4	0	0	0	0
Butterworth	9	2	3	2	1
Zint	8	2	4	2	2
Heldt	4	0	2	1	2
Totals	33	6	10	5	7

Within the story, statistics make good reading for the sports fan, adding something to the game he saw. Every important fact should be covered, and there is no excuse for errors.

The thorough coverage in Example 113 is the result of care in note-taking during the contest. The story opens with a summary lead

184

highlighting the game as a whole, then continues with a chronological account. The short statistical summary at the end shows work by the reporter. Statistics are also the basis of the coverage in Example 114. Again a statistical summary completes a well-written and interesting story.

Hi-Tides March Over Kaydets in Season's First Victory

By MARTY SILBERGER
Co-Sports Editor

EXAMPLE

113

The Miami Beach Hi-Tides, led by a spirited line and hard-running backfield, swamped the Miami Military Kaydets 39-12 for their first victory of the football campaign.

Beach broke the scoring ice as they drove 33 yards in three plays. The big play was a 30-yard toss from Richard Hamar to Jay Wells, putting the ball on the Miami Military three-yard line. From here Hamar carried the ball over on a quarterback sneak.

This gave the Tides a lead that they never relinquished. Steve Steinfeldt's kick was perfect, and the Tides led after the first quarter 7-0.

SECOND QUARTER

In the second quarter, with the Beach defense holding perfectly, Miami Military punted to the Beach 44. Here Richard Hamar again took over and galloped 29 yards to the Military 27. After being held on the next two plays, Hamar connected with Alex Medina on a 19-yard pass, then putting the ball on the Kaydets four-yard line.

Then it was Medina off-tackle for three more and touchdown. Steinfeldt converted to make the score 14-0, with 7:38 left in the first half. The Kaydets finally got their offense moving and rolled 63 yards in seven plays, capped by a nine-yard touchdown run by Mike Price. Miami Military failed to convert, making the score 14-6.

Beach, however, was not to be denied; they returned the kickoff to the Tide 37. Here, Richard Hamar skirted left end on an option play and streaked his way 41 yards to the MMA 22. On the next play Medina bobbled the ball and apparently was trapped for a long loss; however, he turned on his tremendous speed and went down to the Miami Military four.

After a penalty, Hamar found Steinfeldt in the end zone and completed a nine-yard scoring pass. Steinfeldt hauled in the pass with two defenders on his back and a bruised hand. The extra point was good and the Tides retired for the half with a 21-6 margin.

SECOND HALF PLAY

Beach received the second half kickoff and returned it to their

185

own 29-yard line, with Lloyd Davis and Andy Zoltners, two new boys in the backfield, running the ball. The Tides hooked up their fourth score as Davis bulled his way 15 yards to pay dirt. A bad snap nullified the point after touchdown, and the Tides led 27-6 after 6:58 of the third quarter. The Tides continued rolling as Medina ripped off on another touchdown run. This play covered 43 yards. The kick failed and the Tides led 33-6.

With Coach Feinstein substituting heavily, MMA moved 65 yards for their second score of the game. Their extra point

failed, and they now trailed 33-12. The Tides rolled for one more score as Bob Grossman upped the play with a pass interception. Senior Hal Fenster then plunged over for the score, and the Tides had won their first game by 39-12.

THE YARDSTICK

	Beach	Military
First downs	18	12
Yards rushing ...	247	135
Yards passing ...	85	45
Passes	6-9	5-20
Punts	3-38.5	3-30.0
Fumbles lost	1	2
Penalties	20	70

The Beachcomber
Miami Beach High School
Miami Beach, Florida

Spartans Capture District Meet

EXAMPLE
114

Winning 10 firsts and 8 seconds, the Corvallis cindermen grabbed top honors in the annual district meet held at Bell Field, May 10. CHS, by virtue of first and second place winners, sent 17 men to the state track meet May 17-18. The point-hungry Spartans scored 92½ points to Albany's 54½. Shedd and Harrisburg trailed 4 and 2.

Albany captured four first places and five second places to come in a poor second in the predicted close meet. The Spartans placed men in the state meet in all events except the high hurdles, in which the Bulldogs took the two top spots.

Bob Rondeau and George Sprick led the locals to victory. Bob scored first in the 440 yard dash, 100 yard dash, and broad jump, and ran anchor team to score 20 points. George scored 13 points by winning the 220 yard dash, placing second in the 100 yard dash, and running on the relay team.

No records were broken, and most times were slow. Ron Clarke ran a fast mile. The relay team came within a half second of breaking the record time in that event, which is 1:36.8.

First and second place results.

120 yard high hurdles—Won by Workman, Albany; Jenkins, Albany, second. Time, 17:1.

100 yard dash—Won by Rondeau, Corvallis; Sprick, Corvallis, second. Time, 10:7.

Mile run—Won by Clarke, Corvallis; Swander, Albany, second. Time, 4:51.

440 yard dash—Won by Rondeau, Corvallis; Smith, Albany, second. Time, 55:6.

Hi-O-Scope
Corvallis High School
Corvallis, Oregon

The advance story. The coverage story demands the playing up of something new out of the past; the advance story demands that the writer build up enthusiasm for the coming event. Nothing is more effective than factual material. Generalities mean nothing. One team is supposed to be stronger—but why? Measure the teams man for man; measure the records game for game. The sports department with a complete file of all games played by the two opposing teams thus far this season has a store of material from which to build the advance. Such records kept complete from year to year provide the writer with pertinent and interesting historical data. An exchange of information with the paper of the other school may provide important information. Example 115 illustrates the effective use of such data.

Sentinels Hold Slight Margin Over Hard-Driving Alco Team

EXAMPLE
115

At 2:30 P.M. November 28, the blue and white clad team of Allegany high will be facing the red and white uniformed Fort Hill team, awaiting the whistle for the opening kickoff. Approximately two hours later, the Greenway avenue stadium, which had been so packed but a few hours before, will be still and quiet again, and another championship will have been decided.

Campers Underdogs

In this tussle, the fourteenth meeting of the two rivals, Fort Hill has been rated a slight favorite over the West Siders, for in September the Sentinels took a 19-0 measure of Allegany and have been beaten but once, while Alco has had tougher sledding. With the city championship at stake, however, previous records and scores will mean nothing in the "Big Game," as both teams have discovered in past years.

Injuries may handicap both teams, as several regulars of each are on the black-and-blue list. Halfback Ray Stevenson, out with a broken collarbone, and Full-

back Don Sensabaugh, with a sprained ankle, may not see action for the Hilltoppers, while John Eckhart, low-flying Camper halfback and Ed Hounshell, trigger-quick guard, may be out of commission with leg injuries. The two-week layoff before the game may be time enough for some of the players to recuperate, however.

Powers Proves Dangerous

The Sentinels will no doubt be on the alert for Tommy Powers, quicksilver fullback of the Camper eleven, for a few jaunts by "Travelin' Tom" may well decide the game for A. H. S.

The Alco offense, using both

187

"T" and single wing, may prove baffling to their cross-town rivals, as might the precision "T" of the Sentinels eleven mystify the blue and white defense.

Both teams are as dangerous in the air as on the ground, and several completed passes by either one might mean the game. All in all, both teams are fairly well balanced and the season should well be completed with a battle royal.

The probable lineups:

Allegany		Fort Hill
Vernall	LE	Freeland
Fridley	LT	Cox
Piper	LG	Daily
Ruehl	C	Hansrote
Hounshell	RG	Catlett
Dawson	RT	Trieber
Cubbage	RE	Lapp
Clower	QB	Frye
Anderson	LH	Mangus
Peterson	RH	Nicholson
Powers	FB	Lewis

Alcohi Mirror
Allegany High School
Cumberland, Maryland

These techniques far overshadow the threadbare habit of reporting the coach's predictions. What can the coach say? The reporter should be true to the facts, not predicting close games if such predictions are not reasonable. The writer's ability to create interest determines how long before the game the advance story should appear. Professional baseball advances are seen in the dead-of-winter months before the season opens.

Example 116 reveals another approach to an important game. In this case the reporter treats nothing of the past rivalry between the two schools except their previous game this season. His story, although short, is well written; it is likely that he was unable to bring in important details because of the requirements of space. The pressure of other stories is a major factor in determining a story's length.

Bears Seek SIAC Title, Tie in City Competition

By TED LOCKYEAR

EXAMPLE
116

All Indiana basketeers will have their eyes focused on Central gym tonight to determine which Evansville team is the best. The spoils of tonight's game are the SIAC championship and either a complete city title to Bosse, or Central sharing it with Bosse.

In their latest showing, the Bulldogs beat Reitz 46 to 31 for their fifth city win. In their last showing the Bears rolled over Wiley of Terre Haute 50 to 19 for their eighth straight victory.

The Bears will be out to avenge their only loss of the season, a loss to these same Bulldogs. Since January 4 when these two teams last

188

met, Bosse has been beaten by New Albany, while the Bears have gone undefeated. The score of the first game between these two teams was 46-34.

Clarence Riggs, former Central second team coach, is the Bulldog's coach and usually starts Butterfield, DeGroote, Holder, Axford, and either Buck or Jerrel. Bill Butterfield, six feet, five inch center, is the Bulldog's big gun. In 16 games this year he has scored 220 points. Central's point scorer is Bob Kohlmeyer, who has scored 182 points.

IN SIAC standings Central is in first place, and Bosse is in second. A Central win would give the Bears undisputed claim to first place. Bosse's five wins and no losses puts them atop the heap in city standing, and Central's four wins and one loss puts them in second place. A Central victory would enable them to tie for the city title.

In the Associated Press poll of sports writers this week, Bosse is in second place, and Central is in third in the Indiana state ratings. Elkhart is in first place.

Coach Glen Bretz's starting lineup will be Bob Kohlmeyer and Joe Keener at the forwards, Gene Southwood, promising sophomore, at center, and Captain Frank Schwitz and Chuck LaMar at the guards.

Paul Forney, Central athletic manager, announced that the game has been a sellout since Monday. Only 4400 fans were able to obtain ducats.

The Centralian
Central High School
Evansville, Indiana

Although not at all a common practice, one reporter solved his problem of relative merits of past and coming games by combining them into one story. Notice that he begins with the new, the coming events, and concludes with the past game. (See Example 117.)

Other means may be used to build up interest in a coming game. Example 118 occupied the top half of one inside page of the *Liberty Life,* Liberty High School, Bethlehem, Pennsylvania. A similar display covering the rest of the starting players occupied the top half of the facing page. Example 119 features the coming game in an all-out coverage on the sports page.

Example 120 displays a pictorial build-up of the basketball season on an inside page of the Bethesda Chevy-Chase High School *Tattler;* this advance was in addition to the sports page.

A careful analytical comparison of the players opposing each other in the coming game is common in school papers. Although not an integral part of the advance story, it supports it as a supplementary feature. (See Example 121.)

Indians on the Warpath

EXAMPLE
117

The North Central Indians, victorious in six out of seven pre-season starts, leave this afternoon for Mason City, where tonight they will play the first of three games in a barnstorming tour of eastern and central Washington.

Coach Bob Brumblay will take ten men on the trip, including four pivots and six smaller men. Tomorrow the Red and Black squad moves on to Chelan, meeting the Chelan Goats in what should prove to be one of the toughest pre-season games for the Indian team.

On Sunday the team will lay over in Chelan, traveling to Omak on Monday to take on the Omak Pioneers in their third and final game of the road trip.

The North Central team will return to Spokane on Tuesday to eat Christmas dinner at home, but return to action again on Thursday when they open the West Valley Invitational tournament against the Rogers Pirates.

On Saturday, January 14, the Indians travel to Moscow, Idaho, to meet Moscow high. The City league opens on January 10, with the Red and Black five meeting the always-tough Lewis and Clark Tigers on the Armory floor.

Beat Kellogg, 33-23

Pouring 14 points through the hoop in the final quarter, the North Central Indians defeated the Kellogg Wildcats, 33-23, Friday, December 12, on the Wildcats' home floor.

The home team was held to three field goals for the evening, but made 17 out of 30 gift shots good.

The North Central News
North Central High School
Spokane, Washington

EXAMPLE
118

WANTED — THESE MEN FOR A BIG HURRICANE VICTORY

WANTED

A win for the Bethlehem Hurricanes!

Description: "Doc" Sydorak is the coach of the Red and Blue team. He is 5'9" and weighs in at 185 pounds. He has brown hair and brown eyes. He can usually be seen in the Athletic office or the football locker room.

He gives his opinion of the team is. "We had hard luck all year but have a good group of hard workers. We had a good season with some luck, but fumbles have been the biggest problem.

WANTED

A victory. Joseph Mucka, tackle, number 49, shares the wish of all LHS students; a victory.

General description: stands at 6', weighs in at 180 pounds, has brown hair and hazel eyes.

Joe says, "It isn't as bad as the record shows," when asked his opinion of the team.

He is also in room 211 with Bob Muschlitz and Tom Mraz.

WANTED

All Thomas Denofa wants is to win if its by one point or fifty points.

Description—Tom is a big 6'1½" left halfback on the Red and Blue football team. He weighs in at 175 pounds. He is awarded with brown eyes and brown hair.

He can be found out on the football field in the Hurricane uniform with its number 18 or around homeroom 309.

WANTED

A win of about 51-14 with 200 yds. rushing.

Description: Charles Horwath has brown hair and hazel eyes. He is a big 6 foot and has a weight of 162 pounds.

Chas can usually be found on the Hurricane football field in jersey number 19 playing left halfback on the Red and Blue team.

In school he can be seen around the vacinity of homeroom 104.

WANTED

A LHS victory over Bill Allen.

Brian Walker, like everyone else at Liberty, wants a victory over William Allen High School.

Walker is 5'10" tall and weighs in at 178 pounds. He plays guard on the Hurricane Red and Blue football team.

He can be found around the vicinity of homerooms 217A and 217B.

WANTED

A shutout. A score of 60-0 and to chase Wm. Allen right out of the stadium.

Description: Terry Vitex is 5'11" tall and has a weight of 165 pounds. He has brown hair and brown eyes.

If not found around the general area of homeroom 36 he can be found on the LHS football field wearing the Hurricane jersey number 20 playing quarterback for his school.

Liberty Life
Liberty High School
Bethlehem, Pennsylvania

Dynos Meet Hoover at Bowl;
33rd Renewal Held Under Sun
SPORTS

Hoover Water Polo Team
Trounces Glendale College

Hoover's water polo team demonstrated how great its power is Wednesday, November 1, when it downed the Glendale College team, 16-10! The previous Friday the team easily disposed of the other team from across town, Glendale High School, 19-1.

Rich McGeagh's power was just too much for the college to handle, as he racked up 6 points. Bill Krause and Bill Craig each contributed 4 points and Brad Smith rounded out the total with 2 more counters.

The Tornadoes also proved to be too strong for the brand new Glendale High squad as they swarmed in for 8 points in the first quarter and built up a 11-1 lead at the half. The aquamen added another in the third quarter and then finished the last quarter with 7 more, making a total of 19-1.

Colts Beat Bees
Streak Ended

The galloping Colts of John Muir High swept the Moyse Field gridiron, Friday, November 3, handing the Hoover Bees a 20-7 loss, their second defeat of the season.

Cyclone machine was considerably weakened without the ... of injured first-stringers. Gary Munson, Audie Hicks, and Bob Haynes, and was unable to halt the speed of the Muir eleven.

Having won 14 in a row, one short of a new Hoover Bee record, the Cyclones came out on the counters.

McGeagh again led the Tornadoes with 5 points, followed closely by Bill Craig and Brad Smith with 4 apiece. Bill Krause and Larry Raymond had 2 each, and Bill Jonkey and Jim Black each contributed 1.

The Hoover Bee team finished the day off right by also walloping Glendale, 14-1. Kris Storm led the team with 6 points.

Water Polo Results	
Hoover -	36
Glendale -	3

FOOTHILL LEAGUE STANDINGS

Team	W.	L.	T.
Muir	5	0	0
Glendale	4	1	0
Pasadena	3	1	1
Burbank	2	3	0
Crescenta	2	3	0
Burroughs	1	4	0
HOOVER	0	4	1

Tornadoes Must Hold
To Upset Dynamiters
By LANNY LAISON

To say Hoover will be facing one of its stiffest challenges tomorrow afternoon would be superfluous.

The prospects are anything but good, that the Tornadoes will be the victors in the contest. The local writers are guessing Hoover will lose by at least one touchdown, and many say the contest will be nothing to watch because Glendale will so dominate play.

This year Hoover has risen well in the face of imminent disaster. Tying a tough Pasadena team was no mean accomplishment. There was a let down in the Burbank and Burroughs games, but the varsity fought back to hold Muir for almost three periods to a 7-0 score. With such a record as this, it might be possible for the Purples to stage one of the surprises of the year on Coach Roy Vujovich's charges.

In rivalries such as this one, it is often the perfect place for a complacent team to fall prey to the team that "just couldn't win in a hundred games." Despite the fact the Hoover Tornadoes aren't favored, the game will be a good one, and there is always that chance of an upset victory for Coach Bisminski's fighting team.

Players Comment

We recently asked some members of the starting varsity eleven to give us a brief statement about the game tomorrow. Here are their replies:

Dick Fortner, QB, 5'10", 165 lbs. Jr.—"The Glendale High game is always a good game. Hoover wants the victory Bell and is willing to fight for it. So anything can happen and I think it will."

Bob Williams, RH, 6'2", 190 lbs. Sr.—"We will give Glendale a good game. We have steadily improved since the Muir game."

Frank Shandra, RG, 5'8", 2nd lbs. Sr.—"If we toughen up, play up to par, we will beat Glendale."

Bob Mallory, LH, 5'10", 160 lbs. Sr.—"If we work hard and really want to win, we will."

Ron Hatfield, FB, 6'0, 200 lbs. Jr.—"I think that our team will stand a chance against Glendale if our offense moves and our defense holds. If we play this game as we did the first half of the Muir game, this season won't be lost."

Lee Galloway, FB, 6'1", 180 lbs. Sr.—"We are going to have to play our best game to beat Glendale. We have not played our best game yet, and I think we will against Glendale."

PROBABLE VARSITY STARTERS

	Pos.	Ht.	Wt.	Yr.	No.
Dick Fortner	QB	5'10	160	Jr	10
Lee Galloway	FB	6'1	180	Sr	24
Bob Williams	LH	6'2	190	Sr	42
Gary Didden	RH	6'2	190	Sr	45
John Read	LG	6'1	188	Sr	68
Craig Lorentzen	OT	6'1	215	Jr	70
Fred Fuller	C	5'10	160	Jr	32
Mark Krissdor	RE	6'0	180	Sr	86
Jerre Hershman	LE	6'0	170	Sr	85
Joe Green	IT	5'9	200	Sr	63
Eric Fiedler	RG	5'7	168	Sr	62

EXAMPLE 119

Blanchard Runner Up
With Team at Mt. SAC
By TOM DAVIS

What is it like to run against 11 schools with 77 runners in one race? The Hoover cross country team found out Saturday, October 28, at the Mt. San Antonio College Invitational Cross Country Meet. And the team came back with a 2nd place trophy for its effort.

Bob Blanchard led the Tornadoes, finishing 2nd, with a time of 9:04.5. Bob was followed by Phil Anderson 4th, Bob Gillies, 16th, Hap Moon, 23rd, Gary Hicks, 24th, Terry Brager, 28th, and Rick Budke, 54th.

In the junior varsity race, Hoover took 4th as the Cyclones finished as follows: John Carrera, 31st, Doug McChesney, 38th, Jim Herold, 40th, John Rutledge, 50th, Dave Kepler, 61st, and John Roberts, 76th.

The Thursday before, the Tornadoes downed Muir at their Oak Grove Park course, 43-19. Blanchard led the pack, running 8:44. Bob Gillies and Phil Anderson finished 3rd and 4th, running 9:01 and 9:04 respectively. The rest of the team finished as follows: Hap Moon, 5th, Terry Brager, 6th, Gary Hicks, 7th, and Bill Baribault, 9th.

Rick Budke led the junior varsity as they also dumped the Mustangs with a score of 44-22. Budke won the race with a good time of 9:38.

BOB MALLORY
GARY DIDDEN
JEWEL TREAT
JOHN READ
FRED POPPE
ERIC FIEDLER
JACK BONHAM

from top to bottom
these senior members of
Hoover Varsity football

EXAMPLE 120

Purple Press
Herbert Hoover High School
Glendale, California

Spirited Crowd Follows Bethesda Cagemen

● COACH FLORIS DAVISSON explains some of the tactics to be used in the next day's game.

● CLIMAXING MONTHS OF PRACTICE and planning by Coach Floris Davisson and his squad, the Baron basketball team comes out on the court to try for another win. This game is one in a long season's effort to retain the Maryland State Basketball Championship.

A GREAT CHEER of appreciation welcomes the cagemen. During the early minutes of the game, the crowd is silent, concentrating on the team's opening play. Midway through the second period comes a sudden burst of pent-up feeling as the crowd screams its approval or disappointment.

USUALLY, the half-time rest during which Coach Davisson reviews the team's first half play

and shows them how they can improve it in the second half, gives a new life to the team. They come back to win another exciting game, or as has happened, the team fights back, but still loses in the final seconds, leaving the fans depressed.

BUT, WIN OR LOSE, the cheerleaders, the home pep band, and the entire student body are behind their team, hoping for another Baron victory at College Park.

● MIKE BRADDOCK AND PAUL RICKER practice jumping with Coach Davisson acting as referee.

● DURING TIME OUT cheerleaders Ana Soi, Vicky Tini, and Marrlyt Riepert enthusiastically lead the students in cheers.

● TIMEKEEPER AL SADUSKY confers with the referee during time out.

● STUDENTS' FACES SHOW concern and then happiness as the Barons tie a close game.

● BARONS BRAD BROOKS and Eddie Austin guard their men closely in an attempt to hold down their opponents' score.

The Tattler
West Technical High School
Cleveland, Ohio

191

MAN TO MAN

By WAYNE DODD and GEORGE WRIGHT, Sports Editors

EXAMPLE

121

HUNTINGTON PARK		WASHINGTON
Jack Hamilton, 180	LER	John McLaughlin, 180
Glue fingers		Basket hands
EDGE—Even		
Steve Wellman, 200	LTR	Bob Johnson, 195
Could be rough		Top notch starter
EDGE—Even		
Armand Lucier, 175	LGR	Ted Davis, 170
Great against Narbonne		Could upset
EDGE—Lucier		
Darryl Anderson, 183	C	Mike Carlson, 175
Returning letterman		Could get beat
EDGE—Anderson		
Ron Dain, 182	RGL	Rich Wilson, 175
Extra point man		Nothing but determination
EDGE—Wilson		
George Hood, 210	RTL	Norm Budman, 210
Won't be hiding		Should be good battle
EDGE—Even		
Bill Stupin, 185	REL	Ken Stumpf, 190
Will be stumpfin		Will stumpf him
EDGE—Stumpf		
Mike McKee, 160	QB	Rodney Martinez, 169
A real good one		Has done outstanding job
EDGE—Even		
Bryan Collin, 164	LHR	Andy Anderson, 185
Poor guy		Gained over 200 yds. vs. S.G.
EDGE—Anderson		
Larry Eckenrocke, 160	RHL	Estes Banks, 180
Scored two last week		In rotating spot
EDGE—Banks		
Rosco Moore, 180	FB	Andy Piligian, 190
Will be bucking		Scored last week
EDGE—Piligian		

PREDICTED SCORE
21 HUNTINGTON PARK WASHINGTON 18

The Surveyor
George Washington High School
Los Angeles, California

Fairness predominates on the sports pages of student newspapers. Seldom is an unsportsmanlike statement made; seldom does the reporter belittle his rival school's team.

192

In sports, as in straight news, the play the story gets depends upon the public's interest. This may be original interest or interest created by a clever reporter. The paper should take advantage of the school's feature sport, which may change from year to year depending upon the ability of the team. Intramural contests and minor sports must not be neglected. Placing these sports in a prominent position on the page may mean placing them in a prominent position in the reader's mind. The comparative value of events is a constant problem for the sports editor. Is the significance of the past game overshadowed by the fact that the readers saw the game and it is now yesterday's news? How many readers will be interested in the story? The ingenuity of the reporter is the determining factor.

THE SPORTS FEATURE

The true sports enthusiast never finds too much to read about his subject. The straight news facts may be limited, but there is no limit to the side feature angles that a clever reporter can use.

For instance, school papers have long overlooked the news interest in sports officials. Who are these men who appear during the season? What are their problems? What is interesting about them?

Who else connected with athletics can be interviewed? What small or large event has a lot of human interest in it? In what statistical material would the fan be interested?

Examples 122 through 126 only indicate the unlimited field for featuring sports coverage: sports in other lands, interesting things about the coaches, the athletes themselves, the physical condition of the team, and more. The feature field of sports coverage is limited only by the reporter's imagination.

Try Bandy, It's Hockey

By Natalie Gelman

Man, like bandy!

No, it isn't beatnik lingo, nor a new science course to be of-fered at Mumford next year. It's not a language and it's not a dress fad, but it is a sport, in Wales, that is. In America it's usually known as field hockey.

EXAMPLE
122

193

This game is known by various names in different countries. In Ireland it would be called hurley, and in Scotland it would be described as shinty. The actual word hockey came from the Old French word *hoquet*, which means shepherd's crook.

The exact origin of the game isn't known. Ancient Greeks carved friezes showing players hitting at a small object with curved sticks. However, the modern game may be considered a late nineteenth century development.

At first field hockey was only played by men, but it was tried out by women in the 1800's. It was introduced into the United States in 1901 and grew in popularity in women's colleges and high schools.

In 1922, the Field Hockey Association was organized in the United States as the ruling body for the game.

Today, field hockey is primarily a women's game. In the United States, a similar game played by men is known as shinny.

The rules for the original game of field hockey are used for the modern game played now in the United States. A true understanding of the game can be obtained by attending the Mumford field hockey games played by the girls weekly at the beginning of each school year.

The Mercury
Mumford High School
Detroit, Michigan

IT RUNS IN THE FAMILY
Addington Burns up Track

EXAMPLE
123

Jack Addington of the Cody track team is continuing a family tradition by winning two letters in track and one in cross country.

Four consecutive generations of his family have been runners.

Four times around the track seems a short trip for Addington, who runs the 440-yard dash in 53.7 seconds. He can do the 220-yard dash in a fast 22.9 seconds.

"There was a great response to Coach Bob McCullough's call for trackmen last season. If the freshmen stay and work hard, we'll have a good team."

McCullough used new training methods which should pay off this year, Addington believes.

"An outdoor track is really needed at Cody. If home meets could be held here, students would take a lot more interest.

Addington is president of the Varsity "C" Club.

In addition to school activities, he has attained the rank of an Eagle Scout, the highest rank in the Boy Scouts.

Addington will soon make a decision between science, health education, or medicine as his field of study in college. He will attend Michigan State University.

His other interests include swimming, basketball, and badminton. Baking and singing are two of his hobbies.

The Cody Star
Frank Cody High School
Detroit, Michigan

194

Students' Fitness Tested

"We have to run 600 **whats?**" "Yards," says Billy B. Barnes, boys' physical education instructor at Hillcrest. The run was part of the physical fitness tests designated by A. A. Bushman, director of the physical education department of the Dallas public schools. Similar tests are being given to all Dallas students from the fourth grade through high school.

In addition to the run, the tests included pull-ups, or reverse chins, push-ups, and sit-ups in a two minutes' period. The following boys have established records in the boys' gym classes.

EXAMPLE

124

	Seniors	Juniors	Sophomores
600 yd. run	John Hogan, Phil Baerris—1:30	Joe Weir—1:22	Mike West—1:30
Pull-ups	Dickey Fine—15	Bill Merriman—17	Rusty Green—20
Push-ups	Dickey Fine—73	Richard Lewis—61	Rusty Green—56
Sit-ups	Pat Jessmer—95	Keith Tucker—90	Pat Bishop—106

The Hillcrest Hurricane
Hillcrest High School
Dallas, Texas

Time of Year Brings Crutches, Bandages

By JIM MARTI

Everybody knows that high school football is no sissy sport, but it seems that just as love "blooms" in the spring, football graces the fall with its annual assortment of crutches, plaster casts, and other selected maladies.

Relates varsity football coach "Gus" Spraker: "Football is a rough contact sport, and various accidents happen. Everybody has a sprain, sore muscle, or lacerated hand at one time or another. Right now we're pretty lucky in that Bill Plummer is our only major casualty."

SPRAINS, TORN LIGAMENTS

Plummer, one of the many prospects for the fullback position, has a torn ligament and will be out for most of the season.

"I was making a tackle in a practice scrimmage and twisted my knee," explained Bill, who has since relinquished his crutches and is back on his two feet again.

JINX CONTINUES

B-11 varsity tackles Ed Hlava and Dan Palmer are two other innocent victims of the pre-season jinx. Hlava is suffering from a bad knee which he injured in last year's Lincoln Bee game, while Palmer is bothered by inflamed leg muscles.

Varsity left halfback John Tovar and fullback Ed Akman both suffered brain concussions on the same day of practice, but both

EXAMPLE

125

195

have recuperated sufficiently and are "ready and rarin" for the league opener.

BEES PLAGUED

The Bee football squad has really been plagued by injuries as five of the seven returning lettermen missed the opening encounter against Glendale Hoover. All of the Bee ailments, however, are expected to be remedied by the time of the league opener next week.

Safety Gilbert Martinez, half-back Ernie Heredia, and tackle Bob Muniz have all been pestered by pulled muscles, while end standout Oscar Dominguez is annoyed by a back strain.

Rolland Lopez, an all-league prospect, chose a more colorful method of being sidelined. The nonconforming tailback, in pursuit of a soft drink, slipped on the cement and broke his ankle. He is also expected to show his potential before the opening league game with Lincoln.

Franklin Press
Franklin High School
Los Angeles, California

Qualifications of an Athlete Do You Meet Them?

By FRED CALDWELL

EXAMPLE
126

Wearing a uniform and being a member of the squad does not imply that one is an athlete. To be a winner in athletics, and life as well, there are important things one must think about. There are ten questions to ask oneself if one is interested in turning out for athletics.

1. Can the prospect take criticism without looking for an alibi?

2. Does the candidate have the desire to win which is provoked by the spirit of competition?

3. Is the probable athlete willing to practice with all his enthusiasm, and not just report every day and put in the necessary time?

4. Is there a willingness to sacrifice personal interests in order to remain in tip-top condition?

5. Does an ardent desire to improve exist?

6. Does the prospect have the ability to think under stress?

7. Can the prospective athlete keep personal feelings about the opponent out of his mind?

8. Is there belief in the school, the team, and the coach by the athlete-to-be?

9. Is the candidate willing to study as hard as he did before turning out for the sport?

10. Will the athlete-to-be strive daily to improve co-ordination and speed?

It is the coaches' belief that if a student can fill these qualifications, he should be capable of participating in athletics.

The Lincoln Totem
Lincoln High School
Seattle, Washington

196

The sports column. A popular column in the school newspaper is the sports column—written entirely by the sports writer, who comments on the passing field of sports and gives interesting sidelights that may be drawn from sports history. An interesting and stimulating column can draw great reader following, but it must be more than a repetition of the feature points of the games brought out on the sports page in the regular coverage of the news.

The advisability of carrying a sports column depends completely upon the abilities found within the department. Due to limited space in most newspapers, there is usually only one sports column in the paper, most often conducted by the sports editor; there are, however, exceptions.

Examples 127 and 128 illustrate the type of sports column that draws reader interest in schools from coast to coast.

a great dey for

.... From JIM DEY

EXAMPLE

127

LETTING THE CUP RUN OVER

Congratulations are in order for the hockey team after winning the city conference title for the first time since 1950. The Prexies simply outclassed the league, scoring 42 goals in eight games. . . . Also congratulate John Mc-Manus, the smiling Irishman who started out with nothing and built a large wrestling team. In case you haven't seen a match, this isn't the same brand of acting those clowns on television hand out. . . . Save a few for the bucket team which has busted its post-vacation jinx by winning its last two games, scoring 112 points in them.

THINGS HEARD IN THE LOCKER ROOM AND RINGING IN THE HALLS

The basketball team almost busted another jinx: they usually win only when Curley is on with the three stooges, but the boys beat Monroe when Shep was on . . . . Wash has sold as many hockey tickets as Johnson, a school twice our size . . .

RUMORS AND REFLECTIONS

. . . . John Mc Manus' wrestling program will pay big dividends on the gridiron . . . the swimming team will never finish lower than fourth . . . . Wash and Johnson will be playing for the region 4 crown—Wash by 2 points—Johnson has goalie trouble . . . . if the bucket team plays at Como as they played in practise, look out in the plays-offs . . . . Wash will have one of its strongest football teams ever this fall . . . . Mr. Turner won't really quit hockey after this season.

The Surveyor
George Washington High School
St. Paul, Minnesota

197

A Question in Passing

by Ernie Taverner

EXAMPLE

128

As we reach the mid-point of the FHS sports year, there are a number of questions I should like to ask. These questions are not directed to any particular individual, but . . .

How can we as students of Frederick High School have school spirit, support our team, and complete homework assignments in time to play in or attend a game on a week night?

What are the chances that the Cadet Varsity hoopsters will place fourth or better in CVAL standings?

Is it possible that the FHS cinder grinders will better the records set by the grinders last season?

Who supports the team at the away games? Are you loyal to your school and team? Do you make an honest effort to attend the road games to cheer your team?

Has the eligibility ruling caused you—as a student of FHS—to study harder in order to be able to participate in extracurricular activities?

Is the seeming lack of school spirit due to the obvious lack of pep rallies?

High Flier
Frederick High School
Frederick, Maryland

The editorial. The school paper has more of an obligation than just covering the news; it has the obligation of keeping school spirit at the proper pitch, of furthering worthy school activities, and of being an enthusiastic booster at all times. In other words, it has the responsibility of promotion. The advance story, when treated at length and placed in a prominent position, acts as a promotion story. An editorial may also serve in this capacity. Editorials also serve as platforms from which to raise sports issues and suggest their solutions. Examples 129 and 130 are typical sports editorials.

The season's review. The review is a type of feature story worthy of separate attention. Any sports season is subject for a review article on the significance of the season. Once the football team has hung up its uniforms and the school has turned to basketball, there is still an opportunity for the sports department of the paper to take one parting glance back. Examples 131 and 132 are typical "Season's Reviews."

MAKE IT OR BREAK IT

Never have the stakes been so high as they will be today when two fired-up football squads take the field at Kezar Stadium. The outcome of this clash could very conceivably lead the winner to the city championship.

Both Lincoln and Lowell are far overdue for a championship. Lowell has not seen the winner's flag since 1942, while the Mustangs have failed to reach the top rung of the ladder since 1943. Today's game will put one team into the Thanksgiving Day play-offs at Kezar Stadium. The winner of this contest is assured of at least a co-championship for the 1961 AAA season.

Lincoln's hopes will depend largely on the performances of its four possible all-city men: Pat Lewis, Norm Gatzert, Jim Busher, and Dave Conway. Still, this game is the type which cannot be won by a single player. If the Links are to come home victorious, it will have to be a team effort all the way.

Much of the credit for the fine performance of the team this year must be given to sophomore coach Bill Holland. Through his wise leadership and all-around know-how, he has brought a team which was supposed to be no better than mediocre to within one victory of a place in the Championship Game.

Team Needs Support

One point which has been stressed throughout the entire season must be especially remembered today. A team cannot win without people supporting it. The *Log* staff would like to take this opportunity to ask everyone who possibly can to attend the game today. This is a situation in which a loss today will end any hope for tomorrow. Don't plan on missing today's contest and then going to the Thanksgiving Day game "if they make it."

The Lincoln Log
Lincoln High School
San Francisco, California

EXAMPLE
129

Are Half-Court Cage Victories Sporting?

Would you expect a football player to run 200 yards for a touchdown? Or a tennis player to hit the ball over a ten-foot net? Or a baseball player to run five bases for a home run?

Of course not.

Then why would it be any more logical for a basketball player to be subjected to various lengths on the court?

For instance, in 7-AA basketball, a player must be adept on all sizes of courts, ranging from Carter-Riverside's half-court game to Tech's proxy court at J. P. Elder.

Carter's court is twenty feet too small, Poly's is ten feet too small, and Elder and North Side's gyms are fifteen feet smaller than the legendary regulation size court.

While Paschal's court is regulation size, only five of the district's ten games are played there; and Texas Christian University's

EXAMPLE
130

199

regulation size gym is rarely used.

All of which returns us to the ever-obvious conclusion. No matter which court a cage team works out on, they are not familiar with the gym they play 7-AA games on, unless they play at home.

The problem looked as if it were solved with the erection of the regulation size Coliseum court, but it soon became evident that the Coliseum would only be used for crowd-drawing games.

So the season has passed, and as so often in the preceding years there is still no regulation court that everyone has access to.

It is our hope, by starting this early campaign, that by next year Fort Worth will have a universal regulation basketball court where no team can coast to a victory just because of the gym's size.

The Pantherette
Paschal High School
Fort Worth, Texas

Harriers Capture League

EXAMPLE 131

Coach Raleigh Holt's cross country team brought home an Eastern League championship for Hoover as the Harriers defeated Lincoln High School in their final league meet of the season. The victory gave the Redbirds their eleventh league championship in the past twelve years and left them with a perfect 4-0 mark for league competition.

Both teams had compiled a record of 3-0 as they went into the meet held November 10, at Morley Field.

Sterling Jenkins and Larry Gaughen again led the Cardinals as they took first and second times of 10:32 and 10:42, respectively. Jenkins' time was the best of the season, while Gaughen equaled his top time.

John Garrison raced to place fourth with a time of 11:25 to clinch the win for the Cardinals.

The Redbird junior varsity squad was also able to stay undefeated by routing the Lincoln junior varsity team with a 20-38 victory.

Previously, Coach Holt had taken his squad to Mt. San Antonio for the Mt. San Antonio meet held October 29. The meet included schools from over the Southern California area.

Hoover compiled a score of 80 and took a close third behind Milikan of Long Beach and Santa Monica, who had scores of 74 and 79, respectively.

The Cardinals and San Diego High School, which placed eleventh without a score, were the only teams from the San Diego area in that race.

In the Aztec Invitational, held November 3 at Morley Field, the Harriers placed fourth in a field of ten schools.

Helix took first followed by Point Loma and Grossmont.

Jenkins and Gaughen again were the top runners for the Cardinals with times of 10:35 and 10:53. Garrison and Cobbs followed with times of 11:12 and 11:27, respectively.

This Friday the Cards go into the league finals; the following Saturday they enter the CIFSD meet to conclude the season.

The Cardinal
Herbert Hoover High School
San Diego, California

200

SLUGGERS, PIPP TOP PURGOLDERS' ATTACK

Tom Pipp's championship pitching and high-caliber slugging by John La Prest, Ray Tevich, and Dennis Williamson were vital factors in the Local diamondmen's successful quest for their second consecutive city crown under Coach Chuck Bilek.

Although the Tonians' 17–5 record left them a full two games ahead of second-place Juneau at the season's end, they never even held first place until June 6, when Pipp handcuffed King, 8–2.

This victory gave the team a 9–1 record and the league lead, which they never relinquished. Don Heinritz, La Prest, and Tevich all clouted homers to pace the win, with La Prest's three-run blast in the second inning the big blow in a six-run rally.

Although Riverside spoiled the Purgolders' climb to the top, 2–1, three days later, the diamondmen bounced back by edging out West, 3–2, in a ten-inning affair. Williamson led the modest Tonian attack with a pair of singles, while Pipp struck out 20 batters en route to victory.

Lincoln fell victim to Washington's steamroller, 14–0, June 26, as Pipp and Williamson combined to pitch a no-hitter, with Tom starting the first two frames and the Locals' star shortstop handling the last five.

Pipp next tripped up Juneau, 5–0, on three hits, June 28, and followed with a 6–1 drubbing of Tech two nights later.

Williamson topped the Purgold onslaught against Tech, batting in three runs on three hits, including a two-run round tripper.

After losing to Custer, 10–4, and whipping Pulaski, 7–1, the Boulevarders toppled Bay View, 4–1, on July 10.

Once again Williamson belted a homer in the first with a mate aboard and repeated his three hit, three RBI performance.

However, the Local nine continued fumbling around, dropping a pair of 3–2 decisions to cellar-ridden South July 12, and to North two nights later.

The diamondmen clinched the title in the next to the last game of the season, walloping King, 11-2, behind Pipp's six-hitter.

Almost everyone on the team hit the Generals' ace, Bob Stadler,

Final Baseball Standings

Team	Record	
WASHINGTON	17	- 5
Juneau	15	- 7
Custer	14	- 8
King	13½	- 8½
Bay View	13	- 9
West	12	- 10
Boys' Tech	11½	- 10½
Pulaski	11½	- 10½
East	7½	- 14½
Lincoln	7	- 14
North	7	- 15
South	2	- 19

hard, with Williamson and Mark Wasserman gathering three hits apiece, the latter five RBI's.

The 4-0 whitewashing of Riverside in the season finale was typical of another successful baseball campaign under Coach Bilek.

The Washington Scroll
Washington High School
Milwaukee, Wisconsin

EXAMPLE
132

201

CHAPTER LABORATORY

1. Attend the next school athletic event, take careful, detailed notes, and write a 300-word account of the event.
2. What percentage of the copy in your school paper is devoted to sports? Would you consider a shift in emphasis? Write a sports editorial of 200 words on the subject.
3. Select the sports pages of two good daily papers, compare them, and list the merits of each.
4. Write a 250-word advance story on a coming event, using facts, not mere opinion.
5. Compose a sports column of at least four different items. Make it timely.
6. Look through the exchange papers, and find one that is either better or worse than your own school paper in sports coverage. Compare them in class discussion.
7. List six good subjects for sports features that might appear during the next month. Select ten of these subjects from the entire class and discuss.
8. Write one of the stories, selected in Exercise 7, using from 100 to 300 words depending upon the need of the subject.
9. Bring the columns of two good daily sports writers to class. List the points that make their columns good.
10. Ask one of the coaches to talk to the class. Take notes and write some sports copy for the paper from his remarks. Indicate the type of story.

PART THREE
EDITING
AND PRESENTING
THE NEWS

"Has any reader ever found perfect accuracy
in the newspaper account
of any event of which he himself
had inside knowledge?"
—EDWARD VERRALL LUCAS

14 COPYREADING AND PROOFREADING

The operation of a newspaper resembles a wheel. At the hub are the editors who assign stories and then check the copy when it is returned. These editors are the "sitters."

The "runners," or legmen, are the reporters, the spokes of the wheel working out from the editor's desk and returning with copy. The rim of the wheel represents the limits of news coverage; for regardless of the broad interests of the students, a school newspaper has its particular field of coverage.

At the hub of the newspaper operation are the editors, copyreaders, and proofreaders. They are the people who receive the miscellaneous stories from the reporters, check them for authenticity and correct usage, and follow the copy on through to publication.

THE COPY DESK

Whether on a daily or a school paper, somebody acts as a copyreader to check the story turned in by the reporter. The title of the position is not important, for it may vary. What is important is the function of the position.

Every piece of copy that goes into the paper has to be carefully checked for errors before it is set in type. The person who reads the copy and makes the corrections is a copyreader. His equipment includes: (1) a style sheet that indicates the style the paper follows; (2) a knowledge of the few standard copyreading marks; (3) a dictionary; (4) a soft, black pencil; (5) a sense of news; and (6) good judgment.

Following a piece of copy. On the daily paper a story, typed double or triple space, goes to a desk known as the copy desk where it is read and corrected, headlines are added, and the copy is sent on to the linotypist. Many school papers have copy desks, with students especially designated as copyreaders. Others build their staffs around page editors, with the page assistants copyreading their respective pages.

Here is part of a story, typed double space, as it appears at the copy desk:

```
1.                    Taft Highs' anual, the Tiger,
2.   has received the Medalist Award from the columbia
3.   Scholastic Association.  This ix the highest award
4.   a High school yearbo ok can recieve.  Books posses-
5.   ing meritoriusqualities aboveand beyond the BAsic
6.   technical technical requirements be may selected
7.   form the ist place rateings for Medalist, and
8.   olny one percentage of those books submitted are
9.   good enough to receive the Medalist Award.
```

The copyreader marks his corrections, line for line.

```
1.                    Taft Highs' anual, the Tiger,
```

Through carelessness the writer has transposed the *s* and the apostrophe in "High's." Instead of writing over the letters, the editor adds a transpose mark (∩∪) which tells the printer that the letter and the punctuation mark must be reversed. The caret (∧) indicates that an omitted letter, or word, is written above it.

205

2. has received the Medalist Award from the c̲o̲l̲umbia

The three lines under "c" means capitalize to the printer.

3. Scholastic ⌃Association. This i⤫ the highest award

Press (above caret), *s* (above x)

The word *Press* has been omitted, and the editor indicates its addition by inserting a caret with the word written above the line. The misspelling of *is* is corrected by drawing a caret through the *x* and writing *s* above the caret.

¶ 4. a ⫽High school yearbo͡ok can recⁱeiⱽve. ⌊Books posses-

The diagonal line through the *H* indicates that it is to be a small letter. The curved lines between the *o's* in yearbook indicate that the space is to be deleted and the letters drawn together. A transpose mark is again used to correct the misspelling of receive. The editor wants the sentence beginning "Books . . ." to start a new paragraph and marks it accordingly.

5. ing meritori⤬us|qualities above|and beyond the B̸Asic

o (above)

The vertical line indicates a separation of letters or words.

6. technical ~~technical~~ requirements ⌊be⌋ may⌋ selected

A line and a delete mark (⤳) indicate that technical is to be set only once.

7. fo̸r̸m the (1st) place ratⱽings for Medalist, and

The circle tells the printer to spell out the encircled word; the same sign tells the printer to abbreviate or set in digits a word or number already spelled out.

8. o̶n̶l̶y̶ (one) percentage⸒of those books submitted are

This circle says, "Set the word in figures."

9. good enough to receive the Medalist Award.

Copyreading marks. As timesavers, a few standard copyreading marks or symbols which are common to printers and reporters have been developed through usage. In editing copy, the copyreader uses these signs inside the body of the typed matter, enabling the linotypist to see the changes as they come in the copy. (See Example 133.)

206

COPYREADING MARKS

Three short lines under a letter or word indicate that it is to be capitalized.

A line drawn through a capital letter indicates that it is to be set as a small letter (lower case).

A circle drawn around a number or an abbreviation indicates that the word is to be spelled out.

A circle around a spelled-out number or word indicates that the item is to be set in figures or abbreviated.

A new paragraph is indicated by an angle mark inside the copy and a paragraph mark (¶) in the margin.

Words to be transposed are marked with a line extending over one word and under the other.

Curved lines connecting words indicate that the words are to be joined.

A vertical or oblique line between two letters indicates that they are to be separated.

Quotation marks are set off in v-shaped marks indicating that they are set above the line.

A cross or a period in a circle indicates a period.

Three lines under the initial letter and two lines beneath the rest of a word indicate that the word is to be set "caps and small caps"—the first letter a regular capital, the other letters smaller capitals.

A straight line under a word indicates that it is to be set in italic type.

A wavy line under a word indicates that it is to be set in boldface type.

A line called a "run-in" or "bridge" line is used to connect material that is to form a continuous line of type. Often, material between the two parts has been crossed out.

A caret indicates the place where additional copy, written above, is to be inserted.

Either of these marks in circles shows the story's end.

EXAMPLE
133

american

travel club

57

street

¶ now. Jones says

the boy new

class room

last night

pigskin

Avexor Ave.

The East High Record

By Jean Woods

Central High School

the basket.
Arad shot the

it
do today

30

207

Copyreading is exacting. The demands upon the copyreader are many: correcting punctuation, grammar, spelling, and rhetoric. He stands between the copy and the printed page, judging each story for its fitness for print.

He must have good news sense and readily detect violations of news style as well as violations of good judgment. He must be alert for inaccuracies and untruths, and see that all copy conforms to the policy as well as the style of the paper. He avoids tabulations in stories since they add white space in a column, contributing to a spotty appearance. For instance, he marks honor roll lists to be set in paragraph form, breaking the paragraph as needed for newspaper length.

He may have to condense or improve a story, *but his work is not to rewrite*. He marks the copy for the printer, indicating type sizes and faces, width of type page, and inserting subheads and by-lines where they are called for. He writes the headlines. He is guided by the style sheet as well as the dummy of the page for which he is editing copy.

Newspaper style. There is no right and wrong in newspaper style in those matters of punctuation, capitalization, and abbreviation in which alternate forms are generally accepted. But for the sake of uniformity, every newspaper must adopt its own style. Suppose, for example, that a reader found the term "basket ball" in one story in your paper, "basket-ball" in another, and "basketball" in still another. Each of these forms enjoys wide usage, but only one should be used in any newspaper. The English language contains many such examples, and there are similar problems in other areas such as punctuation. There is only one solution—the establishment of arbitrary rules or standards that will cover the majority of cases in which questions arise. In a sense, then, "style" is simply an established standard in those matters in which variable usage exists.

The style book. Every staff should develop a style book. This is something that will grow from semester to semester, and it should be revised whenever the material becomes obsolete. Such a style book may be a part or a section of the staff handbook, or it may be a separate publication.

But no staff need be without such an important guide. The Columbia Scholastic Press Association, Columbia University, New York City, issues such a booklet at a nominal fee. Its table of contents lists: Preparation of Copy, including Abbreviations, Titles, Capitalization, Dates, Compounds, Figures, Italics, and Paragraphs; Standard Forms for Preparing Copy; Punctuation; Use of Illustrations; Writing the Lead Paragraph; Headlines; Copyreading; Proofreading; and Glossary.

This small booklet has been through many editions, undergoing constant revision. A section, treating capitalization, follows:

Capitalization

Below in several instances two forms are given. The one labeled "Down Style" is preferable for newspapers. The other, designated "Up Style," is preferable for magazines. It is suggested that publications conform to the style preferred by the English Departments.

1. Capitalize *English, Latin, German, French, Spanish,* but not *art, astronomy, biology, botany, domestic science, general science, history, mathematics, science,* except when used as names of specific courses. Thus: *Algebra 1, Modern History 2.*

2. Do not capitalize the names of classes in the school: *freshman, sophomore, junior, senior,* or the *faculty.*

3. *Up style:* Capitalize the full name of a school: *Jonesville High School, Freeport Academy, Cornell University.*

Down Style: Do not capitalize words like *school, academy, university, college,* and the like, when they follow the name of the institution: *Jonesville high school, Freeport academy, Cornell university,* but *University of Pennsylvania.*

4. Do not capitalize *high school, academy, university, college,* and the like, when used as adjectives: *the high school team;* or when used without the distinguishing name: *the high school is new.*

5. *Up Style:* Capitalize the full names of associations, clubs, societies, and similar organizations: the *Nevada Athletic Association,* the *Smith Commercial Club,* the *Oriole Literary Society;* but write *the club will meet, the society will debate,* when these words are used without distinguishing adjectives.

Down Style: Do not capitalize the word *association, club, society,* and the like, in expressions such as the *Nevada Athletic association, the Smith Commercial club, the Oriole Literary society.*

6. *Up Style:* Capitalize the names of places in expressions such as: *the Gray Memorial Field, the Whitman Library, the Penfield Building.*

Down Style: Do not capitalize *field, library, building,* and the like, in expressions such as *the Gray Memorial field, the Whitman library, the Penfield building.*

7. *Up Style:* Capitalize the words *street, avenue, boulevard, road, lane,* and the like in addresses: *1309 Harrison Street, 5432 York Road.*

8. *Up Style:* Capitalize the words *river, lake, mountain, hill,* and the like, when they follow the name: *Delaware River, Rocky Mountains.*

Down Style: Do not capitalize the words *river, lake, mountain, hill,* and the like, when they follow the name: *Delaware river, Rocky mountains.*

9. Capitalize *gulf, lake, mount,* and the like, when they precede the name: *Gulf of Mexico, Lake of the Woods, Mount Whitney.*

10. Capitalize titles preceding a proper noun: *Coach Edgar A. Williams, President Ralph B. Johnson;* but do not capitalize such words when they follow the name: *Edgar A. Williams, coach; Ralph B. Johnson, president of the class.*

11. Capitalize all proper nouns, including names of months and days of the week.

12. Do not capitalize the names of the seasons, unless personified: *spring, summer, autumn, winter.*

13. Capitalize all words in titles of plays, songs, books, lectures, addresses, etc., including the initial words *A, An, The,* but not articles, prepositions, or conjunctions within the title: *The Spy;* but *The Last of the Mohicans.*

14. Capitalize the initial words *A, An, The* in titles of periodicals: *I saw it in The Times.*

15. Do not capitalize *north, south, east, west* and their compounds and derivatives, except when they designate divisions of the country.

16. *Up Style:* Capitalize *Christmas Day, Easter Day.*

17. Capitalize the names of all nationalities: *American, French, German, Japanese.*

18. Write *a. m., p. m.* (lower case letters, not capitals).

19. Do not capitalize *adviser* (note spelling is *-er,* not *-or*), *varsity* (no apostrophe), *commencement, room.*

20. Notice the use of capitals and lower case letters in expressions such as *ex-President Taft* (lower case *e,* hyphen, capital *P*).

WRITING—THE CORE OF JOURNALISM

Good, clear writing is a courtesy to the reader and a necessity to the writer. One writes as one speaks—to communicate. If one's writing is faulty, the reader will ignore it—or distrust what he is reading. Good

210

journalism requires good writing, but the rules of writing a newspaper story differ slightly from the rules of writing an essay or a composition. In both, good grammar is essential, but the structures of the compositions differ. Check your writing against the composition and grammar guideposts that follow:

Composition Guideposts—

1. Sentence length must vary, but most sentences should be short. The reader of the newspaper story wants his information in an easily digestible form.

2. Paragraphs must be short. The standard paragraph elaborates or develops one idea, and each new idea requires a new paragraph. In journalistic writing, however, the need for "zip" in the story makes short paragraphs essential, paragraphs seldom composed of more than one or two sentences. You do not, of course, chop the idea off to shorten the paragraph: rather you use the most meaningful words available, avoid unnecessary elaboration, and, when necessary, continue the idea into the next paragraph with a connecting word or phrase such as "Furthermore," or "In addition."

3. First paragraphs must always contain the climax of the newspaper story. Each succeeding paragraph must be progressively less important to the story. The last paragraphs must meet the cut-off test, that is, they must be expendable to satisfy the demands of make-up. This does not, however, mean that the succeeding paragraphs of a story must be less well written. If these paragraphs are worth writing at all, or worth reading at all, they must be clear, precise, and informative.

4. The newspaper story must be regarded as a distillation of the event that has occurred or that will occur. There are forms of written composition in which the entire story can be told with as many adjectives as are necessary to describe the entire situation: the short story, the novel, the biography, the history book. But the newspaper story is meant to give as complete as possible a picture in an abbreviated space. Therefore, the most important and, subjectively, the most interesting facts must dominate the copy.

5. After you have written your story, revise it—Read the rough draft carefully. Have the selection and presentation of the material

fulfilled your purpose in writing the story? Does the beginning of the story contain the Who? What? When? Where? Why? and How? of the event? Make notes in the margin as you read. Make certain that your sentences say exactly what you intended. Vary sentence beginnings. Watch for run-on sentences and sentence fragments.

Start a new paragraph whenever you start a new idea. In the straight news story, start a new paragraph whenever a too-long paragraph dominates the story. Be sure to include the necessary transition.

Check your story for errors in agreement, reference, punctuation, capitalization, and spelling.

Revise your story to get the most punch in the first paragraph.

Grammar Guideposts—

1. The verb agrees only with its subject, not with the words between subject and verb.

> *One* of the books I read *was* interesting.

2. Compound subjects joined by *and* are plural.

> The school *paper* and journalism *class are* demanding work.

3. Compound subjects joined by *or, nor, either-or, neither-nor* are singular.

> *Neither John nor Gail is* willing to interview Miss Haggart.

4. When a singular word and a plural word are joined by *or* or *nor* to form a compound subject, the verb agrees with the subject that is nearer to it.

> Neither *John nor our two advisers agree* with the proposed editorial.

5. Some indefinite pronouns are always singular. Others are always plural. Some may be either singular or plural.

Singular		Plural	Singular or Plural
each	no one	several	some
neither	nobody	few	all
one	anyone	both	none
everyone	someone	many	any
everybody	somebody		most

212

6. The number of a collective noun depends upon the usage of the noun.

> The group *sings* well together. (united action)
> The group *have* different interests. (separate action)

7. The linking verb agrees with its subject, *not* with the predicate word.

> All *types* of reporting *are* Bill's forte.

8. Many words that end in *–ics* may be either singular or plural: *economics, athletics, politics.* In general they are singular when unmodified in any way.

> *Politics is* one of a newspaper's most important topics.
> *His politics are* strangely thought out.
> *Civics is* taught in many schools.
> *A country's civics are* often more theoretical than actual.

9. To decide which pronoun form to use in a compound object, try each part of the object by itself with the verb.

> The Association divided the prize between Roosevelt's staff and us.
> Do you want her and me to dummy the page?

10. The verb *be* is a linking verb and takes the nominative pronoun after it.

> It *is I*.   It *was she*.

11. The use of the pronoun within the clause determines whether the nominative or objective form is used.

> We did not know *who had been elected.*
> Buy five copies and give them *to whomever you select.*

12. The pronoun agrees with its antecedent in number, gender, and person.

> *Each* of the reporters had *his* pencil handy.
> These are the *dummies that are* to be used.

13. To avoid any confusion for the reader, every personal pronoun and words such as *this, which, that,* and *it* should refer clearly to a definite antecedent.

> The design is good, but they did a bad printing job.—confusing—who?
> Remove the yolks from the whites and mix them.—mix which?

213

14. Use the word *other* when comparing an individual member of the group with the rest of the group.

> Our school paper has a greater circulation than all the school papers in this city. (Do you go to school in another city?)
> Our school paper has a greater circulation than all the *other* school papers in this city.

15. Usually, a colon is needed to introduce a list when that list is preceded by the words *the following* or *as follows*. A colon is not needed to introduce a list immediately preceded by the verb.

> The staff required to run this paper effectively is as follows: an editor-in-chief, a managing editor, four page editors, a business manager, and an advertising manager.
> The paper requires an editor-in-chief, a managing editor, four page editors, a business manager, and an advertising manager.

16. In a direct quotation, the speaker's words are set off from the rest of the sentence; usually a comma, occasionally a colon, precedes the quotation. When the quotation ends the sentence, the period is placed *inside* the quotation marks. When the quotation does not end the sentence, the comma is also placed inside the quotation marks. The colon and semicolon at the close of a quotation fall outside the quotation marks. The meaning of the sentence, however, determines the placement of the question mark and exclamation point.

> The coach said, "I predict three touchdowns during the first half!"
> The quotation ends, "I lift my lamp beside the golden door."
> The principal said, "I ask your cooperation," at the assembly.
> Read "The Killers"; then you will appreciate Hemingway's style.
> "Are you willing to devote all that time?" Mr. Hazlitt asked.
> Did the editor say "You should not use this feature"?

A paperback bookshelf. Every writer needs reference books—to aid him in checking facts, dates, and correct spelling and punctuation. The library is the best source of such material, but for speed and convenience every writer should have a reference library of his own. The following books, all paperbound, may be purchased by the individual student or by the school paper for use in the office. The use of such books, and the many others like them, will help you, the journalist, to produce a more accurate and more interesting newspaper.

Bartholomew, J., *Meridian Compact Atlas of the World*, Cleveland, Meridian

Bartlett, J., *The Shorter Bartlett's Familiar Quotations*, New York, Pocket Books

Bernstein, T., *Watch Your Language*, Manhasset, New York, Channel Press

Lewis, N., *Roget's New Pocket Thesaurus in Dictionary Form*, New York, Washington Square Press

Mawson, C. O. S., *Dictionary of Foreign Terms*, New York, Bantam Books

Moore, W. G., *Dictionary of Geography*, Baltimore, Penguin Books

Nicholson, M., *Dictionary of American-English Usage*, New York, New American Library

Strunk, W., Jr., and White, E. B., *The Elements of Style*, New York, Macmillan

Webster's New World Dictionary of the American Language, College Edition, Cleveland, World

The World Almanac, New York, The New York *World Telegram & Sun*

PROOFREADING GALLEY PROOFS

Once the copyreader has edited the reporter's copy, it goes to the linotypist, who sets it into type. The slugs—lines of type—taken from the linotype machine are placed in long metal trays, called *galleys*. The type is inked, and the proofs taken are known as *galley proofs*.

A proofreader reads these galley proofs to detect errors made by the linotypist and errors not caught during copyreading. He very carefully marks each error, and in the margin he indicates the correction that is to be made. The linotypist glances down the margin, readily sees the corrections, and resets those lines. A helper takes the news slugs to the galleys and substitutes them for the lines in error.

The corrections made in the margin of the galley proofs are largely in code (see Example 135), a standard set of thirty-five or forty proofreading marks in use in print shops today (see Example 134). Variations in the codes exist from one shop to another but are slight.

The copyreader acts as an editorial critic of copy, while the proofreader's work is the exacting task of checking the linotypist.

Student journalists must withstand any temptation to change the manuscript as they read proof. Two can read together to advantage; one follows the galley proof and marks corrections as the other reads the original copy aloud to him, calling paragraphs, punctuation, capitalization, and the words of the copy. He even spells out difficult words and names. For instance, he reads:

"Paragraph—Don Ping's Memorial Tigers—cap M, cap T—were in a surly mood Tuesday afternoon—comma—and they clouted four Bosse pitchers for a 23—figure—dash—9—figure—victory—period."

The one marking the corrections can use a card as he goes from line to line. He makes his corrections neatly in the margin nearest the error. If there is no proofreader's mark to indicate his message, he writes out his explanation as briefly as possible. Two students who read proof together a few times become accustomed to some such system of their own, and quickly become rapid, yet accurate, proofreaders.

Two sets of galley proofs are supplied the proofreader, one of which he reads (this set will be returned to the printer later); the other he turns over to a staff member who will cut out the stories to use in making up a dummy of the pages.

PROOFREADER'S MARKS

EXAMPLE

134

⊙	Insert period	⌐	Move to right
⋏	Insert comma	⊓	Move up
:/	Insert colon	⊔	Move down
;/	Insert semicolon	*stet*	Let it stand as originally
⌵	Insert quotes		indicated
⌵	Insert apostrophe	*Run in.*	Make elements follow one
#	Insert space		another
∧	Insert margin copy	*cap.*	Capitalize
=/	Insert hyphen	*s.c.*	Set in small caps
ld.	Insert space between lines	*l.c.*	Set lower case
ℯ/	Delete, or take out	*ital.*	Set in italics
↧	Push down space	*rom.*	Set in Roman
×	Change imperfect letter	*b.f.*	Set boldface
¶	Paragraph	*w.f.*	Wrong font used
No ¶	No paragraph	*sp.*	Spell out
⌒	Close up	*fig.*	Use numerical figures
tr.	Transpose	=	Straighten lines
⊚	Reverse	☐	Indent one em
⊏	Move to left		

216

The proofreader has indicated corrections to be made.

by Neil Stein

ital.

l. c.

EXAMPLE
135

"Station W9VOF. This is Station W9VOF broadcasting from Benjamin Bosse High School, Evansville, Indiana.

Perhaps you've heard this on your short wave receiver during the past few weeks Charles Young and his fellow radio enthusiasts have installed the thirty-five watt transmitter, which Charley built in his home last year in the laboratory next to the physics classroom one hundred and fifty-one.

,,

⊙

fig.

At Fort Knox

b. f.

Of the portable type, the gadget has been places, to say the least. When Young went to Knox Fort this summer with the National Guardsmen, the transmitter went too. At its resting place is here at Bosse where it is used before and after school and during Radio club meetings on Thurs. mornings.

#

tr.

w. f.

present

cap.

sp.

Adams Vice-President

Naturally the members of the club elected Charley president and Gene Adams became vice-president.

=/

no ¶

Clarence Hurt was chosen to serve as secretary. At present the twenty boys are endeavoring to purchase a receiver. Up to now they have been using Lyle V. Courtney's all-wave receiver to pick up signals from the stations with which they communicate.

⑤

↓

¶

Charley, a member of The School Spirit staff, is also interested in public address systems and operates the school public address system during assemblies.

c. & s. c.

217

The linotypist has made the corrections indicated by the proofreader.

EXAMPLE
136

by Neil Stein

"Station W9VOF. This is station W9VOF broadcasting from Benjamin Bosse High School, Evansville, Indiana."

Perhaps you've heard this on your short wave receiver during the past few weeks. Charles Young and his fellow radio enthusiasts have installed the thirty-five watt transmitter, which Charley built in his home last year, in the laboratory next to the physics classroom 151.

At Fort Knox

Of the portable type, the gadget has been places, to say the least. When Young went to Fort Knox this summer with the National Guardsmen, the transmitter went too. At present its resting place is here at Bosse where it is used before and after school and during Radio Club meetings on Thursday mornings.

Adams Vice-President

Naturally the members of the club elected Charley president and Gene Adams became vice-president. Clarence Hurt was chosen to serve as secretary. At present the twenty boys are endeavoring to purchase a receiver. Up to now they have been using Lyle V. Courtney's all-wave receiver to pick up signals from the stations with which they communicate.

Charley, a member of THE SCHOOL SPIRIT staff, is also interested in public address systems and operates the school system during assemblies.

218

CHAPTER LABORATORY

1. Copyread the following exercises in your notebook, making *all* necessary changes.

Copyreading "A"

```
 1                         the unnamed club,
 2   sponsored by Miss Lida Lamar, mett
 3   Thursday during the e. c. a. period.?
 4   Mary Hidrite made an Announcement about
 5   a social meeting to be held before
 6   Thanksgiving.  jane Straub who is presi-
 7   dent of the Club then told her Ex peri-
 8   ences during a trip she took this sumer
 9   to the National Parks of the west, the
10   Expositions at Dallas and San diego, and
11   of rher visit to Culver city.
```

Copyreading "B"

```
 1                         Washington Elem.
 2   School will observe Amer. Ed. Week which
 3   is set  for Nov. sixth to Nov. fifteenth
 4   with two special programs.
 5                         The pupils of the
 6   2nd floor will be hosts to the people of
 7   the community Thurs., Nov. 12th.   "Our
 8   American Schools at work" will be the
 9   general theme for both proframs.
```

Copyreading "C"

```
 1                         GirlReserves in
 2   their last meeting.  Wednesday, Octiber
 3   28, were giv en a talk by Lois Bauman,
 4   a Former Girl Reserve who grad uated in
 5   the first Centralgraduating class.
 6                         Miss Bauman,
 7   accompaniedby 2 friends, motored through
 8   England, Scotland, and Wales.  She and
 9   her friends were intsted in the his-
10   torical back ground and the picturesque-
11   nessof thesecountries.
```

Copyreading "D"

```
 1                    Featuring Chalk
 2  Drawings and rag cartooning by Howard
 3  Ellis, an Asse ,mbly was sponsored by
 4  the 11a class class of east high last
 5  Thurs. in East's auditorium.
 6                    Mr. Ellisdrew
 7  pictures using religious and humorous
 8  themes.  He has traveled ex tensively in
 9  the U.S. and has given performances in
10  all of states the in the west.  Hishome
11  is In Sullivan, Indiana, where he began
12  his artistic career.
```

2. Proofread the following printed selections, pretending that you have galley proof. Mark the incorrect word and proofreader's mark in your notebook and make the correction after it.

Proofreading "A"

Nail-driving contests, speakers, and musical trios were among the Features at the meetings of the various E.C.A. clubs Thursday morning.

The members of the recital club heard a brass solos by Lee Bennett ; a song, "Me and the Moon, by Mae Zeitz ; a cello selection, "Heart bowed Down," by Rosemary Doss ; and a trombone solo, "PALS," by John Hoffman.

Proofreading "B"

Relating incidents from his round-the-world trip, H. R. Erskine, Scripps-Howard reporter, spoke before a Joint assembly last Monday morning.

Mr. Erskin, who was here for a short stay enroute to Memphis, Tennessee, spoke to the gathered students of Central, East, and Memorial schools high. In all he spoke to 3,789 students.

Leaving September twenty-first, Mr. Erskine had flown around the world in 19 days.

Proofreading "C"

In pst decades, thousands of American students, children of newly arrived imigrants to the United States, were hindered in their studies and in their social lives by a language barrier. Languages spkanin their holmes ranged from French to Chinese. Today relatively few students come from homes in which langages otger than English are spoken. But many high school students all over the land still suffer from a language barrier in their academic and social lives. Are you one of those stooping ibdividuals who who slur, "Icanblevut," to your girl friend who counters with, "Wajasa?" Or are you the sophisticatd type who lables everything "squaresvill," or "endsville, man"?

No matter how profond your wit, how clever your ideas, the restofus can not appreciate them if we cannot understand them.

15 WRITING THE HEADLINES

Headlines are the placards that call attention to the newspaper page. They are eye-catchers, revealing just enough of the subject to make the reader hesitate or hurry on. Headlines, by their type faces and arrangements, can bring an aesthetic touch to a page. By their size, they carry to the reader the editor's opinion of the importance of the news.

First impressions are important. Two stores may handle the same quality of merchandise, but the one that arranges or displays its goods more attractively is the one from which people buy. Two makes of automobiles may be of the same worth mechanically, but the one with the more pleasing appearance is the one that sells. Two stenographers of identical ability apply for a position, but the one who makes the better first impression gets the job.

Physical attractiveness means just as much to the newspaper. Through its outward appearance it makes its first impression, so often the lasting one. This physical arrangement of the paper is known as *make-up*. It demands an artistic placement of stories, features, cuts, and ads, and an artistic selection of type faces and sizes. One of the most important elements of make-up is the headline, for while the body type of stories is only 8 or 9 point, typical heads range up to 36 point.

HEADLINE MAKE-UP

Who writes the heads? Not the reporter. He merely leaves space on his copy for the head, starting the first page a third of the way down to allow room for the addition of the head. The copy reader writes the headline according to a previously developed plan for the page (page layout) which indicates the size and type of head to be written for the story in question. Headline writing calls for a knowledge of the purposes of headlines, the basic rules of construction, and the type faces or headline schedule used by the particular paper. Most school papers find it simpler to have two or three editors do all the headline writing. They then become proficient at the job, and a better newspaper appearance results.

The reporter as well as the copyreader, however, should learn the approximate size of each letter (compare *m*'s with *l*'s in your school paper and see page 230) and the approximate number of letters that may be carried in a column for a given type size.

The headline schedule. An effective headline schedule, accurately followed by all staff members, is the first step toward attractive make-up. Every paper has a standard headline schedule giving all the types of heads used by the paper, coded by number for ease of reference. It is this schedule (printed in a booklet for easy reference—See Example 137) that standardizes the appearance of the school newspaper. It helps the page designers select the types of heads and enables the headline writers to construct the heads as soon as the completed stories are in their possession. The headline schedule holds the staff to a style that gives the paper its distinction in make-up. For this reason it is not good practice to change the headline type faces frequently. By consistently using an established style of heads, the paper takes on the appearance of a standard product. It is recognized by its headdress, which is why daily newspapers carefully preserve their style of headdress over a period of years. However, school newspapers that have not changed their headlines for three or four years should review their type faces and sizes.

The parts of a headline. Each section of a headline is known as *deck* or *bank*. Each headline in Example 138 is composed of two decks. In recent years the trend has been away from many decks and toward one or two. Even in daily newspapers one rarely finds headlines with more than two decks, and these exceptions are found in the lead stories at the top of the page. Since headlines repeat information that follows in the stories, most school newspapers today conserve their valuable and limited space by using one-deck heads. A six- or seven-column paper might use more decks than a five-column paper, but most high school papers are five column and follow the one-deck plan.

Older head styles. Some years back, the typical headline had two or three decks, the first being a *drop-line,* the subsidiary decks being *inverted pyramids, hanging indentions,* or *crosslines.* Since they are no longer advocated for the school press, Example 139 is included only for identification.

The modern head. Example 140 illustrates the most typical of school newspaper heads, the *flush-left, no-count* head. The term *no-count* is used because a line may be any length provided it will go in the column. The line should go at least two thirds of the way across the column. Many papers set the first line longer, as indicated in most of the examples. Most heads of this type have two or three lines. Obviously, the term *flush-left* means that each line begins flush with the left side of the column.

The no-count head has the advantage of being easy to write; it is seldom necessary to sacrifice clarity in order to make the head fit the space. Sans-serif type (type without cross strokes at the ends of letters) is often used in modern newspaper make-up. (See A, C, D, and E in Example 140.)

223

EXAMPLE

137

WE'RE BA

Inaugurates Ne

May Day Celebration To Include Crowning

Stimulate Essay Contest

Production Fills Stage

Historic Civil War Home

Stop! Beware! Shopping Females

Just Looking Things Over

BGH—60 pt.
4 col.—24 units
5 col.—30 units

BGH—48 pt.
4 col.—32 units
5 col.—40 units

BGM—36 pt.
2 col.—21 units
3 col.—30 units

BGH—30 pt.
2 col.—24 units
3 col.—37 units

LYD—36 pt.
2 col.—21 units
3 col.—33 units

LYD—30 pt.
2 col.—26 units
3 col.—41 units

LYD—24 pt.
1 col.—16 units
2 col.—32 units

KAUF—30 pt.
2 col.—25 units
3 col.—40 units

Hale Receives Quota Award From Group

Which Came First, Chicken or Egg?

No More Federal Tax To Burden Activities

PTA Study Groups Develop, Improve Personalities

Clubs Consolidate, Select Officers For New Term

BGM—24 pt.
1 col.—14 units
2 col.—29 units

BGM—18 pt.
1 col.—18 units
2 col.—37 units

BGM—14 pt.
1 col.—21 units

LYD—18 pt.
1 col.—19 units
2 col.—41 units

BGI—18 pt.
1 col.—18 units
2 col.—37 units

Headline Schedule

Sample heads from the headline schedule
of *The School Spirit*, Bosse High School,
Evansville, Indiana.

EXAMPLE
138

Clark Picks Sixty-eight
Members for Vocal Vikes

(A)

Name Six to
Honor Group

**January Grads Attain
Highest Scholastic Goal**

Six January seniors were elected
to National Honor Society by prin-

**This Year's Group
Smaller Than Before
By Instructor's Choice**

Names of 68 students who were selected for membership in the Vocal
Vikings were announced September
30 b

(B)

The headlines on this page have been
taken from the following papers: (A)
The North Star, North High School,
Omaha, Nebraska; (B) *The Benson
High News,* Benson High School,
Omaha, Nebraska; (C) *The Talisman,*
Appleton High School, Appleton, Wis-
consin; (D) *The Warrior,* Central
High School, Memphis, Tennessee.

(C)

Announce Dates
For This Year's
Forensic Recitals

**Activities Include
Declamation, Debate,
Oratory, Extempore**

Dates for the forensic activities
this year have been announced by
Miss Ruth McKennan, Mr. H. H.

(D)

Students Aid
Quaker Project

**Volunteers Will Help
Needy Groups**

This summer, high school students
from all sections of the country will
volunteer to aid needy communities in

EXAMPLE

140

Junior Hobby Horse Prances Gaily Through Central (A)

Although every Centralite thinks his or her individual class is the best, no one can have failed to especially note the great variety of individuality and

Graduation To Mark Fiftieth Anniversary (B)

Celebrating Humboldt's fiftieth graduation anniversary, the class will have the 19— graduates as m guests.

Donald Taylor and Barbara Folger To Be New Student Council Officers (C)

Donald Taylor and Barbara Folger will head the Student Council next term as president and vice-president, respectively. They were elected Friday, May 16, by the student body. The same elected

Filsinger, Shapland Are Voted As 'Topularity in Popularity' (D)

Shirley Filsinger and Laurence Shapland were determined the most popular senior girl. take the ticket as seniors with the prettiest hair. Senior prettiest

Engineers Map School Plot, Clearing To Begin Soon (E)

With the drafting of contour maps by city engineers the direction of architect Fred W. Markham under

(A) *The Warrior,* Central High School, Memphis, Tennessee; (B) *The Arrow,* Humbolt High School, St. Paul, Minnesota; (C) *The Blue and Gray Clarion,* Pierre S. duPont High School, Wilmington, Delaware; (D) *The Rattler,* Neligh High School, Neligh, Nebraska; (E) *The Provonian,* Provo High School, Provo, Utah.

EXAMPLE

139

Decorating Club Constructs House ←Drop-line head

Plans To Exhibit Model ←Crossline

Vacation Tomorrow for Pupils as Teachers Go to Classes at Southeastern Indiana Convention ←Hanging indention

Annual Senior Play Moves Ahead—Regardless ←Inverted pyramid

The banner head. The line of large type extending across the top of a newspaper page is called a *banner* or *streamer.* It is used to attract attention to news of exceptional importance. Some daily newspapers use the banner each day because of its make-up and sales value rather than because of any particular news significance. School papers, however, use this type of head only for special occasions. It is followed by a regular headline, and then by the story. (See Chapter 13.)

227

The variety headline. The unusual attracts attention. While the typical headline schedule usually provides for some variation, the paper that never deviates from its schedule is apt to be dull and lifeless. In headline writing as in good story writing, there is no substitute for originality and ingenuity. The young journalist should be encouraged to experiment with new headline forms.

The occasional different head attracts attention. This "variety head," as it is called, may be different typographically (See A, B, C, and F in Example 141) or because of what it says (See D and E). Such headlines are more commonly found on the feature and editorial pages but may be useful elsewhere, provided they are not overdone. Once they become the rule rather than the exception, they cease to fulfill their purpose. As in all journalism, pleasing appearance and good taste are the criteria.

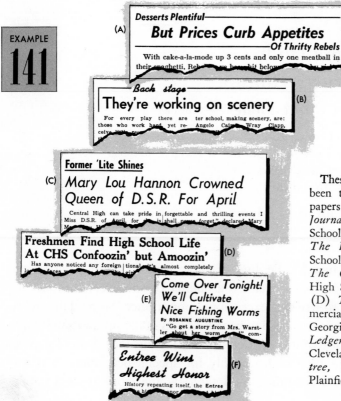

EXAMPLE
141

(A) Desserts Plentiful——
But Prices Curb Appetites
——Of Thrifty Rebels
With cake-a-la-mode up 3 cents and only one meatball in their spaghetti, Reb...

—Back stage—
They're working on scenery (B)
For every play there are ter school, making scenery, are: those who work hard yet re- Angelo Cal... Wray Clapp,

(C) Former 'Lite Shines
Mary Lou Hannon Crowned Queen of D.S.R. For April
Central High can take pride in forgettable and thrilling events I Miss D.S.R. of April, for ... is shall never forget," declared Mary...

Freshmen Find High School Life At CHS Confoozin' but Amoozin' (D)
Has anyone noticed any foreign tional it's almost completely

(E) **Come Over Tonight! We'll Cultivate Nice Fishing Worms**
BY ROBANNE AUGUSTINE
"Go get a story from Mrs. Warst-ler about her worm ..." com-

Entree Wins Highest Honor (F)
History repeating itself, the Entree ...

These variety headlines have been taken from the following papers: (A) *The John Adams Journal,* John Adams High School, Cleveland, Ohio; (B) *The Pioneer,* Southwest High School, St. Louis, Missouri; (C) *The Central Student,* Central High School, Detroit, Michigan; (D) *The Co-Ed Leader,* Commercial High School, Atlanta, Georgia; (E) *The John Hay Ledger,* John Hay High School, Cleveland, Ohio; (F) *The Entree,* Plainfield High School, Plainfield, New Jersey.

228

RULES FOR WRITING THE HEADLINE

The newspaper field has a well-accepted set of standards for head-line writers to follow These hold true for daily as well as school papers. The rules that follow are basic:

1. Incorporate the main feature of the story in the headline. Write the head from the lead.

2. Most stories contain some key words. Build the headline around these words.

3. Use the active rather than the passive voice, unless the passive voice permits the significant thing to be placed first.

4. Each deck should be a complete sentence, with a verb if possible.

5. If necessary, a verb may be understood in a headline—"Vincennes Team in Poor Condition." *Is* and *are* are commonly omitted, and *in* often serves as a verb. It is preferable, though, to use an active verb in each deck.

6. Although it is preferable to begin a deck with a noun subject, an infinitive may be used.

7. Use numbers in headlines only if they are important, and in such instances figures should be used. If possible, do not begin a headline with figures.

8. All headlines are written in the present tense—"Central Defeats Boonville," not "Central Defeated Boonville." The future is indicated by the infinitive—"Central To Play Boonville."

9. Use short words. Avoid long words that will completely fill the line. One-syllable and two-syllable words are preferred.

10. Do not repeat a key word in the same deck or a subordinate deck unless its use is definitely preferable to its synonym.

11. Do not divide words or names from one line to another.

12. The articles *a, an,* and *the* are only used for the sake of balance. Avoid them if possible.

13. Avoid excessive punctuation in headlines. Use a semicolon instead of a period, single quotes instead of double, and the comma sparingly. The comma is used instead of the conjunction *and*.

14. Avoid excessive abbreviation in headlines.

15. Most headlines today are written in capitals and lower case (small letters), replacing the former all-cap heads. The usual style is to capitalize all words except conjunctions, articles, and prepositions of less than four letters.

THE MECHANICS OF HEADLINE WRITING

A mechanical problem. Headline writing also presents mechanical problems. The writer is limited by the width of the column and the type in which the head is to be set. He must consider each line of each deck separately as he writes.

Each line contains a certain number of units, depending upon the face and the size of the type. With each letter and each space counting so many units, headline writing calls for a single mathematical formula. Back in the days when all-cap heads were the style, the process was simply stated: Count all letters one unit except *M, W,* and *I*—*M* and *W* being one and one-half each, and *I* being one-half unit. Today ease of reading and the attractiveness of the page have swung the style to lower-case letters, with only the main words capitalized. This makes it imperative that each staff build its own scheme, determined by the particular type face used in its paper.

Counting units. When capitals and lower case are both used, a formula such as the following is fairly accurate:

Count every lower-case letter one unit, except *f, i, j, l, m, t,* and *w.*
Count lower-case *f, i, j, l,* and *t* a half unit.
Count lower-case *m* and *w* one and a half units.
Count all capital letters one and a half except *M, W,* and *I.*
Count capital *M* and *W* two units.
Count capital *I* one unit.

Count all punctuation marks one half, except the dash and the question mark, which are counted one each.

Count all spaces between words ordinarily one, changing to one half or one and a half to make the count more nearly true.

In dealing with smaller sizes of type, such as 14 point, the headline writer is safe in counting everything as one unit. The narrow letters balance the wider.

The headline blank. Relationships between the newsroom and the print shop can be greatly improved if a standard, printed headline blank is used in writing headlines. This is true regardless of whether the printing is done in the school print shop or by a commercial printer. Some staffs use headline blanks for all hand-set heads and write the second decks, which are machine set, on the top of the copy. For headline blanks, small slips of paper having spaces for the style and size of type may be used. A slightly different form is pictured in Example 142.

EXAMPLE 142

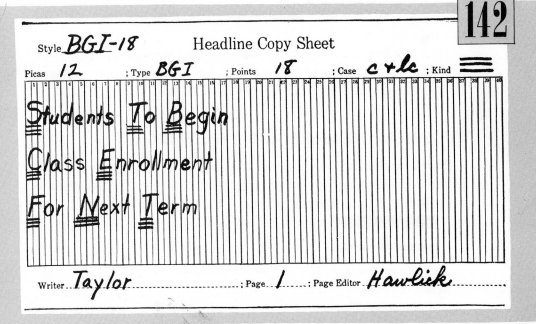

This blank has spaces for the kind and size of type, the width of the head, the kind and style of headline, the names of the writer and the page editor, and the number of the page on which the head is to be used. In addition, the blank utilizes a novel counting device of light and dark vertical lines. The dark or heavy lines are one unit

This headline blank was prepared by Edward T. DeVoe, Bloomsburg (Pennsylvania) State Teachers College, who described it in the December-January, 1936-1937, *Quill and Scroll* article, "A Headline Chart for Copyreaders."

231

apart and are numbered from the left at the top of the sheet. The light lines are used to indicate half units and come between the heavy lines. Thus, if the writer wishes a letter that counts one and a half unit, he utilizes three half spaces. If he is writing a letter that counts only one-half space, he uses one of the half spaces. When this form is used, the writer starts each line at the extreme left, regardless of the type of headline he is writing. Thus the exact unit count of each line may be determined by looking at the number at the top of the column in which the last letter of the line falls. In the original of Example 142, the vertical lines are light red, providing greater contrast between the lines and the letters written over them.

As previously indicated, such a system is an individual matter for each paper. This system merely shows one that functions well for one paper.

With a knowledge of unit counting, and the page dummies and headline schedule at hand for reference, the headline writer is ready. In time the process becomes almost mechanical for him.

PRINTERS' MEASURE AND TYPE FACES

Points and picas. In printing, the term *pica* means a measure of length approximately one sixth of an inch. The pica in divided into twelve smaller units known as points; for example:

██████ This line is twelve points or one pica high.

█████ This is six points high.

——————————— This is one point high.

Measurements in printing are seldom taken in inches; usually the pica or the point (one seventy-second of an inch) is used.

Type is measured by the point system. Type that is approximately $\frac{6}{72}$ or $\frac{1}{12}$ of an inch high is called six-point type. Type that is approximately one sixth of an inch is called twelve-point type; for example:

This is 8-point type.

This is 10-point type.

This is 12-point type.

This is 18-point type.

The text of this book is set in 11 point Times Roman with 3 points of space between the lines (called leading—led'ing). There are numerous styles of type, most available in various sizes.

The terms *em* and *pica* are sometimes mistakenly used interchangeably. They are not the same thing, however. An em is always the square of the type, whatever its size may be. For example:

☐ Here is an em in 8-point type.

☐☐ Here are two ems of 10-point type.

☐☐☐ Here are three ems in 12-point type.

The em and the pica are only identical in 12-point type.

C H A P T E R   L A B O R A T O R Y

1. Clip and mount five headlines, each of which violates one or more of the fifteen rules for writing headlines noted in this chapter. Indicate the rules violated.
2. Clip a story with a poor headline from a recent issue of a school paper. Mount it and rewrite the head.
3. Using practice materials, write three different kinds of headlines, according to the styles set forth in the headline schedules of your school paper.
4. Clip one article from your daily paper; remove the headline but save it. Exchange your article for one obtained by a classmate, and write the head. Compare each headline with the one carried by the daily paper.
5. Analyze all the headlines from one issue of your school paper: Which rules are most frequently violated? Why?
6. *Group activity.* If your school paper has no printed headline schedule, prepare one in the following manner:
   a. From old copies of your paper, clip one sample of each of the different headlines that are used.
   b. Mount these on a large piece of wall board or cardboard, grouping together those composed of the same kind of type.
   c. Assign numbers and letters to each headline.
   d. Indicate the kind and size of type at the side of each.
   e. Indicate the maximum and minimum count of each line.
   Hang the schedule in the newsroom and prepare pamphlets for the copyreaders' use.

16 PAGE MAKE-UP

A paper's make-up is its showcase.

No matter how thorough and lively the news coverage, its interest and freshness depend on the format of the paper. The size of the page, the stock of paper, the number of pages, the number of columns per page, the type face and size, the art, and the arrangement of copy make up the package in which the reporters' work is presented to the reader.

Few staffs ever have the opportunity to inaugurate a school paper and determine make-up from the start, but they all have the opportunity—and the obligation—to examine critically the make-up of the paper they have inherited. Minor changes are made from week to week in securing a lively and attractive arrangement, but an intensive review of all the aspects of make-up should be undertaken every three or four years.

Traditional papers. The older the school paper, the more nearly it is a tradition; and most high school students want to retain school traditions. However, the older the school paper, the more difficult it is to keep it alive. Once a paper has built up its traditions of size, make-up, content, headdress, and style in general, it is natural for each new staff to look upon this heritage as its constant guide. The paper that becomes fixed, however (although it may make an excellent appearance), denies the staff any opportunity to be creative. This opportunity denied, the paper has betrayed its mission. The make-up of the school paper should be dynamic.

When the school newspaper seems to have reached its peak of excellence and organization, it is time to review the entire thing and build anew, using student initiative and creative.ability for the labor.

THE ELEMENTS OF MAKE-UP

The size of a school paper not only reflects the size of the school, it also indicates the emphasis placed upon journalism. For instance, one school of 1000 students has a circulation of 650 papers, while another of the same enrollment issues a large paper because its circulation is 1100. A school of 2000 students issues a four-page, five-column weekly; the same size. paper is published by another school of 600 students. A newspaper may not be better simply because it is bigger. However, the larger paper carries more copy and advertising, and requires a larger staff, thus utilizing more reporters, editors, and salesmen.

Pages and dimensions. In the past, the typical high school paper had four pages, the size of the school determining the dimensions of the page— from three columns for the very small school to eight columns for the very large. Recently, larger papers have taken on a different format.

The size of a paper is measured by the amount of copy it carries rather than by the dimensions of the page. In one city, two high schools publish papers with approximately the same amount of copy but entirely different formats. School A publishes an eight-column, four-page paper, twenty-one inches to the column—total column inches 672. School B publishes a five-column, eight-page paper, sixteen inches to the column—total column inches 640.

The first, with its eight columns, comes closer to the make-up of the daily newspaper, but it lacks the inside pages to support its large dimensions. The second paper sacrifices sheet size for the diversity provided by an additional four pages. The make-up of each presents a new editorial challenge.

School newspapers today lean toward more pages and fewer columns. These advantages are greater page diversity and better display of illustrations and advertisements. The four-column paper is unusual, but when issued in a six- or eight-page format, it offers many possibilities for individuality. Example 143 reproduces two pages of a good

EXAMPLE 143

Page Two — THE TRUMPETEER — March 3, 1961

Teaching Kids To Drive

Driving Teachers Need Sense Of Humor

By BONNIE BURNS

An irate driver pulled up alongside a Driver's Training car—breaking traffic laws to get there—and shouted at the instructor, "Why don't you teach that kid to drive!"

This is one of the many experiences that requires a Driver's Training instructor to have patience and a good sense of humor—and instructors have many opportunities to show these qualities.

Mr. Phillips recalls the time when he had three senior girls in the car. As they came to Campbell Avenue, the girl driver exclaimed, surprised, "Why, I didn't know Campbell looked like this in the daytime!"

A time for patience comes when students are afraid to go "fast." One boy refused to get up to 35 mph (the speed limit). Consequently he and Mr. Phillips got back to school 30 minutes late.

"But I don't like to go fast," was

There she stopped while crowds of people swarmed around the car to get across the street.

"Well, I'm just going to sit here until they move out of the way!" she blushed.

But in spite of the many varied experiences, there has not been one moving accident between cars in all the 16 years of the Drivers Training Program in Tucson.

"Of course," admits Mr. Phillips, "students have backed into things," but he feels that students at CHS have a good attitude toward Driver's Training.

"Boys sign up just as quickly as girls and all in all we've trained about 1,200 kids," the instructor went on.

These have kept Mr. Gridley busy signing $120,000 worth of insurance reductions.

But the purpose of taking Driver's Training is more than just getting reductions on insurance. It gives students an opportunity to become better citizens and learn civic responsibilities.

Driver's Training tries to create a good mental attitude toward driving and an appreciation and care for the car.

"We try to develop a pattern of driving so that good driving comes naturally—so they can do it in their sleep," concludes Mr. Leon Morton, also a driving instructor.

Girls League Members Journey To Arcadia High For State Convention

About 40 Catalina g'rls will attend the State Girls ...'cadia High School in Scottsdale

...ded bus at 6 a.m., the girls will ...for the morning "brunch" and

...League Constitution will be dis...t provided.

...on is scheduled for all day, "We'll ...big basketball tournament that ...r, CHS branch president.

...ean of girls and sponsor of CHS ...any the group.

Notice Knees? Short Skirt Fad Hits CHS Campus

By BOBBI CROSE

Have you noticed the clean, shiny knees showing around Catalina's halls lately?

They are showing because short, short skirts have recently hit the school. These skirts are pleated and hit the leg just above the knee.

This type of skirt made its first appearance in the east where it was given the title Bandstand Skirt because teenage girls wore it on the television program "Bandstand."

Along with the Bandstand Skirt came the short "two-legged" skirt. This type originated back in great-grandma's time when riding side-saddle was proper for young ladies. They have been renewed off and on in the fashion world and given the name "culottes."

Now Catalina girls think the revised "two-legged" skirt and the Bandstand Skirt are comfortable and "neat"—especially if a girl has the knees to show off!

Slater, Bykerk Most Bearded

Bob Bykerk and Roy Slater, both juniors, drew a split decision in the beard-growing contest held at last week's Rodeo dance.

Judges declared the contest, sponsored jointly by the **Trumpeteer** and the Junior Class, to be a draw.

—Dean Zimmerman—

...unches Hair Styling Career

DEAN ZIMMERMAN
He's Devoted

...work hard and is willing to modernize.

"People in this field must be devoted to their work, otherwise they won't get anywhere," he says.

"The work of a hair stylist isn't boring, because every head you work with is different, and even one head of hair doesn't stay the same throughout the lifetime."

Dean thinks that there is much satisfaction in styling and making a person's hair attractive, and feels that he has produced a work of art when he transforms an uncared-for head of hair into a beautiful, up-to-date coiffure.

According to Dean, the perfect length of hair is five to six inches from the crown of the head, and one and a half to two inches at the neckline. "With this length of hair, it is possible to fashion 15 to 20 different hair styles," he says.

The purpose of a hair style is to enhance the features of a person's face. Dean is of the opinion that many hair stylists don't take this into consideration when giving the customer a high fashion coiffure. As a result, the person may end up with a hair style very inappropriate to her face.

From experience, Dean knows that the most fashion-conscious women are those who are most demanding about having the highest fashion in hair styles.

A look into the future finds a new hair style called the Honey Hug. This style is close-fitting at the neck and "poofy" at the crown; it is close around the ears and brushed back from the forehead, says Dean.

March 3, 1961 — THE TRUMPETEER — Page Five

Sports Scope

By AL RUDIS

Bill Kemmeries, Catalina's inimitable basketball coach, was the subject of last week's jibe and this week is the subject of everyone's praise. At the risk of giving the humble mentor a swelled head, we chronicle some of his past triumphs.

Coach Kemmeries was born on the soil of Italy, but soon moved to the U.S. and resided in Nogales for nine years before coming to the Old Pueblo.

Here in Tucson he took up the sport of basketball in earnest and has been one of its top exponents ever since. At Tucson High he led the Badgers to their last state championship in 1949.

"In high school ball a player is supposed to learn to win and lose," states Kemmeries, "but when I went to Tucson High I just learned how to win." Kemmeries led the Tucson team into 51 straight victories in two years against no defeats. He ended his high school career by being named all-state captain.

College competition brought more laurels upon Kemmeries. Going to the University of Arizona on a Baird scholarship, a mark of scholastic distinction, Kemmeries led the UA cagers in scoring and piloted them to their last Border Conference championship in 1954. He ended the year on the All-Border Conference team and an honorable mention All-American.

Rudis

From the University Coach Kemmeries went to the tank force for Uncle Sam and upon his discharge was offered several professional contracts, all of which he refused in favor of coming to the newly formed Catalina High School.

Here at Catalina, in the short space of five years, he has brought the team from being a virtual nonentity in local competition to ranking among the state's leaders.

Coach Kemmeries' first year at Catalina was not very encouraging as, with a team composed of mainly sophomores and without a separate gym, he won only three games. This was the only losing season he was to have as next year he brought the Trojans to a 10-10 record.

In 1957-58 Kemmeries had his greatest year, winning the city championship with an 8-0 intracity and conference mark. The team went on to the state tournament where they captured the consolation crown and finished the season with a 17-5

TROJANS ENTER STATE TOURNEY
CHS Quint Shocks South, Tucson In Regional Clashes

(Continued From Page 1)

City guard Buddy Doolen, the CHS quint eliminated the Rebels who were tabbed as co-favorites along with Phoenix Union to win the state title. In the South fracas Doolen led all scorers with 23 points.

Against Tucson it was a 5-7 bundle of dynamite who led the Catalina attack. Having his best night of the season, little Carl Ferguson shot from all over the court and wound up with 18 markers.

Following close behind Ferguson in the Tucson tilt was Buddy Doolen who hit for 17.

Although Doolen and Ferguson showed up with the largest point totals in the two Regional Tournament contests it was a well-balanced scoring attack in both instances which brought the victories.

Backing up Doolen against South Mountain were Jamie Foster who hit for 14 points and center Scott Pickart with 11.

In the Tucson tilt it was again Pickart who played the supporting role behind the big scorers. Against the Badgers the 6-3 center collected 10 points.

Turning in outstanding rebounding performances in both contests were junior forward Clive Seal and his teammate at forward Jamie Foster.

★ ★ ★

Buddy Doolen again leads team basketball statistics with a 15.7 average and a top mark in every department. He is followed by Scott Pickart, who moved into second ahead of Jamie Foster.

The Trojans, who have hit 69.3% of their free throws, have scored 1,134 in 21 games for a per game average of 54 points. They finished the regular season tied for second in the conference and third in the city.

Here are the individual statistics:

	FG	FT	PF	TP	Avg.
Doolen ..	121	87-113	62	329	15.7
Pickart ..	67	51-63	52	185	8.8
Foster	49	32-45	14	130	8.7
Seal	43	81-114	56	167	8.0
Ferguson	51	17-28	27	119	6.3
Johnson..	27	30-51	36	84	4.2
Ward	21	5-14	22	47	3.1
Barthlmew	1	6-8	1	8	2.7
Jameson..	10	5-8	12	25	2.5
Spiegel ..	4	5-6	8	13	1.9
Cornelius	2	8-12	5	12	1.7
Latham..	4	4-14	16	12	1.2
Beaver ..	0	3-5	2	3	0.6
Murphy ..	0	0-1	2	0	0.0
	400	334-482	315	1,134	54.0

Tracksters Hurdle Into 1961 Season

CINDERMEN OPEN DUAL SEASON AT RINCON THIS AFTERNOON

"Our overall strength is very good although we don't have much depth." With these words Trojan track coach Gale Bell summed up the prospects for this year's squad which opens the season at 3:30 today, traveling to Rincon for a dual meet.

Coach Bell's optimism hinges on the return of eight outstanding lettermen from last year's team. Chris Cole is the only returnee in the sprints and will be gunning for a 10 flat hundred this year. Bob Svob and Hugh Ferguson promise to be two of the top pole vaulters in the state as both have gone over the 12 foot mark.

"The boys have really been working hard, and I'm very pleased with the way they're coming along," emphasized the Trojan track mentor.

Hopes in the distance events will be met by John Donner who as a sophomore set an Arizona prep record with his 4:25.3 mile run. Backing up Donner will be two other mile returnees, Harold Slavens and Dave Fithian.

Basketballer Buddy Doolen returns as a high jumper and will be counted on to be Catalina's best man in that event. Wrestler Don Pearson should be one of the best low hurdlers in the city.

Expected to back up the returning lettermen will be Bob Tompkins and Bruce Grossetta in the sprints, Rick Haller in the mile run, Bill Swain in the hurdles, Ray Bush in the shot put, and freshman Reid Ehlenberg who has already broadjumped 19-8¾.

Besides Doolen, two other basketballers will report out for track at the close of the State Championship Tournament. Carl Ferguson will be counted on in the high jump and Tom Bartholomew will run the hurdles.

This year the Trojan Thinclads will attempt to improve their records in both AA Division 4 and in the state. Last season the CHS squad placed second to Tucson High in conference competition and finished seventh in the state.

When asked who he thought would be the Trojans' toughest opponent this year, Coach Bell replied, "All of them; Tucson, Pueblo, Amphi and Rincon."

All spring sports in Arizona high schools have their state championships decided during University Week in May.

The Trumpeteer
Catalina High School
Tucson, Arizona

Prizes, prizes everywhere and not a magazine to read . . . Mr. Linton Melvin, magazine campaign sponsor, surveys the items that will be used to entice potential salesmen to bring in reams of subscriptions.

ETHS photo by Tom Gordon

Magazine Managers Aim High, Competition Greater Than Ever

"WE WON'T BE outdone in '61," is the cry of Mr. Linton Melvin, magazine campaign sponsor, in reference to this year's magazine sales beginning Monday in the homerooms.

ETHS must display maximum effort to meet its $60,000 goal, according to Mr. Melvin. Competition this year from other schools is greater than ever, with New Trier looming as a serious threat to Evanston's 18-year record of championship sales.

Materials Being Distributed

Materials are being distributed today and tomorrow, with orders being collected all next week through Monday, Oct. 30. Guess contest prizes, high sales awards, life membership drawings, and other bonus prizes will be given out daily in the homerooms. In addition, drawings for special prizes will be held in every homeroom selling more than $6,500 worth of magazines.

New prizes this year include portable tape recorders and typewriters, reference works and best selling books, draftsman's tools, and a huge assortment of stuffed animals.

"Special" Prices Granted

Mr. Melvin advised salesmen to stress the fact that ETHS will supply subscriptions to any magazine at any advertised price. Increased mailings to homes have quoted "special" reduced prices, supposedly available only from the publisher, but these prices may also be granted by student salesmen.

This year's all school manager is Bill Lanphar, West-164. Hall managers are John Hirshman, East-104; Sue Wadsworth, East-124; Roy Faires, North-104; William Lemke, South-144; and Barbara Power, West-164.

Homeroom Managers to Assist

East Hall homeroom managers are Bill Perlman and Mike Pinkster 104; Philip Stowell, 124; Eric Durant and Cathy Michael, 204; and Anne Haswell and Penny Schumaker, 224.

The Evanstonian

Vol. 45   Evanston Township High School, Evanston, Illinois, Oct. 19, 1961   No. 3

Rated All-American, 1960-61

GC Carnival To Feature 'Magoo' Comics, Booths

WALK THROUGH the big clown's head into social hall and hear the sounds of recorded laughter at "Have a Happy," the East Hall-sponsored Girls' Club carnival, from 8 to 11 p.m., Saturday, Oct. 21.

"Have a Happy" caricatures will be done at the North Hall booth. The girls in West Hall invite you to take a cake walk. However, if you would rather, go pogo popping at South's booth. The Musicians' Club will be swinging — balls on strings will knock over coke bottles on a table.

For all-American athletes, we recommend the tricycle track at South Hall's booth. Featuring 13 booths, the carnival's special attraction will be Mr. Magoo cartoons to be shown in the faculty dining room.

The carnival theme was organized by Chairman Penny Kasten, East-164, and her committee. "Have a Happy" is sponsored by Miss Carmen Rivero with Miss Sylvia Sherman as consulting sponsor. Entrance tickets will cost 50 cents and individual booth tickets, five cents.

Movies To Highlight UN Day October 21

UN DAY, Oct. 21, will feature an all-day program of movies, talent, dancing, and a memorial tribute to Dag Hammarskjold.

The program, to be held in the auditorium of the Evanston Library, Church and Orrington, will begin at 10 a.m. and last until 5 p.m. with continuous Encyclopaedia Britannica films from all over the world.

After a dinner break, the program will resume at 7:30 with a special showing of Danny Kaye's "Operation Children," followed by the memorial to Hammarskjold, a talent show featuring foreign students living in Evanston, and a social mixer.

'Key' Plans New Organization of Sections Staff Keeps Yearboo[k]

Watch closely and you'll see a geni concentrated stares of *The Key's* B ecutive editor Mike Place, and Editor

"IN THE FAST decade, we've never Jim Isenthal, editor-in-chief of the 35th

According to Jim, this year's *Re* confidential, but reports indicate that there will be eight more pages than in last year's yearbook, the sections are to be arranged in different order, and more copy will be used to explain the activities at ETHS.

The theme itself is going to be different than it has ever been before. Also, says Jim, a new way of picturing Evanstonia will be presented.

Several of this year's editors are serving in the same capacity in which they worked last year. Because they are now more experienced, it is felt that they should be able to do a better job of compiling *The Key*.

Meeting the first deadline on time, the staff has sent section one to the printer. This contains the table of contents, the hall sections and the foreword.

"*The Key* staff, which until this fall was crowded together with THE EVANSTONIAN, is proud of its new room," stated Mr. Charles Rathbone, ass't sponsor.

Page 8 • The Evanstonian • Oct. 19, 1961

Composer-in-Residence Finds Inspiring Musical Environment

"THIS IS THE FIRST school I've worked in through the Foundation grants," said Mr. John Chorbajian, second Ford Foundation composer at ETHS, with a smile. "And I'm very impressed by all the teen-age zest I see here."

East Hall Initiates Parents Meetings

EAST HALL INITIATED the "Parent Meeting" on Friday, Oct. 6. Featuring a different slant on parent question-and-answer sessions with school authorities, the meetings are being held in the student lounge from 10-11:30 each Friday morning.

"The sessions provide an opportunity for an exchange of information between the parents and department chairmen, hall principals, and counselors," said Mr. Edward Curry, East Hall Principal.

"Who chooses the reading material in the English Department? Why are students being tested Oct. 10, 17, and 24 and what uses will be made of the tests in regard to the student?" were questions asked," stated Mr. Curry.

Seniors Will Take Exams As Scholarship Necessity

ALL SENIORS applying for Illinois State Scholarships are required to take the American College Testing Act examinations to be given Saturday morning, Nov. 4.

Monetary awards are given to those students who show financial need, while honorary awards are given to students meeting all eligibility requirements except that of need.

Scholarships may be used at any school in the state of Illinois.

Continuing, the quiet, dark, 24-year-old New Yorker insisted, "I'm so impressed by the technical set-up and the vocal talent, I'd like to do an opera for the Spring Music Festival, if a suitable topic is suggested."

Has Composed Many Works

An opera would be nothing new to the talented composer, for he has written a one-act opera entitled "Antigone." Among other works he has composed a sonata for violin and piano, and "Medea," a symphonic poem. Most of these were produced at the Manhattan School of Music where he earned his M. A. and B. A. in music.

Mr. Chorbajian (pronounced Shar-bay-gean) has many plans for future music productions and is now orchestrating "Four Christmas Psalms" for chorus and orchestra, based on biblical Christmas passages, for the Christmas Festival.

Hesitates to Classify Style

When asked about his style, Mr. Chorbajian hesitated, "Anyone who writes music today is a contemporary composer because he is influenced by modern trends. But no matter in what period of music development a composer is classed, you can't deny the influences of other periods."

The composer sat silent for a moment, then elaborated, "Personally, I believe the greatest element in music is its expressiveness. If a composer is a good composer, he expresses himself just as a writer might, but he uses notes instead of words."

Mr. Chorbajian

United Fund Misses Goal, Beats Last Year's Amount

THE UNITED FUND ended its campaign last Friday with $720, according to Mr. David Cameron, sponsor. The $800 goal was not reached, but there was an increase of $160 over last year.

"The campaign went well this year because we had good representation in the homerooms," said Chairman Deborah Miles, West-164. The money will be distributed to the Youth Agencies in Evanston, the Junior Red Cross, and the March of Dimes. East-204 was first with $78.07, and South-244 was second with $66.54.

Letter to the Editors

Student Suggests Improvement of Rally

To the Editors:

I suggest that ETHS can learn from this year's fairly successful pep rally. We could have an even better one next year! In my opinion, it wasn't well organized. No one knew whose floats were going by, there wasn't much enthusiasm, and people in the back couldn't see or hear the cheerleaders. It would be much better if the rally could be held in the stadium. I also think that the winning float should be in the game the next day.

I have heard talk about having an all-school directory which would contain the students' telephone numbers, addresses, and homerooms. I think something like this would be helpful. It would assist club presidents and chairmen when they have to contact different people. This directory could be made available to the different heads of organizations through their sponsors. Central Council could decide how to put both of these ideas into effect.

I believe that these ideas would both help the school and create more school spirit for the pep rallies.

— Barbara Mayer,
West-144

McDonald's ALL AMERICAN

look for the golden arches . . . McDonald's

100% PURE BEEF HAMBURGERS — not made from frozen meat but top quality beef ground fresh daily. **McDonald's** Hamburgers are served hot off the grill on toasted buns — the way you like 'em best!

CRISP GOLDEN BROWN FRENCH FRIES — cut from choice #1 Idaho potatoes — prepared to your taste and served piping hot. You never had them so good.

TRIPLE THICK DAIRY SHAKES — smooth and creamy — the good old-fashioned kind made just right!

the drive-in with the arches

McDonald's
1117 HOWARD STREET

UNDERWOOD-OLIVETTI
LETTERA 22

This machine recently won a contest at the University of Illinois as being "the best mass produced item from a safety pin to an auto."

The **Lettera 22** has every important big typewriter feature. It weighs just 8½ lbs., stands only 3 in. high, and is sturdily built of the finest materials.

LIST PRICE $88   **STUDENT PRICE $68**

see the Lettera 22 at

ACE TYPEWRITER SERVICE
919 Main Street, Evanston   ·   GR 5-1155

Evanston Township High School
Evanston High School
Evanston, Illinois

EXAMPLE
144

four-column, six-page paper while Example 144 illustrates the advantages of a four-column, eight-page paper for a large school with well over three thousand students. Extremely attractive five-column formats are reproduced in Examples 145 and 146.

EXAMPLE

145

A Trip To Moscow See p. 2

The Lincoln Log

A Trip To Japan See p. 3

Volume 36 Friday, September 22, 1961 No. 1

Song Girls Begin Fall Activities

Although most students fearfully awaited the beginning of school this semester, six Lincoln girls were anxiously awaiting it; for with the new term, came the prospect of serving as song girls for several months. They would cheerfully lead in spirit and enthusiastically perform at all necessary functions. They would enjoy their work and show that they enjoyed it.

Performing at rallies and games and displaying school spirit at all times are only the rewards, however. These six girls worked long hours preparing for the song girl competition. There were routines to be learned, dances to be created, and schoolwork and good grades to be maintained. Finally, on one June afternoon, these girls received their first and most memorable reward, that of being chosen from almost 50 other talented contestants as true Lincoln song girls.

On September 15, Vicki Cero, Carol Clark, Janet Motzer, Sue Carney, Sharon Ferraris, and Jo Janofsky saw their first rally as song girls. This performance was the result of weeks of practice and tired muscles. Appearing in smart gold outfits consisting of pleated skirts, light-gold blouses, long pull-overs with a Mustang emblem on the front, red leather shoes, and red gloves, these girls lived up to all expectations by performing beautifully and precisely.

WELCOME—Sweden's exchange student Lars Dahlquist is greeted by Bob Moore, student body treasurer.

Swedish Student Here on Exchange

An interesting addition to the Senior Class at Lincoln this year is Lars Dahlquist, an exchange ...

... troductions are only necessary for adults.

There is little difference in ...

3000 Students Jam Lincoln

Years ago, when Lincoln High School was first built, plans were made around the fact that there would never be more than 1800 students in attendance during a single semester. Today those 1800 students have increased to over 3000, making Lincoln, population-wise, the largest high school in San Francisco.

Overcrowded halls, small classrooms, a new bell schedule, and three new shacks are visible evidence of this great expansion. Registries have been changed and new classrooms found, all to provide for the ever-present and always-needy student.

Every place available and suitable has been put to use. For example, many of the boys have been heard to remark on the presence of girls in their hygiene and ROTC room, B202. This is simply due to the mass overcrowding which has made it necessary to hold classes in this part of the school. Girls attending a class in this room have a constant fear of ending up in the boys' locker room, an embarrassing fate worse than death itself.

The teaching staff, too, has increased and several new and pleasant faces are seen in the halls. Several of Lincoln's past teachers, Mr. Norm Glattree, Mr. Peter Walker, Mrs. Marilyn Clark, Miss Joan Shelley, and Miss Jean Thomas, have returned to assist in educating this large body of students. At this time, Lincoln's teaching staff has increased to almost 120 persons, each willing to do his best to see that students are properly educated.

The only real help, however, may lie in the new Lowell High School being built, near Lake Merced; for when this establishment is completed, many students from Lincoln will be re-enrolled at Lowell. Only in this way will the overcrowded condition be somewhat overcome.

'Log' Staff

Sharon Yosiph has been selected to head the journalism staff of the "Lincoln Log" for the fall semester, 1961.

Sharon Mindlin, managing editor, will assist the editor. Other members of the staff include Susan Carlsen, news editor; Marianne Hinckle and Ann Ehrhardt, feature editors; Helen D'Amico, editorial editor; Charles Rapp, sports editor; Joan Collingwood, copy editor; Marion Canuto, business manager; Rosemary Nyberg, circulation manager; Marlene Chiarucci, advertising manager; and Sharon Marks, publicity manager. Mr. Philip Lum will again serve as advisor.

Tennis Shoes For Dance

Tonight is the night, my friendly low sophs, to watch a very impressive group of seniors, commonly referred to as the Forty Links, auctioned off.

Each term this honorary service society at Lincoln presents the Hello Day Dance. This is the time when 20 boys and 20 girls will be auctioned off to new now sophomores as slaves.

The dancing will start at eight o'clock in the boys' gym and conclude at 11:00. The dress will be school clothes and TENNIS SHOES MUST BE WORN! This is due to the fact that the gym floor has just recently been refinished.

Monday, September 25, will be Slave Day. So if YOU win a slave, boys, don't forget to bring your cub scout pack, and, girls, don't forget your teddy bears.

The newly-elected officers of the Forty Links are: President, Barry Ganapol; Vice President, Linda Asher; Secretary, Val Olander; Treasurer, Ron Prater; Sergeant-at-Arms, Rod McCauley.

New Shacks Going Up

Something "new" has been added to Lincoln. Because of the crowded conditions here, three extra shacks have been inherited from the Ulloa Anne Elementary School. Although ordered in April, these buildings did not arrive until two weeks before school started and will not be finished for another six weeks.

As of now, the old shacks end at number 18, and since the main building starts at 21, two of the shacks have been numbered 19 and 20. The third number has not yet been determined. Classes to be held in the shacks will be the ones now held in the boys' hygiene room and in the basement of the main building.

Students hope that these shacks will add classroom space to Lincoln, which is so desperately needed.

'Scholastic Roto' To Be Issued

Buyers of the **Log** this semester will actually be receiving two papers for the price of one, as the **Scholastic Roto**, a national pictorial supplement, will be included once a month.

The **Roto** consists of many articles of particular interest to teenagers. Published monthly, the magazine has a circulation of 1.5 million and is carried by some 1,800 high schools coast to coast.

Go To The Game

The Lincoln Log
Lincoln High School
San Francisco, California

Pat Gridders Play Fort Collins; See Page Four

The SURVEYOR

Student Freedom Suggested; See Editorials

Vol. 3, No. 1 (20 cents) George Washington High School, Denver, Colorado October 19, 1961

Special Exclusive

Briggs, Other Sophs Win Class Offices

ALREADY AT WORK ARE THE NEWLY-ELECTED SOPHOMORE officers, who gathered at a private home to plan the year's activities. Tupper Briggs, president, (gavel-in-hand) is helping Secretary Terry Touff compose on the typewriter while Ayliffe Jones, vice president, looks on. Behind the threesome, Steve Friedman, treasurer, is totaling some checks. Also standing are three Student Council members, Howard Hutson, Joan Bower and Carol Degen, who are looking at the year's schedule. Lee Sullivan, the fourth Student Council representative, is working at the desk.

Sophomore class officers were announced today to the **Surveyor** in an exclusive interview with Mrs. Violette McCarthy, Student Council sponsor.

Tupper Briggs, president; Ayliffe Jones, vice-president; Terry Touff, secretary; and Steve Friedman, treasurer were chosen by 579 sophomores to lead the class of '64.

The sophomores also elected Joan Bower, Carol Degan, Howard Hutson and Lee Sullivan to Student Council.

Sophomore election procedure spanned a week, beginning with a special assembly on Oct. 8, and ending with the final voting on Oct. 14.

The eight officers were culled from the 81 candidates who entered the primaries. From this group sixteen finalists were chosen on Oct. 11.

The new president was Gove Jr. High ninth grade president.

Commenting on his election to the Sophomore Class presidency, Briggs stated, "I'd like to thank the Sophomore Class for selecting me their representative. I hope to work out any problems that might arise and to help the class meet all the standards that have been set in the past."

National Merit Recognizes 29 'Lettermen'

Twenty-nine seniors at Washington will receive letters of commendation from the National Merit Corporation.

These students, who took the National Merit Scholarship Qualifying Test last spring, are in addition to the seven GW semi-finalists.

Mr. Sam Waldman, principal, has announced that Washington's commended students are Hamlet "Chips" Barry, Ron Berenbeim, Susan Bush, Tom Connole, Claudia Curfman, Mary Dickson, Norman Dodge, Terry Downing, Phil Gordon, Patty Hall, Jay Hubert, Steve Jenkins, John Kobayashi, Michael Levin and Carol Lichtenstein.

Others are Carolyn McKinney, Steve Miller, Randi Nervig, Joy Oppenheim, Allen Pichon, Susan Proyor, Richard Shinton, Karin Stanley, Jon Streltzer, James Tatters, Debby Uchill, Steve Virbick and Mayme Weed.

HSH Starts in Nov., Includes Library Use

Given added impetus by the success of last year's program, the Honor Study Hall has been expanded this year to include library privileges.

New applications for membership will be distributed in the next few weeks, according to Claudia Curfman, chairman of the Student Council Interest Committee.

Honor System

"Since the Patriots showed last year that the honor system can work well at Washington, we are optimistic that the new library privilege will also be used in the right manner," Claudia explained.

Students who have specific work to do in the library will need only to show the librarians their HSH pass cards if they enter at the middle of a period. A student who enters at the beginning must fill out a slip, writing HSH rather than a room number.

Provisions will be similar to those enforced last year. Students who submit a teacher recommendation and application will become eligible to utilize a study hall or the library during their lunch hour.

Enter, Leave Once

Both in the library and the study hall rooms, the students will be permitted to enter and leave only once during the period and to conduct themselves in such a manner that no supervision will be required.

Membership will be limited to one-third more than the number of desks in the study room, and the student's office record will not be checked when he applies.

Burl Ives' Tapes Teach American Lit.

How would you like Burl Ives to teach your American literature course?

If your American literature teacher is Mr. Robert McDowell, you can expect to hear from Burl Ives, along with Pete Seeger, Oscar Brand and other nationally known folk singers. Mr. McDowell uses tapes of folk songs and slides of paintings to supplement literary materials in the study of regionalism.

"Surprisingly, the students seem to enjoy the slides more than the tapes," commented Mr. McDowell.

Through these three media, music, art and literature, the people of every region expressed their social and human problems.

Another new teaching device at Washington is the use of the language laboratories, according to Mr. Gerald Sachs.
equipped with ear phones and squipped with ear phones and recordings of foreign languages as spoken in their countries of origin.

This method of hearing the language before seeing it written is regarded as the natural way of learning to speak.

In addition, the customs and folk songs of the people who speak the studied language are taken up as supplementary material.

Council Plans Leadership Day; Pats Attend JRC Conferences

Washington's first Leadership Conference for its own students will be held on Nov. 8.

The day's activities, currently being planned by the Student Council, are geared toward presenting all interested school leaders with a meaningful learning experience.

Open to School

All school club officers, Student Council, General Assembly, **Surveyor** and **Heritage** members and others will be eligible to attend, according to Mrs. Violette G. McCarthy, Student Council sponsor.

Mr. Gerald Van Pool, National Student Council Director of student activities, Dr. George Mathes, principal of Morey Jr. High School and Mr. Earl Reum Denver Public School Director of Student Activities will be among the guest speakers.

Details will be released later.

Red Cross Conference

Washington also participated in a leadership conference last week.

Rosemary Bloedorn and Phil Beck, representing George Washington High School, attended a tri-state Jr. Red Cross Leadership Conference at Pueblo Junior College Oct. 14 and 15.

The conference's programs included Jr. Red Cross leadership training workshops and discussions, a banquet and a square dance.

The pair stayed at the Whitman Hotel in Pueblo and returned to Denver Sunday by chartered bus.

Seniors' Parents Hold Meeting

Parents of seniors met with the Washington administrative staff and counselors last night.

The purpose of the P-TA Twelfth Grade Parent-Counselor meeting was for senior parents to further talk with counselors on college plans and senior activities.

After a group meeting of the parents the administrative staff and counselors in the auditorium, parents talked individually with counselors.

"This meeting served as an excellent opportunity to meet with the seniors' parents," said Mr. Roger Williams, Senior Class sponsor.

Surveyor Holds Sticker Contest; Teacher Committee To Judge

A contest sponsored by the **Surveyor** to select a new design for car stickers will begin this week.

After meeting with the Delegate Assembly, the staff decided that the entire student body should have the opportunity to design a new car sticker.

Students are urged to submit a design to the judging committee, Mr. Robert Rothstein, Mrs. Violette McCarthy and Mrs. Edith Niblo, by placing their proposed design in one of the three teachers' boxes.

The best design will be compared with the old sticker and the final decision on the sticker to be used will be announced in the Nov. 9 **Surveyor.**

PSAT Ticket-Sale Ends Today

Sophomores who have not bought tickets for the Preliminary Scholastic Aptitude Test are urged to do so today.

The test will be given at 8:00 a.m., Saturday morning, Oct. 21 at Washington to all those who have purchased $1.50 tickets from Mrs. Mary Pfarrer, Washington treasurer.

Sophomores Should Take

According to Mr. Merlin Arbogast, evaluator, all sophomores should plan on taking the PSAT whether or not they intend to go to college. Mr. Arbogast also recommends that juniors take the PSAT.

Seniors competing for many scholarships should also take the PSAT.

Inexpensive Guide

"This is an inexpensive test that can be used by the student, his parents and his school for the interpretation of his abilities," commented Mr. Arbogast.

Ticket-selling will end after school today, and only those who have tickets will be assigned and admitted to a room in which the test will be administered.

BARBIE BOWES IS CROWNED QUEEN of Washington's Homecoming by Coach Gregg Browning, as her escort, Axel Staehr, and some of the 500 who attended the dance look on. Sponsored by the Pep Club, "Harvest Harlequin" on Oct. 14 in the girls' gym, was financially one of Washington's most successful events.

The Surveyor
George Washington High School
Indianapolis, Indiana

EXAMPLE

146

CONGRATULATIONS!—Girls' and Boys' State delegates congratulate each other for being selected to attend the summer convention as Washington representatives. Girl Staters are (left to right) Sherry Selch, Evelyn Thomas, Carole McKinney, and Sandra K. Marsh; and Boy Staters are Steve Dalzell, John Heinzmann, Mike Merrick, and Gary Bland. The conventions are scheduled during the summer.

Juniors Travel to IU for Girls', Boys' State

Chosen by the faculty as top members of the Junior Class, four boys and four girls will visit Indiana University for one-week sessions this summer at Hoosier Boys' and Girls' State.

Steve Dalzell, Gary Bland, Mike Merrick, and John Heinzmann will attend Boys' State the week of June 17 while Sherry Selch, Sandra K. Marsh, Evelyn Thomas, and Carole McKinney travel to Girls' State two weeks later.

Sponsored by the American Legion and the American Legion Auxiliary, Boys' and Girls' State strives to teach junior representatives how Indiana government is run and operated in hopes that the delegates will spread the learning to their classmates.

UPON ARRIVAL at Indiana University, the representatives are divided into precincts, cities, and counties. Launching actual campaigns and elections will occupy most of the week-long delegation; however, after the state, county, and city officials have been elected, they will set up offices and govern the mythical Boys' or Girls' State.

Next fall, each representative will make an oral account of his activities at Boys' or Girls' State to both his school and to the American Legion Post which sponsored him.

American Legion Posts who will sponsor the five boys are B & O

Students Plan Roman Banquet, Caesar's March

During the annual Roman Banquet in the school cafeteria May 10, Latin students will relive history with the theme "The Triumph of Caesar."

Senior Sandra Thomas assisted by seniors John Stott and Diane Osting will preside over the meal and program.

LANA TOTTON, Sue Douglass, Emilie Parsons, and Reba Koch prepared the script for the program. The play will be in the form of a radio broadcast centered around Caesar's battles and parts of his life.

The banquet will end with the group singing songs in both Latin

The Surveyor

Vol. XXXIV, N. 12 George Washington High School, Indianapolis, Indiana

4 Continentals Win Hor in Regional Science Co

Four Continentals out of nine who participated in the ninth annual Indiana Regional Science Fair at Butler University won six awards for Washington.

CONTESTANTS from eight counties entered the contest with various science displays which were exhibited and judged.

Pat Coleman, senior, a previous winner, led the way of Washington winners with an honorable mention in 12th Grade Biological and a first place award in Medical Technology which gives her the opportunity to work at the Methodist Hospital School of Medical technicians as a lab technician. Pat's project was "Synergistics Relationship of Elements and Antibiotics."

Sophomore Craig Johnson, a previous winner also, won two awards with his project "Determination of the Endpoint Titration in Bacteriophage." He won an honorable mention in 10th Grade Biological and a second place in Medical Technology.

Junior Pat Kira won a third place award in 11th Grade Biological with the project, "Uptake of Trace Elements in Coleus."

GORDON CLARK, sophomore, entering the contest for the first time, placed second in 10th Grade Biological with his project, "Mathematical Approach to Geotropism."

Other Continentals who participated in the

Kernohan, "

the White

"Psychologic

on the Phys

Adolescents;

ney, "Effect

Heartbeat o

Emilie Pars

Stuffs on the

Dennis Pana

sis."

During th

sors discusse

helping him

display.

Pupils Present Short Comedies

Members of the Dramatics Club, cancelling their one-act play, "I Knew George Washington," which was originally scheduled for tomorrow afternoon, will present two short comedies Thursday, May 11.

Charlene Zeronik and Jackie Stillwell will protray the leading characters in Scene II, Act I of "The Importance of Being Ernest" by Oscar Wilde.

Another short one-act play, not yet selected, will be staged with Nancy Cross, Emilie Parsons, and Diana Schwalm as leading characters.

A 10¢ admission fee will be charged for the play which will begin immediately after school in Room 248. Proceeds will go to the Dramatics Club to help produce future productions.

Musicians Play at Pop Concert

Playing familiar, standard, and classical, as well as popular numbers, the Concert Orchestra, Concert Band, and Dance Band presented their annual Pop Concert in the Boys' gym last Friday.

INTRODUCING a new idea, members of the Junior Band and Beginning Orchestra ushered the audience to tables and sold them cokes, pretzels, and potato chips during the concert. Concluding the evening, the organization sponsored a record hop.

Each of the groups, under the direction of Ray Funk or Miss Ruth Rosser, performed separately. The proceeds of the evening, consisting of an admission fee of 25¢ and receipts of the refreshments, went for band and orchestra needs.

Meet N

W

by Jean Sorr

Forming

gaining educ

lective fields

opportunities

institutes.

PROGRAM

work, and st

the students

institutes. D

work, the rep

to form many

Continental

chances to

experience off

stitute. Stude

ence, mathem

gineering, an

number of c

ties that they

vacation.

However, t

a few basic

gibility. To a

be either juni

terested in th

Between Issues

April 27-City Track Meet

April 28-Business Education Day (School Closed)

May 1-Report Cards

May 1-City-County Golf Meet

May 11-Dramatics Club Play

May 12-Sectional Track Meet

The Surveyor
George Washington High School
Denver, Colorado

Friday, November 3, 1961 The WESTCHESTER HIGH SCHOOL COMET Page Three

AFS STUDENT

Viggo Frederiksen

Danish student likes jazz, WHS

By Wendy Yee

"One of the first things I noticed was that your cars are bigthan ours and that you have fewer bicycles that we in Denmark do." Thus Viggo Fredericksen, B-12, American Field Service student from Denmark, summed up his first impressions of life in America.

Viggo is living with the Mr. J.F. Connellys of Westchester, whose son Roy, A-12, is also a Comet. His family in Denmark includes his father, a salesman; his mother; and two younger brothers, Hans Jorgen, 12, and Niels Erik, 8.

Viggo's spare time is taken up with his playing tennis and soccer; Viggo is also an experienced piano player who enjoys both classical and popular music. "I like to listen to good records," says Viggo, who attends the weekly meetings of his jazz club when home in Denmark.

Teen-age social activites in the United States, according to Viggo, are quite different from those in Denmark. "We have only a sports club in school, but there are many clubs outside of school we may join. In Denmark, there is only one dance a year sponsored by the school—at Christmastime, when the students in the graduating class put on a play. If one wishes to dance at any other time, there are places he may go to in town."

Viggo's ambition is to become an electrical engineer. He indicated that, upon his return home to Denmark, he will become an apprentice in an electrical factory. He will then return to school for more study, and following that, says Viggo, "I hope to be able to return to the United States to specialize in the TV and radio fields."

Many on the Westchester campus who have met and talked with Viggo have been impressed by his fluency in English, but they may not know that Viggo can speak German, Swedish, and French (and English) in addition to his native Danish.

STOOPING TO CONQUER

SHOWN SPECULATING upon the problems encounted by the English gentlemen they portray are (L-R) Chris Fee, B-12, and Phil Fagen, B-12. They act in the play **She Stoops to Conquer,** to be presented Nov. 8 by the play production class. The play is a light satire on life in England of the 1800's and will be presented in both matinee and evening performances. Matinee tickets for the students are fifty cents; adult tickets are one dollar. Photo by Dennis Wadham.

Use your 'noodle,' man

By Francine Kittay

You sit politely, you laugh at the teacher's jokes, and you do all that is expected of you, except think. Is this a picture of you? Are you a tape recorder rather than a thinker? Do you go to school to learn the available knowledge, or to temporarily memorize it?

"The most difficult thing to teach young people is to think for themselves," stated Mr. James Barreca, WHS's journalism teacher. Being involved with the production of our school newspaper, he has come in contact with many such situations. Most students will do their work if they are told how, when, and where to do it.

Initiative and responsibility are developed by young people determining the how, when, and where on their own, he indicated. Mr. Barreca's philosphy on this subject is summed up by the statement, "The mark of a clear-thinking student is his ability to follow directions-whether they are oral, written, or implied. It's the implied instructions that 'throw' the non-thinker," he said.

On the same topic, Principal Carroll Lockridge indicated he feels there is no future for a non-thinking person, and such people will never succeed in holding any position of importance. "As far as the students at Westchester High School go, they are, on the whole, imaginative; and they do have the drive needed to advance in society," Mr. Lockridge said.

When asked if he felt the students at WHS do their own thinking, Mr. Robert R. Douglas, English department chairman answered, "Yes, as much as adults do in any average area in the United States."

Maybe this is so, but take a look at your study habits and grades. If you find that they are just average or satisfactory, try improving them.

As an adult you will be expected to make decisions and form sound opinions. This may only be achieved if you **start thinking now.**

New books added to WHS library

By Monte Swern

Many of you book 'fanatics' will be happy to know that there are many new additions to the library, according to remarks made today by Mrs. Ester Bennett, librarian. For those who comprehend French, there is **Vingt Contes du Vingtieme Siecle.** This is a book of short, humorous stories. Then for you drama stars, there is a book, **Nine Plays,** by Eugene O'neill.

For the mad-scientist-type, there is **Elements of the Universe** and **One, Two, Three, ... Infinity** by Gene Seaburg and George Gamow, respectively.

Last, but not least, for good, old, ordinary reading, there is **Boy Gets a Car,** the adventures of a boy and his car. By Boris Pasternak, there is **Dr. Zhivago,** and **The Longest Day** the latter of which is the story, of D-Day, World War II.

Others include **Hell Cats of the Sea** by Lockwood, Adamson, and Nimitz, all retired military personnel.

Did you know that last semester one-quarter of the student body came to the library each day? They did. There to help these and other readers are Bonni Ernst, Ellen Grauer, and Jeanne Bedard. These girls work in the library before school under Mrs. Bennett's supervision. They are a great asset to the students in obtaining their information. Mrs. Bennett indicated they deserve a "pat on the back."

School goals discussed by educators

More than 2,000 supervisors from school systems throughout the state attended the annual conference on direction and improvement of instruction and on child welfare at the Statler Hilton Hotel, a school official indicated today.

The conference, called annually by State Superintendent of Schools Dr. Roy Simpson, included nationally known experts in the field, five general sessions, numerous exhibits and workshop meetings.

Featured speakers during the week-long conference included James Quillen, dean of the Stanford University School of Education, and Mrs. Georgiana Hardy, of the Los Angeles City Board of Education.

'Music in M-1' offered again

By Wendy Yee

"Music in M-1", sponsored by Mr. Robert Wood, is being held again at noon on Tuesdays.

"I began such a program," commented Mr. Wood, "because opportunities to hear fine music are not as prevalent as those to hear popular music." He originated "Music in M-1" two years ago.

The program not only provides students with symphonic music, but also furnishes them a quiet place to eat, he indicated. All records played, which belong to the music department, are chosen by Mr. Wood. He plans to continue "Music in M-1" for the rest of the semester.

"Music in M-1" is open to students of all grades. Sometimes according to Mr. Wood, there are more boys present than girls. An average of 35 to 40 Comets attend each session.

Parents, elders, pronounce teen-agers 'strange creatures'

By Joan Levi

"What is wrong with the youth of today?" These words are undoubtedly uttered quite frequently among adults. To them, teen-agers appear to be strange creatures who were slipped onto "their" earth by some incredible force unknown to mankind. Worst of all they are still searching for the answer to the question: Why are teen-agers so eccentric?

Are our elders forgetting their youth: raccoon coats, noisemakers, hopped-up jalopys, and all the ingredients needed for a successful football game? No, I don't believe that they have forgotten, but it is hard for them to acquaint themselves with our new fads.

Among these fads are surfing (with the bleached hair), tennis shoes, et cetera. How could you expect our elders to know what a 'gremmie' or 'hotdogger' is, when we didn't know until a few years ago. When you consider the problems, I imagine that we seem quite strange to the older generation.

This situation, however, isn't as hopeless as it might appear. How often do teen-agers fill their parents in on all the 'details'? In the majority of cases the only idea the parent has of your extra-curricular activities is what they can guess. This may be more detrimental than the straight truth. Exaggeration isn't hard to do.

CLUBS ATTENTION!

All clubs wishing publicity or coverage in **Club Clippings** are to submit the information to Wendy Yee, club columnist.

All information must be typewritten and should be submitted no later than 8:10 a.m., in D5, on Monday, two weeks prior to publication in the **Comet.**

New teacher calls WHS 'tremendous'

By Pat Eikner

One of the new teachers here at Westchester is a classical music fan. He also enjoys opera and the ballet as well. This cutural-minded teacher is Mr. James G. Willett, who teaches in the social studies department.

Mr. Willett was born in Long Beach, California. His favorite sports, as a boy, were sailing (since the water was so close by) and football. He originally wanted to be an engineer, but when he found that he was unable to do this, he decided to be a teacher instead.

Mr. Willett, who teaches U.S. History I and II and Study Hall, attended Long Beach State College, where he received his AA degree; the University of California at Berkeley, earning his BA; and Long Beach State College again, this time getting his MA. He did post-graduate work at UCLA and USC.

Mr. Willett's service experience includes the Army Topographical Service and the Naval Reserve. He has taught at Torrance Unified School District for four years; Narbonne High School for two years; and two years at Manual Arts Adult School.

Mr. Willett does not have a regular room here at WHS, but instead can usually be found dashing around rooms C-1, C-2, C-4, C-10, F-8, and A-1 for Study Hall. When he isn't roving around the campus, he may be at the opera or ballet, which he tries to attend whenever possible. He also has a large collection of records of classical music at his home.

Mr. Willett's immediate reaction to Westchester High may be summed up in just one word, "Tremendous!"

NEW TEACHER

Mr. Willett

Westchester Music, Inc.
9101 So. Sepulveda
All "45" Singles
79c
OR 1-5249
LARGEST SELECTION
"Oldies but Goodies"
Mon.-Fri., 10 a.m.-9:30 p.m.
Sat., 9 a.m.-6 p.m.
Sun. 11 a.m.-5 p.m.

LOOK TO MUNROE'S TO LOOK YOUR BEST
MUNROE'S
YOUNG MEN'S WEAR
8634 S. Sepulveda Blvd.
OR 8-0062

Pizza To Go Phone Orders Taken
SCARPELLINO'S
Pizza Houses
No. 1
OR 1-9910
312 W. Manchester
Inglewood, Calif.
No. 2
OS 9-9031
15213 S. Crenshaw
Gardena, Calif.

WHAT IS THE BEST?
A CORSAGE FROM
STAN'S FLOWERS
MAYFAIR Market
Parking Lot Entrance

The Comet
Westchester High School
Los Angeles, California

The choice facing a staff. The amount of copy carried determines the cost of publishing a school paper, but it does not necessarily determine the format of the paper or the frequency of publication. Here the staff may have a choice; for instance—

1. An eight-column, four-page paper carries approximately 672 inches of copy, twenty-one inches per column. A five-column, four-page paper carries approximately 320 inches, sixteen inches per column. If the school is able to issue only an eight-column paper biweekly, it might prefer to bring the news to the students weekly in a five-column format at approximately the same cost.

2. A seven-column, four-page paper carries about 560 inches of copy, twenty inches per column. A five-column, six-page paper carries 480 inches, sixteen inches per column. Here again the staff has a choice.

Paper stock. By far the most popular stock on which school papers are printed is a good grade of newsprint. Some publications, however, hold to the coated white stock on which most magazines are printed. To some degree the choice of stock, however, depends upon the printing process. Before selecting a stock, discuss the matter with your printer.

ESSENTIALS OF PAGE MAKE-UP

Page size, number of pages, stock, printing process, and frequency of publication are matters to be determined by each school. Regardless of variations in format, however, there are some established principles to be followed in make-up. Such principles are basic to good student journalism.

Nameplate. The nameplate is the title line of the newspaper, to be found on the front page, near the top. This title line should be harmonious to the page in typography and proportion and should not change typographically unless the newspaper undergoes a change of name or a revision of design. In most instances it is centered above the stories. Some newspapers, however, move the nameplate to serve the make-up needs of the particular issue. This *floating nameplate* or *roving nameplate* must never drop below the fold, and should preferably be kept at least two or three inches above it. Example 147 reproduces some first pages of the *Orange and Black,* one of the numerous papers using the floating nameplate.

EXAMPLE

147

Speakers Earn Honor Ratings

Uhlemann, Johnston Will Lead Students

The Orange & Black
The Official Organ of the Students of Grand Junction High School
Grand Junction, Colorado

The Orange & Black
The Official Organ of the Students of Grand Junction High School
Grand Junction, Colorado

23 Bands To Play In Slope Festival

League Sponsors Annual Girls Week

Juniors Attend City-CountyDay

SQ3R Program Helps Learning

'Carousel' Set For May 16-17

Boys League To Show Film

French Classes Read Perrichon

60-Hour Schoolwork Week Swamps GJHSers

Clubs Submit By-Laws For SBA Constitution

arly 400 To Receive Diplomas

Orange & Black
Official Organ of the Students of Grand Junction High School
Grand Junction, Colorado

Grads Will Hear Speech by Bothell

Superior GJHSers Merit Recognition

Moss Honored At Science Fair

Max, Jan To Attend Council Conference

Awards, Plays Cap Thespian Initiation

185 Seniors Picnic At Glenwood Springs

The nameplate has a trade-mark value that must be considered when style is evaluated. This value, however, should not keep a paper from replacing a poor nameplate. The nameplate should be of the same family as the main type on the first page, or of a decidedly contrasting type.

Dateline. The dateline, sometimes called the running head, is found on the front page, just below the nameplate. It includes the name of the school, the city, the state, the volume and number of the issue, and the date. Such information as the school slogan and the price of the paper is often superfluous, however. Example 148 illustrates some typical nameplates with systematically arranged datelines.

Datelines giving the name of the paper, the date, and the page number are carried across the top of the other pages. The name is centered, with the number on the outer end and the date on the inner.

Columns. For easy reading a newspaper page is composed of a number of columns. Once commonly 13 picas (a pica is one sixth of an inch) wide, columns are now usually set 12 or even 11 picas wide. Originally all newspaper pages used column rules, that is, vertical lines between the columns. Now many papers set their copy a pica or so narrower, using the white space between columns for contrast; this is especially true of the editorial page.

Masthead. The masthead always appears on the editorial page; it usually tells who issues the newspaper, when and where it is issued, the subscription rates, and the names of the adviser and chief editors (at times the entire staff is included). The title usually matches the nameplate in typeface, giving a feeling of harmony to the paper. (See Example 149.)

Central High Register
Central High School
Omaha, Nebraska

The North Star
North High School
Omaha, Nebraska

The Walton Log
Walton High School
New York, N.Y.

The Southwest Lancer
Southwest Miami High School
Miami, Florida

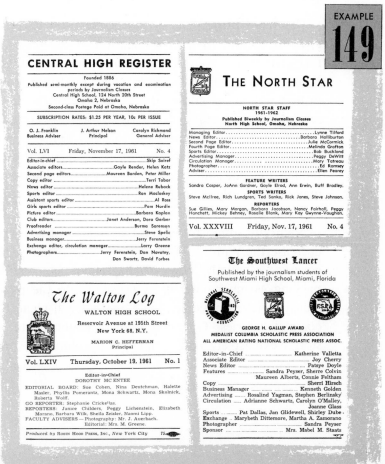

EXAMPLE
149

The professional thoroughness of a school paper can be checked by such points as the nameplate, the datelines, and the masthead.

PAGE DISTINCTIONS

High school papers, usually only four pages long, demand that the nature of each page be rather definitely determined. Generally this distinction is as follows: first page, news; second page, editorial; third page, feature; and fourth page, sports. The time advantage to this arrangement is obvious. The sports page is more immediate than the feature page, and for that reason its copy should go to the printer later. Pages two and three are printed together. (This advantage does not hold true in offset reproduction.)

The school paper should be properly proportioned. For the 13-pica column, the following page dimensions are pleasing to the eye: five columns—12 x 20 inch page; six columns—15 x 22 inch page, and seven columns—17½ x 24 inch page.

The front page. The layout of the front page, the show window, gives the reader his first impression of the paper. The reader's eye first goes to the top left of a page and then travels directly to the right corner where it hesitates. The important story must be placed in that right-hand corner if it is to receive the focal attention it deserves. Once the story in this right corner is absorbed, the eye either swings easily around the page to other items, or jumps dizzily from one to another, depending upon the effectiveness of the design. Although the one story holds the center of interest, every item must maintain its relative importance to the whole. Harmony creates a pleasing page.

Naturally some stories must be long to be complete. Long stories decrease the number of stories on the front page, lessening effective coverage of all the news of the school. One authority will suggest packing as much interest as possible into the page by including as many stories as possible, while another will plead for fewer but more complete stories. One compromise might be to cover the leading stories extensively and to include a column of one-paragraph news

244

briefs set in boldface type. This policy both broadens the sphere of interest and provides adequate coverage of the more significant news items. The adviser for a seven-column school paper once set a minimum of twenty stories on the front page as a standard; a five-column paper may carry as few as ten.

Every front page should carry some material lighter than straight news stories. One long feature and a human-interest story would lighten the page. Cuts should be included in every issue. The boxed story and the boxed head are two tricks for presenting lighter material and adding variety to a page. Boxes should not be placed next to cuts, and their borders should be simple. Unruled boxes are also effective; the space gained by indenting each end of the line serves the same purpose as the rule around the box. Thus material for a 13-pica column would be set 11 picas wide.

Some newspapers add to an attractive layout by carrying *ears* on the first page—small items, set on either side of the nameplate and often boxed, that call attention to special features, present weather information, denote the edition of the paper, or boost particular features.

As mentioned above, the floating nameplate provides innovations in front-page make-up. It is not uncommon to find a streamer head or even a story above the nameplate. Some of the highest rated school papers are those that have changed from the more symmetrical, traditional make-up to the streamlined layout obtained by the use of such innovations.

The appearance of the front page can be tested by folding the paper in half horizontally and judging separately what is above and what is below the fold. Most of the heavy heads will come above the fold, but the lower section must have some distinction of its own. To make up a page, one begins at both the bottom and the top.

The editorial page. Although page one is the show window of the paper, the other pages should be as carefully planned. Each page must have a purpose behind it; each must be distinctive.

Editorial material should dominate the editorial page, advertisements being confined to later pages. The editorial page should be lighter in appearance than any other. For effect, the editorial columns are often set wider than the others, with the type leaded (lĕd'ĕd) one point—eight point on nine, for instance. Leading a column widens the distance between lines of type. Daily newspapers usually have the flag or masthead in the upper left-hand corner, above the editorials. However, there are interesting deviations from this position in the school press.

The sports page. The sports page by its nature requires life in its make-up. This life can be achieved without gaudiness by the use of action photographs of sports events and complete and interesting coverage of the school sports field.

Many daily newspapers carry a deep nameplate at the top of the sports page. The school paper should hesitate to follow this practice for its space is limited. A sports nameplate two inches deep run on a six-column paper robs the page of twelve inches of copy—an equivalent of 500 words. Does the nameplate carry more interest than the 500 words?

The fourth page. After considering the front, editorial, and sports pages of a four-page paper, we speak of the other page as the "fourth page." However, it may be either the third or fourth page in the paper, depending upon the placement of the sports page. Some papers consider it the feature page, others the second news page.

This page may serve as a "catchall" if care is not exercised. It must have distinguishing qualities that differentiate it from page two.

The advertisements should be in attractive relation to the other copy. Pyramiding the ads to the right is an attractive way of arranging them and permits more ads to be run by the side of copy. Borders and rules should not be used on ads that attract attention to themselves.

Interesting news stories too minor to make page one may well be included on the fourth page. It is also appropriate to play up news features, personals columns, entertaining matter such as puzzles, and other interesting copy.

Many papers have built up reader interest in this page to a point at which it is the first read by the student. It should attract this attention by a distinctive but not sensational headdress. Attractive two-

and three-column heads might well announce the lead story. On inside pages the lead story takes the left-hand corner since the ads pyramid up the right.

Some attention should be given to the related appearance of pages two and three in a four-page paper, since in a paper they are viewed together. One editor should lay out both, or the two page editors should work closely together in the planning.

Realignment in six- and eight-page papers. Papers now publishing more than four pages present no uniformity in their classification. This lack of uniformity is good, for individuality is to be encouraged. One paper follows this plan: (1) news, (2) editorial, (3) news, (4) feature, (5) feature, (6) sports, (7) sports, and (8) news. The last page carries news second in importance to page one. The columns appear with the features on pages four and five. A six-page paper follows front-page news with news features on page two, editorials on page three, sports on page four, with any carry-over on page five (features complete the page), and sports on six.

Page make-up. No paper should leave its make-up to the printer— The execution of make-up by staff members benefits both the paper and the high school journalist. The original conception of a page— the selection and location of stories, headlines, illustrations, and ads —planned on a sheet of paper is the *page layout,* or *page dummy.* Page make-up is nothing more than page design, and good design requires that a plan be worked out roughly as a dummy. Each page editor should determine the make-up of his page. If all page editors work in conjunction with the managing editor, harmony of make-up throughout the paper can be achieved.

These early drafts, or dummies, of the pages can be worked out on 8-by-11 inch sheets. Once the page editor has determined this page make-up on such a form and has had it approved by the managing editor and the adviser, he transfers it to a similarly ruled dummy the size of the regular page of the paper (See Example 150). If all trial dummies are approved by one capable staff member, the harmony of the whole is protected. Example 150 also reproduces the printed page resulting from the dummy.

EXAMPLE

150

Faculty Votes on Pep Assembly Time

The faculty voted on Oct. 11 in favor of holding pep assemblies during third period whenever necessary. Only two pep assemblies during a season will be held during third period. The rest will take place eighth hour.

Head cheerleader Nicky Vandapool asked for more pep assemblies during third period because the cheerleaders lack time to present skits and other material when the assemblies are after school.

Mr. Raymond Acsell of the Social Science Department commented, "One asset of having the pep assemblies during third hour would be that working students will not be denied the experience of attending the assemblies."

One teacher asked whether the pep assemblies are so valuable as the class they take the place of. "Each class," replied Nicky. "is cut down only five minutes which doesn't take away too much from the class period."

Some teachers felt that the students would be so emotionally excited they would not settle down and classes following the assembly would suffer repercussions.

Miss Carol Barclay, speech teacher, said that student cooperation might eliminate the need to have the assemblies after school.

Mrs. Blanche Pigott, German teacher, thought the plan should be tried for a year.

"I would like to see some data on the relationship between pep assemblies and the sale of athletic tickets before we make it mandatory for the students to attend," countered Mr. Keith Lindblom, sociology teacher. "Some of these kids feel so out of place at a pep assembly as Eichmann would at a Bar Mitzvah."

"ALL IN FAVOR, raise your hand." The faculty votes on the question of when pep assemblies should be held. It was decided that two pep assemblies each season will be held during third hour.

East High Spotlight

Official Publication, East High School, Denver, Colorado
Member of Columbia Scholastic Press, National Scholastic Press Association and Quill and Scroll

Volume XLVIII, No. 3	October 19, 1961	Price 20 cents

PSAT To Measure Students' Ability

On Saturday, Oct. 21, the Preliminary Scholastic Aptitude test will be given at 1 pm to pupils of East High school.

As a two hour version of the Scholastic Aptitude test, the PSAT contains multiple-choice questions which measure a student's progress in the fields of verbal and mathematical ability.

Since these two tests are similar, prediction of SAT scores are determined from the results of the PSAT.

Individual marks, compared with pupils throughout the nation, help counselors evaluate a student's ability and serve to guide them in planning programs and recommending col-

both Craven, head of the testing office. "Results indicate subjects in which they are weak, and help counselors to plan their schedules accordingly."

Score reports are mailed to the schools in December. An interpretive booklet accompanies the results and explains their meaning.

East registers for and makes arrangements to give the test through the Educational Testing Service. A fee of $1.50 covers the cost of providing test materials.

PSAT marks may also be released to colleges or scholarship agencies which require them.

Sophs' Officers Elected

New sophomore officers elected on Oct. 11 are president, Buddy Noel; vice president, Barbara Baker; secretary, Pam Hollis; and treasurer Betty Bonsib. The new members of Student council are Cookie Pile, Connie Plunkett, Steve Baker and Corky Chew.

B-ddy is now a member of

committees on Student council and they will work with their class sponsors, Mr. Wayne Gnadt and Mrs. Elizabeth Pixley.

Class dues and the sophomore party projects will be just two of the jobs of the new sophomore officers, Miss Walter said.

Buddy said that if it were at all possible, he would like to ...re class back ...h teams.

... won, of ...said "and I'm ...best to make ...phomore class

Head Custodian Retiring in Oct. After 12 Years

Mr. Ralph Messenger, head custodian at East High school for 12 years, will retire on Oct. 28.

Since 1947, Mr. Messenger has been chiefly responsible for taking care of East. It is his job to see that the building is kept clean, properly heated and in constant repair.

To assist him in these duties is a custodian staff of ten men, seven boys and three women.

"These people, who work from 6 am to 2:30 pm five days a week, help keep East the attractive school it is today," stated Mr. Messenger.

Mr. Messenger was born in Pennsylvania, but moved to Denver when he was eight years old and has lived here ever since that time.

He worked as a janitor at Gove Junior high and Logan Elementary school, but held the position of head custodian at Garden Place school, Byers Junior high and Manual high school.

After his retirement, Mr. Messenger plans just to relax and take things easy. Mr. James Cooper, assistant head custodian, will serve as head custodian until a new man is permanently selected for the job.

"East is a building which is in constant use both day and night," said Mr. Jack Bearshear, assistant principal. "It is occupied not only as a school-house, but as a meeting place for many clubs and community groups. The excellent condition in which East remains is by itself a fitting tribute to Mr. Messenger, who has worked to keep it such. All of us here are certainly going to miss him."

Angelus Staff Sets Deadline for Photos

Students should have their pictures taken by Oct. 31 if they wish to have their picture in the Angelus.

Appointments should be made only with Abdou, Francois, House of Photography, Jack's, Jafay or Stoffel, who have contracts with East.

"The photographs must be in by Oct. 31," stated Mrs. Carolyn Nelson, Angelus sponsor, "because the Angelus staff must begin pasting up the pictures. We estimate 1200 pictures will be submitted, all of which must be alphabetized and matched with the correct name going with the correct picture."

...s for "Ask Any Girl," Drama Club Play

... Jeanine Soker... of the Mad... hotel, Chris... el as an off-

... Carol Foster... m Mesa, Doris... erry Stone.

... Rost and Mr.... re serving as... and Sandi... udent director

...out the experi-...eeler, a small-...order to broad-...y, retires to a...rts' hotel. Men...ghton, an ad-...d Evan, Miles...Together Meg...time, using the...echnique; is...Meg. The re-...hat might be

AWAITING HIS CUE, John Walker ponders his lines during a Drama club rehearsal of the play, "Ask Any Girl."

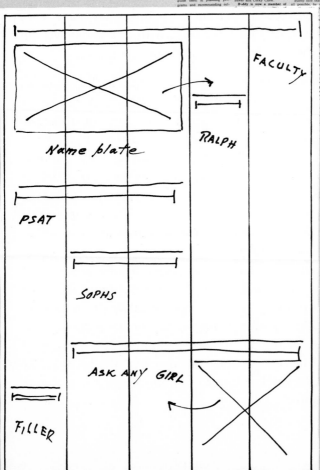

FACULTY

RALPH

Name plate

PSAT

SOPHS

ASK ANY GIRL

FILLER

East High Spotlight
East High School
Denver, Colorado

The first dummy serves as an assignment sheet against which the page editor later checks the copy as it comes in. After the galley proofs and the proofs of headlines and ads have come in, he pastes everything on the second dummy in its exact position. He is careful to provide enough space between stories and headlines for dashes. The completed dummy is then turned over to the make-up man, who follows it in making up the page. A well-designed page and good relations between the make-up man and the editorial staff are the direct result of carefully worked-out dummies.

THE CHALLENGE OF MAKE-UP

Training in make-up. Few high school newswriters ever become really proficient in page make-up. In fact, make-up ability is scarce even in the professional field.

However, once a school staff masters the general principles of page arrangement and the selection of types, this knowledge can be passed on indefinitely through a system of page assistants. Under each page editor, there should be at least two staff members who work as apprentices. The work of a page editor is so diversified that a novice can really appreciate its demands only through close contact with the job.

There is one weakness in this approach: the new page editor is inclined to reproduce and thus perpetuate the style that characterized the page when he assisted with it. On a conservative paper this continuity of style may be desirable.

Page arrangement. Good page arrangement requires interesting balance. Balance should not be considered only a symmetrical arrangement of stories, headlines, and cuts. Symmetrical balance, used too often, is monotonous.

Another type of page arrangement is focus make-up, which on the first page features the right-hand column story. Every page should have a center of interest from which the reader's eye can easily and naturally travel to other sections of the page.

Balance does not have to be the distracting kind that sets down a head for a head and a cut for a cut. For instance, a photograph in the upper left-hand corner of a page can be placed to balance a dark head in the lower right-hand corner. Light balances light, and dark balances dark. There must be unity throughout the paper, every headline and every cut having a pleasing relation to the whole page, and every page having a pleasing relation to the whole paper.

Type selection. For ease of reading and dignity of design, heads should be of one family of type, set upper and lower case, rather than of mixed type families set all caps. Such a family as Garamond, Bodoni, Cheltenham, Caslon, Goudy, Century, or Cloister, in bold-face, lightface, and italics permits sufficient variety for an attractive page. This headdress should range from 30 point on down; three faces, in harmony, to the page should be the maximum.

No headline should run over two decks. Since school papers are not sold on the newsstand, heads need not attract the passing eye. The first deck in the one-column heads at the top of the page may be set in 30 point, or 24 for small papers. Occasionally a two-column head at the top might warrant 36 points. To be attractive, headlines do not have to be black or freakish. Type size should decrease going down the page, with the exception of one or two two-column heads at the bottom of the page to provide balance.

The high school paper should use the streamer or banner head only for special events. By the time the paper appears, important school events, such as athletic victories, are too old to merit banner attention. The banner, if used sparingly and with discrimination in type face, can be an attractive make-up feature of the page. It is most effectively used when the school paper wishes to feature some coming event—and a previously undeveloped angle of the event at that.

The streamlined paper. What was at first called streamlining in make-up has now become so common that it is almost the rule rather than the exception. Essentially, the term *streamlining* has applied to "trying something new" in the way of make-up.

Some of the common features of streamlining are (1) a decidedly different make-up, (2) the use of sans-serif type, (3) the use of no-count heads, (4) running cuts or boxes up above the nameplate, thus narrowing the nameplate and the top-of-the-page make-up to fewer

250

columns, (5) the use of one or more heavy column rules to break up the page into distinct areas, (6) a disregard for certain standard rules of typographical make-up, and (7) a floating nameplate.

Streamlining might be considered an attempt to modernize a previously conservative typographical arrangement. It demands a real study of type and make-up, and—as always—good taste.

Sources of help for the school paper that wishes to improve its make-up along modern lines might be:

(1) *Editor and Publisher,* 1475 Broadway, New York City.
(2) *The Linotype News,* 29 Ryerson Street, Brooklyn, New York.
(3) Streamlined daily newspapers.
(4) The national student press associations (see Chapter 27).

For ease of reading, the body of the paper should be set 8 point on a 10-point slug. (The examples in this book are set "eight on ten" or "8/10".) Furthermore, this planned leading lessens the tight appearance that comes with setting body matter solid. Eight on nine is also considered good for school papers.

When a printer sets up a column that is some points short of being full, he drops one-point leads (lĕdz) between the first body lines of the story until the space is absorbed. Short news items of from two to five lines in length, ready for use as filler, may be used by the school editor to prevent excessive leading.

Whether a traditional type face with serifs or a modern san-serif type is to be used is a matter to be determined by the total design of the newspaper—its history, purposes, size, and of course, the local resources of each individual printer.

This line is set in 14-point Caslon, a type face with serifs.

This line is set in 14-point Spartan, a type face without serifs.

Where a traditional look is desirable, a type face with serifs should be used. Where a modern, "streamlined" appearance is desired, san-serif faces should be seriously considered. Spartan (**Spartan**), Metro (**Metro**), and Vogue (Vogue), are typical of the many good san-serif type faces available.

The tabloid. Too frequently the word *tabloid* is associated with the sensational in journalism. The term really comes from the smaller page dimensions of the tabloid paper; the misconception arose because some of the first tabloids in the daily field did lean toward the sensational. The five-column paper is the typical tabloid size, and the school paper of this size adapts itself readily to streamlining. Enlarging the school paper at one time invariably meant a seven- or eight-column publication. The more recent trend has been to "go tabloid," with growth in the number of pages rather than in page dimensions. The five-column paper now outnumbers all others.

Art. Illustrations, both photographs and cartoons, are an integral part of a newspaper. Whenever possible, photographs should show action, and cartoons should be drawn by the students of the school. Chapter 19 treats this subject in detail, but certain principles must be considered under page make-up. Illustrations must arouse and maintain interest, clarify and enliven the copy, balance and quicken the page. The test of an illustration, cut or cartoon, is its immediacy. In layout, however, certain demands must be met. Illustrations must never weigh too heavily on the page, creating unbalanced spots of black. Their size and placement must conform to the demands of the headlines, the look of the nameplate if the illustration appears on page one, the design of the masthead if the illustration appears on the editorial page. The illustration must tell its story by complementing, not competing with, the page. In the case of cuts, the overline (the headline of the picture) should follow the style of a headline; the caption or legend further explaining the picture goes beneath the cut.

Printing miscellany. Long stories should be broken by one- to four-word subheads, set boldface and inserted every two or three inches. On the inside pages, feature stories are sometimes broken with asterisks or additional white space.

For the sake of distinction, the name of the school paper should be set in boldface, italics, or caps and small caps wherever it appears.

School editors should always watch for small make-up distractions such as the appearance of white gaps in a column rule, or the wearing of repeatedly-run cuts or type (common stock), such as the masthead and the nameplate. Tabulations should be avoided in stories, for they give the page a spotty appearance.

The staff must demand care by the printer, whether the school printer or an outside craftsman. Sight down the column rules of the printed page to see if they are straight, look for broken letters, see if the rules on the boxes fit neatly at the corners, and check the whole paper for even distribution of ink.

Occasionally, color can be used to advantage. The Christmas issues of the papers in a few schools run in two colors: green and red, black and red, or black and green. The heightened effect is well worth the additional cost. The first page of one Christmas issue had a tree printed in a green light enough to permit the black type to show up when printed over it.

CHAPTER LABORATORY

1. Prepare a list of terms used in page layout and make-up work. Include the terms *balance* and *contrast*. Discuss in class.
2. Find exceptionally good examples of page make-up in back issues of your school paper and discuss in class. Why are they good? Treat one page at a time—front, sports, etc.
3. Examine the nameplate, dateline, and flag of your school paper. Do they include all of the information desirable? If necessary, draw up sample copy in corrected form.
4. Do you think that your school paper has the format and number of columns most practical for the size of the school and the amount of circulation and advertising? If not, prepare an alternate format. If you prefer the present form, prepare a defense of it for class discussion.
5. Indicate your preference in page distinction for both a six-page and an eight-page paper. Discuss in class.
6. Discuss the advantages and disadvantages of the floating nameplate.
7. How many stories can be carried on the front page of a four-column paper without getting a spotty page? a five-column paper? a six- to eight-column paper?
8. Assume that you are in charge of revamping the make-up of your school paper. List six or eight points in your plan to assure distinctiveness and good taste; dummy the pages.

17 MAKING THE MOST OF THE NEWS

News is not news until it is recognized by the reporter—and the reader's recognition of its significance depends upon the play given it by the editor.

All news is affected by its treatment at the hands of an editorial staff. Even the length of a story and its position in the paper influence the reader's judgment of its significance. Thus the newspaper has a responsibility and a conscience. This is particularly true of the high school newspaper, with its strategic position in the school.

MAKING THE MOST OF SCHOOL NEWS

The editorial responsibility involved in presenting school news may take many forms: (1) the responsibility of the paper to support a special school event by appropriate publicity; (2) the adequate coverage of a matter important to the welfare of the school; (3) the concerted editorial campaign to influence opinion or action; (4) the analysis of which type of story will best present the news—news story, feature, editorial, or possibly two or more different stories; and (5) the decision of location and play to be given to any story.

254

More than make-up. This aspect of featuring the news is something more than the mechanical make-up of the paper. It is the step beyond the arrangement of a page or the selection of a type face. Rather than the art of typography and balance, it is the art of news sense and value judgments. It is this aspect of a newspaper that distinguishes good editorial work from the average or mediocre.

The editor must not confuse the size of the type with the importance of the news. A story not worthy of major attention because its subject is unimportant or the coverage inadequate cannot be improved by increasing its length or type size. Headlines call for the reader's attention as his eyes move down and across the page, but the proof of the message is in the story itself. A story must live up to its display.

An editor must not sacrifice news values to fit a typographical pattern. Make-up is designed to serve news value, and is effective only when it does. Consequently, the power of a paper is in its ability to understand and communicate the value of the news.

What is the function of the school paper?

The function of the school newspaper. In accordance with contemporary trends in journalism, the school paper should be effective in expressing and directing student opinion, at times even community opinion. It may be a medium through which the students speak, and it may be a medium through which student opinion is directed and crystallized.

This is a trend of journalism at large—the interpretation of the day's news. A great many school papers are realizing the important role that the high school paper may play in forming public opinion.

The editorial platform. The opinions expressed in the editorial columns should be away from individual opinion and toward group opinion. This implies that the group, namely the staff or a smaller editorial board, must come to a common understanding on editorial policy. The most democratic method is through the staff meeting or the editorial board meeting, where pros and cons are discussed and where a group decision is eventually reached. Many papers use the idea of the editorial platform, illustrated in the three examples that follow (Examples 151 through 153):

The Red and Blue Advocates

EXAMPLE
151

As a representative of Reno High School, *The Red and Blue* would like to place its policy before the members of Reno High. The following points were subjected to careful thought and consideration:

1. A program of special days and assemblies to promote and unify school spirit.

2. A school newspaper in the interest of the entire student body.

3. Efficient coordination of student activities with an equitable distribution of offices.

4. An opportunity for students to express themselves freely through the publication of letters to the editors and other contributions.

5. Stimulation of interest in school, community, and national affairs.

The Red and Blue
Reno High School
Reno, Nevada

EXAMPLE
152

The Weekly's Platform for Hyde Park:

1. Efficient Student Government.

2. More School Spirit.

3. Better Community Relations

The Hyde Park Weekly
Hyde Park High School
Chicago, Illinois

EXAMPLE
153

The School Spirit Advocates . . .

Broadening the scope of the activities of the Student Council, and complete student cooperation with and interest in the Council.

A complete new numbering system for classrooms.

Increased attention to spring sports to include better-planned pep assemblies, wider participation in all minor sports, and, if possible, tennis courts on the school grounds.

A review of the principles of sportsmanship by the students and an active campaign to display these principles at all times.

Reformation of the demerit system, to punish such misdemeanors as tardiness in proportion to their seriousness.

Elimination or consolidation of overlapping honor organizations so that duplication of purpose and membership can be held to a minimum.

A minimum of donations asked of students and those few donations on a purely voluntary basis.

The School Spirit
Bosse High School
Evansville, Indiana

These are printed statements of policy usually appearing in the editorial columns just below the flag. They express the group attitude of the staff toward problems and situations primarily connected with school life. While it is not absolutely necessary that the staff print its platform, anything worth advocating is worth presenting regularly in some definite and organized form. Printing the platform weekly helps to keep the issues before staff members as well as before the student body. A more ambitious platform statement is found in Example 3, Chapter 1.

Good intentions mean nothing in themselves. They are significant to the school only if utilized by the editors in the good works of the paper—the selection of news, the play it is given, the sincerity of the paper and of the staff as individuals, and the ability of the reporter to carry out an accepted program.

The power of the press. The school paper, not unlike the daily paper, may be an extremely powerful device. It may even become a virtual dictator of student affairs, a result to be strenuously avoided. Quite often the staff of a school paper is composed of the natural leaders of school affairs. They must guard against forming a clique and priding themselves on being able to "run things."

Schools are preparing students to participate in a democracy, and any educational activity which tends to defeat this purpose has no place in the American educational system. For this reason, advisers and staff members should avoid attempted domination of the student body by the select few who compose the school paper staff. Such domination by a relatively few students, no matter how capable they may be and no matter how good their ideas may be, is not democratic and is therefore contrary to the democratic concept of education.

Thus, the problem of the staff is one of leadership, not domination. The paper's influence is transmitted through its recognition of the significance of various news events, through its support of certain activities in the school, through its presentation of the facts of an issue, and through its ability to present the news in a manner which catches and holds attention.

The editorial techniques reflect the differing editorial purposes. For the school paper, three purposes deserve special attention:

1. The concerted editorial campaign conducted by the paper to influence opinion or action
2. The adequate coverage of a matter important to the school
3. The support given a special school event

THE EDITORIAL CAMPAIGN

A planned program. Once the paper has decided what its attitude is to be toward a certain issue, some constructive campaign is in order. Such a campaign must be discussed in staff meeting, planned, and a step-by-step procedure laid out. The campaign might be limited to a series of three or four editorials, or it might be broad enough to include cartoons, symposium interviews, interviews with teachers or prominent students, student polls, and even special editions.

Even though the cause is worthy, the coverage must warrant reader interest—it cannot be justified by purpose alone. A single story or a single editorial does not constitute a campaign; a campaign is a series of efforts by the paper.

Example 154 is one story in a series on safe driving run during the year by *The Compass,* North Dallas High School, Dallas, Texas. It was apparently the editor's intention to emphasize the importance of the subject periodically, although campaigns are sometimes disposed of in shorter order.

Example 155 reproduces one issue of the *Jackson Globe,* Miami Jackson High School, Miami, Florida, in which the inherent evils of Communism are brought to the attention of the reader by both story and cartoon. This story was one of four on Communism in America.

In the first, an editor's note indicated that this campaign series was written in cooperation with the Miami Jackson Junior Exchange Club's project on anti-Communism. Thus the paper capitalized on a worthy project of a school club and projected the effort into print.

It is common for school districts from coast to coast to hold elections for school support. The citizens are asked at the polls to renew

258

EXAMPLE

154

Driver's Ten Commandments

I.   The good driver keepeth his car in safe condition.

II. He driveth only when sober, and never to great weariness.

III. His mind doth not wander, for safe driving keepeth a man busy.

IV. He keepeth always to the speed which giveth perfect control.

V.   He passeth intersections and grade crossings with care.

VI. To children and pedestrians he giveth thought, for over them he hath the power of life and death.

VII. He obeyeth the law of the land, knowing obedience may increase his years.

VIII. For the hazards of driving in the night, he maketh allowance.

IX. Though his soul be tried, the good driver remembereth that courtesy is the first law of self-preservation.

X.   When he goeth on foot, the good driver remembereth the Golden Rule.

—From Traffic Conference

The Compass
North Dallas High School
Dallas, Texas

EXAMPLE

155

JACKSON GLOBE   **September 21, 1961**

It's Time to Sit Up and Take Notice America!

By Jose Cabezas
Assistant News Editor

High Lights
Coral Gables High School
Coral Gables, Florida

"The fate of the capitalist is self-destruction . . . they are old, decaying, they will fall..." so say the communists, are they right . . . will we fall?

The answer to this question is in your hands, the American youth. In your hands is the fate of America, of freedom, justice and truth. In your hands is the future of millions of unborn children who are yet to live under the blessings of our heritage. You will decide if they will live under the stars and stripes.

But are you willing to fight? Do you realize the many dangers that constantly threaten our way of life, our freedom?

Of course you do! You say so every morning when you pledge allegiance to the flag, to the republic for which it stands, the republic in which you live . . . *or don't you?*

Don't you realize that every morning when you stand up and put your hand over your heart and say "I pledge allegiance to the flag of the United States of America", you are actually saying "I pledge to support and defend my country, my way of life. I recognize my obligation and my duty to my country."

Or do you just rattle it off mechanically and think meanwhile of the fun you are going to have that night at a party? Do you do this and still call yourself an American? Are

you such a hypocrite that you can do this and still say, "I'm an American"?

If you think that pledging allegiance is a waste of time or something that isn't important, don't say the words, because the words are not important. What is important is the feeling behind these words . . . "and to the republic for which it stands, one nation under God, indivisible, with liberty, and justice for all."

Remember apathy has destroyed many nations before us, and the question still remains . . . will we fall?

NOTE: This is the first of a series of articles written in cooperation with the Miami Jackson Junior Exchange club's project on "Anti-Communism."

. . . Letters to the Editor . . .

or raise tax levies, or to vote school bonds. This is the subject of Examples 156 and 157, which are taken from two different school papers in Akron, *The Garfield President* and *The South Cavalier*. This tax election covered the entire school district, and the various school papers supported the cause.

In this one issue alone, *The Garfield President* carried a lead story on the front page, a cartoon and an editorial on the editorial page, and an interview with the president of the Board of Education on page three. *The South Cavalier* carried an interview on page one, a

South Cavalier
South High School
Akron, Ohio

260

Attend
Back-To-School
Night, Nov. 3

THE GARFIELD
PRESIDENT

Vote
"YES"
Again

Vol. LXIII—No. 3   GARFIELD HIGH SCHOOL, AKRON, OHIO   Thursday, November 3, 1960

Levy Renewals Impose No New Taxes; Rising Enrollment Creates Needs

Garfieldites On WAKR-TV

EXAMPLE 157

Eighty Per Cent of School Income Depends on Renewal of Levy

Renewal of the 14-mill operating levy and the 2-mill building levy is imperative to Akron schools. Without passage of the 14-mill levy the income of the school would be cut 80 per cent after December 1960. Obviously, this would leave insufficient funds for maintaining the schools. Only with the support of the community can we hope to keep Akron schools operating at the high level which they have reached.

It should be stressed that the two levies impose **no new tax** rates on the voter, but are a renewal of the rate voted in 1955.

261

The remarkable advances in education since the 1950's should be enough to convince the Akron voters that their dollars are being well spent. Many people are not aware of the changes in Akron curriculum and schools. Akron has pioneered in the "Advanced Placement" field with great success. Many of the the students taking these courses obtain full college credit for their year's work in high school.

From the standpoint of buildings, in the past five years three new junior highs and four new elementary schools have been built. Another twelve additions and improvements to existing schools were made. This has been paid for by the 2-mill levy which Akron voters were wise and far-seeing enough to vote in 1955. Still the increased enrollments require more school rooms, schools, teachers, and equipment. Akron's school population has been increased by 38 per cent while the city population has grown 5 per cent.

On the average Akron spends $321 per pupil per year. Four of Ohio's eight largest cities spend more.

Are you willing, as you have been in the past, to make an investment in the future by supporting your schools now?

The Garfield President
Garfield High School
Akron, Ohio

cartoon and an editorial on page two, and an informational question-and-answer news feature on page two.

The drives for increased school funds so frequently carried in school newspapers are aimed at public thought and action. Naturally the paper must get into the hands of the parents and citizens if such publicity is to be effective. It is one thing to present the case properly; it is something else to attract the desired reader. Some papers give much time and space to stories of this type but no consideration to whether or not the paper will reach the homes, offices, shops, stores.

If the paper is delivered to the students early in the morning, or at noon in a school where the students remain for lunch, only a small percentage of the papers distributed will be brought into the homes; but if it is distributed the last thing in the school day, a great percentage of the students will carry their copies home. Additional copies, in the case of a campaign for school funds, should be systematically distributed in the waiting rooms of doctors' offices, stores, and shops.

If the staff is waging a campaign for school funds, such as the support of a school bond issue, it is quite proper for the school to contribute extra funds to pay for the extra copies.

262

A point of view. The fact that an editorial campaign is dedicated to one viewpoint, even though there may be sound arguments for an opposite one, places that much more responsibility on the staff to determine worthwhile issues to support. To fulfill its obligation and opportunity to influence right action, the school paper must adopt policies and wage campaigns, rather than sit back and passively cover school news.

These campaigns should be in harmony with the purposes of the administration; such harmony can be maintained by close working relationships between the principal and the editor. In fact, such contacts have news value, enabling the staff to sense the true editorial significance of school movements. The position of the faculty adviser is significant in this working three-way relationship.

The possibilities for subjects and coverage in editorial campaigns are unlimited.

COVERING A MATTER OF VITAL IMPORTANCE

Periodically a subject of vital importance to the school appears on the school scene. It may or may not invoke editorial support, but it calls for immediate attention in the paper—above all, full and factual treatment. This is spot news, something that appears suddenly rather than something that recurs such as a game, an assembly, or a student government election.

Here is a challenge to the newspaper staff, for it presents such questions as these:

> Will the paper take an editorial stand?
>
> What types of stories can best fulfill the coverage?
>
> Is there a place for illustrations or cartoons?
>
> Can the staff move rapidly enough to bring the accurate information required to the student body before biased opinion is formed?

The action taken by the Dade County School Board in Miami, Florida, to enforce the Florida state law against illegal high school

263

fraternities was such a challenge. Examples 158 through 163 are taken from five Miami high school papers and show the editors' varying reactions to this school district announcement on fraternities. The pages of the papers (all five columns wide and six pages long) are reproduced to show the ways in which each paper featured the subject.

The total coverage devoted to the subject by each newspaper is included to indicate its relationship to the paper's total space.

The Southwest Lancer (Example 158) devoted ten column-inches to a front-page news story, featured across the top of the page above the floating nameplate, and twenty column-inches to two second-page editorials under the blanket head *Frat Feud Fires Factions;* one editorial was subtitled *"Clubs Serve Needs,"* the other *"Clubs Lack Goals."*

EXAMPLE

158

PAGE TWO   THE SOUTHWEST LANCER   SEPTEMBER 28, 1961

Frat Feud Fires Factions

Students Say

Clubs Serve Needs

During the past weeks much local attention has been focused on the controversy concerning "illegal" high school fraternities.

On Sunday, September 10, what many students believe was a slanted and seriously erroneous article was printed by a local daily newspaper on the subject of high school fraternal organizations. These fraternities were accused as a whole of being responsible for some serious and disgusting crimes.

A wise person once said that there are two sides to any dispute. This public newspaper has given one viewpoint. Now the members of the high school fraternities and their supporters feel that they should present their side of the question.

In the first place, every member of a high school fraternity believes that his constitutional right to free assembly for peaceful purposes was violated in 1941 when the Florida State Legislature enacted the anti-fraternity law that is now in effect.

Why have these fraternities come about? Most members agree that the basic purpose of their organization is to provide wholesome entertainment for the entire membership.

One of the major grievances against these clubs is that they supposedly exclude some students. Students at Southwest Miami High School are not excluded from membership in a fraternity on grounds of religion, financial status, or any of the other so-called reasons.

These groups willfully and cheerfully perform such
lection for ch
hospitals, and
of them are c
to any good c

Therefore, it
fraternal organ
actions of a few
ity is dedicated
well as themsel

The school
ganization w
on the basis
membership
up by the sch
Where are th
Miami High S

Students at S
for service club
ao, a gregario
group rec—atio

When these
gally sponsore
have no other
ternities.

The S

Clubs Lack Goals

The current controversy about secret fraternities and sororities brings up questions about them that need to be considered. Laws, which are made for the safety and protection of all, have been violated by some students. Secret organizations, have been declared illegal by a State Law.

Why have they been declared illegal? Members of secret fraternities and sororities have no adult supervision. The activities of these groups get out of band because there is no older, wiser person to counsel officially and because the members don't think ahead. They don't realize that what they say and do will reflect not only on themselves but also on their family and friends. Experience has shown that under certain circumstances fraternities and sororities do not work for the best interests of individuals or the community.

Another reason for the law is the attitude of parents. They do not seem to understand that the school has no jurisdiction over these clubs, consequently they pay little attention to them.

Limited membership seems to be a must in these secret organizations. Membership is not based on academic standing or, if it is in the regulations, it seldom is enforced.

Pledging activities go on during school hours, and often involves doing homework for other students. Club members tend to favor each other in school politics or tell little stories to get a club brother out of trouble.

Shoot For The Moon Says Principal Aber

This is the year for Southwest students to make a concentrated effort to "shoot for the moon." Our five years of planning and working will be paying off dividends for students as never before. This is the hour for our young people to get into the training program so that we can help them start on their way toward top futures of their own choosing—their own special "moon projects."

For the past few years we have had more and more students going into orbit with top awards and scholarships in many fields. Southwest has risen very rapidly to a place among the top schools in Dade County and in Florida because of the work of its students and faculty.

Now we have an opportunity to soar farther, faster. We have a number of new courses which will help to push back the limits of educational space. We

have special teaching methods and materials which are new. In fact, we are pioneering in some methods of study. A 30-million dollar crash program in college education has been planned by Governor Farris Bryant. This is the time for you to sign up to get your share of it after you graduate.

In addition, we have a faculty of men and women who have imagination, who are full of enthusiasm, who are well trained, and who are interested in helping you launch yourself into your future successfully.

Given the equipment and the scientific staff for an all-out push, all you need is the desire to volunteer for the top launching project at Southwest. Start your mental and physical fitness program today so that we can help you "shoot the moon" for your future success and happiness.

Lee A. Aber

New Faculty

(Continued from Page I)

Language teachers Miss Ruth Meltzer, Robert D. Lowenthal and Miss Margery Ann Jenkins were all born in the north, although Miss Jenkins lived in Cuba for 17 years. Mrs. Flora Mamakos and Mrs. Dorothy Roeth will teach business education. Mrs. Mamakos has two young children, while Mrs. Roeth holds a private pilot's license and a real estate license.

Four new social studies teachers

Who in the South and Southwest" in 1961; Mrs. Nancy Davis received the Valley Forge Freedoms Foundation Classroom Teacher's Medal, and John D. Sheridan spent several years as personnel manager of Hayes Aircraft Company.

For the past two years Miss Susan Winter, biology, has been doing research in hematology and holds a B.S. degree in zoology. Boating, waterskiing and dancing are hobbies of Mrs. Marcia Plager, science

Illegal Frats Face Extinction

By JOY CHERRY

A move to enforce the Florida state law against illegal fraternities is being made by the Dade County School Board. These clubs which exist in the greater Miami area high schools have received derogatory publicity in the local newspaper.

Various sources including the Me-

tro Police claim the illegal organizations investigated use narcotics, distribute pornographic literature and movies, hold alcoholic sex parties, and practice homosexuality.

As a result of the recent flareups, the school board is taking action on all fraternities existing in the junior and senior high schools. It has been

reported that principals and teachers have been instructed to report any students whom they believe might be members of a secret society. Those reported will be ordered to disband or face immediate expulsion. The law banning secret societies is 20 years old.

Many students have expressed

their sentiments toward the statements printed in the newspapers.

"Although our club has always been known for quality rather than quantity, we have been forced to dissolve our membership due to an ultimatum facing our varsity athletes. We also deny any and all charges of narcotics, sex, or homo-

sexuality," stated an ex-president.

Regarding the law, a student wishing to remain anonymous made this comment, "This ineffective law is not needed in the schools today, since the students should be entitled to schedule their time outside of schools as they and their parents wish."

The Southwest Lancer

The Spearhead of Progress

FRAT FEUDS See Page 2

VOL. V, No. 1   SOUTHWEST MIAMI SENIOR HIGH SCHOOL, MIAMI, FLORIDA   SEPTEMBER 28, 1961

2946 On Triple Sessions
6 New Courses, 28 New Faculty
Spark Active Top Enrollment

Student Groups To Assist In Metro Traffic Program

264

The Miami Edison Herald (Example 159) devoted twenty column-inches (including a photograph) to a front-page news story, featured across the top of the page above the floating nameplate; the story was

Miami Edison Herald
Miami Edison High School
Miami, Florida

continued for seventeen inches on page six. Another story, "Will Clubs Disband?" appeared on the editorial page under the club editor's by-line. It totaled fifteen column-inches including a small line drawing.

The Pioneer (Example 160) carried an eight-inch news story on page one, second in importance to the results of the National Merit examinations, and a second-page editorial totaling ten column-inches.

The Palmetto Panther (Example 161) devoted twenty-one column-inches to a front-page news story, including a by-line and photograph. An inquiring-reporter story on the editorial page totaled nine column-inches.

265

EXAMPLE

160

The Pioneer

Forensic Follies
News-Pictures
Turn to Pg. 3

VOL. 10 — NO. 2 NORTH MIAMI SENIOR HIGH SCHOOL OCTOBER 20, 1961

School Clubs To Implement State Laws On Membership

"Technically speaking, clubs and organizations are not yet in business," Principal W. E. Rice announced Monday night to the annual Key Club Leader's banquet in the high school cafeteria.

To acquaint club leaders and sponsors with the law of the state and the regulations of the Dade County administration, Mr. Rice addressed the group, outlining methods, procedures, and regulations.

"It is not up to us to debate the issue, but to do all in our power to implement the law," Mr. Rice observed, as he pointed out that this law was passed in the best interests of the students of Florida.

LAW NOW BEING ENFORCED

The law, while not new, is now being examined with the intention of carrying out the letter as well as the spirit of the law.

Under this law, students are not to have a voice in the selection of members, other than serving in a recommending capacity to an adult leader.

All clubs are to have in the office of the Director of Student Activities by October 23 a charter, by-laws, and constitution, said documents to be built around the ten requirements established by the school board.

Pioneer Elected State D. E. Leader; D. C. T. Now D. E.

Are you ambitious? Do you have average grades or better? Are you a junior at North Miami?

If you can answer "Yes" to these questions, you might be the person who would be interested in a new type of program offered at our school — the D.E., or Distributing Education program.

Up until last year this program was known as D.C.T., but according to Mrs. Breese, the sponsor, "The new vocational wing makes it unnecessary for this program so we have initiated a new one."

In 1953, Mrs. Breese began the D.C.T. program, and in 1954, a new course was started, C.B.E.

These courses are offered to in-

National Merit Results In; Two Chosen For Semifinals

SHERYL LEADER

A. Fox and S. Leader Tops; Twelve Get Commendations

BY ELAINE EDWARDS

"Andrew Fox and Sheryl Leader have been named semi-finalists in the 1961-62 Merit Program as a result of their outstanding performance on the National Merit Scholarship Qualifying Test," announced W. E. Rice, principal.

Twelve seniors have been commended for their high performance on the National Merit Qualifying Test. They are: Charles Beck, Marion Brown, John Citron, Ronald Crowell, Steve Grisillo, Steve Kallison, Steve Kaplan, Daniel Kesden, Maureen King, Rodney King, Albert LaMontagne and Norman Wayman.

Andrew Fox is now attending the University of Chicago without finishing his senior year at North Miami High. Sheryl Leader has maintained over a 4.0 average in the two years she h... ...th Miami.

P. S. A. T. Scheduled at N. Miami; 350 Students Plan for 'Warm-Up'

The Prelim... ...Test will be given Oct...

Those of you who could are almost non-existent. But don't feel bad. Your parents and a great many of your teachers couldn't tell you either. That's where the problem lies, with all of us. It is all of us that must combat this ignorance. All of us must study it.

Clubs Have House Cleaning

Many cries will be heard throughout Dade County concerning the club provisions now put into effect. Actually, these laws are not new but have only been implemented.

The main change in the various club's constitutions will be the manner in which new members are accepted. In the past many were rejected because they did not reach personal qualifications. Qualifications now are based mostly on grades, character, leadership, and achievement. In this way blackballing is ruled out.

In a democratic society a person should be able to earn his own place and not be dependent on one who might not like him. If there is a person who is undesirable and shows just reason for his removal from the club, he or she could be reported to the school authorities and steps would be taken to remove him.

Mr. Rice pointed out at the Leader's Banquet that any fraternity or sorority sponsored by outside organizations do not come under this ruling unless members wear emblems, pins, hold meetings in the school or involve the school in any way.

The investigation started after many complaints were made to the school board by parents and interested citizens. Pledging, hazing, disorderly conduct and blackballing were reported. The purpose was not to hinder clubs in any way, only to give the club a fuller chance to serve the school. Members will be selected by a carefully planned program, each rated in comparison with others who have applied.

Some disagree strongly on this matter, others realize the importance of following the school ruling, set up by the state legislature. It is not the place of the students to disagree, but rather to understand that this is the democratic way. This is the ruling set up by the state, and carried out by the school administration.

... school of this caliber snobbish cliques, sometimes composed of even our most intelligent students. It is a sad thing that American teenagers have sunk to this level.

A disgusted member of the clique.

Dear Editor:

I am writing this letter because I am shocked at the way some of the students in our school are acting. It seems that they have no school spirit, or respect for their school.

In front of our school is the school seal. It was put there as the symbol of our school, and we are supposed to respect it. Yet, everyday I see many students walk right over it as if it was not there. It is necessary to again put a rail around it because our students are not "grown up" enough. Is it possible that they **don't know** about it? In any case, I think it is time that our students begin to respect their school.

A Concerned Student

Joe Will Never Know It; Time Has By-Passed Him

Joe Never Know was a student at North Miami Senior High. His grade section doesn't matter, nor his subjects. His teachers? Well, they don't have much to say about Joe.

You see, when Joe Never Know was a little boy he would amble

thrown away. But he was the last to admit this. Secretly, he wanted to go to college. Surely he would change. But, instead, his old self returned. He continued to put assignments off; never even knowing when they were due. College board exams came and went.

...letter of entry for college ...ntirely forgotten, and entrance ...were discarded. Joe just sat ...and waited for the offers to ... He could do all this tomor... ...or the college itself would con... ...him.

...ll, I saw Joe Never Know go... ...nto the employment office the ...day. I asked him what he ...doing lately. "Oh, I don't ...," he sighed.

...ways between West Berlin and West Germany? The answer to these questions is "No!" This must also be our answer to the question of negotiation.

U. Fund Drive Organized for '61

Students in junior and senior high school will be allowed, for the first time, to participate in the annual United Fund drive.

"We feel it would be good for the students' citizenship development process to approve one drive, and one drive only, within the secondary schools," said Joe Hall, Superintendent of Schools.

The United Fund of Dade County was organized in 1957, to eliminate the multiplicity of separate campaigns for health, welfare, and character building agencies. It consists of 39 agencies.

In previous years only the Junior Red Cross membership drive has been allowed in the public schools. Since then, the Red Cross has become a UF agency.

The only money-raising activity will be the distribution of pledge envelopes among the students. They may return them with or without a contribution. Students are not to solicit gifts from parents or neighbors.

Edward S. Swenson, UF general campaign manager, emphasized that "This program does not call for any quotas or any pressures to be exerted on any individual student, homeroom, or school, except the stimulation of participation by returning the envelopes with or without a contribution." The envelopes will be collected and opened at United Fund Central Headquarters, not at the school.

THE PIONEER

...blished bi-monthly by the Journalism Class of North Miami High School, 800 N. E. 137th Street, North Miami, Florida.

Address all communications to
The Pioneer, North Miami High School, North Miami, Florida.
W. E. RICE, Principal
C. E. NILES, Advisor
...ture .... Elaine Edwards, Steve Grisillo
...ing Editor .... Carol Pobletts
...ising Managers .... Mary Linda Bull, Kathy Wells
Evelyn Allred, Jan Abele, Iris Borrok, Marian Flum, Bob Howards, Linda Keller, Maxine Levine, Pat O'Leary.

The Pioneer
North Miami High School
Miami, Florida

EXAMPLE

161

PHRASES FLASH ON screen in timed sequence for JAN PITTS, 10-19, and MARY ALICE GOETZ, 9-6, during a developmental reading session under the direction of MR. WILLIAM BODDINGTON, English instructor.

DEVELOPING READING PROGRAM IS NOW WELL UNDERWAY

BY Paul Fox
PANTHER Staff Writer

Palmetto's Developmental Reading Program, under the direction of Mr. William D. Boddington, English teacher, is well under way.

It has as its purpose: To improve the general reading of all students at Palmetto by stressing such developmental skills as "thought getting," vocabulary, and comprehension techniques.

Various materials are used including "The Controlled Reader", **Standard Test Lessons in Reading**, and grade-level literature texts, selected library materials and periodicals.

Orientation begins with the Iowa Silent Reading Tests and grouping within each English class in a generalized slow-medium and fast (especially for use of Controlled Reader).

Each class in the Developmental Reading Program lasts ten days with a "follow-up" of one day a week in regular class.

Mr. Boddington stated that the Development Reading Program is having its affect upon every other class the student attends. He finds that students read and understand far more in a shorter length of time since having attended these classes.

General classroom instruction is held in room 408.

CLUB COVERAGE P. 5

Palmetto Panther

BLITZ BEACH

VOL. 3, No. 2. Palmetto Sr. High School, Miami, Fla. OCTOBER 20, 1961

Two Seniors Seek Merit Scholarship

Two Palmetto High students have been given recognition for their high achievement in the first stage of the seventh National Merit Scholarship competition.

Peter Andrus, 12-9; **Paula Davis**, 12-14, were named semifinalists in the 1961-62 Merit Program as a result of their outstanding performance on the National Merit Scholarship Qualifying Test.

Chris Hager, a former Palmetto student, is also recognized as a semifinalist.

The test was given last March in more than 15,000 high schools. These students are among approximately 10,000 seniors throughout the country who attained the status of semifinalist.

With each step of the rigorous test, these students move a step closer to their ultimate goal — a four year Merit Scholarship to the college of his choice.

• • •

Five other Palmetto seniors have been honored for their high performance on the National Merit Scholarship Qualifying Test given last spring.

The students are Sherry Campbell, 12-12; John Evans, Jr., 12-11; Tabor Novak, 12-3; Jane Sniffen, 12-10; and Dale Williamson, 12-11.

Each student who is endorsed by his school receives a formal Letter of Commendation signed by the principal and the president of the National Merit Scholarship Corporation.

Neophyte NHS Taps 22 Seniors

Twenty-two seniors were inducted into Palmetto's year old National Honor Society Oct. 5, in a school assembly.

The students were Roberta Bigman, Tom Brown, Cathy Copley, Jane Cowan, Mary Dothard, Barbara Elliott, John Evans, Kathy Greenawalt, Gwen Grizzle.

Others were Lynn Haynes, Ralph Hutchins, Robert Lane, Dianne Lucas, Marlou Morton, James Owens, Claude Phillips, Robin Shelley, Patricia Shull, Joan Ann Smith, Jane Sniffen, Dennis Stanley, and Jeff Wright.

Membership is based on four qualities: leadership, character, service and scholarship.

Under the direction of President George Miller, 12-5, NHS members will study parliamentary procedure and practices this semester.

Other officers for this year are: Bob Kiesau, vice-president; Dellarae Black, secretary; Jan Wackenhut, treasurer; Linda Kiser, chaplain; and Susie Straight, historian.

Juniors eligible for membership will be tapped second semester. All students must have attended Palmetto for at least one semester.

Mrs. Anne Polack, and Mrs. Jemmie Batchellor are NHS sponsors.

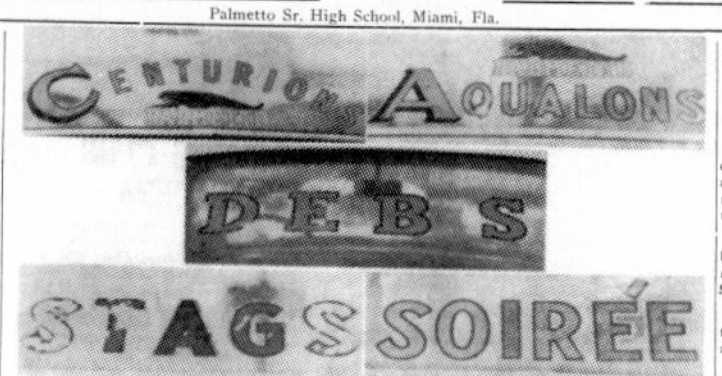

MANY CARS IN the Palmetto parking lot bear insignias such as the ones above, indicating membership in illegal fraternities.

FRATS TAKING FALL

By Jane Franzino
PANTHER Staff Writer.

"Offenders of the state law concerning illegal organizations will be subject to suspension and/or expulsion or referral to juvenile authorities," stated **Principal Clyde Crabtree**, commenting upon the recent furor aroused by the illegal fraternity and sorority issue.

"First of all," he said, **"Key and Wheel Clubs** will have to change their constitution to conform to the law set up by the school board. By changing their constitutions regarding membership, clubs will become legal within the law the way it is set up at the present time."

Mr. Crabtree has instructed teachers and students that the following items should be observed carefully throughout the school:

1. **Be constantly alert for cars with decals and other emblems that identify organizations outside the school which are not legal.**
2. **Teachers are instructed to notify the principal of any pins seen on students.**
3. **Any incidents in the school indicating hazing or similar apparel which would identify someone with any organization will be reported.**

Another rule that has been set down is that no students belonging to clubs, legal or illegal, oustide the school, may wear their pins in school unless they are approved by the school.

A meeting was held to discuss this situation Oct. 20, attended by **Dr. Joseph Hall**, superintendent of Dade County Schools, and his staff, all high school principals, and school board members.

When asked how an organization may become legalized and accepted by the school, **Mr. Crabtree** said, "To become legalized you must abide with the rules of local school and the school board.

"The club must meet on school time and on school property. They must agree that all events at night must be approved by **Mr. Harold Knott**, student activities director, and all activities must be attended by sponsors.

The night events must only be of social nature, such as a dance, and be limited to the number of clubs in school.

SC COMMITTEE FORMULATES ETHICS CO...

A Student Council Code... committee has formed t... a Code of Ethics, which... sist of morals, principle... tices.

Three divisions of the... be Patriotism, Honor, a... standing for PHS or Pal... School.

Patriotism will include ... the flag, knowing and si... alma mater, and school's ...

Honor will cover chea... spect for teachers, fellow... and school property.

Service will include a... services done actively and... to the best of student's a...

The Student Council, w... operation of the PTA, ... up the Code of Ethics ar... ute it to the student bo... near future.

Decals with the initials ... be given to all students ...

• • •

A reorganization of th... this year finds each office... ex-officio on a council c... He will serve as a superv... sisting the committees i... work.

Standing committees for ... include public relations, ... tions, sales, safety, and ... and grounds.

JERRY PARTNEY, vice-president of Student Council, serves as chairman of the Inter-Club Council, which takes care of all inter-club matters at school.

And in conclusion I might add, Mr. Roger Carson, physics teacher, became the father of a nine pound baby boy on the morning of Oct. 4. Mr. Carson's wife, Mary, and the baby are doing fine. The father is gradually recovering.

— o —

SENIORS DISCUSS CLUB PROBLEM FACETS

Question: What do you think of the current "illegal club" situation?

Dellarae Black, 12-3, "The various clubs are going about this problem the wrong way. **The laws involved are not school laws.** The only thing the clubs can do is show the public they represent the mature youth of our state."

Fred Belland, 12-7, "The abolishment of these clubs tends to destroy the right of being an individual. **As long as the club members engage in no illegal activities, they should have the privilege of forming.** In fact, I think such clubs are a credit to this school."

Tabor Novak, 12-3, "I hope the service clubs will have some say in the choice of their members. **Perhaps this could be accomplished through a student-faculty selection board.** If the clubs are open, the entire meaning of the club would be destroyed and robbed of its effectiveness."

Susie Howard, 12-8, "The clubs in this school are generally respected by students, parents and the community. **If a service club has a good sponsor and constitution, it should be allowed to operate.**"

Pete Shaefer, 12-4, "These laws concerning illegal clubs are quite general and in a way unfair to clubs that have been formed to date. The clubs are right in some ways, and wrong in others. Many students in these clubs displayed leadership in that they formed a club. **But since the method of choosing members conflicts with state laws**, these students must modify their organizations so they obey the law."

Butch Straley, 12-1, "I'm glad that **some kind of check** was placed on the activities of a few of the clubs.

The PALMETTO PANTHER congratulates Pat Partney, 10-3, Judi Cohen, 12-6. Linda Kiser, 12-2, and Sandy McQuinn, 11-5, for being honored as Top Teens in the MIAMI HERALD.

These students were selected by a Palmetto faculty committee.

CALENDAR HI - LITES

Oct. 19—JV Football-Key West.
Oct. 21—Football-Miami Beach.
Oct. 25—JV Football-Coral Gables.
Oct. 26—Senior Class Stunt Night.
Oct. 27—NO SCHOOL (Parent-Teacher Conference Day)
Nov. 1—JV Football-Columbus.
Nov. 3—Football-Stranahan.
Nov. 13—Football-Columbus.
Nov. 17—Football-Key West.

SENIORS PRESENT FIRST PROJECT

Senior Stunt Night, the first senior project of the year, will be presented Oct. 26 at 8 p.m., in the auditorium.

Skits, modern dances, solos, pantomines, and music by combos are rehearsing for the production. Included in the performance are songs by the Triple Trio, piano solos, the Nairobi Trio, a chorus line, and example of progressive education class and imitations of famous people.

Many seniors not on stage will be busy as stagehands, ticket-takers, and ushers. Others will be selling cokes during intermission. Over 100 people are participating.

Production managers are **Brenda Acton**, 12-12, and **Jennifer Wynn**, 12-1. **Miss M. Trbovich**, drama teacher, is faculty advisor.

Admission is 75c for students, and $1.00 for adults.

Following the program there will be a free sock hop in the gymnasium for all seniors and their dates.

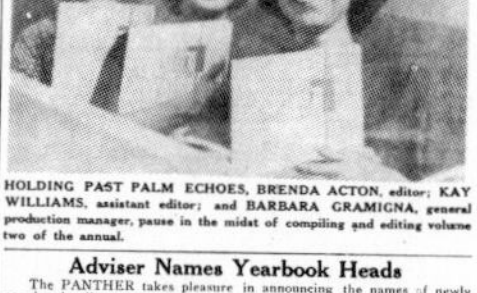

HOLDING PAST PALM ECHOES, BRENDA ACTON, editor; KAY WILLIAMS, assistant editor; and BARBARA GRAMIGNA, general production manager, pause in the midst of compiling and editing volume two of the annual.

Adviser Names Yearbook Heads

The PANTHER takes pleasure in announcing the names of newly appointed editors and holders of other editorial positions of THE PALM ECHO, as selected by Mr. Nick Taylor, yearbook adviser.

Editor, Brenda Acton
Asistant Editor, Kay Williams
General Production, Barbara Gramigna
Business Manager, Mary Dothard
Senior Editor, Susie Howard
Circulation Editor, Lynn Ward
Art & Advertising, Judy Seigal
Superlatives, Glenda Sylvia and Andrea Eurt
Girls Sports, Sharon Pitz and Rosie Cohen
Sports Co-Editors, Sam Woods and Jim Pearson
Photographer, Ray Green

Palmetto Panther
Palmetto High School
Miami, Florida

The Jackson Globe (Example 162) limited its treatment to the sixteen column-inch news story on the front page.

EXAMPLE
162

Legal Clubs Must Meet School Board Standards

Miami's current controversy over secret societies and high school service clubs which violate Florida laws has resulted in the Dade County School Board setting up standards to be maintained by all clubs.

Although Jackson has never had a secret society problem, the new rulings affected it slightly.

Perhaps the most noticeable change will be in pledging. Clubs may tap new members, but may not pledge them in anyway.

A member must be chosen on the basis of his grade average, conduct in and outside of school, leadership ability and achievements. No club is allowed to vote its members in!

Principal Loran L. Sheeley voiced his opinion of the rulings, saying, "Personally, I don't think the new rules affected us at all. In fact, I believe it strengthened our club program." He added that he felt most Jackson clubs had always been very democratic in their choosing of members and had chosen worthy students rather than friends.

Jackson students met the new restrictions with mixed emotions. Bill DeGroodt, Wheel club president, commented, "I think the new way of membership is fairer since Wheel previously voted its members in. It will probably bring up academic standards, but it might hurt clubs' working ability since applicants can no longer be interviewed."

Jr. Miss president, Elaine Arnold, believes, "The club rulings are strict, but if we abide by them, I feel that in time they will be lifted to an extent."

Dale Wilson, Key club president, remarked, "Many people feel that these rules will restrict clubs, but it should boost their standing in the community. Clubs will probably be more highly respected now."

Jr. Exchange club president, Jose Cabezas, feels, "The new Board of Education ruling on clubs will not in any way hinder Jackson clubs, but will improve them."

Judie Robertson, Opti-Miss president, declared, "I don't feel Jackson has to worry about its clubs because they have been good and upstanding for years. There is no reason for us to panic over what a few story-seeking papers print."

Jackson activities director, D. E. Moomaw, asserted, "None of our administration is against legal clubs. In fact, we are very much for clubs operating for the school's benefit."

Homeroom period was extended October 20 so each student might select a club which he would like to join. Jackson's first club period was held between first and second periods October 26.

There are 60 approved clubs at Jackson, including honor societies, interest and service clubs. Each student was given a list of these clubs to consider for membership.

Any student belonging to a non-approved club or organization which is in violation of school rules and regulations shall be subject to suspension or expulsion from the schools of Dade County.

Jackson ◉ GLOBE
THE VOICE OF THE STUDENTS

Volume 25—No. 3   Miami Jackson High School, Miami, Fla.   October 31, 1961

Jax Homemakers Attend FHA Meet

Jackson's Future Homemakers of America will attend this year's first district meeting November 11, at Miami High school.

Representing Jackson's FHA are Calista Morris, president; Phyllis Downing, president-elect; Miss Vickie Howard, FHA counselor, and other chosen delegates.

According to Miss Howard, this meeting will offer an opportunity for meeting other FHA ... ...e urges you to ... ... Will Defeat ... ... Ex...

Jax Votes Nancy Cover Girl

By Ann Gardner
Globe News Editor

Pert and popular Nancy Dale will grace the cover of Jackson's 1962 National Forensic League calendar. Elected by the student body as cover girl from 82 nominees, Nancy has been a calendar girl since eighth grade.

Besides holding the coveted honor of "Cover Girl" Nancy is Jr. Miss parliamentarian, NFL president, Wheel club princess and a Swingette. The busy senior also participates in Science and Math honor society, Pep club, SNHS, NHS and student council cabinet.

Nancy recalls that when she was ...eer girl, "I wasn't sure ... thing. I just ...

Jackson Globe
Miami Jackson High School
Miami, Florida

Summary of the total coverage. In all five instances the editors published the facts needed by the reader, including direct quotation of the state law behind the school board's directive. Four of the papers carried the story as the lead news on the front page, and three editors decided that the reporting called for by-line treatment, with the attendant additional flexibility.

In all cases the reporters and editors turned to the school leaders—administrators, club sponsors, presidents of clubs, and seniors—for quotes.

Two of the five papers showed ingenuity in their selection of photographs dramatizing the subject. All five papers treated the subject on page one, four on the editorial page as well. As is natural, the papers varied in their editorial attitudes, the feelings of some reporters being more apparent than others. However, the examples as a group show a concerted, factual, lively approach to a timely subject, and are representative of high-quality student journalism.

This chapter is concerned with the play of news; therefore, the next example (Example 163) illustrates the treatment afforded the

267

POINT OF VIEW . . .
MR. SCHUMACHER . . .
MAN ON A TIGHTROPE

EXAMPLE

163

Mr. Herman G. Schumacher, Principal of Cody High School, is a man on a tightrope.

He walks across a thin wire stretched between ignorance and education. He carries a single pole for balance, the Board of Education at one end and the student body at the other. He must plan his steps carefully so as not to disturb the delicate balance.

MR. SCHUMACHER MUST cross that wire first. He must stabilize the wire when disturbances upset the equilibrium. He must make the wire safe for those who follow him toward the goal of education.

But Mr. Schumacher now realizes that a serious problem impedes the smooth crossing of the wire. The fraternity-sorority question stretches the wire dangerously thin.

The first step in solving any problem is to recognize that a problem exists.

THE CODY STAR IS PREPARED to help Mr. Schumacher maintain the delicate balance by supporting this first step.

We will do these three things:

1—The Cody Star will print the names of the leading fraternities and sororities in this area.

2—The Cody Star will submit the names of the officers and members of these groups to Mr. Schumacher.

3—The Cody Star invites all interested students to express their views in the Editor's Mail Box.

Illegal student organizations have created a serious problem at Cody High School. We cannot solve this problem by pretending it does not exist.

YET DESPITE STUDENT appeals to The Cody Star, a small minority of students have persisted in the notorious violation of a state law.

Mr. Schumacher may now take this first step—formal recognition of the problem—with the help of information supplied by The Cody Star.

HE WILL NOW STOP, check his balance, and begin to strengthen the thin spot on his tightrope.

Students, teachers, parents, and administrators will follow him. All must walk a tightrope toward Mr. Schumacher's goal—the best interests of the student body and recognition of the law.

Do you, fraternity and sorority members, realize that you too walk a slender thread toward recognition of the law?

Do you, as members of illegal, secret organizations, realize that recognition of the problem you have created carries the ugly possibilities of investigation?

Do you, as parents of these students, realize that your children are taking a step backward, away from the goal of education at the other end of the wire?

Steps forward must be taken now before the threadlike wire wears thin and SNAPS!

The Cody Star
Frank Cody High School
Detroit, Michigan

same school issue in another section of the country. Again, a student journalist has risen to the demands of the subject and produced excellent coverage.

SUPPORT OF SPECIAL SCHOOL EVENTS

If the event has not yet occurred, the advance is intended to build up interest. If the event has occurred, the follow-up gives proper recognition to its significance.

The events to be covered are not necessarily unusual; in fact, they are usually recurring activities—graduation, the homecoming game, an annual festival, the senior play, the selection of a school queen. Therefore the difficulty arises of finding new editorial approaches.

In addition, each school has its own distinctive events requiring publicity; and in all schools the unusual event calls for major attention. (See Examples 115–21 in Chapter 13.)

The recognition of royalty. The selection and crowning of a school queen is typical of the activities to be played up by the school paper. With her royal train of ladies-in-waiting, and at times a gentleman attendant, the queen usually appears on the high school campus in the fall, at football homecoming; but there are exceptions. She may arrive with an annual Crown 'n Capers variety show, the ROTC ceremonies, or the opening of an ice festival, if the locality is Minnesota or a New England state rather than Florida or California.

If the school is in Indiana, the annual occasion may very well be linked with basketball.

The appeal is packed with reader interest. The early selection of semifinalists, the disclosure of the queen at the last moment, the excitement of the runner-up ladies-in-waiting and all the pomp and ceremony attending the occasion—these are the ingredients of copy.

Two photographs highlight Example 164. One pictures the semifinalists for homecoming queen in the advance story and the other the queen and her three attendants as they appeared in the issue featuring the coronation at the homecoming ceremonies. In both issues, homecoming was the feature story on the front page.

EXAMPLE
164

Opie Named Homecoming Queen

3,500 Attend L.J. Homecoming

by Diane Moler

Approximately 3,500 people attended La Jolla High's Homecoming game and parade held Friday, November 3, on Scripps Field.

The colorful parade began at 7:00 and ended with the coronation of Linda Opie, as Homecoming Queen. The three princesses were Melinda Merritt, Penny Jackson and Carol Clifford. The four captians of the game were: Bill Rauth, Kenny Liberty, Dan Berry and Ned Downham.

Alums Join Parade

Floats entered in the parade were built by the Senior Class, Junior Class, Boys' Federation and Girls' League, and Key Club. The four candidates were driven around the field in new, pastel cars. Also in the parade were Pennie Geering and Jose Romero, the A.F.S. exchange students. The representatives from the Key Club were in a shiny red fire engine belonging to Mr. Larry Upp, Principal of Scripps Elementary School. The present song and cheerleaders and the J.V. cheerleaders were waving and cherring from smaller red sports cars. Also seen by the crowd were the alumni song and cheerleaders, Alan Darby, Jim Storm, Marianne Hernandez, Pat Archer, John Cambell, Salli Vining, Gerri Marker, Marci Pilcher, Linda Griffiths, Carol Richards, Diane Johnson, and Carol (Timnes) Keagen.

Extra Greets Fans

The La Jolla Light, which has wholeheartedly supported the Viking team this year, put out 1,200 copy extra edition proclaiming the Viking lead in the third quarter, and the entire story of the Homecoming. These

...ritt, Linda Opie, queen, and Carol ...LIGHT photo by Gerry Sandford).

Vol. XXXVII No 3   La Jolla Jr. - Sr. High School   October 27, 1961

Homecoming Game Next Friday

5 to 6 Thousand Turnout Expected

by Susan Brown

Four beautiful girls, bright lights, and an array of festive floats will mark the annual 1961 Homecoming, November 3, at 7 o'clock on Scripps Field.

Approximately five to six thousand people are expected to watch members of the football team crown one of the four girls queen. The nominees are: Carol Clifford, Penny Jackson, Melinda Merritt, head cheerleader, and Linda Opie, head songleader.

The four candidates will be presented to the entire student body Friday, November 3, at a rally on Scripps Field. Not even the candidates will know the results of the election until Friday night at the coronation.

Homecoming this year is sponsored by Mariners, the girls' honor organization at L.J.H.S. Various clubs on the campus are submitting floats. Some of these clubs are: Key Club, Girls League, Boys' Federation, the senior class and the junior class.

Art Club Hosts Career Seminar

The 1961 Art Careers Seminar will be held at the La Jolla Art Center, Nov. 4.

This meeting is sponsored by the Art Director's Club of San Diego and the La Jolla Art Center to provide opportunities for students in grades 10 through 12 to explore specific fields of work connected with art. The seminar is organized to point out the different requirements for entrance to jobs at different ability levels.

Art is one field covered by Careers Conferences, a plan to give San Diego's students the broadest possible view of...

Murphy, Page, Rolander, Oliphant LJ AFS Finalists

Brian Murphy, Nancy Rolander, Tom Oliphant, and Barbara Page are the La Jolla AFS finalists this year. These four juniors were selected after undergoing several eliminations over a period of three weeks.

"I've never been so excited," said Brian Murphy. "It's wonderful", said Nancy Rolander. "It's the greatest thing that ever happened to me", said Tom Oliphant, and "I'm so happy", said Barbara Page.

The final elimination took place in the "model living...

Tryouts For All-Girl Show In Auditorium Nov. 1, 2, 3

by Diane Moler

Girl'sing tryouts will be held November 1 through 3, in the auditorium, immediately after school. Girl'sing is open to senior high girls who have organized ideas on an act. Their acts do not have to be perfected at the time of tryouts. There will be four days of rehearsal and the dates of rehearsal will be disclosed to those who pass the tryouts.

Those whose acts are selected for this annual production, put on by the Mariners, are to use their own equipment and props, except for the record...

WHICH ONE? The four candidates for Homecoming queen are left to right: Melinda Merritt, Linda Opie, Penny Jackson, and Carol Clifford.

The football team will play the Clairemont Chieftains, in the game which will begin at 8 o'clock. (See story page 4).

Colonel Sharon Wetzell, says the drill team will outdo the alumni. There will be songs of the '30's, '40's, '50's and of '61, she said.

The Hi-Tides
La Jolla High School
La Jolla, California

CHAPTER LABORATORY

1. For discussion purposes, bring to class a daily newspaper in which the editor has featured a particular piece of news. If your community has more than one daily, secure a second paper to compare its treatment of the same news.
2. If your paper has an announced editorial policy, discuss in class whether the paper's coverage actually promotes the policy as stated. What ideas do you have for doing so?
3. If your paper has no editorial platform, propose one. Then develop a platform statement in class to be referred to the staff for consideration.
4. In exchange papers, find examples of editorial campaigns and compare them with the examples in this chapter. Then compare your school's editorial campaigns with those of the exchange papers.
5. The examples treating the school-board directive on fraternities and sororities in this chapter illustrate a paper's responsibility to cover significant news effectively. Discuss the different approaches taken by the five papers, and compare their effectiveness.
6. In its advance news stories, a school paper supports worthy school events. List as many types of recurring events (such as football games) as you can. Then find examples of support given to *non-recurring* events in back issues of your school paper.
7. Discuss coming events in the school calendar, and indicate possible coverage approaches.
8. This chapter has emphasized three main areas in which news is featured—the editorial campaign, news of unusual significance to the school, and the publicity given to coming or, at times, past events. Discuss in class any other areas calling for special effort in "making the most of the news."

18 MAINTAINING READER INTEREST

A school newspaper in Southern California, the *Spectator,* suddenly gives up the name it has carried for so many years, and appears in the school hallways as the *Comet.* In Florida an equally successful school paper adds a full page "For Girls Only." A third paper, beginning publication with the opening of a new high school, issues its Volume 1, Number 1, edition under the startling title *U-Name It.* (See Examples 165 through 167.)

What does it all mean? It means, simply, that school newspapers must keep alive to maintain reader support. At times the campaign of sales is a competitive one, floated on loyalty to homeroom or class. In other instances the bare facts of publication costs are revealed, the students being told that the paper will either have to be cut in size or number of issues, or to be discontinued entirely. But in the final analysis READER INTEREST determines the number of subscriptions, which is as it should be.

Service to school. When the school paper is subsidized by the Board of Education or all students are forced to buy it, the paper may be threatened by stagnation and mediocrity. Therefore, the

272

SPECTATOR Becomes COMET

By Comet Editors

EXAMPLE

165

Beginning with this edition of Westchester High's school paper, it will be entitled the *Comet*. This name change is no accident. It has the combined approval of your student government, principal, journalism and printshop advisers, and editorial staff. They believe the title change is more in keeping with the space age in which we live.

And they don't make changes just to be different. After proceeding through the proper channels, with careful consideration being given at each stop, they felt the name change **had** to be made. Their three major reasons were as follows:

One. Better, modern school newspapers reflect their schools' nicknames; by no stretch of the imagination could *Spectator* be related to WHS's nickname, **Comets.**

Two. *Spectator,* as a title, did not mirror the soaring, orbiting school spirit of WHS's student body; rather, it left one with the image of a lazy "character" relaxing in the sun as the world passed him by.

Three. The name *Spectator* was too long; that is, it contained too many letters in it to make a dynamic-looking nameplate for the paper.

As the new title, *Comet,* easily overcame all three objections, it became the unanimous choice. Now, your editorial staff aspires only to make the *Comet* the kind of paper you want. Toward that end, they have aimed their combined efforts.

"New Look" appeals to COMET readers

By Natalie Strombeck

EXAMPLE

166

More than 75 per cent of Westchester High students wholeheartedly approve the 'look' of the *Comet*. In a random survey, students were asked: "What do you think of the paper's new name, *Comet?*" Replies to the question are given below.

LINDA OLMSTEAD, A-12: "It's terrific! *Comet* represents Westchester's soaring spirit and goals."

SHOKO MORI, B-12: "Since we are Comets, I think our school paper should be named *Comet,* too."

MARY BROWN, B-12: "*Comet* exemplifies the spirit of the school."

DENNIS DICKS, A-11: "The name *Comet* is very unoriginal."

MARGOT HODGES, A-11: "Dynamic! *Comet* makes the paper stand out."

DONNA DE MATTEIS, A-11: "*Comet* is great! It's just perfect!"

DENNY LOCKHART, B-11: "Tough! The newspaper name should jive with the school name."

COZETTE CHATTIN, B-11: "I like the name *Comet* a lot better. It follows along with the school name."

LEAN HARPER, A-10: "I'm certainly glad they changed the name *Spectator*, but I wish they had changed it to something better than *Comet*."

BEVERLY OLMSTEAD, A-10: "*Comet* is a much more appropriate name than *Spectator*, and it gives more publicity to the name of our school."

FRED GRIMSTEAD, A-10: "I don't like the name *Comet* because it sounds phony. Also, everything around here is named Comet, and it is kind of tiring."

DIANE ROBERTS, B-10: "I liked *Spectator* better. *Comet* seems to break with the tradition of the newspaper."

PEGGY JARVIS, B-10: "I don't like the name because everything here is named *Comet*."

KATHY ZINN, B-10: "The name *Comet* is a lot catchier than *Spectator*, and it ties in better with the school."

BONNIE LEVENSON, B-11: "I like the name *Comet*, but I don't like the way it is printed at the top of the paper, it's too spaced out."

WENDY WEBEL, B-10: "*Comet* is a good name for our paper, I don't see what *Spectator* had to do with WHS."

CHRIS BURGMAN, A-10: "I like the new name because it gives the paper a bold appearance."

The Comet
Westchester High School
Los Angeles, California

school paper supported by the students through a fund plan must strive for reader interest—and so must the independent newspaper. Reader interest is the lifeblood of a paper, and only by winning and retaining it can a paper become the living force in the school that it deserves to be.

The school paper must fight for the attention of the student. Such a fight must be conducted on a purposeful plan worked out to the last detail.

There is no preferred way of building this interest, but it is evident that paper after paper is aware of the necessity and in turn is doing something about it. For instance, the Westchester High School in Los Angeles threw away the security of its *Spectator* and gambled on greater student following with the new *Comet*, plus a new format and more news-features instead of straight news. It worked.

The students at Denver's new Thomas Jefferson High School circulated a new paper on the opening day of school, with the invitation —*U-Name-It.*

274

Think of the advantage the staff had that day in carrying on their subscription campaign. The paper spoke for itself; the staff member who entered a homeroom to take subscriptions did not have to sell an idea alone.

It is not the size of the school that determines the size of the paper or the size of the effort behind it; it is the extent to which the staff appreciates the paper's unique function in the school.

| NAME THIS NEWSPAPER | ? ? U-NAME-IT ? ? | BEAT WASHINGTON |

Volume I, Number 1 — September 12, 1960 — Page 1

Thomas Jefferson Opens on Schedule

EXAMPLE **167**

U-Name-it??
Thomas Jefferson High School
Denver, Colorado

AN INDEX TO GROUP INTERESTS

Determining interest groups. A school is made up of a number of major interest groups, and the staff must discover these natural divisions. Readers naturally have common interests, one being the welfare of their own school; yet these common interests may merely touch the surface, not reaching the individual's deeper concerns.

No two schools will have exactly the same interest groups; within the school, interest groups are continually shifting, and there is always some overlapping; yet any staff can begin a classification of the school's groups on the following broad bases:

1. The students are divided into two big groups: boys and girls.
2. The students are divided into classes: freshman, sophomore, junior, and senior for the four-year school; or sophomore, junior, and senior for the three.
3. The readers may be classified into athletically-minded, activity-minded, socially-minded, and scholastically-minded.
4. Any paper has three main groups of readers: students, faculty, and parents.
5. The courses followed divide the students into natural interest groups: college, commercial, industrial, etc.

Boy-girl groups. Most high schools are coeducational, with approximately as many boys as girls. Through the office the staff can determine the exact division. Assuming that the school is roughly divided half and half, the editor will schedule as much copy appealing to girls as to boys.

Girls' dress and make-up often command a special page or at least a feature or two in the paper. Example 168 is representative of an effective page for girls.

EXAMPLE
168

Miami Edison Herald
Miami Edison High School
Miami, Florida

The place of the automobile in the lives of boys has inserted automobile columns into the make-up of the school paper. The typical treatment of the automobile is the continuing column or feature, usually presenting the story and photograph of a particular student's particular car. Never a new car, it is an elderly one (See Example 169) composed of the student's ingenious assemblage of parts. Column names include "Car of the Month," "Show 'n' Go," and "Auto Biographies."

EXAMPLE 169

Wednesday, April 26, 1961　　　THE SURVEYOR　　　Page Three

Gentlemen, Start Your Engines!

4 Compete in Auto Contest

by Kenny Drake

Two teams from the school auto shop will compete with five other schools from the Indianapolis area at Tech this Saturday in the Plymouth Trouble Shoot test.

The contest, sponsored by the Chrysler Corpora[tion], high school student's auto knowledge against one a[...]

Trophies are awarded to all contestants and alternates, and the winning team will be awarded scholarships to the Chrysler Corporating Training Center Indivi[...]

L. A. Ley, Regional Service Manager of the Chrysler Corporation commented, "All-in-all, the Chrysler Corporation believes that the Plymouth Trouble Shooting Con[...]

The WESTCHESTER HIGH SCHOOL COMET

CAR OF THE MONTH

SHOWN ABOVE is Westchester student Ted Landis's 1955 Ford two-door sedan, the Comet's first Car-of-the-Month.　Photo by Varney

'Car of Month' Honors Go to Landis's '55 Ford

By Bruce Riblett

"Car of the Month" honors go to Ted Landis, B12, for his red-and-white '55 Ford two-door-sedan.

CONFEDERATE　　　　　MARCH 10, 1961

Stock 'Ah Ben-Hur Tin' Sports Motor, 4 Wheels

Boasting a bright turquoise-blue finish, Dick Sherman's 1954 Chevrolet two-door car stands out as a bright addition to the Rebel parking lot.

Dick, a junior, takes pride in the great pep exhibited by the stock engine. "Who needs racing cams, when the stock job will do it just fine," commented Dick proudly.

Besides a classy motor, the car has other distinguishing features: the trunk and side chrome strips are leaded in, and the wheels display four shiny bullet hubcaps.

In bright red letters, the car's christening name stands out: ah-"BEN HUR"-tin.

The interior color scheme offers a cool contrast to the pa[le] blue of the outside finish. Th[e] seat covers are black and white. Two-tone gray and panels fin[ish] off the sophisticated atmos[...] here of the little vehicle.

Perhaps the highlight of th[...]

Dick Sherman, owner of this issue's Feature Car, points out the clever name—"Ah BEN HUR TIN"—to an interested staff member.

Roorda Writes . . .

THE LEWIS AND CLARK JOURNAL, WEDNESDAY, DECEMBER 13, 1961

RANDY JOHNSON'S METALLIC blue '49 Ford coupe, powered by a '57 Merc engine is believed capable of turning 92 m.p.h. with an e.t. of 15.4 seconds in the quarter mile. (Photo by Shimizu)

Auto Biographies

By RICH HOMAN

Ready to go is the word for Randy Johnson's '57 Mercury-powered '49 Ford club coupe.

The car is easily distinguished by its metallic blue paint and the fact that it is nearly stock in appearance except for the lowering job and the relocation of the gas filler pipe in the trunk. The car has also been nosed and de[...] Competition [...] have been added [...]

Show 'n' Go

Dennis Brock's Chevrolet

By KEN

Take a look at the car above. Not only is it the first Show 'n' Go feature of this semester's *Log*, but it also will set the trend for future customs.

A '56 Chevy, this metallic silver blue two-door coupe is owned by Denny Brock, high senior and all-around man of the campus.

When you pop the hood, you'd better put your shades on: this engine is almost completely loaded. It has a '60 Corvette engine with a 4-inch bore, cam, fuel injected pistons, solid lifters sparked by a vertex magneta. It also includes Headman headers reworked by McGurk, duel four barrels with oversized jets, 4.11 rear end, with column shift.

Dennis plans a complete tuck-and-roll, but now he only has stock upholstery. A four-speed Corvette box is also in the plans right now.

A summer job in the construction business keeps Dennis happy, because with the money earned he not only purchased this car but is also supporting it.

When the Chevy is completed, Denny will race it down at Half Moon Bay (not in it, but on the drag strip).

FALL CLASS OFFICERS

277

These features emphasize safety, the care of automobiles, and the technical ability of the students. The columns read "It has a '60 Corvette engine with a 4-inch bore, cam, fuel injected pistons, solid lifters sparked by a vertex magneto," or "Under the hood is a 292-cubic-inch '56 T-Bird engine, which Ted spent the entire summer rebuilding. It is bored .060 and has polished heads and forged true pistons."

Class groups. The item that appeals to the freshman may appear childish to the senior, but the future life of the paper depends upon the cultivation of that underclass interest. Picture the average freshman. What clubs and other activities are open to him? What courses are open to him? What is his age, and what are the reading interests of that age? In what general school information is he deficient but naturally interested? Thus the typical member of each class should be created. The staff of the paper, made up largely of seniors, is close to the life of its own class and somewhat removed from that of the lower classes. The editor must see that these differences do not appear in print. Keen observation of and close contact with other classes will enable the editor to avoid inequalities that might otherwise appear unintentionally in covering the news.

Athletic, social, activity, and scholastic groups. Effective coverage of the athletic, social, activity, and scholastic interests of the school will not only appeal to students belonging to these groups but might arouse interest in other groups of students. The key is effective coverage, general enough to attract the browser, detailed enough to hold the attention of the already interested reader. If the school places great emphasis upon athletics, the paper will find a strong reader following for sports news. If club and activity affairs are important in the life of the school, the paper will devote careful coverage and necessary space to the field.

The paper should be encouraged to stress scholarship, but the subject must be balanced with other news of interest, and it must be well presented. The demands of education have never been as great—for both student and teacher—for this has been a world of scientific innovation, a world of increased communication, increased trade, increas-

278

ing contact with the nations of the world and the pathways of the universe. Classroom innovations are front-page news, as are the accomplishments of individual students. Playing up human interest and conflict, such as great achievement against equally great odds, is one of many possible approaches to such stories.

Parent, student, and faculty groups. If the school newspaper is generally read in the home, parent meetings and certain school events that are already common knowledge to the students must receive adequate coverage. If one of the functions of the paper's platform is publicity, then the parent group must be definitely treated. Nothing builds up a teacher's interest in the paper more than the assurance of finding the activities with which he or she is concerned reported adequately and accurately. The teacher thus comes to look upon the paper as a reliable source of information for all school activities.

The paper's run, or beat, should include the head of the Parent Teacher's Association, the Dad's Club, if there is one, and periodically other school supporters from the outside.

NAMES ARE NEWS

Names add interest. It is an unwritten law in a newspaper office that names are news. For years *The Boston Globe* made a concentrated effort to get the name of every man, woman, and child living in greater Boston into its columns some time during any successive twelve months. A number of names come into print naturally, some again and again, but it takes real ingenuity to see the news possibility in most people.

Assume that the school is a small community within itself—one hundred, five hundred, a thousand, or five thousand. Daily newspapers realize that the smaller the community the greater the news importance of each individual. Here the personals column, the question-and-answer column, the biographical column are effective for both the daily and the school newspaper. Example 170 illustrates the effectiveness of names in making news. Putting a person's name in print is justified, however, only in so far as there is news value involved.

Much interest can be created by a good student columnist who makes a place for the contributions from his reader. This columnist is called a conductor of a column, for he does not profess to write it all himself. He builds the student contributions (deposited in a box placed outside the door of the newspaper office) into his own copy. Some clever conductors have had phenomenal success in building up an active following. Example 171 wittily appeals for such contributions.

EXAMPLE 170

Magazines Match Students

Someone has said that life is like a book—some of your fellow strugglers unknowingly might remind you of a magazine. For instance:

U. S. Camera.........Jim Wroth
New Yorker.......Jackie Brown
Reader's Digest.......Ervin Deal
Country Gentleman..Ed Vantine
Good Houskeeping
...............Hazel Erickson
American Girl......Janice Ulrich
Esquire............Jack Gothard
True Romance..Darlene Weaver
Argosy ....Don Stewart
Field and Stream..Paul Hartman
Seventeen..............All '29ers
Playmate.........Ronnie Willet
Mademoiselle........Millie Forst
New Republic.......Cozier Kline
Holiday ....Teachers Convention
Tip Top Comic........Bill Nigh
Your Physique......Dick Darling

The Northeastern
Northeast High School
Lincoln, Nebraska

EXAMPLE 171

If You Have

moved
eloped
sold out
been drafted
been robbed
been married
bought a car
sold one
wrecked one
stolen one
had company
been visiting
lost your hair
lost your teeth
lost your dog
been in a fight
had an operation
got a new girlfriend
got a new boyfriend.
It's news! Turn it in . . . we'll print it!

The Star
Belmont High School
Belmont, Mass.

Letters to the editor. One of the public's contributions to a newspaper is the so-called letter to the editor. In the school newspaper it sometimes expresses student dissatisfaction with something being done in the school. The editor must select and publish only those that are really constructive. Daily papers often publish a Public Forum column carrying these letters and in turn other readers' answers to them on the editorial page. If the school editor attempts to handle material of this nature, he must at all times keep one foot on the paper's platform and the other on his own good judgment. It is ethical for the paper to back the administration.

The editor is never justified in carrying a column of faked letters, i.e., letters written by staff members because the students themselves have not been aroused to the point of contributing. In order to begin such a column, however, the editor or columnist might solicit letters or contributions from friends. If such material is not spontaneous after a couple of issues, the feature should be discontinued.

The lighter touch. There is always place for the lighter touch in holding reader interest. The April Fool's Day issue is popular over the country, requiring cleverness and inventiveness that everyone can enjoy. *The Confederate* and the *Lincoln Log* of Denver's South and Lincoln high schools, for example, bring out their April first issues as *The Counterfeit* and *The Lucky Logger*. (See Example 172.)

Untapped sources. The homeroom is an untapped source of news. Homeroom correspondents who are not members of the staff are not usually successful reporters because they are too far removed from the life of the paper and are usually not trained. Therefore a staff member should be assigned to each homeroom. Naturally he will meet the group in person and become acquainted with the individual pupils as well as with the group's activities and interests. A series of home-room stories may thus be developed, bringing out personal as well as group news. All thirty-seven members of a homeroom might cleverly be treated in a story of three or four hundred words. Such a series need not be stereotyped, for students vary greatly in interests and activities.

School newspapers commonly provide forms for the systematic cov-erage of all possible sources of news. Example 173, circulated to all teachers in the school, is typical of such forms.

Detailed coverage of the homerooms, clubs, and other groups in the school can provide material for a calendar of events, always inter-esting to the students and of definite service to them. Examples 174 and 175 provide two excellent illustrations of such "calendars." Publi-

EXAMPLE
172

Annex Sinks in Swamp

Thomas Jefferson High School, located at 3950 South Holly Street, has sunk into the swamp.

Jefferson, familiarly known as

"The Annex" in this area, began submerging late Thursday after noon while students were still in their classes.

Confusion reigned for several minutes until junior high students calmed the older students. Then every thing quieted down and

rescue work got under way. Rescue units from South and George Washington rushed to the aid of the trapped students and faculty.

Lenny Dee, South's rescue Captain, stated, "I have never seen such a mess: T. J. sinking slowly into the mud and students sticking their fat little heads out of the windows. Teachers were madly trying to save books and equipment ...and the Principal, was shouting through the wet P. A. system."

Fire trucks were brought in and ladders were raised to the windows for the victims of "The great sink" to escape, because they didn't want their brown shoes and gold socks to get all muddy and wet.

Finally the entire school, including football team and Pep Club, was evacuated, except for the valiant Principal, who was determined to stick with his P.A. system and go down like a true-blue captain.

Tan Serving, from the Washington squad, charged through the quietly sinking portals in an effort to save the stalwart principal. After a half an hour of anxious waiting, spectators of the event were relieved to see the two climbing out of the Girl's Gym window with their arms full of hats and balls.

Casualties were transported by Volkswagens and little red wagons to the "motherland," South, and given first aid by experienced athletes.

Cliff Boffee missed a rung on the ladder and plummeted into the swamp, and Karry Bapp heroically pulled him to safety out of the churning mess.

Experts just released to the press that T. J., "The Annex," is not permanently sunk, but will rise again only to fall by Monday or Tuesday, or Someday, anyway.

South Concert Last Strains

Concert Band has played its last concert! On their way to a guest appearance at a rally for the George Washington Patriots, the entire band, complete with instruments, seiged themselves into the elevator.

Confederate
South High School
Denver, Colorado

COUNTERFEIT

Vol. 29, No. 9
Friday, April 7, 1961
South High School
Denver, Colorado
Price 20c

Hero Worship Overcomes Rebels

It is 8:30 a.m. at South High School and huge crowds of students are lined up along the front walk. Ten policemen are trying desperately to hold back the surging mobs. Suddenly a cheer goes up from the crowd as a black limosine pulls to a stop at the end of the walk. An excited voice cries out, "He's here. He's here."

Coach Yates and Coach Wilson hurriedly roll a red carpet down the sidewalk to the car. A loud fanfare is given by South's orchestra. Then the car door swings open and out steps Coach Baseball, our great exchange student from that wonderful, cool high school—George Washington.

This is probably the greatest thing that has ever happened to South High. Out of the kindness of their green and white hearts, the Washington students are trying to bring a little happiness in-to the dull, drab lives of the Rebels. They feel that the mere presence of one of their great students will serve to set an example. Oh how lucky we are!

As Cass walks up to the school the South students bow before him to express their eternal gratitude. There is a moment of silence as the South football team raises Washington's colors on the flag pole.

Then without warning the crowd breaks and rushes toward the beloved Cass. Girls scream and fight to get near him. They faint if he smiles at them, and there are hundreds of girls lying in crumpled heaps on the lawn. The boys run after him asking for advice on how to be cool.

But luckily Cass escapes to his private hall and quietly goes to room 200—his locker. He changes into his lounging Jacket & scarf and prepares for his classes.

As he walks down his hall Cass thinks to himself, "I'll have to admit it. There's just one word for me and that's GREAT. I really am great."

H!-de-hi; hi-de-ho;
Hi-de-hi, hi-de-ho, take your gal and let's go; to Jefferson County Fair Grounds, that is. The occasion? Graduation exercises of South High which have been moved, this time to the "wide open spaces."

But none of the usual fal-de-ra nissy stuff that comes with graduation! A good ole rootin-tootin rodeo will take place, featuring the stock of South High School. Each graduating senior will receive his diploma only through demonstrating ability in one of the following contests:

Calf ropin—not the kind that wears garters.

Steer wrestling—only for the real he men.

Bronc riding—no doubt will be available to assist contestant activity among the

Horse Jumping—mice

Fal-de-ra, No-doze For Senior Grad.
provided for a stimulus.

Brahma bull riding—girls may be reassured, for only "feminine" bulls will the given them.

Special yodeling, contest—designed for those s'ill letergirling with changing voices.

Trick actin—using cows because of their great "showmanship." (In extreme desperation, a treat may be given instead.)

Showmanship acts—diplomas for best horse permanents and manicures.

Dr. W. H. Anderson is already encouraging all seniors to try

somewhat regretful, however, for hints of new cheating devices are already in circulation. Character-istic of these are pea-shooters used to encourage that extra kick from the opponent's bull, and stink-um on the calves to assure a successful catch.

Junior Escorts are busily in preparation a i s o, purchasing their stylish new horses, and taking courses in first aid, par-ticularly in stretcher-bearing.

Oh yes, and one last word of advice to seniors — be sure to eat lightly before the hour of the

Seniors Feel Urge: *Move to New Hangout*

Due to the overcrowded condition of the hallways during the time of the Senior Bull S and being converted into a psychological testing laboratory.

Senior Joe Darrell's superior knowledge on the matter may "Well ... we ... who ... know there."

Senior Jim Burrel's experience can have some intimate discussion there."

PROM ROYALTY ANNOUNCED

Lancer's Lucky Logger has come up with one of the biggest scoops ever to be dug up by a Denver paper.

Starting news has just been dis-covered concerning the Senior Prom, "Creations in Crystal." As you all know, the senior class (1961) has announced that it has received the privilege of having the first senior prom of Abraham Lincoln High School.

Our information is fourfold. We will announce the names of our selected prom king and queen (a complete surprise). The place at which it is to be held, the time you should reserve, and the name of the world-famous band which we will have to entertain us.

By strange coincidence, our king and queen were elected by a writein ballot. Because they are so in-separable, Bob Grossman and his briefcase will shine as our featured

King Grossman Chooses Classy Queen of Senior Prom

Those two will reign at Missis-sippi Stables. This luxurious bistro was selected because of its locality and luxurious decorations. We hope the exotic, if unusual, frag-rance of this lovers' paradise will enhance the evening for all.

Although nothing definite has been decided, there has been a rumor about changing the name of our prom to "Piggly Paradise."

Because this dance will be held on June 3, immediately following graduation exercises, the time has been changed from 9 to 12 to a more convenient hour of from 12 to 4. This, we know, will greatly everyone concerned.

We promised a big-name band, so here it is. We shall be honored by the music of Dr. Superglobal-itrictraitronabliocating and the boys. Big enough?

Entertainment will consist of a senior sock hop, which will be pro-vided by vocalist Larry Praneen and his two-piece orchestra, "Drummer Jenks" on the coffee can and "Whistling Otis" on the pop bottle.

Mr. Richard Mitchell, sponsor of the seniorclass, will reign king over the sock hop (provided he joins in with the other leaguers)

Following the conclusion of the sock hop, the senior class of nine-teen hundred and sixty-one will present Mr. Mitchell with a gift in appreciation of his tireless (?) ef-forts on the part of his duty as senior class sponsor. Consideration was given to several gift ideas, and a decision has been made. Mr. Mitchell's gift from this year's senior class (keep in mind that the funds are limited) will be "the poor guy's" the present junior class.

IF YOU READ THIS
AND THINK IT
"COOL" YOU WILL
BE AN APRIL FOOL!

Senior Luncheon Moved

Lincoln's Senior Class Luncheon, which is to be held on Sunday, June 25, has been moved from the Pinehurst Country Club, in Jefferson County, to the Golden Jassi. Reasons for moving the lunch-eon are due to the limited funds in the senior class treasury.

Swiss steak, the previous menu for the luncheon, will be replaced by hamburgers and fries. Choc-olate shakes and soft drinks will provide the remaining refreshment.

All this food will cost each senior, who has not paid his dues, approxi-mately forty-five cents, saving a whole dollar and fifty-five cents! Seniors having paid their dues will receive a one per cent reduction on entire costs of the luncheon.

NATIONAL HONOR ADDS FIFTY-ONE

National Honor Induction was held Thursday, March 7, at 7:30 p.m. in the Lincoln high school audi-torium.

Qualifications for National Honor are based on scholarship, lead-ership, and service. Members must be in the top 8% of their class.

There were 23 seniors and 28 juniors inducted. Seniors are as follows: Patty Altman, Fred Anderson, Nancy Black, James Brown, Katherine Carwin, Karen Dengler, Sheila Foster, Norman Gotoch, Robert Grossman.

Joan Hammond, Judith Hawkins, Nancy Henderson, Margie Hobert, Stephen Ireland, Sterling Jenkins, John Justice, Sandra Keenan, Pa-tricia Kelly, Patrick Lay, William Lewis, Gretchen Ries, Cheryl Roush, Cheryl Smith.

Juniors are as follows: Donald Alvarado, Martha Anderson, Donna Arthur, Leland Bebee, Dan Bishop,

All-City Talent Show

Abraham Lincoln's student body
Keeps Council Busy

SOPHOMORE PARTY HELD IN CAFETERIA

"Blue Heaven" will be the theme of the Sophomore party to be held Saturday, March 18. Their party will be in the school cafeteria, from 8 to 12 p.m.

King and queen finalists were named Wednesday, March 1. Queen finalists are Jacque Sagrillo, Mina Tucker, and Charlene Wueker. King finalists are Don Greves, Jim Hamel, and Ron Stewart. These six were chosen by sophomores from a list of more than 40 sopho-mores.

Sophomore council has been di-vided into committees to prepare

THIS STORY HAS BEEN TEM-
PORABILY INTERRUPTED
FOR A FLASH . . .
USE YOUR BRAIN-
POWER TO CONTROL
Your HORSEPOWER
Now. Back to the Story . . .

for the dance. Committee members are: Band, Linda Hollam and Dee Locklin; bids, Deedra Harburg and Sherry Stewart; decorations, Pam Augustine, Jim Hamel, Bob Max-ton, and Diana Scheezeman; fav-ers, Diane Madden, publicity, Carol Dominguez, Dave Fisher and Mina Tucker; refreshments, Don Greves, and Margie Lindstrom; and royalty, Lana Lee.

Music for the party will be pro-vided by the K-men, an eight piece band from Denver university.

Dress will be cult robes and ties for the boys, and party dresses for the girls. Corsages will be given with the tickets.

The *Lucky Logger*

Vol. 1 No. 5   ABRAHAM LINCOLN HIGH SCHOOL   April 1, 1961
Denver, Colorado

SCHOOL BOILER ROOM TO BE SETTING FOR JUNIOR PROM

After thirty-four hours of fast delibera-tion and extensive checking for a satisfactory place to hold the annual Junior Class Prom, the school board has finally decided on the school boiler room.

Rumor has it that the boiler room is to be decorated in yellow and red "Deep Purple" to go along with the school colors.

Glancing at the picture you probably asked yourself, "Is-n't that the senior class president and three of his cronies?"

New faces employed in the jani-torial service at Lincoln: Larry Hoskins, Sterling Jenkins, and Dick Palincki, are are at last fulfilling their childhood dream of being janitors.

Unending qualities and aptitudes are necessary for filling the shoes of a good janitor. One quality all these fellows sure have is the abil-ity of giving "mean looks." Look up the finesse and skill they pos-sess in handling the different tools of their trade.

Good luck! With such skill and aptness you are sure to succeed!

Forty-Five to Escort Seniors

Forty-five junior class girls have been selected to serve as Junior Escorts...

The Lincoln Log
Abraham Lincoln High School
Denver, Colorado

YOUR DEPARTMENT IS NEWS

EXAMPLE

173

In order for the *West Higher* to give a fair share of space to each department, we must plan as far ahead as possible. We frequently miss a good story because the event is conceived and executed between the time the copy goes to the printer and the date of publication.

Our publication dates are set for the whole year. This is necessary because of our contracts with the printer and the advertisers.

At certain times of the year many important events occur within a two-week period. If we do not know about events in your department, our copy may go to the printer with no space allowed for your news. (Killing type already set is expensive, and we can't afford it.)

We are seldom interested in events that have already happened. Our policy is to print it while it is still news to most people. That requires thinking ahead on your part as well as ours.

We shall send you a copy of this sheet from time to time. Please list on the lower lines the requested information and return to Mr. Vacha in Room 120 at your earliest convenience, whether or not you know the exact dates.

Event Coming Up   Date   When can you see a reporter?

_____   _____   _____

_____   _____   _____

_____   _____   _____

_____   _____   _____

PLEASE LIST BELOW the name and homeroom of any student you know who has done something newsworthy—i.e., hobby, novel experience, worthy achievement, etc.

_____   _____

              Name   Homeroom

_____

       Nature of experience or achievement

_____

_____

The West Higher
West High School
Cleveland, Ohio

283

EXAMPLE

174

CALENDAR

Friday, Nov. 10
    Raindrops, 8 A.M.
    Armistice Day convocation
Saturday, Nov. 11
    Parade—Band, Red Feath-
    ers and Color Girls. Meet
    at Bernard and Riverside
    at 9:30 A.M.
Monday, Nov. 13
    Conduct board meeting,
    8:15 A.M., room 127.
    Girls' basketball, 3:20.
    North Central Highlights,
    7 P.M., KFIO.
Tuesday, Nov. 14
    Ballet, 8 A.M.
    Girls' League central coun-
    cil meeting.
    P.T.A. meeting, 7:45 P.M.
Wednesday, Nov. 15
    Slave dance, 8 A.M.
    School skating, period 6
    and after school.
Thursday, Nov. 16
    Indian dance, 8 A.M.
    Senior B meeting, period 3.
    Victory, 8:30 A.M.
    Girls' basketball, 3:20.

The North Central News
North Central High School
Spokane, Washington

Dates to Circle

Nov. 22—First basketball game—
    Wisconsin Rapids
Nov. 23—State Hi-Y convention
    at Janesville
Nov. 25—Aud-Movies on "Elec-
    tronics"
Nov. 28—Thanksgiving Vacation
    begins
    N.S.P.A. Convention at
    Milwaukee
Nov. 29—Basketball game at
    Janesville
    N.S.P.A. Convention
    Thanksgiving vacation
Nov. 30—N.S.P.A. Convention
    Basketball game at La
    Crosse
Dec. 2—Aud-Discussion on the
    Atom Bomb and Inter-
    national Control
Dec. 5—Aud-Movie

West High-Times
West High School
Madison, Wisconsin

EXAMPLE

175

cation may be weekly, biweekly, or monthly, depending both upon the frequency of issue and how often such a column is warranted.

WRITING DETERMINES READER INTEREST

Telling the full story. In the final analysis, the most elaborate techniques of determining and widening reader interest succeed only through good writing and good editing. The stereotyped reporting of games, assemblies, and club meetings fails to satisfy the average student reader. Routine happenings must be measured on a scale that carries more weight than "who, what, when, where, why, and how."

It would be interesting for the editor at the end of the football season to compare his paper's coverage stories of the eight or ten

284

games. So many of these stories are written from a stereotyped form which asks little of the reporter covering the game. There is such a similarity among the stories that even the editor wonders how they got by. The sports scribe must do more than retell to the students who saw the game who won, by how much, how each score was made, how statistics compared, and how the substitute star won the game. The school paper has more than an obligation to record history.

What was there about the game that the spectator did not see? That's the challenge to the reporter—humanize the story. Maybe he'll find the answer on the player's bench, in the box office, in the dressing room, between halves, in the home of a player—but surely not in the play-by-play recording of the game along the sidelines. And wherever he finds the answer, it's going to be packed with surprise, heroism, sacrifice, courage, conflict, drama, heartache—in short, human interest.

Are editorials read? Another story often written in stereotyped form is the editorial. Many a school staff has debated whether editorials are worth the space they occupy, judged on the basis of reader interest. Some editors do away with editorials entirely, while others disguise them under regular news heads. Both of these practices evade the issue entirely; the first jumps at conclusions, the second acknowledges defeat and adopts trickery to overcome it. An editorial disguised under a news head is really a "doctored" news story.

Student newspaper practice too often reveals the following characteristic weaknesses in handling editorials: (1) Reporter A is assigned a 250-word editorial, regardless of his lack of interest in anything current; (2) The editorials have no connection with the timely things happening in the school; (3) Two or three reporters, on some papers even one, are assigned the job of writing all editorials; (4) An editorial is written to fill a given space, and consequently the writer has repeated the same thing in several different ways; (5) The editorial writer is selected because he cannot write a straight news story without editorializing—thus, he has to be used on editorials; and (6) The editorials resulting from these practices follow stock subjects such as George Washington, the New Year, Christmas, and school spirit.

If editorials are to be improved, the reconstruction must begin before the writing.

285

Deviating from news style. The plea for beneath-the-surface reporting, humanizing of the news story, deviation from the who-what-when-why-how pattern, and a freer style of writing in order to touch reader interest is not an invitation to disregard the fundamental laws of news reporting. The innovations suggested here are not for the beginning reporter. They are for the reporter who knows the fundamental rules of newswriting and is ready to go a step further—one who needs a new challenge in his work. Only by knowing and reflecting the fundamentals can he proceed without abusing journalism.

SELECTING DETERMINES READER INTEREST

One punch story each issue. It was maintained by the late E. W. Scripps that every issue of a paper must carry one punch story that stands out boldly, and that such a story can often save an otherwise dull issue. The Scripps-Howard papers have followed this practice. The burden of this plan falls upon the editor, who in turn must find one or more ingenious reporters who can produce such stories.

A case in point. A Miami high school acted as host for fifty Peruvian students, ages fifteen to seventeen, who came to the United States as guests for two weeks. What happened may be gathered from the school paper itself, the *Miami Edison Herald,* in Examples 176 through 179, arranged chronologically.

Example 176 appeared across the top of the first page of the December 19 issue of the paper, and under a banner head reading "We'll Pilot Peru Operation." It was continued to page three of the six-page paper. Example 177, an editorial, appeared on page two of the same issue, December 19.

Example 178, a news-feature giving background on Peru, was carried at the top of page three of the same issue, under the head "Scenes of Peruvian Turmoil Uncovered."

Example 179 is the upper portion of the front page of the January 19 issue, the Peruvian guests having arrived approximately one month after the first announcement.

The straight news coverage is at the top. On either side are news-features reflecting conversations between the hosts and the guests.

WE'LL PILOT PERU OPERATION

EXAMPLE

176

Within the next year Peru will face a political crisis. Already hundreds of Latin young people have been flown to Russia for a Soviet brainwashing. "Operation Amigo" involves no brainwashing, just an opportunity for Latin Americans to get a first hand taste of democracy and form their own opinions.

Herald Public Service Editor Pat Murphy contrasts Soviet objectives with democratic objectives in a similar statement: "This is not a brainwashing program. We want them to observe and accept life as it is. Whatever life is like in the U.S., that is what we want them to see."

Edison Hosts

January 15 is the tentative date for the arrival of the fifty-member pilot group ranging between the ages of 15-17. For two weeks the group will stay in Edison students' homes and attend school and other activities with them. Peruvians will also be guests at clinics showing a cross section of democracy at work.

Hosts to the Peruvians will show them the slum area as well as places such as Hotel Row and Lincoln Road. If democracy in Latin America is to be revived by this student-to-student program, a true and complete picture of our way of life must be observed by the guests.

If the program is successful, it will continue and spread to other Dade County schools. Winter here is summer there, so Peruvian students won't miss any school.

A committee of leading Lima business, professional, and political men headed by Dr. Raul Be-

raun, president of the bar association, has recognized the need to combat communism with democracy, but needed assistance from Miami. Assistance came from *The Herald* who will cooperate with Dade school officials in arranging the program.

Plans Made

During a recent visit to Miami, Dr. Beraun was given a tour of Edison by Mr. Donald Burroughs, director of student activities, William Duncan, principal, and Miss Charlotte Poitevint, journalism instructor. In the hope that the visitors will take the idea of a practical education system back to Peru, Dr. Beraun suggested that the Peruvians tour the shops, home economic department, music department, and art department. If such training was introduced into Peruvian school systems, many more Latin Americans would be able to earn a decent living.

Student council officers and club presidents met with *Herald* Managing Editor George Beebe, Associate School Superintendent Wesley Matthews, Senior High School Director Robert Wilson, and Principal William Duncan to discuss the project and possible acceptance of Edison to be the pilot school.

With a unanimous decision, Edison voted to undertake the project placing Edison in the eyes of the nation and giving Edisonites an adult responsibility with a chance to prove themselves capable of being leaders of tomorrow.

Student Council President David Folsom selected a Steering

287

Committee to handle "Operation Amigo" at Edison. The committee will be divided into sub-committees and added to as necessary.

Since the seeds of communism are usually planted by a few well-educated leaders, the Lima Committee will select students from the growing middle class and upper class who are familiar with the English language.

In preparation for their visit, Edison has sent *Heralds, Beacons,* guide books, pictures, and football programs to Peru. Here it brings out an example of how Americans have failed in fighting communism. Spanish translations of books about American history and democracy are not found in Latin-American Countries. Latin Americans are more familiar with the French Revolution than with the American Revolution.

"Operation Amigo" has drawn much response. The most noteworthy is the backing given by President John Kennedy. Here in Miami, the *Herald* has received calls offering money, homes, and personal services.

Donald Burroughs, director of student activities at Edison, expressed his enthusiasm for the program: "Here is a chance for Edison students to accept adult responsibility. If we are able to operate effectively today, we will operate as effective citizens tomorrow."

Operation Amigo

EXAMPLE

177

Communism is a convincing web that seeks out the inconsistent minds of youth and entangles them in subversive propaganda. The youth of Peru and Chile are in danger of communist influence—but the opportunity to find out the truth for themselves has been presented to them.

The *Miami Herald* and other interested parties have outlined a program whereby Latin-American students will visit in the homes of American students for a two-week period. It would be their privilege to observe and form their own opinions about American life.

It has been proposed that approximately fifty "pilot" students be brought to Miami via the Peruvian airlines at a rate of $200 a person, round trip. The program would go into operation during January and continue if successful.

In a sense, this is a junior-sized Peace Corps, and can be most effective in promoting good will and understanding.

Up until now we, as youth of America, have been unable to participate in the political affairs of states. It will be of great benefit not only to the Latin-American students but also to ourselves as we play "host" to these foreign students. This program will give us a chance to judge the foreign relationship that exists in South-American countries. Perhaps this experience will enable us to keep America strong when we are the ones "holding the reins."

We should keep in mind that, at present, we are dealing with students who, someday, may well be political leaders of their countries.

288

Scenes of Peruvian Turmoil Uncovered

EXAMPLE

178

In the era of the conquest of America, the actual territory of Peru formed, with Eucador, part of Bolivia, Argentina, and Chile, the mighty Incaic Empire, the capital of which was Cusco. The conqueror of this empire was Francisco Pizarro, who in 1525 founded the city of Lima.

The movement towards independence from the power of Spain did not advance until 1820, the year in which General San Martin arrived on the coast of Peru at the head of an independence army. Troubles inside the country were leading the revolution to failure when Simon Bolivar, called by Congress, and with more troops from Colombia, put an end to anarchy. Principal battles of the revolution which gave Peru independence were Junin, fought under the leadership of Bolivar, and Ayacucho, fought by Antonio José de Sucre.

Principal cities: Lima, the capital; Ell Callao; Arequipa; El Cuzco. Peru is bordered by Ecuador, Colombia, Brazil, Bolivia and Chile.

Peru Promotes International Friendship

EXAMPLE

179

"Cold" reception for Amigos, but only weather-wise.

When the big Peruvian airliner dropped landing gear to American soil, a new adventure began. Approximately fifty-one Peruvian students met with their American hosts at a school reception, and they were on their way for a two weeks visit.

Being met by Mayor Robert King High, was just the beginning of introductions to city officials. Yesterday they toured the Hialeah industrial center with major factories on the itinerary. Today, a tour of the Homestead Air Force Base has been arranged. The latest in rockets and planes will be shown.

January 20, 21, and 22 will be spent at home and in school. January 23 is certain to be a busy day; in the morning, a tour of Ft. Lauderdale is on the schedule. The trip from Miami will be made by train. They will visit all important sights of interest, from tourist to commercial standpoint.

At noon of the same day, the Miami Beach Rotary Club will take students on a tour of Miami Beach, Lincoln Road Mall, and the famous celebrities homes. At eight o'oclock a panel discussion will take place . . . on the panel will be Mayor High and Miami's political leaders. All questions that our guests might have, concerning any subject of their stay in the United States will get an answer.

January 27 is the conclusion of their stay here, and they will return to their native Peru.

Peruvians get first look at American hosts at airport.

What About These United States?

It is not too early to say whether or not the Peruvian students like the United States, most of them reply: "We love it."

"Everything is so big, I wish I could live here forever," said Irma Diaz. She is also very surprised about the American way of life; she wondered how it was that in the U. S. everyone, or almost everyone, owned a car. "When on Saturday morning a car came up

shown to them is the best and that it surpasses their greatest expectations.

America Extends A Warm Hello

Fads Change Often, Twist Termed "Crazy"

Teenagers are alike all over the world, whether they observe the same customs or not. Their likes and dislikes are much the same as ours. Peruvian boys play basketball, baseball, soccer, swim and engage in activities much as American boys do. The girls also have parties, window shop, talk over the telephone, and have boyfriends.

When one of the boys was asked what he thought of the "Twist" he raised his finger to his head and replied, "Crazy."

Memories Captured On Stage

Miami Edison Herald
Miami Edison High School
Miami, Florida

Peruvian students are quoted. On page two of this issue, there were also a short lead editorial entitled "Welcome, *Amigos*" and another, longer editorial, written in Spanish and entitled, *"Bienvenidos Amigos."*

Such opportunities for news coverage do not often come to a school. But in a sense, Miami Edison High School helped to create the story. The project itself developed from the possibility that such a group might be brought to Miami, and then become localized to this high school. The intensive coverage reflects the ingenuity of the staff. A punch story in each issue is not beyond the imagination of student editors.

Reporting fragments of stories. In covering a story a reporter often finds himself trying to obtain fragments of the story before the full details are ready for announcement. Generally the faculty member who is the source of the story does not want to make these fragments known until the complete announcement is ready, or at least he or she sees no reason for doing so. The adviser and the staff must educate the faculty to see that no story is ever complete; some related angle must have gone before, and some other angle will undoubtedly follow.

If the paper can announce when the tryouts for the senior play are to be held before these dates are generally known, the announcement is fresh and interesting. If no news at all is forthcoming, the drama critic might make news by reviewing the possibilities for different roles in different plays that might be selected. For instance, a senior talented in character acting might induce a teacher to select a play with a character lead. The sports writer who knows the students trying out for a particular sport can review the possibilities for positions long before the coach is ready to announce his first-string line-up.

This ability to create stories, or to build up insignificant details in a routine story, should be encouraged. Such a story often becomes that punch story by turning the spotlight from the known to the unknown.

Pictures stimulate interest. Pictures are a natural creator of reader interest—nothing enlivens the page like a cut. The cost of engravings is far overbalanced by the additional interest in the paper. Editors should try to use drawings and photographs by the students. The school paper is, after all, a medium of student expression.

290

Promotion stunts. Promotion stunts to publicize the name of the paper can be as effective for the school paper as for the daily. One paper conducts a spelling bee for the entire school, giving prizes to the best spellers. It arranges for contests in the homerooms to determine homeroom winners. These winners in turn appear in an all-school assembly, and are "spelled" down until the best speller is determined. Two student editors take turns calling the words, which are taken from suggestions submitted by all teachers. The participants are judged by three faculty judges who sit at a table on the stage. Each contestant wears a large card bearing the number of his homeroom. The spectators, seated by homerooms, become so excited and enthusiastic in following their respective candidates that it is necessary from time to time to quiet them. This particular school has forty homerooms.

Bring-a-book week for the library, Bring-a-bulb week for the school grounds committee, and printing a special program for the homecoming day game are three possible promotion stunts. There are unlimited possibilities.

Every school paper should build up and carry on a number of these annual traditions outside the regular work of editing the paper. They build the paper's prestige and afford interesting material for copy. The spelling story carried interest for five consecutive issues.

MAKE-UP ADDS INTEREST

Helping the reader. Editors must place greater emphasis upon editing and displaying the news. It is one thing to gather sparkling, fresh, and unusual stories; it is another to have them radiate these qualities after they are in print.

Keeping a newsy appearance. Usually the school paper looks upon its third page as a feature page. Uniform locations and uniform headings on the week-by-week columns enable the student to turn immediately to them. However, too many columns with cuts or other set heads may eventually detract from the newsiness of the paper—swinging its appearance toward that of the magazine. It is easy to fall into the habit of issuing the "same paper" week after week, with new words in the heads and columns.

Editorials on page one. Placing a special editorial on page one doubles reader interest, a trick that should be tried occasionally by every paper. To repeat it more than two or three times a semester, however, would be "riding a good horse to death."

News briefs. People read almost everything which has been broken into short paragraphs resembling personals columns. A school paper, limited for space as it is, should run as many different stories as possible on the front page. A "News Briefs" column, consisting of eight to twelve short news items, might be effective on the page. The items can be separated by short dashes, conservative ornaments, ten-point heads, or by setting the first line of each item boldface.

MEASURING READER INTEREST

The drop-out method. The alert daily paper checks the effectiveness of its features from time to time. A common procedure is to drop a particular feature for a few days to see if there is any demand for its return. This system does not give a true picture of reader following, for the bulk of readers who like the feature will probably not write to the paper. This is not a good method for the school paper.

The questionnaire method. Readers usually respond to questionnaires on their preferences by elevating their tastes—even though they are told not to sign their names.

The interview method. A more desirable survey, lending itself to use in the schools, is one built around the interview. It assumes that the reader reads the articles of interest to him, and that his preferences can be determined by a study of what he actually reads. The survey might be conducted by a school paper in some such manner as this:

The school is broken up into small groups of about thirty-five students, with one staff member assigned to each group—homerooms are natural divisions. The reporter interviews the students individually, using one copy of the last issue of the paper for each student. The interviewer sits down with the reader, places before him a copy of the paper, and goes down every column with him, checking each article he has read. To the question, "Did you read this article?" he secures a "Yes" or "No" answer. Even though the reader says he usually reads a certain feature, it is not marked unless it has been read in that particular issue. After a time the reader will take the initiative in pointing out the articles he has read.

Readers should be consulted within one or two days following publication. Once the school paper has thus interviewed its students, it has valuable data by which to revise its offerings. Interviewers should be trained before they approach the students, and another session should be held after each has made his first interview. To be effective, this plan calls for much hard work; it need be used, however, only about every two or three years.

The observation method. If the school paper is small, it is possible that most students read all of an issue, even though they are not particularly interested in parts of it. This suggests another method of determining real interests, although it is rather subjective and difficult to administer—watching the pupils as they secure the paper to determine what they read first. This can be done if delivery is made during the homeroom period for the sake of this study. The staff member delivering to a particular room remains long enough to see which page is read first by each student. He jots down the number who read the front page first, the number who read the editorial page first, and so on. He can even note which section of a page is read first.

READER INTEREST BY THE DAY

The newspaper staff of Lane Technical High School of Chicago has a novel approach to holding reader interest. The paper, the *Lane Tech Daily,* is issued daily, Monday through Friday. It is a two-column, four-page paper, six and a half inches by ten. The make-up consists of one or two stories on each page. (See Example 180.) Sports holds its traditional fourth page position, with the privilege of expanding when necessary. For instance, one Friday issue was devoted to sports exclusively, the city championship game in which the school was to participate taking over all four pages.

The total output of copy for the week would include the typical coverage of any newspaper—editorials, letters to the editor, feature stories, interviews, and straight news treatment. But the format is effectively suited to the paper's public.

EXAMPLE
180

Lane Daily
Lane Technical High School
Chicago, Illinois

294

CHAPTER LABORATORY

1. Bring to class two different daily newspapers that obviously either appeal to different types of readers or have a different point of view of reader interest. Use the examples as the basis for a class discussion.

2. Divide your school into interest groups (naturally there will be overlapping), and take one of these groups as a test of how effectively your paper caters to reader interest. If no stories can be found, list some possibilities.

3. From the last issue of your school paper, choose the three stories of greatest interest to you. Suggest a follow-up on one, or suggest another story that would appeal to the same interest group. Write the story for possible publication.

4. Examine and discuss the printed forms that your paper has provided to solicit news. If there are none, prepare a suggested form for the paper.

5. Discuss the advantages or disadvantages of a small daily (such as Example 180) in building up reader interest, in comparison with a weekly paper.

6. Show how your paper is succeeding in pleasing the students and how it could be improved.

7. Write a 200-word story of some classroom episode that should be appreciated by a fair percentage of the readers. What would you consider a fair percentage?

8. What appeal does your paper make to the parents? Could or should it do more in this respect?

9. Tabulate, by dividing the work, all the names that appeared in the last issue of the school paper, and the number of times each appeared. Discuss in class the situation revealed.

10. Find a school exchange that reflects good reader interest, and explain the reasons for your selection to the class.

19 NEWSPAPER ART

Newspaper readers deserve well planned and well executed photographs and illustrations. Regardless of how thoroughly gathered and how excellently reported, the news is often clarified by the support of appropriate art.

In the newspaper world the word *art* refers to pictures and illustrations of all types appearing in publication. The engraving made from a picture and the picture printed from the engraving are both known as *cuts*.

Newspaper art is indispensable to reader interest, for much news calls for amplification that can come only from art. The two main divisions of newspaper illustrations are photographs and line drawings. One is a view through the eye of the camera, the other a view through the eye of the artist.

STUDENT PHOTOGRAPHS

There was a time some years ago when the school paper enterprising enough to use photographs turned to commercial firms for such work, but today there are enough amateur, and even professional, photog-

296

raphers among the students to provide student art work to accompany student editorial work. Many papers now list staff photographers in their flags and give them credit lines under their pictures.

It is common for school papers, especially in sports coverage, to borrow cuts that have already appeared in the city newspapers, using a courtesy credit line to honor the donor, but the practice ranks a poor second to the creation of material that has never before appeared.

Selecting the subject. The school photographer receives assignments just as the reporter does, but he should also have ideas for the editor. For the purpose of reproduction in the school paper, the staff photographer should follow a few fundamental principles:

Subjects that show action have much more appeal than those formally posed. With a little practice and thought, the photographer can work action into his still shots and materially brighten his work.

The photographer should not include too much in any photograph. Too many people participating in an activity lessen interest in the activity itself, for unless the illustration is a full-page spread, details are lost and with them the immediacy of the activity. It is preferable to place a few students informally in the proper setting to indicate the activity.

Naturally there are times when the entire group must be photographed, and here it is wise to sacrifice the bodies for the sake of the faces. The photographer arranges as many as thirty or forty in three or four tiers, perhaps on the school steps, and then aims high. Large groups should usually look more formal than small groups.

Student groups are more the business of the yearbook than the school paper. The formality of the group photograph discourages its use in the paper. Credit to the entire football team justifies use of its picture, but there is greater student interest in an action shot of a play.

In the portrait picture, the staff photographer should secure a contrast between the subject and the background. A neutral or mottled background, however, is usually superior to a light background.

Furthermore, the solemnity of expression so commonly accepted a few years ago has given way to the more pleasant expression—not, however, the toothpaste-ad approach.

Excellent examples of student photography are scattered throughout this book; therefore only three are included in this chapter. Note, however, that the finest student photography requires ingenuity in layout to present it effectively to the audience. The layout is the frame of the photograph (and the drawing as well) and determines the effectiveness of its presentation.

Example 181 is really two stories with accompanying illustrations under one head. The layout results in equal treatment of the two bands—with eye-catching distinctions, however. Note the in-action feeling of both photographs.

The quality, variety, informality, and good taste of the candid shots in Example 182 are clearly evident in this treatment of football practice. Even the non-sports enthusiast will find himself following a page that creates reader interest in content and layout.

Example 183 is an illustration of an old subject given a new twist—the class will. Here the photographer and the cartoonist teamed up to illustrate a special senior edition of the paper.

EXAMPLE
181

Student Bands Are Success

A group of boys known as the Galaxies was selected to play at the Broomstick Bop last Friday night, October 27. This band consists of five juniors, and one senior from Harding. Members of the group are: Butch Stokes, piano; Rich Walker, bass; Mike Stokes, guitar; Greg Hartman, saxophone, Rick Williams and Jack Carty, drums.

The band got their start at the American Field Service Talent Show at Harding in April of 1960.

The Galaxies were in a city "Battle of Bands" contest which was sponsored by the Coca Cola Bottling Company. In all, there were nine bands competing. The Galaxies took first place in this contest.

The band plays at dances, wedding receptions, socials, and parties. Their music ranges from rock-n-roll to old tunes and blues.

Mike Stokes, one of the juniors in the group, is both the leader and organizer of the band.

The Galaxies

The Fortunes

A group of boys called the Fortunes played at the Harding Homecoming Dance this year. They were organized a year and a half ago and have played frequently since then.

The Fortunes played at the The Fortunes consist of: Bob Pankonin, guitar; Pete LeMay, drums; Merle Christenson, saxophone; Terry LeMay, bass, and Stan Rydell, trumpet. Hazel Park Commercial Club dances which were held every other Friday night during all of

last year. They also have played at the Prom Ballroom, Crystal Colliseum, New Brighton, Newport, Macalester, East Side Y.M.C.A., and the Polish American Club.

The Beacon
Harding High School
St. Paul, Minnesota

298

Tattler PICTORIAL

David Mack, Photographer   November 20, 1959

B-CC Football Team Practices In Preparation For Big Game

CHARLIE BRADFORD practices the blocking he must use on Saturday.

PREPARATION for a varsity football game does not begin Saturday morning when the team boards a bus or enters the locker-room to dress for the game. Nor does it begin when they run onto the field to the cheers of the student body. On the contrary, the Barons started practice before school reopened this fall and will continue until the last game.

MANY STUDENTS have asked, "What does the team do to prepare for a game?" They start the preceding Monday by studying their opponent's offense and defense, and matching it against their own. Fundamentals such as pass defense, kicking, and passing are stressed.

FOR FOOTBALL PLAYERS the day is just beginning when they go to sixth period class. All members of the varsity have gym this period. This enables them to have a longer practice period. They first go to the locker room and put on their uniforms and then go out to the practice field.

FROM 3 O'CLOCK until they can no longer see the football, they practice every play Coach Sadusky thinks could be helpful in the next game. To keep in condition, they take laps around the field, do calisthenics, and practice blocking. This continues from Monday until Thursday. On Friday, the team rests as Coach Sadusky explains the important points learned during the preceding week's practice.

WHEN SATURDAY comes, the team know that they are ready for the game. All of the work done during the past week will show, win or lose, that the team did everything they could to be ready.

JOE MEGBY struggles into his jersey for the afternoon practice.

STEVE EVANS prepares for the afternoon drill in weaknesses and fundamentals.

BUD WHITTAKER centers to Tom Arata.

THE PROGRESS OF THE GAME is mirrored in the faces of the players.

PRACTICE PASSES are an important part of the afternoon's work.

COACH SADUSKY directs defensive play from the sidelines.

THE LONG PRACTICE SESSION ENDED, Don Kreuger dresses for the trek home and hours of homework.

The Tattler
Bethesda-Chevy Chase High School
Bethesda, Maryland

299

I Hereby Will Southeastern To The

EXAMPLE 183

Sketches by Kathy Russo

MOST RETIRING GIRL

MARY PILOT

CUTEST COUPLE

RANDY LEDFORD   MARILYN BALDWIN

MOST SOPHISTICATED BOY

JOHN BIRKENSHAW

SHELBY MURPHY   FRIENDLIEST BOY

SANDI HABUCKI

SWEETEST GIRL

MOST ATHLETIC BOY

TOM STILL

DON SLOAN

CUTEST BOY

MOST LIKELY TO SUCCEED

CAROL SCHUMACHER

IDEAL JANITOR

JIM PICKERING

JUDY IAMQARTER

MOST SOPHISTICATED GIRL

I, JAMES DAGEN, will Nancy Tchokreff and Clara Armstrong the names Frank and Chrlie, and to anyone who wants them a pair of patten leather points, size 9.

I, JEROME BRONER, will to my enemies my geometry book in the hopes they will get more from it than I did.

I, GERI RINI, will to Peggi Sherwood a certain bathing suit on Lexington Beach and Charlotte a certain Wednesday night and L. G. at Metro. To Mr. Yoskovitch a more optimistic view on life.

I, BRUCE LYON, will all underclassmen the ability to "clinch," "comprehend," and "grasp the situation"; or "in other words," "for all practical purposes," to "dig that jazz."

I, CLEMENT ATLIA, will all my books and old chemistry tests to my little sister who will need them.

I, KATHERINE MACK, will to all Seniors a large bottle of nerve pills and a hot water bottle for after finals.

I, DOLORES McBRIDE, will to Sue Davey one street cleaning sign and to D.A.O. a Full Privilege Membership at the "Y" for future use.

I, DIANE STRELL, will to Bob Heiden all my books used in my senior year, in hopes that he may get more out of them than I did.

I, KAYE MILLER, will to Kathy Fraser my ability not to panic in traffic. Also the ability to get along with E.L. as well asI get along with F.B.

I, LOREN BEADLE, will to Mary Beadle my ability to get along with all the teachers at SE.

I, MARGARET MORAN, will my calves to Rick so he will make all-city football next year, and to all undergraduates the wonderful times I've had at SE.

I, DIANE PETERS, will to a certain teacher whose initials are' Mr. Stephens a copy of, "Good Jokes I Have Heard," in the hopes his will improve.

I, LINDA SUHR, will to anyone the ability to do the splits and cartwheels and to get along with Miss Hansen while on the basketball team.

I, BARBARA CORDER, will my locker to my sister, Becky, and good luck to Sandra Goodman in getting up from lunch on time.

I, LAMAR GLASSCO, will to Barbara Edison my ability to pass biology and to complete my homework without taking any books hom.e

I, CAROL LAMBERT, will Gary Weisgerber five free lessons on good photography so that he has a fair chance for the photo crown. HA. HA.

I, ROSS LEWIS, will to Arthur Honold the will to get in trouble in study hall with Mr.Wisniewski.

I, ANITA BISHOP, will all my height to the short boys in SE.

I, JO ANN WARREN, will Mr. Maiolani and Mr. Blomfield people to give them the same (if not worse) treatment they gave me. I will Carol Daher a ride in my first jalopy.

I, ARMANDO AVECILLA, leave my books to Southeastern and wish to the future seniors all the best of luck in the future.

I, JOAN FUTRELL, being of sound mind, do hereby will my book entitled "Getting The Lead In Your Senior Play" to Diane Gacchina. Also, to those who have contributed to my memory wall, my thanks.

I, ROBERT KOLLOEN, will my locker across from the library to anyone wishing to walk past the library when there are meetings held there.

I, BETSY KAMBERS, will Judy Valade and Janice Smith a walkie-talkie set so that they can communicate at all times.

I, ORA LEE MILTON, will all of my bad grades that I received at SE to Vera Green.

I, BOB CLARK, will to any freshie my good old flat tire excuse in hopes that he can use it.

I, SHARON CRAWLEY, will Karen Jaco the ability to goof up while cheerleading as well as I did.

I, BILL LUX, with Bob P. and Ron L. the first row of seats in House 303. Also, Bob C the will to give all girls a chance.

I, CAROL E. FOSTER, will my elevator pass to any freshie who can find the elevator.

I, ROBERT HARRIS, will anybody all my Comp.4 notes in hopes that they can do a better job than I did.

I, CATHIE WOODHAM, will Liz McKenna one worn out piece of music and a beat-up senior pin.

I, LORRAINE MORGAN, will future commercial classes the good and bac luck I've had in Mrs. Ryder's Office Machines class.

I, PATRICIA MEYER, will to Lola Petrie the ability to give all her friends a bus card with her name on it and still manage one left for herself.

I, KAREN BASTIAN, will to Franny V. my ability to go with a boy as sweet as Steve.

I, JAMES RAWLS, hereby, will to Bennie Sneeze my success in arriving at school each day one minute before the last bell and still not be tardy for my first hour chemistry class.

I, BARBARA HODGES, will to Ann Culbertson my senior pin and hope she will use it to the best of her ability.

I, SHARON REEVESM, being of sound will and mind will to Gail Rose and Elanie Pate the ability toget back their clothes after certain parties have borrowed them.

I, LINDA WILLIAMS, will my ability to resist skipping school to sister, Gail, in hopes that she will use it.

I, JUDY ANN HOWZE, will all future SE students to know the identity of H. A. Jungaleer. Also, to my sister, Nancy, all the swell times I've had at SE.

I, CHARLOTTE COOPER, will Jean Barnett the ability to pass every semester so she may graduate without summer school entering her mind.

I, HAROLD WEBER, will to any student in 303 a pair of sneakers if they have study hall sixth hour with a certain teacher.

I, DAN HILL, will to nyone who is unfortunate enough t› come at 5 to 8 a parking place within our district.

I, JIMMY BRASWELL, will to anyone my ability to get out of house without being caught. To Russell my all A report card; to any 12B all my cheat sheets.

I, PAT BYARS, will any new 12A all my E comp 4 papers and the ability to graduate in January '52.

I, PAT WIECHERT, will to anybody who wants it, all the hard times I have had in all my Comp classes.

I, ELLEN EAHLMAN, will to all those who will some day be seniors to make a goal in life and seek it out.

I, JAMES WALDEN, will Co. "D" lst B.G. lst Brigade to John E. Ball.

I, ARKLES BROOKS, will my scholastic ability to Carol Glass, my speed in track to Harold Hall and Melvin Herzfield, and my thanks for this speed to Mr. John Tolfer. All my A's to my sister Marsha Brooks.

I, STEVE RAVEZZANI, will to Ron Hunter a new set of drum sticks so he may please Mr. Miller.

I, CAROL WEIER, will to all 12B's the ability to get Mrs. Vereen for Comp 4 and Mr. Stephens for Economics.

I, JOANN FERRENCE, will to my sister Margie the ability to eat pizza and to keep her hands off J.B., K.G., & D.F.

I, JOANN FERRENCE, will to my sister Margie the ability to eat pizza, and to keep her hands off J.B., K.G., & D.F.

I, MARIAN RALPH, will and bequeath to Karl Perrin the ability to sneak in an approximate four hour "nap" and still manage to awake in time to watch Jack Paar and cram for a Friday Chem test.

I, LUCY TALLEY, will to Mary Lou weber my 3 1/2 study halls.

I, MARY ANN TRUPIANO, will all my left over materials from all my sewing classes to anybody needing scraps.

I, LINDA WARD, will to Judy Lacy the ability to keep going with Nick through the rest of the term and next.

I, SANDRA NICHOLSON, will to Linda Pangone all my old school books and hope that she will have better luck with them than I did.

I, JUDY OWENS, will to Carol Lewis another party at Garip; to Karen Green a pair of binoculars for the purpose of watching that special someone for me.

I, CAROLYN WALZ, will to Barbara Temple my seat in Mr. Stephen's Econ. class. Also, to Barbara Edison all my Comp.4 notes.

I, DON FRERICHS, will to L.A.D. my little black book so that she won't have to ponder any longer over who I secretly admire.

I, JANE JONES, will to anyone in study hall 222 my service post outside of it for four semesters in a row.

I, LEWIS HUNT, will to Pat Fuchs the picture of Teddy Roosevelt in 222 so she can always have Jasper the Ghost with her.

I, CAROL SCHUMACHER, will Bette Jones and Lynne Defpelder all of the good times I've had with the swimming team.

I, DALE MARINO, will to any poor sap that wants it my ability to be a perfect goof off.

I, MARILYN BROWN, will to my sister all my "D's" in American history in hopes that she will raise them to "A's."

I, JOAN WILSON, will all my brains to Jerry Alford.

I, MARY JANE MARINO, will to no one the privilege of having Mrs. Barrie as their "second mother" and to any student driver the ability to park in the teacher's parking lot during school hours and get away with it.

I, KAREN ROSIN, will to Sue Davey my ability to aggravate a certain 4th hour teacher.

I, TERRY KLAASEN, will to Rick Mazzie, the spell I hold over a certain teacher, and to D.H., nothing.

I, CHARLENE MIKELSON, will to Karl W. the ability to bowl. To Judy R., and Peggy Mc. the ability to stay on a diet. Good luck P Mc. with you-know-who.

300

Juniors, Maybees and Freshmen - Alas...

DIANE THOMAS

CUTEST GIRL

I, PAT LOWHORN, will to any 12B my Comp 4 test papers, which Bob Parks copied from.

I, SANDRA TEMPLE, will all my Comp 4 papers and my teacher, Mrs. Vereen, to Barbara Edison and Barbara Temple.

I, GAIL ROBERTS, being of sound mind, will to any freshie the privilege of getting easy teachers in the 12A.

I, FRONZA WOODS, will to Fifo a new Dodo to have council duty with and to all Jungaleers a good Comp t. acher before they get to Comp 4. To Carol Willard the "pig" again with an extra large squeeze.

I, DIANA ANDELEAN, will to Carol Lewis all the happiness in the world with a certain L.J., and the ability to get like D.B. was one night.

I, JIM JACKSON, will to anyone who wants it, a slightly broken locker located near 223 and to C.B. my ability to pass without studying.

BRUCE LYON

CLEVEREST BOY

I, CASSANDRA TAYLOR, will J.O. a pair of wings to learn how to fly, and to L.J. his car keys back from last June.

I, LOUIS EDWARDS, will one chemistry book to Werner Von Braun, one trig book to Alan Shephard, and one used brief case to anyone that wants it.

I, SHELBY MURPHY, will to Ozzie Lucas presidency of the Lemon Society and to Chuck Foory the ability to hold his cookies when necessary.

I, GLORIA CALLAWAY, will to Frances Johnson the ability to graduate this year. To any future senior all my "E" papers in Economics who wants them and can use them this year.

I, ROBERTA JONES, will a piece of broken window to Art Bryant, and my luck in getting along with teachers to all who desperately need it.

I, JEAN KORBUS, will to my sister, Lillian, all my books in hopes that she will get more out of them than I did.

I, SAUNDRA KRAFT, will Claire Armstrong my seat in retailing so that she may admire M. T.

I, JOHN BRAMBLETT, will my ability to get along with Mr. R. to T. T. and to C.J. the best of everything.

I, FRANK HENDERSON, will a saxophone mouthpiece to Charles Greer.

I, BETTE GAINES, will my sister Pat to science. I also will to Mary McGinley my Spanish dictionary and to John Korachis my viola bow.

I, MARILYN BALDWIN, will to Sue Davey the ability to remember the right key at the right time.

I, CHARLES GRAHAM, will to James Hudgens one B drawing in drafting and to Jim Jackson—nothing.

I, CAROL SUE FINGER, will to P.G. one white Cadillac and luck with what goes with it.

BEST DRESSED GIRL

JUDY BEHRENS

I, JAMES IVERS, will to Bill Hood my invaluable parking space on Fairview and the tardy passes necessary when this space is occupied by someone else.

I, RUTH HOERAUF, will to Barbara Patterson, one chair for at any party to have fun on.

I, LARRY DIETRICH, will to my younger brother Ron my intelligence, my quickness of thought, my sparkling personality, and my eagerness to learn, in the hope that he may be half as great as I.

I, BEVERLY JOHNSTON, will to Mr. Russell, a revised joke book; Willie Burgess, Copenhagen; Linda Tepper, another perfect Senior Trip like 1961; and Mr. Leib, a bald tennis ball.

I, GERI KNAUS, will Marge K. my gym locker so she won't have to run back and forth from lockers to get her clothes.

I, JESSIE LAMON, will my personality to Joyce Belcher with the hopes that she will use it well to the best of her ability.

MOST ATHLETIC GIRL

LINDA SUHR

I, HELEN MURRAY, will to Claudia Jackson a Gypsy for her heart and T.F. to A.T. Also to P.S. and C.J. a library of great books.

I, URSULA MAGER, will to Miss Larsen the luck of finding someone to translate her letters from German into English and vice versa.

BEST MANNERED BOY

DAVE DEVRIES

I, SUE COX, will to my sister Patty Cox, all my hard times and old homework papers to get through the eleventh grade.

I, GALE DAWES, will to my sister Jeri all my ex-boyfriends; she needs them.

I, SHARON KALKAN, will to anyone who is not in a hurry to graduate my ability to stay in Shorthand 1 & 2 for four semesters.

I, ROSALIE McCALL, will to Celeste Karmey all my old books to help her get through high school; also my ability to get along with Miss Crow.

I, HAROLD HALL, will my pair of fourth place track shoes to Melvin Herzfield, my torn jersey to Arkles Brooks, and my luck of getting in late safely on weekends to Mary Carr.

I, JANICE SMITH, will my sister Pat the ability to talk continuously in Mr. Yoskovich's Econ class and get away with it. Also to anybody who drives, the ability to get 15 kids in a six passenger car.

BEVERLY JOHNSTON

CLASS SIREN

I, CAROL DITTMAN, will to any freshman my ability to avoid getting nine hours for three years at old SE.

I, MARILYN ROBISON, will to any on-coming senior the best of luck in getting a good mark in Mrs. Ryder's office machines class.

I, ELLEN WAHL, will to D.D. a loud and reliable alarm clock, and to T.W. a suit of shiny armor.

I, EDWARD MICHAEL, will everything to anybody for any reason at all.

I, DELBERT WALSH, will to Elvis McCoy, my dreadful ability to put off until tomorrow what has to be done today.

I, SHARON SENIFF, will Leslie Taylor my ability to open my locker and duck the books that happen to fall; and to Frank Mitchell all my worn out gum from study hall.

I, MARY PILOT, hereby will to Joan Heppner another program at Cobo Hall, to Rick Mazzei my age, and to Sarah McIntyre another J.B.

I, ERWIN FAISS, will all my stubby pencils to Angelo DiAnna.

I, BILL MESHEKEY, will to Sue Davey a fixed ballot machine so she will win every 203 house election. Also, the ability to pass modern lit. and Comp4 with all "A's."

I, CAROL BURDEN, will to my sister, Linda, the ability to drive to school during her senior year and still be late.

I, PATRICIA PAGE, leave to my brother, John, and to all other SE Jungaleers a sincere wish for good luck in graduating.

I, STEVE HOLT, will my gold-plated bottle opener to Walter Dunn.

I, INGRID BAUER, do hereby will Walter Dunn a certain S Club pin in the hopes that he will make better use of it than I did.

I, PETE COUTSOS, will Jim Gehrke and Rick Mazzei ten judo lessons.

CLASS CHATTERBOX

LOIS KINGSHILL

I, BARBARA FRANKLIN, will to Ann Makino the ability to have two houses—222 and 303—and to Bill Head, my desk in Economics under the "wild" yardstick of Mr. Yoskovich.

I, JUDY WEBER, will to Joann Nowak my ability to notice pretty Christmas wreaths and some more good times like those in C4H.

I, LYNN LEATH, will to May Wyatt my ride to school so she won't be tardy and all my happy days with Mr. W.

I, BRUCE DUNN, will my ability to get along with a certain Physics instruco instructor to anyone who needs it.

I, BERNICE HOEVEL, will to Mr. Holdredge the luck of having my little sister in his t my little sister in his study hall next semester.

I, RIDLEY SMITH, will John Davis my ability to throw a baseball farther than he throws.

I, JANE HUBER, will Penny Pirtle all the good times I had at SE.

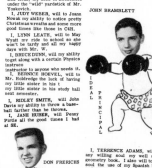

DON FRERICHS

MOST LIKELY TO SUCCEED

KATHIE GAULT

CLEVEREST GIRL

I, DIANE THOMAS, will Sandi Williams a certain frat house at Wayne and to Marilyn Cerneant the ability to sink a certain ship in the Pacific.

I, CAROL LOTHIAN, will my sister Mary a box filled with all the fun and laughter I've had at SE hoping she won't try to push any more of the same in this box for it's about to explode already.

I, TED WOLLESEN, will good times, embarrassing moments, and a great deal of knowledge to anyone lucky enough to get C.T.M. for a Spanish teacher.

I, KEN SLATCHER, will J.F. and D.M. one set of unused survey forms, and Mr. J.M. many semesters of peace and contentment without me on the stage.

I, REBECCA MOORE, will all of my Comp 4 papers to my sister.

I, BRUCE BRONSON, will Carol Burden my ability to get along with Mr. Brown.

I, ELLI LELKE, will to Pam Frissie my ability to come to school on time and my Comp 4 book with all the answers.

JOHN BRAMBLETT

IDEAL PRINCIPAL

I, TERRENCE ADAMS, will to any willing soul my well used geometry book. I also will to any soul the use of my Spanish book and what knowledge that may go with it.

I, NORA MASON, will to Marlene Luckey all my coffee in the morning before school and the love for Jim's jazz records, that I cannot stand.

I, JANET RHOADES, will another great cast party to the members of the next Senior Play, and a certain magazine to D.M. and K.S.

I, SONJA TCHOKREFF, will all my books with the answers in them to Nancy and hope she has more luck with them than I did.

I, FLOYD DZIADULA, will Elvis McCoy my ability to bribe all my teachers.

The Jungaleer
Southeastern High School
Detroit, Michigan

Developing and printing. By doing his own developing and printing, the staff photographer can save much of the cost of commercial photography or even of commercial finishing. He should discuss his prints with the printer whenever possible and learn to distinguish those prints that reproduce well from those that do not. Engravers frequently complain that the most common fault of photographers, both commercial and amateur, in preparing prints for newspaper reproduction is overexposure.

The printing process determines the cost of reproducing art work in the school newspaper; therefore, the school paper should periodically assess its printing process to see if its expenditures on illustrations and the number of copies it prints are best served by this process. (See Chapter 20.) Saving in the reproduction of artwork can often be made by utilizing *offset* printing, a process that eliminates engraving and prints the picture from a rubber-covered roller onto the paper. Some papers use the offset process entirely, others just for occasional picture supplements. Every journalism class should visit both the printer and the engraver, for nothing produces greater familiarity with the processes than firsthand observation.

THE LINECUT

The newspaper picture that does not come from a camera comes from the drawing board, and requires a talented artist—in the school newspaper, a talented student artist. The first function of a paper is to cover the news, drawing upon the picture to strengthen the story. Drawings are an important part of this process.

The line drawing (black and white artwork composed of lines, dots, dashes, etc., rather than artwork involving tones of gray) is the basis of all newspaper cartoons. These can be divided into two types for the purpose of newspaper illustration: (1) the editorial cartoon and (2) the feature cartoon. The first is used editorially to express or influence opinion, or to bring action. It may support an editorial, but at times it appears alone—a strong editorial appeal requiring no words (see Examples 184 and 185).

The editorial cartoonist is directed by the policy of the paper. The

302

Subscribe Now!

The Oracle
Bay View High School
Milwaukee, Wisconsin

EXAMPLE
184

EXAMPLE
185

The Tattler
West Tech High School
Cleveland, Ohio

drawing shows his ingenuity in execution, but its subject is determined by the editorial purposes of the paper.

The feature cartoon is lighter-spirited; its purpose is entertainment. It, in turn, has two forms, the continuing comic strip (see Example 186) and the single drawing (see Example 187). The feature cartoon reflects the good taste and judgment of the paper, but it originates with the student artist. The possibilities for an ingenious artist are great in the feature cartoon. The cartoon strip is popular with student newspapers, the characters usually cast as typical students in typical school situations.

Cartoons often reflect the temporary presence of a good student artist on the staff. A school paper seldom maintains a comic strip or a running editorial cartoon from year to year. They emerge with the presence of talent and wane with its absence. This policy is editorially sound, for an inferior picture no more belongs in print than an inferior piece of copy. The cut that graces the standard heading for a column is a common outlet for the talent of a staff artist. (See Chapter 12.)

PENNY and PETE　　　　　　　　By Kathy Arno

Panel 1: PENNY-PETE BROUGHT YOU HOME VERY LATE LAST NIGHT, DIDN'T HE?

Panel 2: YES MOTHER, IT WAS LATE. DID THE NOISE DISTURB YOU?

Panel 3: NO, DEAR. IT WASN'T THE NOISE.... IT WAS THE SILENCE !

The Polaris
North High School
Minneapolis, Minnesota

EXAMPLE 186

Equipment. The artist for the school paper needs very little equipment, but this equipment must be properly selected. The creator of one regular comic strip managed very well with this equipment: drawing board, T-square, Columbia 3-ply Bristol board which comes in 22 x 28 inch sheets, a Gillott pen number 303, a ruling pen, a No. 2 camel's-hair brush, a piece of art gum, a No. 2 pencil, and a bottle of India ink. Engraving screens and grease pencils are also possibilities.

Cartoon strips are usually drawn with pen and ink, with the brush work limited to filling in the solids.

Lettering. Good lettering immensely improves an average drawing. The careful cartoonist pencils in his picture before he begins to ink it, and provides parallel lines in pencil to guide him in his lettering. After the ink is dry the penciling is erased with art gum.

The editor should never permit a student's poor lettering to detract from his good drawing. An assistant who letters well, and captions set in type, are possibilities.

The block print. The block print, produced from a linoleum cut, is one of the most creative and least expensive forms of school newspaper art. The artist executes both the original drawing and the

304

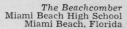
The Beachcomber
Miami Beach High School
Miami Beach, Florida

DRIVER'S EDUCATION CAR

SIEBERT

"WHY, NO - I THOUGHT YOU WERE THE INSTRUCTOR!"

PROWL

200

2/00

"WONDER WHO'S IN THE SUIT?"

Palmetto Panther
Palmetto High School
Miami, Florida

MRS. PITTS

TURNER 11/10

"HEY! LET'S STOP AND SEE HOW THE BIOLOGY CLASS DID ON THEIR GRASSHOPPER EXPERIMENT."

EXAMPLE
187

linoleum cut itself. Art stores carry blocks of appropriate size. The cutting is done with a few sharp tools also obtained at art-supply houses. The picture is first drawn on the linoleum surface, or is transferred to it from a drawing. The lines to be printed are left raised, and all the rest is cut away. Because the block itself is used in printing, the lines must be well supported; the effect is naturally bold in comparison with pen-and-ink work.

This bold technique is more often used in the yearbook and magazine than in the newspaper, but it can be an excellent source of inexpensive, imaginative high school art. The effectiveness of Example 188 can best be appreciated by imagining its appearance in its

305

EXAMPLE
188

The Argentian
Argentine High School
Kansas City, Missouri

original size, a three-column cut, on the editorial page. The striking effect of large areas of black and white that the linoleum cut produces can do much to enliven an otherwise lifeless page.

THE MORGUE

The purpose. The term *morgue* has two general meanings: (1) the supply of cuts available for use in a publication; (2) more often the accumulation of all types of information needed in the publication of the paper. There is a saying among librarians that a misplaced book is lost; the same thing is true of the morgue. Unless the morgue is well organized, it is virtually useless.

Art. Storage of cuts is a problem even with professional newspapers and printing plants. Some kind of drawer space is, of course, necessary. If drawers are too deep or too large, however, the weight of the cuts may break them. Supply houses can provide regular electrotype cabinets in which the drawers are only as deep as one cut. Before you store the cuts, take a proof of each on a sheet of paper and wrap the cut in its own proof with the printed area visible. This protects the cuts from dirt and scratches, and allows particular cuts to be located

306

more easily. Some classification process should be instituted. For example, all signature cuts could be grouped together, all single-column portraits together, and so on.

If the school paper has a staff photographer, old negatives will eventually become a problem. Naturally, these must not be destroyed. A filing cabinet of the proper size in which to file envelopes vertically provides one good solution. Each envelope contains one negative. The subject of the shot, the date, the occasion, etc., are indicated on the envelope. Each envelope is then numbered and filed serially. In the newsroom a large sheet of plasterboard contains one print of each picture taken by the staff photographer. Each print bears a small number corresponding to the serial number on the negative envelope. In addition to lending color to the newsroom, the system makes the matter of duplicating prints a simple one.

Files. The school paper which comes out this week may seem to have little value after it has been read. As time goes on, the paper becomes more and more valuable, however, because copies become increasingly scarce. Each staff should preserve copies of its current issues for future use, beginning immediately. One staff, which prints its paper regularly on newsprint each week, has a few copies printed on a good quality bond paper. These may be preserved more readily than newsprint and will not "yellow" or get brittle. The most satis-factory method of preserving copies is, of course, binding. If your paper does not have bound copies of past issues, accumulate as many of your past issues as possible and bind them now, even though you do not have a complete series. It should then become the regular duty of the exchange editor, the secretary, or some other staff member to pre-serve weekly copies for binding at the close of each year. The school and city libraries will usually welcome annual bound copies as gifts.

Like other phases of high school newspaper work, there is no limit to the extent of the school paper's filing activities. It may wish to do as most daily papers do and file clippings from each issue. In general, there are three satisfactory methods for filing clippings: the file folder, the filing envelope, or the filing card on which clippings are pasted. If two copies of each issue are cut up, and each story filed under its appropriate heading, necessary material will be immediately available to reporter and editor. For instance, if clippings of the annual games between two rival schools are instantly available, together with the accompanying statistics, much more vital sports stories can be written. Such a clipping file will save time and improve the paper.

Current information. There is just as great an opportunity in the field of current information. For example, a card file containing the name, address, phone number, grade level, and activities of each student will be extremely valuable. Such information is always available in the school office, but the closer at hand, the more frequently the information will be used. Every school newspaper office should have a record of all teachers, their class schedules, the degrees they hold, and the schools they attended. There should also be a record of all clubs and extracurricular organizations.

CHAPTER LABORATORY

1. Review the art the school paper has carried in its last two issues to determine the extent of use. In class discussion, determine if this is a reasonable amount.
2. The file of pictures and cuts retained by a school paper is usually rather inadequate. Should the paper maintain a morgue as does the daily? Discuss the pros and cons in class. What sort of system would you ·recommend for your paper?
3. Make a study of the stories assigned for the next issue of the paper; from their page locations, suggest appropriate art work—cartoons or photographs.
4. Have the business manager of the paper appear in class to discuss the costs of art. To what extent is the cost of a cut offset by the cost of labor saved in linotype?
5. If the paper can afford one cartoon each issue, should it be a comic strip? If not, propose the nature of it.
6. Consider ways to get more art in the advertisements.
7. Prepare a rough layout for page one of the paper, indicating the placement of cuts that would help the page.
8. Prepare such a layout for one other page of the paper.

20 GOING TO PRESS

A poorly printed paper invariably indicates poor copy and editorial indifference, for the staff that values its output will not be satisfied until the print job is of equal quality. Most school papers are printed by commercial firms, a few are produced entirely in the school, and some are printed by a combination of the two. The majority of the papers are produced by flat bed "letterpress," although some papers are produced by a popular printing method known as "offset," and some are duplicated or mimeographed. Many elements, not the least of which is cost, determine the method of printing to be used.

TYPESETTING

Hand composition. Originally all type was "set" by hand. Printers had trays or "fonts" of type, each piece carrying one letter or character. All type to be set was picked up by the printer and assembled in a "stick," one character at a time. After the type had been used, it was "distributed"—that is, each character was replaced in the proper compartment and used over and over again. Today, handset type is never used for the "body" of the news story, but only for some headlines, extremely large type, or sections of ads. Actually most headlines on commercial papers are set by machine.

The Linotype. All daily newspapers are now produced on linotype machines, which, as the name implies, set lines of type. The linotype operator, sitting at a typewriter-like keyboard, "types" out one line of type. The machine arranges small pieces of brass called *matrices* (plural of *matrix*), each of which has a letter symbol punched into its side. When enough matrices have been set to fill one line of type, the operator pushes a lever that moves the line of matrices against a mold into which hot type metal (lead and antimony) is forced. The line of type or "slug" cools as it slides into a tray (galley) besides the operator. (See Examples 189 and 190.)

Monotype. In monotype composition, usually used only in encyclopedias and mathematics and scientific books, the operator presses the keys on a keyboard also similar to a typewriter. The machine perforates holes in a roll of paper, each arrangement of holes corresponding to a different letter. The result is something like a paper roll used to operate a player piano. The printer then places the roll of paper into another machine which automatically, like that player piano, sets *individual* (*mono* means "one") letters of type.

Galley Proofs. After the type has been set, it is assembled in long trays called galleys. Proofs are then made by running an inked roller (brayer) over the type and pressing long strips of paper onto the inked type. When these proofs are read by the proofreader, errors are noted (see Chapter 14), and the galley proofs are returned to the printer. If the linotype operator has made an error or if the editor decides to change a word, the entire line at least must be reset. If a word is to be added or a longer word substituted, two or three lines following may need to be reset. Unlike handset type, the linotype slugs are melted and the metal is reused after the newspaper is printed (in letterpress) or a special proof is pulled (in offset).

310

MAKE-UP

Page make-up. The printer, following a page dummy prepared by the editor, assembles type, ads, and cuts in a page-size form called a chase and finally "locks-up" the whole page. Generally, a page proof is pulled at this time and checked for make-up errors.

PRINTING THE PAPER BY LETTERPRESS

But the page is only the beginning. What follows is a description of what is called *letterpress printing*. The term *letterpress* means printing from raised surfaces, rather than flat or plane (as in plane geometry) surfaces. Therefore the letterpress process is a general term including many types of printing methods. In all of these printing methods an impression is made from raised letters which have been inked onto the sheet of paper. In general there are four kinds of letterpress printing presses: platen presses, flat-bed cylinder presses, rotary presses, and the web (newspaper) press which is really a form of the cylinder or rotary press.

Once the page has been proofread and okayed by the editorial staff, the page of type may undergo a number of different processes. If the number of copies to be printed is very small (under a few thousand), the locked-up page may be put onto a flat-bed cylinder or platen press, and the paper printed. Printing directly from the type can only be done when the "run" is small, for type metal quickly wears out and the printing will not be distinct in a large run. If a larger run is necessary, a cardboard-like material will be heated and then pressed hard against the page. This will result in an exact copy of the page, but it will all be backward, like an image of a newspaper page in a mirror. From this *mat* or mold, a metal plate will be cast. It is this plate that is used in the actual printing of daily newspapers.

If a flat-bed platen press is to be used, the plate and the surface on which the paper is held (the platen) are both flat. By a mechanical process, the paper and the plate are brought together, and the paper is printed. While some school newspapers are printed on a platen or job press, only the very smallest can be handled this way. Papers with five columns or more are usually too large for a platen press.

EXAMPLE
189

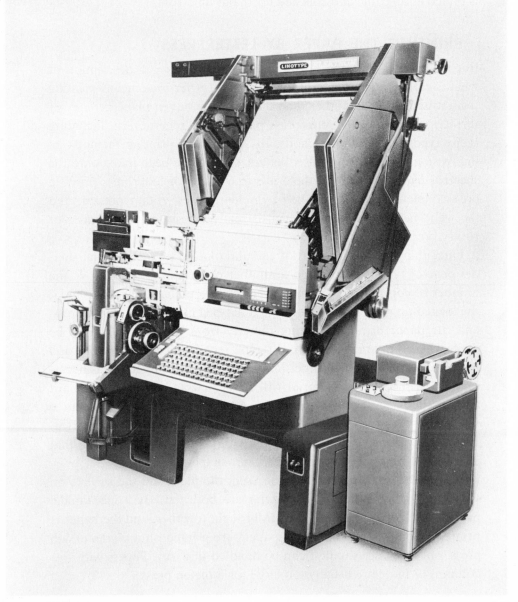

EXAMPLE

190

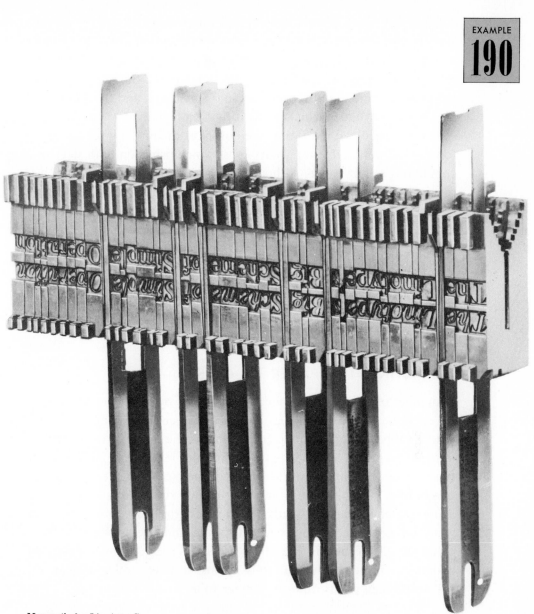

Mergenthaler Linotype Co.

Today all daily papers are printed on cylinder or rotary presses. Both involve a method whereby the paper is held on a roll or cylinder which is rotated against the printing plate. In the flat-bed cylinder press, the printing plate is flat as in the platen press. In the rotary press, the printing plate has also been cast into a cylinder, and the paper rolls between the cylinder which feeds it and the cylinder which prints it. This high speed method is now used on most major daily papers in the form of the web-perfecting rotary press which prints on both sides of a continuous roll of paper. Although this press sounds complicated, it is relatively simple—like the roller on many washing machines.

Most school papers are printed on some form of the flat-bed cylinder press. On this press, all types of raised-surface material may be used—type, halftones, linecuts, wood cuts, linoleum blocks, etc. In most school newspapers, it is not even necessary to make plates, but the paper is printed from the type itself over which the cylinder carries the paper. The number of pages printed at one time varies with the size of the press.

PRINTING THE PAPER BY OFFSET

A number of school papers today are printed by the *offset* process, so called because the plate does not print directly onto the paper but onto a rubber roller which in turn "offsets" the material to be printed onto the paper. The offset plate, unlike the letterpress plate, has no raised letters or cuts. It works on the principle that water and grease do not mix. The flat plate is made of flexible zinc or aluminum chemically treated so that the words and pictures attract the greasy ink. The white background is dampened with water and rejects the ink. Three cylinders are needed in the offset press. The top cylinder holds the cylindrical printing plate; it rolls against a water roller and an ink roller and then prints onto the rubber roller.

The offset printing process has many advantages for some newspapers. No engravings are needed, for the printing plate is made by a photographic process; therefore only good photographs and clear "reproduction proofs" (carefully prepared proofs of headlines and copy) are necessary for offset printing. This means lower costs.

314

The text copy may be set on linotype or monotype machines, as in letterpress reproduction. A very careful proof (reproduction proof) is then drawn and this proof is photographed for the offset plate. However, the text can also be produced on special typewriters that align the right margins as well as the left, often at less cost. In fact, inventors have already created processes by which full lines are "printed" by photographic means, without any type really being set at all. The newspapers of the future may well be set this way. While most school papers printed by offset use a special extra-white paper, some use regular newsprint.

Because of the number of illustrations required in yearbooks, there is a definite trend to offset reproduction in the yearbook. School newspapers, like daily newspapers, are still overwhelmingly printed by letterpress. There are advantages and disadvantages to both methods, and the decision is one to be made by the school in question after careful consideration of funds and local resources. Are both letterpress and offset available to the school, and what are the relative advantages and disadvantages of each? Quality is the first consideration, cost the second.

It is difficult to distinguish a good offset job from a good letterpress job (in books or papers). Poor offset products, however, are much more noticeable than poor letterpress products among high school newspapers. Every school publication should periodically analyze its printing procedures in relationship to the total possibilities within the community. A school paper should never sacrifice quality for the sake of economy, for a few more subscriptions and a few more advertisements can readily make up the difference in costs.

COMBINATION ARRANGEMENTS

Some schools, particularly those with vocational printing departments, have the facilities to carry the printing of the paper all the way through. Still others have no printing facilities at all. Often, however, the school has some printing facilities which are not extensive enough to handle the total job. Linotype work can practically always be purchased on the outside, and the heads and ads often set up and the pages made up in the school print shop. It may be necessary to arrange for the printing with a local printer with a press of the right size to accommodate the chases that have been locked up in the school print shop. An alert business manager can practically always find adequate facilities in his community. Such facilities may include the local newspaper for lintoype service and presswork. This will demand close cooperation between the school and the local newspaper so that neither product suffers.

THE DUPLICATED SCHOOL PUBLICATION

The duplicated school newspaper or magazine is often found in the smaller school without the resources to finance a more expensive printed paper. The term refers to any paper or magazine prepared first on a typewriter and then reproduced in the school directly from the original stencil or form by a mimeograph or similar duplicating device.

Make-up and production. Since this type of paper is run directly from the stencil or form prepared in the typewriter and inserted in the special duplicating machine, the publication is limited in size. The dimensions of the page are ordinarily those of a piece of typewriter paper, 8½ by 11 inches. Duplicated papers sometimes vary in the number of pages, not in the size of a page.

A good grade of paper permits the utilization of both sides, thus simulating a printed newspaper as well as saving material. The staff's major problem is to secure a professional-looking product. There is no skilled printer to prepare the type and print the papers. The production is completely a student enterprise. Good reporting can be—and often is—lost through poor duplication. Leaders in the field of student journalism have never claimed artistic advantages for this method of production; its chief merit is economy.

For the 8½ by 11 page, three-column make-up is preferable to two-column, for it bears a closer resemblance to newspaper style. Only six or eight items can be artistically arranged on the first page, and stories must be short or continued to later pages. Line drawings are often used effectively. (See Example 191.)

316

THINKING HABITS

Now that you have voted for your choice of a Student Council president for next year, can you say to yourself honestly, "I voted for the person I thought was best suited for the office," or did you vote for

EXAMPLE
191

CONGRATULATIONS!
Bob Gallagher
For president!

HI-LIFE

CONGRATULATIONS!
Allene Johnson
For president!

Vol. XXVI No. 62   Kane High   Kane, Pennsylvania   May

Music Groups Set For Concert

Tonight is the night! The band, orchestra and chorus concert is being held in the auditorium under the direction of Earl Stewart at 8 o'clock. Tickets are available from any student in the music department. Profits will be used for instrument replacements and entrance fee for district and state competitions.

The program is as follows:

Rosemunde Overture	Schubert
Londonderry Air	Arr. Roberts
Paul Revere Suite	Allan Grant

ORCHESTRA

Oklahoma	Rodgers
Adoramus Te	Palestrina

MIXED CHORUS

The False Prophet	Scott
He Met Her On The Stairs	Levey

GIRLS CHORUS

Waltz From Sleeping Beauty	
	Tschaikowsky
Strumming	Woods

MIXED CHORUS

Manhattan Beach	Sousa
Light Cavalry Overture	
	Von Suppe

BAND

Amparite Roca	Texidor
Desert Song	Romberg
King Cotton	Sousa

HURRI-KANES START LAST MILE FOR YEAR

Final step for this year's Hurri-Kane was taken Saturday when the books were sent to the bindery at Kurtz Brothers in Clearfield, Pa. Books will be distributed some time before exams but the exact day is not known.

'B SEEIN' YA!

At the Concert Tonight at 8 p.m.

PROM COMMITTEES NAMED BY CARLSON

Committees for the Junior-Senior Prom have been appointed by the Prom chairman, Esther Carlson. They include:

PROGRAMS: Shirley Robinson, Alfred Johnson, Shirley Peterson, Jean Scott and Virgil Nelson.

ADVERTISING: Nancy McKenna and Mary McDade.

TABLES: Virginia Gates, Helene Wood, Yvonne Saf, and Connie Colella.

REFRESHMENTS: Mary Loh, Shirley Swan and Jill Gale.

For SERVING: Charlotte Keller has engaged the following underclassmen: Marian Penn, Karen Galvin, Peggy Newton. Walter Keller and Ron Carlson.

Bob Magnuson, Sue Standburg and Nancy McKenna are planning the decorations and the rest of the class will help put them up.

Eighth Grades Exhibit Projects

Eighth graders are at it again. This time they have made projects for history class which went on display yesterday. They have been working on them for weeks.

On their arrangement committee are: Harold Bank, chairman, Roberta Shaver, Harriet Wilson, George Crosson, Arley Donevan, Romaine Holland, Dorothy Weborg and Bev Scordo. Miss Sylvia Johnson is the supervisor for the projects and their history teacher.

CO-ED TO INSTALL NEW OFFICERS

New officers will be installed tomorrow night at Co-Ed, it was announced by Mrs. Oscar Bauer today. Out-going officers are: Charlotte Popowski, president; Howie Sanford, vice president; Rheta Benson, secretary and Ronald West, treasurer.

Ron is new president; Mary MacEwen, the vice president; Mary Hess, secretary and Josie Clifford, treasurer.

Seventh graders from all grade schools are invited to attend tomorrow, since they will be part of the Junior High next year. The following week will be Senior Night but the details were incomplete as yet at deadline time.

PHOTOENGRAVING

Photoengraving is the process by which metal plates are prepared for printing by photography and etching. The process is based on the scientific principle that certain substances harden so that they will not dissolve in water when they are exposed to light. First the engraver photographs the image on a negative, which he develops and places against a metal plate which has been treated with a solution that hardens under light. The plate with the negative is then exposed to light, the light reaching the plate only through the transparent parts of the negative. The solution covering the parts of the plate exposed to the light become hard; the rest of the solution is washed away with water. A protective resin is then applied to the hardened solution, and the entire plate is dipped in an acid solution which eats away all the metal not protected by the resin. What is left prints the picture.

There are two types of photoengravings: *linecuts* and *halftones.* The linecut is essentially a black-and-white drawing of something, without any gray shadings or intermediate tones except those produced by lines, dots, and dashes. The halftone is a photograph or painting of something, involving broad gray or intermediate tones. The negative for a linecut is made by simply photographing the drawing or art work. The negative for a halftone is made by photographing the photograph or painting through a "screen." The screen breaks up the picture into tiny dots. Engravers have various sizes of screens used for different types of work. A screen is composed of two pieces of glass with diagonal lines etched on them; these are placed face to face producing a "screen" similar to an ordinary window screen. The number of lines per inch varies from 50 to 250. The degree of detail necessary determines the number of "lines" per inch in the screen used.

The size of screen—number of lines—is also determined by the kind of paper to be used in printing. Daily newspapers usually use 65- or 70-line halftones. A high grade of smooth newsprint will usually take an 85-line halftone, while a coated or book paper will reproduce 100-line halftones and finer. The finer the screen, the greater the detail. (See Example 192.) For this reason, it is wise to use as fine a screen as possible on the particular kind of stock selected. Halftones are

318

EXAMPLE
192

To get this cut the engraver photographed the original picture through a
60-line screen.

To get this cut the engraver photographed the original picture through a
85-line screen.

Wide World

To get this cut the engraver photographed the original picture through a
100-line screen.

319

more complicated to make than linecuts and are consequently more expensive. Furthermore, the finer the screen, the more expensive the halftone.

There are three things an engraver must know in order to prepare a photoengraving: the portion of the original to be reproduced, the size of the finished engraving, and the size of screen desired if a halftone is necessary. Responsibility for supplying this vital information rests with that staff member who deals with the engraver.

The portion to be reproduced. Often the print to be reproduced has unimportant background around the essential figures in the photograph. To have the faces or figures in the photograph reproduce as large as possible, such space should be "cropped" out of the picture. The staff member in charge makes small marks in the margins of the photograph with crayon, thus avoiding any damage to the print; or he may fit a piece of paper over the photograph, cutting out a "window" that will show just that portion of the picture to be photographed. He may also paste the picture *with rubber cement* on a piece of paper and draw crop lines on the paper. (See Example 193.)

Marking art work for the engraver. The size of the finished product desired should be indicated in picas. Marking the copy for a one-column cut or a two-column cut is not enough, since the widths of columns vary. The width of a cut is measured two ways, by the face and by the base. The face is the actual printing surface, while the base is the block upon which the cut is mounted. The base width should be specified.

There is usually enough white space above or below cartoons for the width to be marked for the engraver. Photographs usually do not have such a margin, and marking on the back damages the surface of the photograph. The paper should have gummed stickers printed for this specific purpose. Each sticker should carry the name of the school and have three blank lines to be filled in: one for the type of engraving, another for the width, and another for the time of delivery. This sticker is filled out and then pasted on the back of the piece of art with rubber cement, or on the paper on which the photograph is pasted.

320

EXAMPLE
193

Wide World

EXAMPLE
194

321

Reducing and enlarging. Since engraving is a photographic process, the finished cut may be larger or smaller than the original. However, it is a good idea to make a drawing twice the desired size so that it can be reduced one half or one third; the result is neater than the original.

To summarize the steps that go into marking photographs or art work for the engraver: first, the copy must be cropped so that the engraver knows exactly what goes into the finished engraving; then the required width of the finished engraving must be marked on the art work. The proportion of the width of the finished plate to the width of the original art work determines the depth of the copy; therefore if the cropped copy is thirty picas wide and twenty-four picas deep, and the finished plate is to be fifteen picas wide, the plate will be twelve picas deep. (See Example 194.) The copy must be carefully measured so that the crop marks are parallel.

Cautions. Inexperienced editors often make costly mistakes. For example, writing on the back of a print from which an engraving is to be made may show up on the finished engraving. When it is absolutely necessary to make notations on the back, the print should be laid face down on a flat surface, and a soft crayon or china pencil should be used. Also, paper clips should not be used on prints as they mar the surface. A heavy piece of paper or cardboard over the corner of the photograph will hold the paper clip. Staples must never be used on copy. Photographs should always be mailed flat, between heavy pieces of cardboard.

MATS AND STEREOS

A mat is a piece of heavy cardboard carrying an impression made from an original engraving. Mats are frequently supplied by advertisers, and casts are made from them to be used in printing. The process consists primarily of pouring hot type metal over the mat; the result is a *stereo* or *stereotype,* called a cast, similar in appearance to the original cut from which the mat was made. Mats may be used over and over again and should be preserved in the morgue for future use, as should usable stereos, halftones, and linecuts.

If art work that has appeared in any other newspaper or publication (such as a sports photograph from the local paper) is to be used, a "courtesy line," or credit line, must accompany it. This is usually set in very small type directly under the cut.

THE WHITE BUFFALO GOES TO PRESS

There is no better way to close this chapter than with a success story. Chosen from many, this story reveals how a school newspaper can grow from an idea to a financially sound enterprise serving the community as well as the school. *The White Buffalo,* Madras, Oregon, High School, is a good example of what a school, regardless of size, can do if it wants a good paper enough to work for it, and has an energetic and competent faculty adviser to lead the effort.

Progress through printing. Some years ago this paper was barely meeting expenses, with only half of the student body of three hundred subscribing, and merchants reluctant to place ads in the struggling sheet. Subscriptions were then $1.75 per year for the eight four-page, four-column issues, advertising $1.50 per inch.

Facing extinction or the mimeograph machine, the school turned to printing within the school. A used platen press was purchased for $1200, of which the school board provided $650, the balance obtained by borrowing.

The rates were dropped to 75 cents for a yearly subscription and 35 cents per inch for ads. The number of issues was increased from eight to eighteen, and both subscriptions and advertising started to climb noticeably. The first issues were four columns and six pages, the page nine by twelve inches. By the end of the year, the paper had grown to eight to ten pages per issue. and *The White Buffalo* was in good financial condition.

The four-column paper continued to add pages; when it reached eighteen, a larger sheet was imminent, for the increased circulation was heavily taxing the hand-feeding operation of the platen press. Over 90 per cent of the business firms in town were now taking advantage of the advertising outlet.

The second thrust. The school then purchased a Kelly flat-bed automatic press, which permitted a five-column page, eleven by seventeen inches. The funds came from the newspaper and a magazine drive among the students. Today *The White Buffalo* appears in a five-column, twelve- to fourteen-page format, with sixteen issues a year and a balance in the bank. (See Example 196.)

Copy is set at the local newspaper and brought to the school in galleys. There the heads and ads are set, the pages made up, and the paper printed on the school press. The students fold, gather, mail, and deliver. The average cost of a fourteen-page issue is about $135, including linotyping, paper, ink, cuts, and postage.

With a student body of 550, the press run is now over 1150 copies, for the paper is popular with both the community and the alumni. It is sold on the newsstands as well as through subscription, and the circulation grows with the school and the town.

Staff organization and copy movement. The school has only one period a day for journalism class and newspaper and yearbook activities. Madras, Oregon, is a rural community; over 80 per cent of the students travel to school by school bus, making after-school activities difficult at best.

The staff is comprised of an editor-in-chief, an associate editor, a managing editor, a news editor, a feature editor, a sports editor, a head typist, a news-bureau director, a files editor, a business manager, an advertising manager, a circulation editor, a photographer, an alumni editor, and reporters.

Assignments. The news, sports, and feature editors post assignment sheets listing the story, reporter, date assigned, date due, date in, name of typist, and a column to be checked when the copy goes to the linotyper. Thus copy can be easily traced at any time.

The deadlines are staggered so that some stories come in as the last issue is distributed, thus smoothing the flow and preventing last minute bottlenecks.

News	To be typed	Head writers
Sports	Typed	Heads
Features	Editor	Linotype copy

The copy box. A copy box with nine compartments has been constructed on the plan shown in Example 195. Reporters check the assignment sheets for their names and stories. When written, the story goes into the compartment of the editor who assigned it—news, sports, or feature. This editor marks the story off the assignment sheet and copy reads it for completeness, accuracy, and style. It then goes into the to-be-typed compartment. Whoever types the story adds his initials and moves it on to the typed box. The head typist checks it off the assignment sheet with the typist's name, checks the typing, and places both the original and the typed copy in the editor's compartment.

This is the final check, and it is made by the editor or the associate editor. Here the copy is also marked for the linotype operator. The original copy is filed and the typed copy placed in the head writer's compartment. A quick glance at the nine-compartment box reveals any pile-ups. Ordinarily the copy flows smoothly through the channels as it is checked and rechecked.

The work of the reporters is rated by the editors according to quantity and quality, the exact numbers of inches being recorded. In weekly meetings the editors evaluate quality. The adviser emphasizes that role in his own approach, giving suggestions to the editors and helping the cub reporters improve their work and advance on the staff.

The story of *The White Buffalo* is not a plan, for no two school situations are alike. Its purpose is to stimulate.

EXAMPLE
196

MAGAZINE SUBSCRIPTION DRIVE STA...

Assembly Kicks...
14-Day Camp...

White Buffalo

Madras Union High School, Madras, Oregon   October 20, 1961

Vol. XV, No. 3

Head Magazine Drive

Heading the annual magazine drive for 1961 are student body vice president Hugh Vibbert and treasurer Ronda Schien, who started selling subscriptions today.

Hi Schedules Parents' Day

Band Boosters To Raise Funds

65 Seniors Take Aptitude Tests

School Lis...
540 Enroll...

Sales Start Today For '62 Yearbook

Salesmen Listed

Senior Photos Due

New Features

Junior Art Club Plans Card Sale

Hatfield to Sp...
At Madras Hi

B's Day Ahead

Ready for Hi-Sage Orders

Gathering for their first pep talk from Hi-Sage editor Margie McBride...

History Repeats Itself

Relief, Joy at War's End Forgotten

By Carol Schultz

Many Students Continue Studies

Ambulance Drive on

Buffalo Buggles
By Gary Kopln

Buffaloes Win At State Meet
Heard of Buffaloes
Season's Last Da...
Full of Exciteme...

Buffs Suffer Only Defeat By A-1 Bend Bruin Five

Pep Club Votes To Keep Uniform

VON LUIS DANE
IRV MORRIS
REAL ESTATE

TROUT

You get more
EAN OF MILK
in DAIRY QUEEN
more proteins and
minerals . . . less fat
Madras Dairy Queen Store

Loafers Auto Club
Sponsors Car Wash

Irv's Richfield

RAMBLER SALES & SERVICE

MADRAS EVERGREEN CHAPEL
Complete Mortuary Facilities

ALBERT C. SURATT
INSURANCE   REAL ESTATE

Madras Main Street Garage, Inc.
Chevrolet and Oldsmobile

H. J. (Hank) Muzgay

327

CHAPTER LABORATORY

1. Have one of the editors of your school paper explain the paper's printing procedures to the class. Write a summary of the plan followed.
2. To keep the news fresh, the period of time between the reporting of school news and the circulation of the paper should be brief. On paper, analyze your paper's schedule from reporting to printing, and make suggestions for shortening this period.
3. For the class, arrange a visit to the print shop that produces the school paper, and discuss the visit in class.
4. Examine the exchange newspapers, and, if possible, separate those printed by letterpress from those printed by offset. As a class, compare the two groups of papers and discuss the attributes of each.
5. If you have a school print shop, visit it as a group and compare its facilities with those of the Madras, Oregon, High School. What are the factors in your school and community that encourage or discourage school printing of your school paper? Compare your printing costs with those of *The White Buffalo*.
6. Bring to class an issue of your school paper that contains a photograph which would have looked better with more "cropping." Discuss.
7. In class, mark a photograph or drawing for proper reduction to fit the allotted space in your paper.
8. Select exchange examples of high and low quality printing, and bring them to class. What good standards are violated?

328

PART FOUR

THE BUSINESS OF JOURNALISM

"All the news that's fit to print."
—ADOLPH S. OCHS
Motto of *The New York Times*

21 STAFF ORGANIZATION

If a newspaper is to be published, the staff must be organized, and the keynote of this organization is efficiency. Because school situations vary greatly, there is no one best arrangement of duties. The staff organization that is right for a particular school is the one that gets the job done expeditiously and results in a journalistically superior product. A few fundamental principles should be considered standard for any school attempting to organize its work, however. They are as follows:

1.   The organization must be sufficiently flexible from term to term to permit the utilization of available pupil personnel to the greatest possible advantage.

2.   The staff must be organized to fix responsibility definitely and without question.

3.   There must be planned provision for promotion from semester to semester or year to year through some sort of competitive system.

4.   There must be adequate provision for in-service training of all staff members.

5.   The staff must be organized into workable units that are more or less complete in themselves.

330

6. A feeder system must be provided whereby beginning reporters work alongside experienced staff members, thus avoiding a complete turnover of membership at the beginning of a school year.

7. Placement must recognize true ability and talent.

8. Everybody on the staff must have a specific job to do.

ORGANIZATION: EXAMPLE 1

This plan of organization has been developed through many years of continuous publication of a school paper. Slight alterations are made from year to year, reflecting new ideas and new staff members. It is essentially a school-paper organization and has little resemblance to the organization of a daily newspaper. One of the basic distinctions is the system of page editors, in contrast to the plan that provides a single news editor, a single make-up editor, and a general copy desk.

The editor-in-chief is the head of the entire staff, directing all other workers, both editorial and business. He works especially through the managing editor and the business manager. He is the representative of the paper in all school activities. He is a school leader, commanding the respect of the staff, the student body, and the faculty. The editor-in-chief is aggressive but level-headed; he does not run after sensational stories. He has mature judgment, handles staff difficulties well, and has advanced to his position through successful experience in lower positions on the staff.

1. THE EDITORIAL DIVISION

Managing editor. The managing editor is in charge of the entire editorial staff and is responsible for all reading matter. He directs the output of copy, generally working through the page editors. He decides news policy and passes judgment on advisability of copy. He should be able to provide staff members with ideas when needed. The managing editor is responsible to the editor-in-chief. He is a good newswriter, writing just enough to set an example for others. He is tactful, shows confidence in the editorial staff, and is appreciative of the ability his workers show.

331

Page editors. There are four page editors for the respective pages —(1) news, (2) editorial, (3) features, and (4) sports. The page editor, aided by page assistants, is responsible for assigning, gathering, copyreading, and editing all news on the page. He keeps a datebook and works far ahead on future assignments. He keeps copy records of all the work he assigns, and can at any time give an accurate report on the work of any reporter who has had a story on that page— a report showing deadline evasions, unusual initiative, and any other relevant facts. He determines the make-up of the page. He must be a capable newswriter, have a keen sense of news, know type faces, and handle his staff well. He should feel an in-service training obligation toward those who work under him. He is responsible to the managing editor.

To distribute responsibility more widely among a large staff, the adviser may very well use eight page editors, two for each page. These page editors may alternate.

Proofreaders. The head proofreader is responsible to the managing editor for the proofreading. Three assistants work under him, following the schedule of work that he has set up. This department must be steady and observant in its task, and take pride in diminishing errors from week to week. (See Chapter 14.)

Page assistants. Under each page editor a staff of workers reads copy, types stories, writes headlines, and assists in every way possible. Some of these understudies succeed to page editorships the following semester. Since pages one and two are free of advertising, they carry more copy than the other two pages and one more assistant is provided for each of them. The assistants are responsible to the editor of the page.

Director of the news bureau and assistants. The chief duty of the director is to cooperate with city papers, giving them the school news daily. Aided by three assistants, he collects all data to be sent to the dailies; he then gives the material to his assistants, each of whom is responsible for contacting one paper. The director is responsible to the managing editor. He must constantly strengthen his bureau, checking on the publicity that actually comes out in print. See page 347.

Columnist. Above all, a columnist should be a person with ideas; he should actually create his own column. He is responsible to the editor of the page on which his column appears, and to the managing editor. Occasionally staff members create columns so good that succeeding staffs attempt to continue them. Unless the prospective columnist has a specific idea for a column, one that is actually his own, he should not be considered for the position. Effective columns must be alive, and to be alive they must reflect the personality of the writer. Such life is rarely obtainable if the columnist attempts to follow the style of his predecessor.

The staff photographer. This member of the staff must be definitely interested in photography and have "news sense" besides. If the facilities are available, he should work in the darkroom and do his own developing and printing. He is responsible to the managing editor, but works closely with the art editor. A good photographer is an asset to any paper.

Typists. Typists, directly responsible to the page editor, are needed for each page. The number varies with the size of the paper.

Reporters. Every member of the editorial division is a reporter, although he holds some responsible position in addition. Even the editor-in-chief may be assigned stories by the page editor, and in this particular capacity he functions in the same manner as any other staff member.

Copy-desk operation and posting assignments. For the school newspaper a single copy desk with a small number of copyreaders who edit all copy is not advantageous. Instead, a copy desk for each page is preferable, with the editor of that particular page acting as head of the copy desk. This plan makes it possible for more students to profit from the experience and in addition does much to eliminate "passing the buck" from one staff member to another. Each page of the paper thus functions as an individual unit, with definite responsibility resting on the editor of that page. Duplicate stories are avoided by conferences between page editors and with the managing editor when assignments are made.

Under this plan, the page editor makes the assignments for his own page at a specified time in advance of the deadline. Before posting the assignments, he contacts the editors of the other pages to make sure that all available news sources have been surveyed. A printed assignment sheet, Example 197, is furnished for posting assignments. Printed on the back of a Manila envelope, 9½ by 12½ inches, it thus provides a container for the copy.

The name of the reporter, the title of his story, the approximate length, and, if necessary, the source are posted. As the copy is turned in, the page editor places it in the envelope. At a regularly assigned time the page editor meets with the members of his copy desk and directs the editing of the copy and the headline writing. As headlines are written and copy is edited, he records the name of the copyreader after the title of the story on the assignment sheet, thus creating a permanent record of the whole process. The envelope then serves as a container in which to send the copy to the linotypist.

The page editor is also provided with printed envelopes (see Example 198) in which he places his headline blanks. These blanks (Example 142) are counted, and the number is recorded in the space provided on the envelope. In addition, the class schedule of the page editor is recorded on the face of the envelope so that he may be located if needed in the print shop.

After the material has been set in type, two galley proofs are taken; one is read and corrected by the proofreaders, and the other is sent to the page editor. Using these galley proofs, and proofs of his headlines, he pastes up a dummy indicating for the printer every detail necessary in composing the page. This dummy then goes to the composing room where the page is made up. When the make-up is completed, a proof is pulled, and the page editor and the managing editor examine it carefully for any errors that might have been missed. When the final O.K. is received and changes have been made, the type is locked up and goes to the pressroom to be printed.

The editorial board. If the editorials of a school paper are to be interesting and vital, they must be founded upon something real and specific. Since the editorial speaks for the paper, the staff must approve

EXAMPLE

198

HEADLINE
COPY

Page

ISSUE DATE ....

ISSUE NUMBER ....

NUMBER OF HEADS ENCLOSED ....

PAGE EDITOR ....

In Case of Difficulty, the Page Editor May Be
Located:

Period   Room

1. ....

ECA ....

2. ....

3. ....

4. ....

5. ....

6. ....

7. ....

The *School Spirit*

		PAGE EDITORS		PHONE		PAGE
DEADLINE			ISSUE DATE		ISSUE NO.	

X	REPORTER	SUBJECT	WORDS	REMARKS

PICA MEASURE	POINT SIZE	TYPE NAME	FACE STYLE	SPECIAL INSTRUCTIONS

ASSIGNMENTS

EXAMPLE

197

individual sentiments before they are voiced in print. Therefore each school paper must have a policy-determining organization to discuss and determine the paper's position on any issues that arise.

If the staff is small, it may act as a whole in this capacity. If it is large, however, a smaller organization is necessary. One school newspaper maintains an editorial board for this purpose, composed of the editor-in-chief, the managing editor, and the page editors. The board meets regularly one day a week and is subject to call by the editor, managing editor, or adviser. Each semester a platform consisting of several planks is drawn up; it is continually subject to revision throughout the semester. Page 256 shows the platforms from three different school newspapers. Once the board has taken a stand on a particular issue, definite plans are made for the editorial attack through cartoons, interviews, editorials, questionnaires, and other means. The editorial board is the brain of the editorial division; its effective functioning eliminates the problem of individual opinion voiced as staff opinion. The individual writer represents the staff; the staff represents the school as a whole.

2. THE BUSINESS DIVISION

Three departments. Frequently the business and editorial divisions of the school paper meet as a single group. This plan is satisfactory if the paper and the staff are small, but as either or both increase in size and the functions and the activities of staff members are extended, it is desirable to divide the staff into two groups. In the business division there are, in general, three departments—the accounting department, the advertising department, and the circulation department—each of which is treated extensively in one of the three following chapters.

Business manager. The business manager is in charge of all business and financial matters. He heads the business division and is equal in rank with the managing editor, responsible to the editor-in-chief. He is courteous, tactful, and patient. He manages the advertising force, the collection work, and the circulation, and is responsible for all of the purchasing for the paper.

336

The financial manager. The financial manager assists the business manager in financial matters. He oversees all bookkeeping activities, issues monthly statements, and makes financial estimates and reports to the business manager, the adviser, and the staff. If the paper is large and issued frequently, he may need assistants.

Advertising manager. The advertising manager, responsible to the business manager, is in charge of all advertising. He plans the advertising campaigns, directs advertising solicitors, plans advertising copy, designates advertising make-up on dummies for pages three and four, and sees that the advertising total is kept up to the quota set by the department. He also goes out with his assistants to sell advertising space.

Advertising solicitors. Depending upon the size of the paper, there may be four of these workers, preferably two girls and two boys, who work under the advertising manager in securing the paper's advertisements. They must be enterprising, businesslike, willing to work after school, and make favorable contacts with business firms.

Circulation manager. The circulation manager holds an important position but one which is often underestimated. He is in charge of all circulation, both in- and out-of-school subscriptions, and subscription campaigns. He prevents all "leaks" in distribution of the paper. He also assists the business manager in subscription collections, since up-to-date circulation lists depend upon familiarity with the progress of collections. The circulation manager is responsible to the business manager.

Circulation staff. Staff members who work directly under the circulation manager, counting and distributing papers within the school, constitute the circulation staff. The size of this staff depends on the circulation of the paper. One assistant supervises the mailing of exchanges and mail subscriptions and organizes and preserves those exchanges received in return.

Typist. The business department needs one typist who types circulation lists, bills to be sent out to advertisers, and anything else needed.

337

Using the school business department. There are two main organization plans for the business management of a school paper. One, just discussed, is to maintain this department as a branch of the regular staff organization. (See the staff chart in Example 199.) The other plan involves setting it up in the business department of the school, with a second faculty adviser and a core of business students.

The merit of this second plan is the business training it gives students who are following that curriculum in school. The plan is practical only in schools large enough to have well organized courses in the field through which students first learn business theory.

The disadvantage of the plan is the separation of responsibility for the production of the paper. There must always be a close working relationship between editorial and business staffs. Both groups must feel the enthusiasm and pride that make a good school publication. If the business department takes over the financial side of the undertaking, there must be a way of enabling those students to feel a partnership in the production. Attendance at staff meetings and use of the news office as the business office are only two of the means.

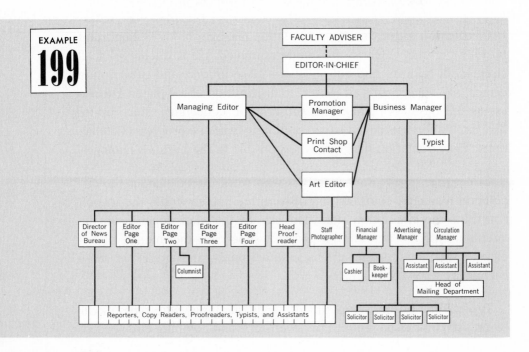

EXAMPLE

199

338

3. OVERLAPPING POSITIONS

Some staff members cannot be listed specifically as members of either the editorial or business division because they serve both or because they serve as a link between the two. Such are the following:

Print-shop contact. Responsible to both the managing editor and the business manager, this person bridges the gap between the print shop and the staff, easing friction between the two. Trained in both newswriting and printing, he works through the shop, rewriting heads that will not fit, seeing the advertising manager for advertising copy that is late, taking heads from the managing editor to the shop, and smoothing the flow between staff and print shop.

Promotion manager. The promotion manager is in charge of promotion schemes that will advertise the paper to the students and convince business houses of its value as an advertising medium. He is responsible to both the managing editor and the business manager. His duties include such matters as helping the business department put over a subscription drive, furthering a weekly broadcast by the school paper at the local radio station, promoting an all-school spelling bee, and improving the exchange list so that better papers will come into the newsroom. It is an excellent job for one who is still on the staff after having served in some important position such as editor or business manager.

Art editor. This editor is in charge of all art work that goes into the paper, such as photographs, cartoons, and linoleum block prints. He works closely with the business manager to determine funds available, with the page editors to determine their wants and needs, and with the managing editor to insure that the art carries out staff policies. He becomes proficient in make-up and assists page editors in make-up. He is responsible to the editor-in-chief.

Board of control. As the size of the staff increases and the individual problems of each division become more and more foreign to the other division, a need for a coordination agency between the two arises. The board of control is composed of the editor-in-chief, three members elected by the editorial board, three elected by the business division, and three representing the student printing department. The editor-in-chief presides, a secretary is elected, and problems that do not fall solely within the specific jurisdiction of any one group are presented here for settlement. When disagreement exists between the two divisions, when special editions and extra pages are being planned, and when major equipment must be purchased, this board makes the decisions. The board meets biweekly, and keeps accurate minutes of the meetings.

ORGANIZATION: EXAMPLE 2

The following is the organization plan followed by the *Orange and Black,* the newspaper of the Grand Junction High School, Grand Junction, Colorado. The over-all pattern, described below, is charted in Example 200. The duties, taken from the staff manual, are stated as directives to the person holding the job.

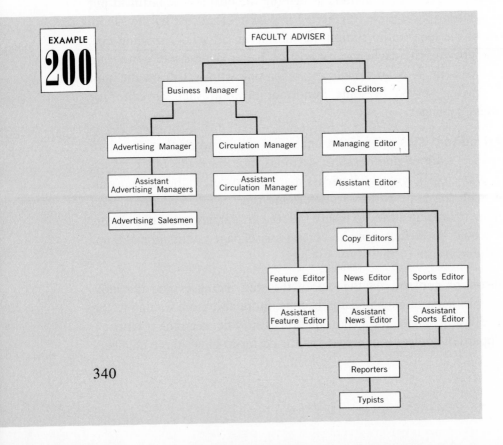

EXAMPLE
200

FACULTY ADVISER

Business Manager

Co-Editors

Advertising Manager

Circulation Manager

Managing Editor

Assistant Advertising Managers

Assistant Circulation Manager

Assistant Editor

Advertising Salesmen

Copy Editors

Feature Editor

News Editor

Sports Editor

Assistant Feature Editor

Assistant News Editor

Assistant Sports Editor

Reporters

Typists

340

Co-editors. Assume leadership in planning each issue and making over-all plans for the year, particularly regarding policies and campaigns to be stressed.

Hold a staff meeting preceding each issue to discuss and decide points of emphasis along with other details.

Delegate outlined duties to each staff member so that he is able to assume assigned responsibilities. The *Orange and Black* is a cooperative venture.

Work with various staff members as indicated in planning assignments, layouts, editorials, etc. Assume responsibility for optional copy on feature page.

Assume responsibilities for directing staff so that deadlines are met, but do not take over their duties except in case of absolute necessity.

Check all copy before it goes to the printer.

Complete final layout, and paste up dummy.

Make necessary contact with printer, and arrange for securing proof and setting up paper.

Train top staff members so that any one of several is capable of taking over publication of an issue.

Copy editors. Assist with all phases of writing, editing, and headline writing.

Copyread and edit all stories before they go to the co-editors. Have them retyped if necessary. Reread the typed copy.

See that words are counted on all stories to check on length.

Check the count of each headline.

Mark all copy for the printer—subheads, front-page lead stories, editorials, etc. Leave nothing to guesswork.

Completely master style book and copyreading and proofreading symbols.

Take charge of seeing that proof is crossread. (One person reads the proof to another who checks it with the manuscript.)

Assist printer if necessary.

Assistant editor. Assist with all phases of writing, rewriting, editing, and headline writing.

Know all plans for each issue, to be able to assume duties of co-editors in case of absence.

Assist with layout and pin up dummy.

See that supplies and editorial forms are always on hand.

Cooperate with news editors in planning each issue and assuring adequate coverage of events.

Scan copy and heads after copyreaders are through, and turn finished copy over to editors.

List all stories before they go to the printer; give head size, style, and column width, and length of story.

Scan galley proofs to check proofreading.

Feature editors. After cooperative planning and cross checking with other editors, assign features and post assignment sheet. Set early deadlines. All features should be in no later than Wednesday preceding final deadline. Plan ahead to accomplish this, and post assignments early.

Plan layout for feature page with help of editors.

Check to see that stories are rewritten, copyread, and proofread. See that all feature material is in early.

Check with managing editor for pictures to be taken after approval by co-editors.

Assist with proofreading and setting up paper as necessary.

News editor. After cooperative planning and checking with other editors, assign stories and post news story sheet. If possible, avoid giving anyone double assignment. Set deadlines early.

Be responsible for checking with editors to see that stories are in at deadlines. Keep work chart for each staff member and reporter.

Suggest any needed rewriting to reporter if time permits. Help rewrite and edit as necessary.

Work with copy editors in following news stories through to finish; editing, copyreading, headline writing, etc., as necessary.

Plan layout for pages one and four with help of editor.

Assist with proofreading and setting up at printers as needed.

Clear with managing editor regarding all pictures to be taken.

Managing editor. Learn all aspects of editing and work cooperatively with co-editors in completing each issue.

Assist with copyreading, proofreading, rewriting, editing, headline writing, and checking copy and heads before stories go to the printers.

Assume responsibility for seeing that production chart is kept up-to-date.

Contact business manager to see that ad dummy is ready early and does not conflict with editor's layout.

Assist with pinup of dummy and setting up at printers if necessary.

Arrange for all pictures after double checking with co-editors.

See that all pictures are ready for printer by Tuesday morning.

See that all linecuts are marked as to width and other directions.

Sports editor. Assume complete responsibility for sports page.
Post assignments for sports stories.

Plan dummy for sports page.

See that stories are in, edited, typed, copyread, rewritten, and "head-lined" as soon as information is available. Only weekend events may be in Monday.

Check with business manager to see that advertising layout is suitable for sports page.

After checking with co-editors, make arrangements for pictures for sports page with managing editor.

Plan a well-rounded, lively, zippy page covering all phases of sports with emphasis upon coming events.

Business manager. Take chief responsibility for planning and holding to budget.

Keep record of all receipts and expenditures, and keep file folders up-to-date.

Take charge of planning advertising for each issue and over-all planning with cooperation of advertising manager.

Plan advertising layout as early as possible—at least by Wednesday preceding deadline.

Make out bills as soon as all advertisements are in, so collecting may be done promptly. Rebill or call personally when necessary.

Make final check on all advertisements before sending to printer.

See that necessary forms are on hand at all times.

Assume complete responsibility for seeing that all aspects of the business end of the newspaper are carried out satisfactorily and on time.

Advertising manager. Plan advertisements for each issue with business manager.

Assign advertisements to be sold, and see that all are in on time.

Make accurate duplicates of advertising, following instruction of advertiser exactly.

Notify business manager as soon as possible if more advertisements are needed.

Choose all mats and deliver to printer Thursday before deadline date.

Supply printer, composing room, and editors with accurate, complete run sheet.

Take charge of keeping prospect file up-to-date.

Circulation managers. Keep an up-to-date record of the number of SBA [student activity] ticket holders in each homeroom and sixth-hour class. Secure a recheck periodically.

Arrange for distribution of *Orange and Black,* including all high school rooms, vocational school, gym, shop, music room, district administration office. Include all teachers without sixth-hour classes, junior high teachers, the public library, and business offices.

Prepare and mail exchanges from an up-to-date mailing list.

See that papers are filed in student and permanent files.

Fold and put away all excess papers.

Have reminder notice read Wednesday over public address system so students will have SBA tickets on hand.

HOW TO MAKE IT WORK

Once the proper organization has been set up for a particular school and the adviser's proper relationship established (see page 350), the real problem becomes one of "making the system work." Here are some suggestions.

Assure thoroughness of organization. The need for careful delegation of responsibility and the detailing of each position's duties cannot be overemphasized. The heads of the enterprise, student editors, and faculty advisers have an obligation to hold staff members to their duties, or to reassign the duties if an individual cannot carry the load.

Keep up with your paper. The jobs described herein are very likely somewhat different from jobs bearing similar titles on your paper. Job duties are rarely the same from paper to paper or even from year to year on the same paper. The contents of each job should be reviewed, and revised if necessary, every time the staff personnel changes. The editor-in-chief and his top assistants should undertake such a review before the new staff members take office.

Assure goodwill toward the paper. Respect for the paper and the individual journalist is essential for the school newspaper. The *New High Weekly,* William Penn High School, York, Pennsylvania, emphasizes this point for new staff members in its handbook.

344

GOODWILL

There are two very definite reasons why members of the *Weekly* should try to promote a feeling of goodwill toward that organization among teachers and students. They represent the two groups upon which we are dependent for support.

The first concerns the matter of subscriptions. A school newspaper must look within the walls of the institution in which it thrives for the majority of its subscribers. In the long list of subscribers outside of the school, the great majority are either alumni or other interested persons who receive the *Weekly* as a gift from students. Thus the continued existence of our newspaper depends almost entirely upon whether or not students feel anxious to support it.

The second way in which we are dependent on the school is with regard to the subject matter of each issue. It is only through the co-operation of students and to a greater extent, of faculty members that we are able to collect sufficient material to print news which is both interesting and new to our readers.

With our objective squarely in view, the problem of reaching that objective becomes itself much less obscure. Unless he is unworthy of the name, no *Weekly* staff member who is thoroughly aware of the dependence of his newspaper on the goodwill of teachers and students will allow any personal prejudice that may exist between these persons and him to react against the *Weekly*. Rather, he will be at all times careful to prevent such a feeling from arising.

He will make a similar effort while doing *Weekly* work. If he is, for example, a reporter assigned to cover the story of a program to be sponsored by a teacher, he will prepare a written series of questions necessary for the article prior to interviewing that teacher, since the teacher should not be annoyed by a series of visits to get information that can be obtained during the first visit. The teacher's natural desire to see the program publicized will, incidentally, cause him or her to extend the same kind of courtesy to the reporter in assembling as soon as possible all information that may not be at hand at the moment. Some teachers, however, must be constantly followed up so that they will learn to make plans far ahead.

It is impossible to list here the many ways of gaining the goodwill of teachers and students. It would probably be useless to do so in any case, since the only necessity is that those who represent the *Weekly* in the eyes of the school (and remember that this includes not just reporters going after stories but ALL *Weekly* staff members at ALL times) should remember their debt to the teachers and students. As long as they feel the full weight of this debt, they will know instinctively how to act in accordance with it.

Promises to teachers and students, obligating the *Weekly,* should never be made without proper authority. When promises are made, they must be kept. Always avoid any act or statement that could in any manner undermine confidence in the *Weekly.*

Have a workplace. Staffs differ in their facilities and in their work space. Frequently the student has little control over the adequacy of these facilities. The staff must have headquarters, however, whether a cubbyhole under the stairs, a corner of an English room, or a full office for the sole use of the staff.

Use standard forms. The proper printed forms do much to expedite and coordinate staff activity. Story assignment forms similar to Example 197 are excellent. There is no magic about this particular form, however. The *Jeffersonian* uses the assignment card shown in Example 201 with equal success. Business forms are also essential. (See the following chapters.)

EXAMPLE
201

(CLIP THIS CARD TO STORY)

Story

Number of Words   Page

Headline

Assigned to

Date Assigned

Deadline

Date Received in 332

Rewritten by

Have regular staff meetings. Every staff must examine each of its issues critically and consider methods for improving its operations. When both divisions of the staff meet at the same time, of course, one meeting must suffice. However, separate staff meetings may be preferable. (See Chapters 22 through 24.)

The meeting of the editorial staff is presided over by the editor-in-chief or the managing editor. Each page editor criticizes his page orally in the presence of the whole staff, pointing out poorly written stories, violations of make-up principles, proofreading and other errors. Other staff members then state their views. As the end of the semester approaches, potential page editors are asked to criticize. They thus become more conscious of the problems confronting page editors. Any staff member, including the editor-in-chief and the adviser, may comment on the issue.

The procedure may be varied from time to time by bringing in professional newspapermen—or past staff members who have entered the field of journalism—to make the criticisms. Followed week after week, this procedure results in an improved paper and a better morale among staff members. In addition, future page editors benefit from the experiences of present page editors.

THE HIGH SCHOOL NEWS BUREAU

Developing interest in the school and its publication is not limited to the work on the school paper alone. A number of staffs have developed news bureaus through which they channel their news to the daily newspapers and radio and television stations in the community. News bureaus have as their function publicity for the school, especially the distribution of facts in a way that will bring credit to and interest in the school.

Example 202 shows the organization of such a bureau by the *Orange and Black,* of Grand Junction High School, Grand Junction, Colorado. The school's explanation of the duties of the respective staff members follows the chart.

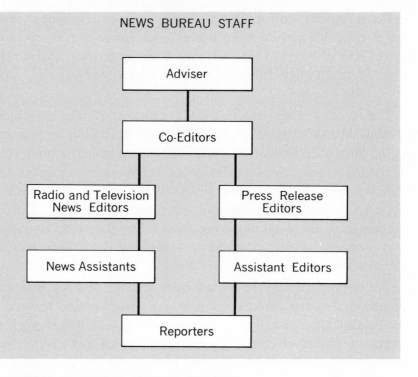

NEWS BUREAU STAFF DUTIES

Co-editors. Head the news bureau staff which furnishes news interpreting the school program to daily papers and radio and television stations.

Coordinate the work of the radio, television, and newspaper editors, clearing with them on stories daily.

Check with the school, radio, and television news staff and school newspaper editors to see that stories are assigned and written. Usually the individual who writes the *Orange and Black* story does a rewrite for the daily papers and the radio and television stations.

Copyread all stories before they go to news outlets.

Arrange delivery of news daily to newspapers and radio and television stations.

See that a scrapbook is kept of all stories printed in newspapers.

Evaluate type of news furnished to determine whether the over-all result is a good interpretation of the school program with an emphasis on the curriculum.

Work with publications director in carrying out area-wide publicity program for School District 51.

Press release editor. Work in close cooperation with the news bureau editors in arranging for regular, timely newspaper coverage of school news.

Help to assign stories, to rewrite and edit copy, and to check all copy before it goes to the newspapers.

Supervise work of the assistant editors and of the reporters on the news bureau staff.

Keep on the alert daily to spot news that should be written for the *Daily Sentinel* and other regional and state newspapers.

Radio and television news editor. Work in close cooperation with the co-editors in arranging for regular, timely coverage of school news over local radio and television stations.

Help to assign stories, to write and edit copy, and to check all copy before it goes to the radio and television stations.

Supervise the work of the assistant editors and reporters writing radio and television news.

Keep on the alert daily to spot school news that should be written for on-the-air publicity.

Work with publications director in planning special student radio broadcasts, particularly the Saturday teen programs.

Assistant editors. Work with the news bureau co-editors and the radio, television, and newspaper editors in planning and writing news for those outlets.

Help with the typing, editing, and checking of news.

Work directly with the reporters in checking to see that the stories are written and turned in on time.

Keep on the alert to spot possible news stories to be used in carrying out the school public information program.

Assist with teen radio program.

Reporters. Write stories for radio, television, or newspaper publicity as assigned.

Do rewrites of stories assigned for *Orange and Black* for air and daily-paper outlets if the story is of the type usable.

Share with fellow journalism students, who all serve as reporters, the responsibility for carrying on the school's public-information program.

Appear as newscasters and participate in teen radio programs when the opportunities arise.

THE RELATIONSHIP OF THE ADVISER TO THE STAFF

Teaching responsibility. The acceptance of staff responsibility is essential to successful high school journalism. The adviser's first duty is to set the stage for staff work, assuring the best of working conditions. The adviser must protect his staff from pressure from above, and protect those above from embarrassment through the publication. Once he has demonstrated his faith in the ability of the staff, and the staff realizes it, he has established himself as a director of learning rather than as a dictator.

The exact relationship of the faculty adviser to the editors is determined by the personalities involved and their capacities to assume responsibility. At times there are strong student editors who have the ability and the judgment to step out—way out—in front. A teacher welcomes such an editor. At other times the adviser does more of the checking than he would actually like to do, but this may be remedied the following semester.

Should censorship be exercised on the paper? Certainly, but not through teacher domination. A competent staff provides the censorship, which is a natural part of publishing a paper; editing means selecting. No newspaper publishes *all* the news. In printing the news, emphasis means as much as selection. The writer must anticipate the consequences of the story he is offering for print. If he does not, perhaps the page editor will. If the page editor does not, surely the editor-in-chief will. As an editor selects stories for publication, he rejects others naturally. This is censorship. Seldom need the adviser be the censor.

Staff organization. In summary, there is no one best system of staff organization. The positions provided and the responsibilities of each, carefully outlined, should serve the requirements of publishing the individual newspaper. The plan followed must enable the teacher to use the student personnel to the best advantage of the students and the school.

CHAPTER LABORATORY

1. Select one of the positions on your school paper and prepare a description of its duties. Be specific.
2. Prepare an organization chart for your school paper (see Examples 199 and 200). In class discussion, compare your chart with Examples 199 and 200 to clarify the relationship of positions.
3. Compare the two staff plans described in this chapter. Which do you think more practical? Present your points in class discussion.
4. Interview a member of your paper's staff on his work on the paper.
5. Is having an editorial board preferable to permitting the editor to set editorial policy? What is the practice of your school paper?
6. From an exchange paper, clip a flag that carries the staff positions and in class discuss that school's plan in comparison with yours.
7. If your school paper has a news office, determine whether it is adequate for the proper operation of the staff. If not, present practical suggestions for its improvement.
8. Analyze your paper's news bureau. If it does not have one, set up a practical staff organization and discuss in class.
9. Does your school paper provide for the carry-over of a sufficient number of experienced journalists to the new year to assure the paper the retention of quality? If not, consider how this might be accomplished.
10. If these positions were included on a staff, what might be required of each: girls' editor, exchange editor, society editor?

22 BUSINESS MANAGEMENT

High school journalism is big business, and behind a successful publication is good business management. No matter how well edited, a school newspaper depends upon adequate financing for its achievements. It is the fuel that puts the project into orbit.

Building the case for a subscription to the paper or selling twenty inches of advertising space to a reluctant merchant brings personal returns to a student just as covering a news story or laying out a page does. And, in turn, it brings to the paper the revenue that makes the paper possible.

The school newspaper is one of the very few opportunities for a high school student to get direct business experience. This is one means by which the business department of a high school can extend its instruction beyond the classroom walls.

SOURCES OF REVENUE

A financial survey. A survey of the finances of the first thirty newspapers to reply to a questionnaire (sent to a sampling of schools

352

drawn at random from lists issued by the national press associations) discloses that, as a group, school newspapers are big business. These thirty schools may be considered representative of nationwide practice among schools of the size represented in the study. Together, the thirty papers under consideration have a budget of over $100,000 — the amount their combined staffs spend in a given school year.

Of this income, 42 per cent is derived from advertising carried in the papers. The remainder, for the most part, is derived from the sale of the paper to students. In some instances, this part of their revenue is the result of direct subscription; in others, it is a share of the school fund accumulated through the sale of activities tickets or some other package arrangement. Some newspapers derive this part of their income through a combination of revenue from both direct sale and student funds.

It is apparent from this survey that the typical newspaper issued in a school of 1000 students or more depends upon advertising for at least a third of its revenue; and it is not unusual for this portion to exceed 50 per cent. Some staffs use other sources to supplement subscription and advertising, but these are exceptional. The types of miscellaneous income are evident in the annual financial statement of the *Magnet,* Owatonna High School, Owatonna, Minnesota (see Example 203).

Advantage of wide sale. The comparison of circulation with enrollment figures indicates that it is not unusual for the number of papers issued to reach or exceed the number of students. This may be a practical circulation goal for any school newspaper staff.

The large school has an advantage in financing its paper. The heavy costs are incurred in the original "make-ready," such as linotyping, photography, cuts, and printing. The unit cost of extra papers run off by the printer after the minimum allotment is insignificant. Consequently, the business staff's objective is sale of the paper to a maximum number of students. This is not only financially expedient but journalistically desirable since the original objective is to get the news to as many as possible. In smaller communities, out-of-school subscriptions are a good possibility.

353

EXAMPLE

203

Financial Report

THE MAGNET

October 1, 1964

SOURCE OF INCOME	ESTIMATED INCOME (in dollars)	ACTUAL INCOME (in dollars)
Advertising	914.00	795.75
Subscriptions	348.00	381.55
Concessions	300.00	142.83
Dance receipts		154.35
Candy sales	276.00	99.39
Card sales		160.88
Board of Education	400.00	400.00
TOTAL	$2238.00	$2134.75

TYPE OF EXPENSE	ESTIMATED EXPENSES (in dollars)	ACTUAL EXPENSES (in dollars)
Photography	80.00	66.20
Printing	1700.00	1723.15
Dues and conventions	200.00	195.00
Miscellaneous	125.00	
Circulation prizes		25.00
Dance decorations		11.61
Operator's Club		2.25
Homecoming Orchestra		100.00
Big Nine		3.08
Supplies		28.28
TOTAL	$2105.00	$2154.57

BALANCE	133.00	−19.88
Balance September 1, 1963		296.55
Balance from last year		276.67

UNPAID ADVERTISING

Ted's Shoe Service.....$15.25
Mac's Music Mart.....$29.00

The price of the paper is an important factor in its sale. The staff must consider such questions as (1) at what price level does the possible pupil consumer react against purchase, and (2) would a lower price mean in the end a greater return through more subscriptions?

Frequency of publication. The goal of every staff should be publication of a weekly paper, with biweekly publication only where necessary. The paper issued less than twice a month may (1) lose the sustained interest of the students, (2) be unable to publicize coming events adequately, (3) have to ignore a significant current school problem, and (4) sacrifice the morale-building function that is one justification for its being.

Maintaining the necessary frequency of publication is a challenge to the business division of a school paper. Two methods are most productive: (1) increasing support by the students, and (2) developing the local merchants' confidence in the school paper as an advertising medium.

BUSINESS MANAGEMENT

The business manager. While there is no one best staff organization, the business manager should always head the entire business staff. It is his duty to see that the business staff performs all of its activities efficiently and promptly. However, his major task is the financing of the paper. He is concerned about the circulation of the paper and the success of the advertising program. He is interested in eliminating waste and in effecting economies. It is just as important for him to spend the paper's revenue wisely as it is to work at raising the money.

The business management of a school publication has four primary duties: (1) planning the budget, (2) securing the most efficient services, such as printing, at the least expense, (3) raising the funds, and (4) systematically keeping the records. Each of these is essential, and the entire operation centers in a good business manager.

Business assistants. The number of designated business assistants will depend largely upon whether or not the business phase of the

355

paper is being emphasized, and upon the size of the paper and the frequency of publication. If the paper is a weekly carrying as much as 300 column inches of space, or more, the business manager will need at least one or two assistants. A paper this size will probably need a financial manager who may be called the assistant business manager.

Many of the detailed operations discussed in this chapter may be performed by such a staff member. In addition, there may be a cashier whose duty it is to receive all money and pay all bills on order from the business manager or the financial manager. If the activities of the business staff are sufficiently developed to merit the addition, there may also be a bookkeeper, although in general the financial manager should be able to care for all of the bookkeeping activities, provided a simplified system such as the one described herein is employed.

Clerical assistants. At least one good secretarial assistant, competent in shorthand and letter writing, is required to assist other staff members. She should have access to the school's mimeographing facilities and should be able to prepare copies of the material needed by various staff members.

Job descriptions. The specific titles of business staff positions will vary from paper to paper, just as the nature of the jobs will vary. The important thing is to have a description of each job. No other single device will do as much to fix responsibility on the staff. For a good example, look at this job description for the position of business manager on *The Student*, Woodrow Wilson High School, Portsmouth, Virginia.

Job Description for the Position of Business Manager

1. Cooperate with the editor.
2. Direct business operations.
3. Keep in touch with other managers to see that they are on the job.
4. Make an operating budget.
5. Assist in getting ads and writing them if necessary.
6. Appoint a salesman for selling in homerooms when papers come out.
7. Receive and deposit (with the school treasurer) all money col-

lected. (Make two deposit slips, one with names of payees on back.)

8. Prepare requisitions for money paid out (make two requisitions).
9. See that advertisers are properly billed.
10. Help handle business with the printer and with the engraver.
11. See that all materials are ordered for use on the staff.
12. See that post office regulations are observed.
13. Keep a cash book showing income and expenses.
14. Attend all conference and staff meetings.

RECORDING FINANCIAL OPERATIONS

A systematic approach to the business operation, namely, keeping the books, is essential to the interests of the school as well as those of the paper. The necessity of avoiding slipshod procedures demands an effective, relatively simple system.

Kind of system needed. Three criteria should be adopted for any bookkeeping system on the school paper; (1) the system must be simple; (2) it must represent the various transactions in such a manner that each one may be thoroughly traced; and (3) it must be reasonably "foolproof." These three qualifications have guided the development of the system described in the following pages, which entails the keeping of only three permanent records: an accounts-payable ledger, an accounts-receivable ledger, and a special type of cash journal.

A system of accounting may be unexciting, but a good system of accounting is essential to the efficient management of a school newspaper. Slipshod methods in the business department are not evident in the make-up of a school paper, but no brilliancy in the editorial or mechanical managements can compensate for loose handling of funds. A fully effective school paper demands skillful management.

The cash journal. There are many types of cash journals, and each staff together with its adviser must develop a form to meet the needs of its particular situation. One school paper uses the form pictured in Example 204. The cash journal should provide a record of five specific types of information: the amount of receipts, the general source of receipts, the amount of expenditures, the general types of merchan-

EXAMPLE **204**

CASH JOURNAL								RECEIPT ITEMS			
TOTALS			DATE	DESCRIPTION	FIRM or PERSON	✓					
RECEIPTS	EXPENDITURES	BALANCE					RECEIPT NUMBER	ADVERTISING	CIRCULATION	OTHER SOURCES	CHECK

dise or service for which those expenditures were made, and the balance on hand.

In the form illustrated in Example 204, there are three money columns at the left indicating the amount of receipts, the amount of expenditures, and the balance, or difference, between the two. In the next columns are the date of the transaction, a brief description of the transaction, and the name of the firm. Next a group of three money columns records the three sources of income together with another column for the receipt number. All receipts for this particular paper come from advertising, from circulation, or from minor miscellaneous sources. When money is received, it is not only indicated in the general "receipts" column, but also in the one or more columns at the right which tell whether the money came from advertising or other sources.

In similar fashion, there are eleven expenditure classifications for this paper. Money paid out is listed in the total-expenditure column, but it is also listed under the particular heading so that the nature of the expenditure can be determined immediately. This type of arrangement makes it possible to determine at the close of any financial period, month, semester, or year, just exactly how much has been spent for cuts, how much has been spent for printing, and so on. This arrangement makes it extremely easy to prepare a budget for the next financial period. It can be seen that a certain amount was taken in from adver-

358

From , 19 to , 19

EXPENSE ITEMS

NO.	TYPESETTING	PRESSWORK	PAPER	ENGRAVING	PHOTOGRAPHY	EQUIPMENT	SUPPLIES	MATS AND STEREOS	DUES AND FEES	STAFF MEMBERS EXPENSES		MISCELLANEOUS

tising last year and that another amount came from circulation. Through the use of this type of cash journal, it is possible to compare intelligently receipts and expenditures for succeeding semesters or years.

The accounts-payable ledger. Every amount the paper owes is recorded in the accounts-payable ledger. Most of such ledgers have an index in the front in which all firms and individuals to whom money is owed can be listed. The number corresponding to the page or the account number assigned to each firm is posted next to each entry. This makes it possible to find easily the page devoted to the account with that particular firm. (Only one firm is listed on any one page.) There are various types of ledger sheets, but one of the simplest is pictured in Example 205. This type of ledger has three money columns, the first of which is used for money paid to the firm—the debit column; the second is used to enter the cost of merchandise delivered or services rendered—the credits column; the third carries a balance and shows the exact status of the account at all times.

The ledger sheet in Example 205 presents a representative account with a typesetting firm. On September 14 a bill was received for $98.93 and entered in the second or "credit" column. Likewise, the same amount was entered in the "balance" column because this is the amount actually owed the firm on that date. On September 20, another bill of $101.30 was received and entered in the "credit" column. To obtain

359

<table>
<tr><td colspan="2" rowspan="2">EXAMPLE
205</td><td colspan="9">NAME *Keller Typesetting Co.*</td><td colspan="3">ACCOUNT NO. 2</td></tr>
<tr><td colspan="9">ADDRESS   6 *South First Street*</td><td colspan="3">SHEET NO. *One*</td></tr>
</table>

DATE		ITEMS	Folio	√	DEBITS	√	CREDITS	DR. OR CR.	BALANCE
Sept.	14	Typesetting Issue #1					98 93	Cr.	98 93
Sept.	20	Typesetting Issue #2					101 30	Cr.	200 23
Sept.	27	Typesetting Issue #3					96 89	Cr.	297 12
Oct.	9	Check #6793			297 12				000 00
Oct.	10	Typesetting Issue #4					107 49	Cr.	107 49
Oct.	17	Typesetting Issue #5					99 83	Cr.	207 32
Oct.	22	Check #6799			107 49				99 83

the balance, the last balance was added to the amount of the bill just entered. On October 9 the paper sent the firm a check for $297.12, which was entered in the "debit" column. When this amount was deducted from the last balance, the new balance was zero. If the amount of the payment had been less than the old balance, the difference would have been placed in the "balance" column and indicated as the amount still owed to the firm by the letters "cr" in the column to the left. If, for any reason, the check were greater than the balance, the difference would be indicated in the "balance" column, and the letters "dr" in the column at the left would indicate that the firm was indebted to the paper by that amount.

The accounts-receivable ledger. The accounts-receivable ledger is similar in many respects to the accounts-payable ledger. In it are recorded all of the amounts due the paper. Most school papers have little to record in accounts-receivable ledgers except the accounts of their advertisers. The same type of book may be used as for the accounts-payable ledger, with an index in the front and a single page for each firm or individual who owes money to the paper. If both ledgers are kept by the same staff members, they may be bound in the same cover. Entries are similar except that, as indicated in Example 206, charges against the firm are "debited" in the "debit" column, and payments made by the firm are "credited" by listing the amount

EXAMPLE

206

NAME Dawson's Shoe Store				ACCOUNT NO. 40				
ADDRESS Main Street				SHEET NO. One				

DATE	ITEMS	Folio	✓	DEBITS	✓	CREDITS	DR. OR CR.	BALANCE
Oct. 8	14" ad @ $1.25			17 50			Dr.	17 50
Oct. 29	10" ad @ $1.25			12 50			Dr.	30 00
Nov. 3	By check					30 00		0 00

in the "credit" column. Like the accounts-payable ledger, the accounts-receivable ledger carries a running balance at all times. If payments made by the firm exceed the amount actually owed, a credit balance is carried and the letters "cr" are indicated to the left of the "balance" column.

RECEIVING MONEY

Duplicate receipts. There should be an ironclad rule in the office of every school paper that absolutely no money will be accepted unless a receipt is issued. A record of receipts can best be kept through the use of a duplicate receipt book. In this book, the cashier, or some other staff member designated to receive the money, writes a receipt to the individual from whom the money is collected, gives the payer the original receipt, and keeps the carbon copy in the receipt book. The person in charge of the receipt book and the collections must be extremely careful to record the nature of the source of the money. For example, if one of the advertising salesmen brings in a sum of money collected from one of the advertisers, the cashier should write the receipt to the collector (the salesman), but should be certain to include the name of the advertiser who paid the money and the fact that the money is to pay for advertising run in the paper. In other words, make the duplicate receipt a complete record. (The advertis-

361

ing salesman should also have a duplicate receipt book and write a receipt for the advertiser when the money is collected.)

Depositing funds. Systems for disposing of cash vary from school to school, but there are two plans in general use: one involves some kind of central accounting system for all school activities and the other a separate bank account for the school paper. The two plans are similar; in the former, however, funds are turned over to a central treasurer or clerk in the school, while in the latter, funds are deposited directly in the bank. In either case, some sort of deposit slip will be used. The staff cashier should prepare these deposit slips in duplicate; that is, a carbon copy should be prepared at the same time as the original. This copy should be kept on file in the newspaper office in order that errors by the central treasurer or the bank may be detected. The deposit slip should show the amount of currency deposited, the number and amounts of checks together with the names of the persons or firms upon whom they are drawn, and the total. All checks should be endorsed in accordance with the school's policy before they are released.

Entering cash transactions. Once a particular receipt has been recorded in the duplicate receipt book and the money deposited with the bank or central treasurer, the receipt must be entered in the cash journal. If, for example, the local shoe store used $30.00 worth of advertising space during the month of October, and the salesman for this particular firm made the collection on November 3 and turned in that amount to the cashier, the cashier writes a receipt, gives the collector the original, and leaves the carbon copy in the receipt book. After this, the bookkeeper or financial manager goes through the receipt book and records the transaction in the cash journal. He enters $30.00 in both the total-receipts column and the advertising receipts column. In similar fashion, when a circulation collector turns in $3.30 for collections in homeroom 153, a receipt is issued, and the amount is then entered in the cash journal. The amount, however, is listed in the circulation-receipts column instead of the advertising-receipts column. The cash journal thus becomes the record of original entry. It is customary for the bookkeeper to make a large check mark (ν) on the duplicate receipt to indicate that it has been entered.

362

Posting in the accounts-receivable ledger. The record of a transaction, such as the payment for advertising discussed above, is not complete until an entry has been made in the accounts-receivable ledger. *In this case, the posting is done from the record of original entry, the cash journal.* The bookkeeper would note the entry in the cash journal, look up the account number of this advertiser in the index of his accounts-receivable ledger, turn to that page, and "credit" this firm's account by entering the amount in the second or credit column. When these items are posted in the accounts-receivable ledger, a check mark should be noted in the cash journal to indicate which have been entered. It is customary to enter the account number in the column with the check mark ($\checkmark$) at the top. This makes rapid reference possible in the future.

PAYING MONEY

Two systems used. Just as there are two systems in general use for the disposition of funds by the paper, so there are two systems in use for paying bills. If the school paper has a separate bank account, the logical method is to pay by check. All bills should be paid regularly each month between the first and the tenth, unless special provisions are made. Once each month, the bookkeeper or the financial manager should go over the accounts-payable ledger and determine how much is owed to each firm, and checks should be written for these amounts. If the school has a central treasurer who writes all checks for all organizations and activities in the school, he will probably provide some sort of order or voucher form. This is similar in form to a check, but it requests the central treasurer to pay a specified amount of money to a certain firm. A school paper builds respect by paying its bills on time.

Handling petty cash. There are times when it is necessary to make small expenditures, at times less than one dollar, during the month. To avoid delay and to minimize the amount of bookkeeping necessary, a "petty cash" fund should be provided. For this purpose, a small sum, perhaps about ten dollars, should be withdrawn from the bank or from the central treasurer and kept for such expenditures. This withdrawal

363

should be charged to "petty cash." When cash expenditures are made from this amount, a receipt should be secured from the person to whom the money is paid. A form similar to Example 207 may be used. When the fund becomes depleted, another check or voucher should be written to bring it up to the original amount. When petty cash checks or vouchers are entered in the cash journal, the exact items for which the money was used may be secured from the petty cash receipts and should be entered in the journal under the proper classifications of expenditure.

Entering amounts paid. Stubs of checks written by the business manager or vouchers returned by the school treasurer must be entered in the cash journal. In addition to the date and description of the payment, the amount is entered in the total-expenditure column and also under the heading of the expenditure classification of the particular item. Occasionally it is necessary to record the full amount of the payment in the total-expenditure column and to enter parts of the amount in two or more of the specific-expenditure columns. This is usually the case in entering petty cash items.

Posting in the accounts-payable ledger. The accounts-payable ledger should, like the accounts-receivable ledger, have its entries made from the cash journal. The operations are identical; here, too, the account number is indicated in the cash-journal column to indicate which items have been posted in the ledger.

PURCHASING SERVICES AND MATERIALS

Concentrating purchasing. All too often, school papers are so disorganized in their purchasing activities that it is impossible to know exactly what has been purchased at any given time. There is only one solution—the concentration of all buying activities in the hands of a single person, in most staff organizations, the business manager.

Using a purchase order. The amount of purchasing necessary determines to a large degree whether or not a standard purchase-order form should be used. No one thing places purchasing under the absolute control of the designated individual more than the use of a form similar to that in Example 208.

364

EXAMPLE

207

EXAMPLE

208

PURCHASE
ORDER

N° 153

DATE........................

ORIGINAL

THE SCHOOL SPIRIT
BENJAMIN BOSSE HIGH SCHOOL
Evansville, Indiana

TO: ....

....

....

Kindly ship to THE SCHOOL SPIRIT or deliver to the bearer
the Goods or Merchandise indicated below. The number of
our Purchase Order should appear on your invoice.

Quantity	ITEM and DESCRIPTION	Unit Price	Extension
	TOTAL		

Entered ....   THE SCHOOL SPIRIT

Filed ....

Business Manager

PETTY CASH

....$.........

For...

....

....

Charge to Account.................................

Signed.................................

Date.................................

The form pictured in Example 208 is made in triplicate, each sheet in a different color. The white or original copy goes to the person or firm from whom the item was purchased, the second or yellow copy to the business manager, and the third or blue copy to the financial manager or bookkeeper. Business staffs must make merchants realize that no goods or services are to be delivered or charged to the paper without one of these forms. If the practice is adhered to, the business manager and the bookkeeper will have a record of all purchases. The lines "Entered" and "Filed" in the lower left-hand corner of the pur-

365

chase order enable the business and financial managers to record the dates the order was received and the invoice entered on the books.

If complete responsibility for the financing of the paper is delegated by the adviser to the business staff, it should be the privilege of the business staff to pass on all expenditures before they are made. The first-page editor may desire to use a particular cut on his page next issue. The purchase of this cut should be authorized by the business manager, who should know without question whether or not the paper can afford such an expenditure. The editor-in-chief may wish to purchase a new style of paper for typing copy. He may have very good reasons for wanting to make the purchase, but can the paper afford the expenditure? The answer should rest with the business department in general and the business manager in particular.

Saving through systematic buying. When all purchasing is concentrated in the hands of the business manager advised by other staff members, savings may be effected with a little time and thought. For example, members of a particular staff felt that their printing costs were too high. They investigated the cost of paper and got quotations on printing with the understanding that the stock was to be furnished by the staff. They discovered that a material saving was the result, because the printer was charging a profit for handling the paper. They followed this practice for approximately three years and then discovered that if they purchased a ton of newsprint instead of the usual five hundred pounds, a saving of twenty dollars could be realized. Other savings can be realized in the making of cuts. (See Chapter 19.) If one or two interested members of the staff actually apply themselves to the task, a number of financial leaks resulting from lax purchasing may be stopped. It may be startling, for instance, to realize that fifteen hundred copies of the paper are printed each week when there are but twelve hundred school subscribers and one hundred subscribers on the mailing list. Obviously, a financial leak.

THE BUSINESS-STAFF MEETING

Purpose of meetings. Members of the business staff should conduct a meeting after each issue of the paper is published to criticize their own work, the financial status of the paper, and consider ways and means to improve their particular phase of the paper's business. The business manager should preside over this meeting unless the two staffs are combined into one group, in which case the editor-in-chief should probably take charge.

The business manager should call for reports on the activities of the financial, the circulation, and the advertising departments for the preceding issue. After the reports are heard, they should be discussed in open meeting, and weaknesses should be considered in the hopes of overcoming them. Frequently members of the circulation department may make valuable suggestions to the advertising manager and vice versa. (Suggestions for reports by the circulation and advertising departments may be found in Chapters 23 and 24.)

The profit-and-loss estimate. One of the questions usually foremost in the minds of business staff members is, "Did we make or lose money last week?" The business manager, the financial manager, or the bookkeeper should report an estimate of the financial outcome of the preceding issue. This is best done by using a "Weekly Profit-and-Loss Estimate" form (See Example 209). On this form are recorded the estimated income for the issue under discussion, the estimated expenditures by budget classifications, and an estimate of the amount made or lost on the issue.

After the report has been read, discussion may be opened. Suggestions for reducing particular expenditures may be made, and occasionally the group will be asked to decide a particular issue by voting.

The financial statement. While the profit-and-loss estimate is important, it must be kept in mind that it is an estimate and that the figures are not exact amounts. Therefore, it is desirable to have an exact statement of the financial standing of the paper approximately once each month. (See Example 210.) On such a statement the amounts of money on deposit and on hand are added to the amounts of the accounts receivable and the supplies on hand to determine the total assets of the paper. The total liability is found by adding accounts payable, money paid in advance by subscribers, and reserve for equipment or other purposes. The difference indicates the net worth of the paper.

367

EXAMPLE

209

WEEKLY PROFIT-AND-LOSS ESTIMATE

Issue Number................ Date.............................

INCOME

Estimated from................sub-
scriptions prorated for
................issues .... $............

Estimated from advertising
this issue ....

TOTAL INCOME .... $..

EXPENDITURES

Typesetting .... $............
Presswork ....
Engraving and mounting.. ....
Transportation ....
Mats and stereos.......... ....
Postage ....
Newsprint ....
Photography ...(estimated) ....
Other supplies..(estimated) ....
Equipment ....(estimated) ....
Dues and fees ....
Other ....

TOTAL EXPENDITURES .... $..

ESTIMATED PROFIT OR LOSS .... $..

....
Financial Mana

Date
Submitted........................ ....
Business Mana

MONTHLY FINANCIAL STATEMENT

Statement as of............................, 19........

ASSETS

Money on deposit .... $............
Cash on hand ....
Total accounts receivable... ....
Supplies on hand ....
Other assets ....

TOTAL ASSETS .... $............

LIABILITIES

Accounts payable .... $............
Prepaid subscriptions ....
Reserve for equipment ....
Other liabilities ....

TOTAL LIABILITIES .... $............

SURPLUS AS OF ABOVE DATE.......... $............

....
Financial Manager

....
Business Manager

EXAMPLE

210

If the assets exceed the liabilities, a surplus will be the result; if liabilities exceed assets, there will be a deficit, and the staff should immediately take steps to correct the situation.

The discussion of other problems. The staff meeting should be the clearing house for all problems of the business staff. Although the financial manager is designated to shoulder the financial responsibility of the paper, and the advertising manager the advertising responsibility, every staff member should be made to feel that the problems of every other staff member are his problems. The opinion of a group is often better than the opinion of individuals, provided members of the group are equally well informed.

368

CHAPTER LABORATORY

1. Have the business manager of your paper discuss his duties with the class. Use the sample job description on pages 356-57 as a check list. How does his job differ from that of the business manager of *The Student*?
2. Prepare a paper recommending needed changes in the business manager's position on your own paper.
3. Make a study of the financial procedures used by the responsible staff members on your paper. How is incoming money handled? How are purchases made, and who authorizes them? How are bills paid?
4. Find out whether your paper made or lost money last semester. Could the accounting procedure be improved?
5. Design a set of forms to be used in the financial management of your paper.
6. Suggest a series of topics to be discussed at a meeting of your business staff.
7. Why is there so much variation among schools between circulation and number of students? What is the ratio for your school paper?
8. How does your paper stand in percentage of revenue from advertising?
9. Does your local paper appear frequently enough to command respect as a newspaper and to serve the newspaper needs of the school? Discuss in class.
10. Is the subscription rate of the paper adequate for its support? If not, could it be raised a dollar a year without losing subscribers?

23 HANDLING THE ADVERTISING

The revenue derived from advertising is one of the principal supports of the high school newspaper. Like the daily paper, the school paper cannot exist without the support of local business. But this is not a one way street—the high school student today represents a huge, and recognized, market; and the school newspaper is a very effective way of tapping that market.

The man who bridges both needs is the advertising salesman. But like all important phases of school journalism, the advertising department has certain fundamentals to follow in establishing its policies— for the advertising department is primarily responsible for assuring that the paper is profitable and the advertiser happy.

SELLING ADVERTISING

Amount of advertising. The high school newspaper is dependent upon the income it derives from advertising to supplement the revenue

370

derived from circulation. The average school paper receives roughly 50 per cent of its revenue from each source. (See page 353.) Therefore, the public school newspaper must assume the obligation of a business. Because revenue is not assured from one term to the next, the challenge is active and continuing.

How much advertising should a school newspaper carry in order to provide good financial support and yet maintain reasonable proportions between copy and advertising? The table below presents the solutions of a few school papers sampled on this point. As is obvious, there is no one answer. The average is 28 per cent, but, for your school paper, the better percentage might be 25 or 30. Whatever the goal, its attainment depends upon the advertising salesman.

SIZE OF NEWSPAPER			ADVERTISING CARRIED	
Columns	Pages	Column Inches	Column Inches	Per cent of Total Inches
5	8	560	150	27
5	8	640	213	32
5	6	510	118	23
8	4	640	183	29
7	4	456	120	26
5	6	450	98	22
5	4	320	75	23
8	4	672	216	32
5	4	340	95	28
5	8	560	116	21
4	6	288	66	23
6	4	480	157	33
7	4	532	145	27
5	4	320	89	28
5	8	640	216	34

Are you sold? The high school student who sells advertising must himself be "sold" on the value of an ad in the school paper. Naturally, his attitude is sure to be reflected in his behavior in the prospective sales situation. Consider these facts:

1. High school students form a common age group of from about fourteen to seventeen—a market group with common characteristics. The advertiser knows exactly at whom he is aiming, and does not have to scatter his shot as in other advertising media.

2. While adults have already formed certain buying habits, high school students compose a group whose habits are still flexible.

3. High school students influence their parents' buying of furniture, clothing, the new car, and the television set.

4. This group already buys a large part of the goods consumed in the community. In a few years, they will be even greater consumers. The firm that looks ahead is eager to establish faith and good will for the future.

Get the facts. In addition, there are specific facts that must be determined in each school situation:

1. How many students in your school subscribe to the paper?

2. What proportion of these students take the paper home? What is the average number of persons in each home who read the paper?

3. How many homes receive the paper through mail subscriptions? What is a conservative estimate of the number of buyers who see the paper in the waiting rooms of doctors, lawyers, and dentists?

Once the student assures himself that he has something valuable to sell, approaching a prospect will be less embarrassing. Untrained student salesmen are a selling campaign's greatest menace. They can soon play havoc with an advertising field that previously held great possibilities. For the future welfare of the paper, it is better to send out no salesmen than to send out those untrained. Once trained, the apprentice member of the business department might well temporarily confine himself to selling advertising. Once he becomes a member of the department, other phases of the paper's business can and must be learned through work and study.

The life of the school paper. The life of a school paper is longer than that of the daily paper. Being a weekly publication, it is new until the next issue. Because of its small size and the student's inherent interest in it, it is read almost completely. This is a great advantage to the advertiser and should be made known to him.

Some Do's and Don'ts. While no rule works all of the time, the following should be of some assistance to the novice advertising salesman. Learning to confront the local merchant and deal with him in a sincere, businesslike manner is an important part of the experience a student gets on a high school paper.

Do—

1. Prepare yourself before you start out to sell. List definite prospects and determine what they might advertise and how much space they might take. Try to find out the name of the right person to see. Entering a firm and asking for the advertising manager by name carries much more weight than merely asking for the man in charge of advertising.
2. Be businesslike in your approach. Know the merits of advertising in your paper; have a complete knowledge of the rates and provisions; and assume a cheerful and businesslike attitude. These things develop the prospect's faith in the publication.
3. Carry a list of those merchants who year after year advertise in the paper. Keeping the firm's name before the student helps assure the firm a steady influx of customers in the future.

Don't—

1. Beg advertising from a firm. The school paper gives value for money received, and only on this business basis should advertising space be sold.
2. Use the fact that you are a customer or that the school made a certain purchase to "force" a sale.
3. Use family contacts as a substitute for sales talk. Appealing for ads on the basis of friendship is discourteous; it has the effect of putting friends on the spot.
4. Consider a sale complete until all arrangements have been made for securing copy for the ad. Businesslike procedure must not cease once the space is sold.

Meeting sales resistance. Any staff that studies its advertising sales campaigns and records all contracts accurately will notice that merchants' objections to advertising in the school paper usually fall under a few general heads. The following arguments are among those most often presented:

Our advertising budget is filled for this year.
If I advertise in your paper, I'll have to do it in the rest of the school papers in this city.
Business is too bad now. We can't afford it.
We advertise in the annual (or the magazine) of your school. That's enough.
We've tried advertising in school papers, and it doesn't pay.
We don't advertise anywhere.
Advertising in a school paper is merely a donation.
We've never advertised in school papers.

None of these arguments is infallible. A little study will reveal a sales approach to meet each one. The old donation concept of school advertising constantly bobs up, and must be met with facts. A study of a firm's previous attempts at advertising may present weaknesses. Advertising in the magazine or annual may be hurting the newspaper's chances at legitimate business. In short, there is no limit to the preparation necessary to float a successful advertising sales campaign. Although much of the success depends upon the ingenuity and the personality of the student, there are certain truths he can carry with him that always make good sales talk. There is no substitute for facts in meeting sales resistance.

SETTING ADVERTISING RATES

Advertising in the school paper is usually sold by the column-inch, as is space in daily newspapers. Most papers have a sliding scale of rates, although some do charge a fixed figure per inch regardless of how many inches are purchased or how many times the ad is to run. In general, the rate schedule that offers a discount for larger ads and another discount for a number of insertions is more desirable. Both of these provisions are an inducement to take more space with the paper, in the long run making advertising in the paper more valuable. (See Example 211.)

Advertising rates themselves vary greatly with the locality, and the time. In large metropolitan areas like New York City and Cleveland, Ohio, rates are higher than in smaller communities throughout the nation. This is not an inflexible rule, however, for local conditions

The NORTH STAR

WEEKLY PUBLICATION OF NORTH HIGH SCHOOL

OFFICE: ROOM 17, NORTH HIGH SCHOOL

2319 Stringtown Road, Evansville 11, Ind.   Phone HA 5-7276

DUPLICATE
ADVERTISER

DATE_____

The undersigned firm hereby agrees to use_____column-inches of advertising space in THE SCHOOL PAPER in each of the issues checked in the margin at the right, the cost to be determined on the basis of the rates listed below under Option I, Option II, Option III.

The undersigned agrees to pay any costs incurred by THE SCHOOL PAPER in preparing engravings and stereotypes.

One copy of THE SCHOOL PAPER containing each insertion of advertising will be furnished the advertiser.

Firm Name _____

Address _____ Telephone_____

Signed _____

Salesman _____
For The School Paper

Accepted
Ad Manager _____

RATE PER COLUMN-INCH

OPTION	One Inch	2-9 Inches	10-19 Inches	20 or More Inches
Option I: 1-3 Insertions	$1.50	$1.35	$1.00	$ .90
Option II: 4-9 Insertions	1.35	1.00	.95	.80
Option III: 10 or More Insertions	1.00	.95	.85	.70

REMARKS: _____

_____

All copy must be in the hands of THE SCHOOL PAPER one week in advance of publication date.

Accounts will be payable the first of each month.

VOLUME X	VOLUME XI
Number 1 Friday September 22..........☐	Number 1 Friday February 9 ....☐
Number 2 Friday September 29..........☐	Number 2 Friday February 16 ....☐
Number 3 Friday October 6 ....☐	Number 3 Friday February 23 ....☐
Number 4 Friday October 13 ....☐	Number 4 Friday March 2 ....☐
Number 5 Friday October 20 ....☐	Number 5 Friday March 9 ....☐
Number 6 Friday November 3 ....☐	Number 6 Friday March 16 ....☐
Number 7 Friday November 10 ....☐	Number 7 Friday March 23..............☐
Number 8 Friday November 17 ....☐	Number 8 Friday March 30 ....☐
Number 9 Friday December 1 ....☐	Number 9 Friday April 6 ....☐
Number 10 Friday December 8 ....☐	Number 10 Friday April 13 ....☐
Number 11 Friday December 15 ....☐	Number 11 Friday May 4 ....☐
Number 12 Friday January 12 ....☐	Number 12 Friday May 18 ....☐

EXAMPLE
211

other than size influence the cost of advertising, and a larger city may have lower rates than a smaller one. A random survey of high school newspapers shows rates varying from $1.00 to $2.00 per single column inch, with decreasing rates for increased inches (usually above six) and continuing advertising. Advertising rates have more than doubled in the past twenty years, and this increase may be expected to continue, albeit more slowly.

In effect, advertising rates are determined by printing costs, size and make-up of the school, and competition. In determining its rates, each school must analyze how much it can charge before it loses advertisers to other media. A study of costs, local conditions, and the competition should provide a solution.

Advertising contracts. The school paper must conduct its activities in a businesslike manner. Contracts between the advertiser and the paper eliminate misunderstandings resulting from verbal agreements. Advertisers may become confused on rates or sizes of ads if a written record is not prepared.

A contract similar to the ones in Examples 212 and 213 is valuable to both advertising department and advertiser. In general, the contract should record three basic types of information: the size of the ad, the frequency and date or dates of insertion, and the rate per column-inch for that specific ad. The contract should be prepared in triplicate, the original submitted to the advertising manager, the second copy to the advertiser, and the third copy to the staff bookkeeper or financial manager for billing.

THE ADVERTISING DEPARTMENT

The advertising staff of almost any school paper includes the advertising manager, the head of that particular department of the business division, and several assistants, salesmen, or solicitors. The number of assistants depends upon the size of the paper, the frequency of issue, and the degree to which the advertising phase is emphasized. Whatever the size of the staff, their efficiency depends on the system.

376

EXAMPLE
212

The West Higher

West High School
6809 Franklin Ave.
Cleveland 2, Ohio

A Student Publication
Established 1919
Wo 1-0057

ORDER FOR ADVERTISING SPACE

Name of Business _____

Address _____ Zone _____ Telephone _____ Date _____

Insertion dates: To be billed:

1._____   Total inches ordered_____   1. After each insertion_____

2._____   Number of insertions_____   2. End of each month _____

3._____   Width_____columns   3. End of semester _____

4._____   Length_____   4. After last insertion _____

5._____

6._____   Ordered by_____

7._____   Salesman _____

8._____   Print, type, or paste copy on reverse side.

Rates: $1.00 per column inch. 10 percent discount for 6 or more insertions.

The need for a system. The importance of the advertising department cannot be overemphasized. If the staff wishes to increase the size of the paper, it must look to the advertising department to supply the revenue. If it wishes to include more cuts, the advertising department must be consulted. And if any kind of special edition is contemplated, it depends upon whether the needed additional advertising can be sold.

For these reasons, the staff must be organized efficiently so that its duties may be performed with a minimum of lost motion. It must also be organized so that new members constantly receive in-service training for the higher positions some of them will hold.

The prospect file. The use of some sort of prospect file or list assists such organization. Such a file should include the names, addresses, and telephone numbers of the advertising managers of firms that might advertise in the school paper, each name noted on its own filing card.

377

EXAMPLE

213

CONTRACT FOR ADVERTISING IN THE *ROCKET*

Northeast High School
63 and Baldwin
Lincoln, Nebraska

_____

(date)

_____

BUSINESS

_____

ADDRESS   PHONE

agrees to purchase _____ page of advertising in the _____
Rocket at $10 per 1/6 page, $15 per 1/4 page, $25 per 1/2
page, and $50 per full page.

All advertising is pictorial with copy written by the advertising
staff. Any specifications as to who should be in the picture or
special slogans in copy should be listed below. The picture will
be taken by appointment made by the *Rocket* advertising manager. The advertiser will be billed April 1. Payment is due
within 30 days of the billing.

_____

COMPANY ADVERTISING MANAGER

_____

ROCKET ADVERTISING MANAGER

_____

ROCKET ADVERTISING STAFF MEMBER

One person should be designated to have charge of such a file. In
small staffs, this will probably be the advertising manager; in larger
staffs, it may be the advertising prospect manager or a business department clerk.

378

The person selected should be continually on the lookout for additional firm names. These may be firms that advertise in other school papers; those with which the school cafeteria, the athletic department, classes, and school organizations do business; and even those that advertise in the daily papers. A separate card should, of course, be made out for each of these prospects, with the name of the person in charge of advertising on each card—extremely valuable information to the salesman.

The use of call slips. Calling on prospective advertisers is too frequently a spasmodic, unorganized practice with school newspapers. To have several salesmen call at random on one firm while half a dozen others are not even approached is at least ineffective and sometimes offensive. Firms who will advertise do not like to be bothered unnecessarily, and others may be offended because they were not solicited.

There is only one solution. The advertising manager must assign certain salesmen to call on certain firms, thus avoiding duplication and insuring maximum coverage. The use of a call sheet or assignment slip similar to that in Example 214 helps to place the matter under the control of the advertising manager.

In one system the various salesmen look over the prospect file and choose a number of firms upon which they would like to call. The advertising manager makes out call slips for each firm, giving the original to the solicitor and retaining the colored duplicate in his book so that he constantly has a record of the firms being approached and of the solicitors making the contacts.

At the beginning of a new school year, the natural thing to do is to begin with the previous year's advertisers as a nucleus. Suggesting an increase in the space to be taken is a good approach.

Staff meeting report. The advertising staff should report the status of its activities to the rest of the staff each week, using a report such as the one in Example 215. In addition, the advertising manager should call any special activities to the attention of the rest of the staff. A report each week does much to keep the staff on its toes and provides a basis for comparison with previous weeks or semesters.

EXAMPLE
214

AD COPY
THE SCHOOL SPIRIT

ISSUE NUMBER .... PUBLICATION DATE ....

FIRM	SIZE COL.	SIZE IN.	SALESMAN	REMARKS

IN CHARGE OF DUMMY ....

SENT TO MOORE'S .... EXPECTED ....

PROOF READ BY .... AND ....

ADVERTISING DEPARTMENT
CALL SHEET

Solicitor.. Date ....

Call on the following firm:

....

....

on or before ....

Talk with Mr. ....

Signed ....

Advertising Manager

Solicitor's Report: Date Called

....

....

....

....

....

....

....

Signed ....

Solicitor

Report made .... Entered ....

EXAMPLE
215

WEEKLY REPORT OF ADVERTISING MANAGER Issue Number.............; Date			
Salesman	Inches Sold	Ads Sold	Call Slips Due

Reporting and recording results. The solicitor should report the results of his efforts to the advertising manager: he has sold an ad, he was asked to return at a later date, or he was definitely refused. Whatever the results, he should make a record with all of the particulars on the lower half of his call sheet and return it to the advertising manager. The manager indicates on his duplicate that the assignment has been completed and turns the original over to the prospect manager. The prospect manager in turn records the results on the proper prospect file card, including the name of the salesman and the date of the call, the outcome, and the particulars, such as why the advertiser refused, when he asked the salesman to call again, or the size and number of ads sold. Finally, the prospect manager indicates that he made the entry by placing his name or initials in the "Entered by" column.

If this procedure is followed, the advertising prospect file should increase in value as time goes on. Solicitors can see what arguments against advertising were used, and can be prepared to answer these arguments on future calls. Also, if the record is kept conscientiously, it will provide a valuable index of those merchants who wish to place ads during certain seasons of the year. Its value to a new staff cannot be overestimated; instead of beginning anew each year, the ad staff can virtually pick up the work where it was discontinued. Obviously, to be effective a prospect file must be kept up-to-date.

THE LAYOUT OF ADS AND PAGE MAKE-UP

Purpose of layout. The advertising layout has two main purposes: to give the prospective advertiser an idea of the appearance of the finished ad, and to tell the printer what the advertising man has in mind. Merchants sometimes refuse the high school advertising salesman because they do not have time to set up ads. This obstacle may be completely overcome when the student approaches the merchant with an idea, outlined on paper if possible.

Preparing printer's copy. Three things must be included when preparing advertising copy for the printer: the exact size of the ad,

its general appearance, and the location of the cut, if any. The advertising manager may also specify the kinds and sizes of type to be used, depending upon his ability and the school's arrangements with the printer.

In preparing a layout for the printer, the advertising man always
draws his copy to the exact size of the completed ad. He also sketches
in all copy to appear in larger size type, making the lettering approximately the size and degree of blackness that he wishes in the final
product. In such a layout, there is often some copy which cannot be
written or printed small enough to be filled into the assigned space (see
Example 216). In this case, the layout man simply sketches lines to
indicate where the copy is to go and writes the copy at the side of
the ad.

Since the copy that goes to the printer is frequently the layout that
is used to sell the merchant, the layout should be as neat as possible.
In addition, the ad should be well balanced, and attention should be
focused upon the part of the ad that the merchant wants featured. Often
the advertiser will supply the complete plate of the entire advertisement, which simplifies the school's operation.

The ad and page make-up. Arranging the ads in the paper is the
job of the advertising department. In general, there are three styles of
make-up used by school papers. The first is known as the pyramid
arrangement (see Example 217A and B). The pyramid is usually
built up to the right, and an effort is made to place the largest ads in
the lower right-hand corner, the size of the ads diminishing up and to
the left. The second type is the double-pyramid arrangement, sometimes called the well type as the space between the ads resembles a well
(see Example 218). The same principles of make-up apply here in
that the larger ads are placed on the bottom. The third type of arrangement, illustrated in Example 219, is really a modification of the second and is called the magazine type of make-up because it is frequently
used in magazines.

All of these styles may be used to advantage in the school paper,
depending upon the nature of the ads and the type of material to be run
on the rest of the page. Regardless of the type of make-up used, the
advertising make-up man should always try to arrange the ads to give

each advertiser the best location possible. Small ads should not be "buried" by being surrounded with larger ads. Large ads, however, surrounded by small ads still attract the attention of the reader. In general, advertisers wish their ads to be near reading matter and frequently specify page preference. For example, beauty shops prefer

EXAMPLE

216

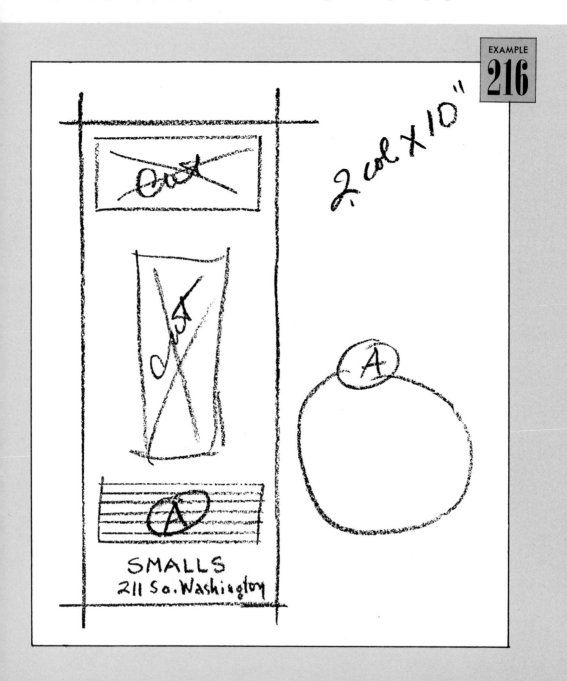

EXAMPLE

217

North Miami's Bogartmen Fight Coral Gables to 0-0 Standstill;
Battle of Gain-and-Lose Excites High School Crowd of 5,200

Gridders Grapple on Ground
Aerial Attempts Avail Little

By FRED FRANCIS

North Miami's Bogartmen battled through a defensive deadlock against Coral Gables on September 26, and gave the fifty-two hundred prep fans attending a 0-0 score.

Starting with a stiff defensive block by the Bogartmen, it was apparent that the teams were equal. Gables held the Pioneers just as steady as the latter had held them a few moments before, and it seemed to be indicative of the rest of that night's gridiron action.

Aerial attempts helped little throughout the game, most of it being a series of stifled ground moves, fumbles, more ground moves, and punts. Making first downs, stalemated moves, and then penalties, the ball never seemed to get where it was meant to go.

On one play in the first half, Gables threw a high pass right to Pioneer Half Dennis Webb. Following the interception with quick ground work, Sophomore Quarterback Rich Mehlich and Senior Halfback Jim Muthart picked up two first downs. But then a fumble occurred and the Cavaliers took over once more.

The half ended scoreless, with two fumbles and two penalties.

The second half was only a repeat of the first, starting off with more of an air game but ending like the first had. It was during the early pass plays that Mehlich had his hand slipped on and was ordered out of the game. His replacement caused a fumble and the regaining of the ball by Gables.

It moved down to North Miami's five and looked like paydirt for the Cavaliers. Then a Coral Gables ball carrier, hit hard by Pioneer Guard Jack Mitchell, fumbled the pigskin, and North Miami's Paul Gysan recovered.

Then followed a new series of penalties, incompleted passes, and a punt, which put the ball right at Gables goal line. Gaining only three yards in three downs, the Cavaliers were in a tight fourth down position. They pulled a sharp fake punt play, and with the aid of a penalty, got their first down.

There were eight seconds left of play and still no score, and Gables made a desperate triple-reverse pass play, almost making it successful, but it was no use. The game ended the same way it started.

an equal match. Neither team ever changed the lights on the scoreboard which said 0-0.

It's every man for himself as Pioneers and Cavaliers fight to catch pass.

NORMANDY T.V. and HI-FI SERVICE
A L L   M A K E
HI-FI - STEREO - T.V. - TAPE RECORDERS - RADIOS
12870 Biscayne Boulevard   Plaza 9-8181

New Tennis Team
To Strive For State

Racquets in hand, the 17 new members of the North Miami High tennis team are striving for a championship this year.

After three weeks of try-outs, Miss Veling, tennis coach, has selected a team composed of 17 boys and girls.

The members are: Nancy Howells, Girls' captain; Joe Beson, Boys' captain; Ronald Cromwell, Randy Andrews, Veronica Casnale, Lee Scott, Carol Ann Castell, Danny Stetson, Beth Adler, Nick O'Dawe, Lynn Chation, Judy Taylor, Becky Cline, Dave Marshall, Jinny Howells, Karen Schwartz, and Becky Kline. The new manager is Vicki Stark.

TONY'S BARBER SHOP
576 N. E. 125th St.

GO!
"PIONEERS"

Compliments of

SONKEN-GALAMBA CORP.

A

North Miami Industry

REDDY...
willing and able

to power all your household appliances—especially that record player on the next party.

FLORIDA POWER & LIGHT COMPANY
Helping Build Florida

Custom Tailoring

SLACKS TO YOUR
ORDER $19.50 UP

Complete

Formal

Rentals

ONE-DAY SERVICE

DAVID CAMERUCCI

891 N. E. 125TH STREET

PL 1-0320

Alterations - Reweaving

before or
after the
game

for the tastiest treat in town!

TRY THE "ALL AMERICAN"

Before or after the ball game . . . or for a tasty snack anytime . . . bring your date to McDonald's. Find out for yourself just *how good* a 15¢ Hamburger can be. McDonald's Hamburgers are made of 100% pure beef, government inspected and ground fresh daily. They're served piping hot and delicious on a toasted bun. Try 'em today . . . and remember, at McDonald's you get fast, cheerful, courteous service . . . plenty of parking . . . no car hops . . . no tipping . . . the tastiest food in town at extra thrifty prices.

You get a delicious, 100% Pure Beef Hamburger, government inspected and ground fresh daily, crisp, golden-brown French Fries served piping hot, plus a rich Triple-Thick Shake . . .

ALL THREE FOR ONLY 47c
For a party of four, only $1.88

the drive-in with the arches

McDonald's

13750 BISCAYNE BOULEVARD

Suits To Replace Tanks

April, 1961

Pioneer
North Miami High School
Miami, Florida

RAISE YOUR GRADES!
Expert individual home tutoring by
large staff of licensed teachers.
All Subjects.   Reasonable Rates.
Tutoring Service of NY
Call after 3 P.M.   PL 1-4358

SPACE AGE CAREERS   2½ YEAR PROGRAMS IN AVIATION

AEROSPACE ELECTRONICS
MISSILE & AIRCRAFT DESIGN • AIRLINE MAINTENANCE

FREE CATALOG

ACADEMY of AERONAUTICS
LA GUARDIA AIRPORT
22 AVE. & 86 ST.
JACKSON HEIGHTS
N.Y.C. HA 9-6600

in Brooklyn

IBM

KEY PUNCH, SORTER, TABS, COLLATOR & REPRODUCER, COMPARATOR & WIRING

SECRETARIAL

ADELPHI EXECUTIVES SCHOOL
1712 Kings Highway • Dl 6-7200
1588 Flatbush Ave. N. B'lyn College

Put this under
your Easter Bonnet!

There's a wonderful job opportunity awaiting you—and your friends—at Metropolitan Life after graduation. Pay us a visit during your Easter vacation.

Good starting salaries—regular increases—rapid promotions.

Life Insurance, Disability, Hospital, Surgical and Major Medical Expense benefits.

Appetizing luncheon as guest of the Company—without charge.

Cash awards for suggestions.

Liberal vacations and holidays.

Well-equipped medical service.

Training classes during office hours—to help you prepare for a better job.

A modern, well-stocked library —no charge to employees.

Fun in many social, athletic, hobby and recreational groups in the gymnasium.

Ideal working conditions.

It's fun to work with your friends.

METROPOLITAN LIFE INSURANCE COMPANY
Madison Avenue and 23rd St., New York 10, N.Y.

IN NEW YORK CITY • LONG ISLAND UNIVERSITY
NEW FACILITIES NOW PERMIT ADDITIONAL ENROLLMENT

The Lane Reporter
Franklin K. Lane High School
Brooklyn, New York

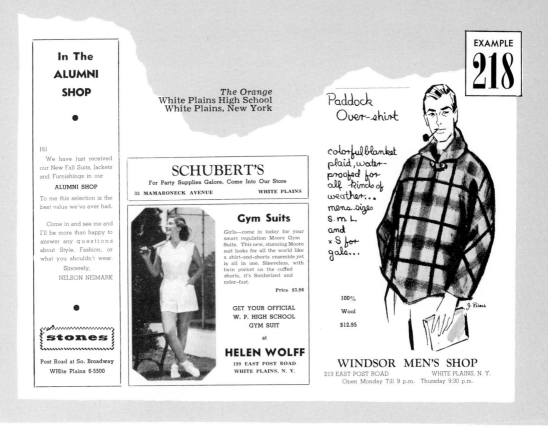

EXAMPLE 218

In The
ALUMNI SHOP

•

Hi!

We have just received
our New Fall Suits, Jackets
and Furnishings in our
ALUMNI SHOP

To me this selection is the
best value we've ever had.

Come in and see me and
I'll be more than happy to
answer any questions
about Style, Fashion, or
what you shouldn't wear.

Sincerely,
NELSON NEIMARK

•

stones

Post Road at So. Broadway
WHite Plains 6-5500

The Orange
White Plains High School
White Plains, New York

SCHUBERT'S
For Party Supplies Galore, Come Into Our Store
35 MAMARONECK AVENUE   WHITE PLAINS

Gym Suits

Girls—come in today for your
smart regulation Moore Gym
Suits. This new, stunning Moore
suit looks for all the world like
a shirt-and-shorts ensemble yet
is all in one. Sleeveless, with
twin pocket on the cuffed
shorts, it's Sanforized and
color-fast.

Price $3.98

GET YOUR OFFICIAL
W. P. HIGH SCHOOL
GYM SUIT
at

HELEN WOLFF
199 EAST POST ROAD
WHITE PLAINS, N. Y.

Paddock
Over-shirt

colorful blanket
plaid, water-
proofed for
all kinds of
weather...
mens sizes
S. m. L.
and
x S for
gals...

100%
Wool
$12.95

WINDSOR MEN'S SHOP
213 EAST POST ROAD   WHITE PLAINS, N. Y.
Open Monday Till 9 p.m. Thursday 9:30 p.m.

that their ads be located on pages that carry fashion columns or other
news that appeals to the female reader. While the school paper cannot
always satisfy every advertiser, it should go as far as possible to meet
these demands. It is natural to give preference to the larger advertisers
and those who advertise regularly.

Ad copy envelopes. Frequently advertising copy is lost or misplaced unless some definite system is provided for its care. The ad
copy envelope shown in Example 214 has been very valuable to
one paper. Prepared copy is recorded on this envelope and placed
inside. When copy goes to the printer, the whole envelope is sent.
When proof is read, the composed ads may be checked against the
record on the envelope. A device such as this is extremely helpful,
especially when ads are set up in a school print shop.

385

EXAMPLE
219

SCHOOL SPIRIT MAKE-UP SHEET

PAGE   ISSUE NO.   ISSUE DATE

PAGE EDITOR   O.K. BY ADVISER

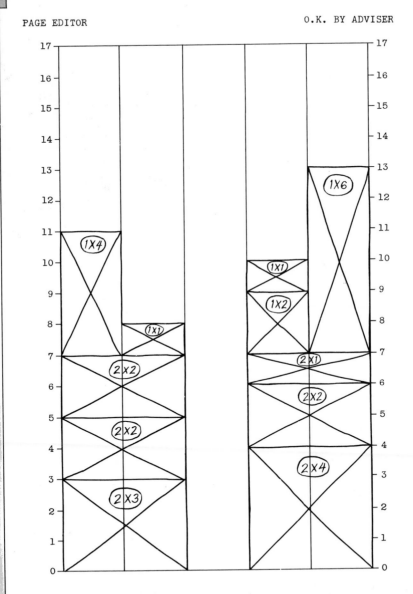

Size of ads. School papers commonly carry good-sized ads, that is, up to ten or fifteen column-inches. These normally use cuts and consequently add interest to the page. In some school papers, however, there is an abundance of small ads, of one to three column-inches. They are little more than notices that these firms exist. If there are enough of them to bring in noticeable revenue, they leave the impression in arrangement of small blocks stacked one upon the other. To the merchant such an ad often means little more than a donation to the school. Two things can be done to alleviate the situation:

1. The paper should provide more than four pages, if possible. Many small ads on a seven- or eight-column page undermines an attractive make-up. A six-page, five-column paper, with approximately the same number of column-inches as the four-page, seven-column paper, provides more pages on which to distribute the ads rather than two.

2. The advertising manager of the paper might encourage the firm to run larger ads less frequently, for instance, a six-inch ad every three weeks instead of a two-inch ad weekly.

The small ad should not be discouraged, however. Good business dictates a place for advertising of all sizes. Many four-page papers carry ads in three pages, and a few have even tried first-page ads.

The ad dummy. The advertising department must prepare an ad dummy for the page make-up man and the printer. This may be done in two different ways: either actual proofs may be pasted on the sheet, or a dummy may be plotted in a fashion similar to Example 216, except that the names of the advertisers are written in the respective spaces. Usually the advertising department prepares its dummy first, and then turns it over to the page editor, who in turn pastes up his part of the page dummy. The exact routine through which the dummy passes will of course differ for each different staff.

Proofreading the ads. Proofreading the ads is just as important as proofreading straight copy. In general, all ads should be proofread twice. After the ad has been composed in the print shop, it should be proofed and read. After the entire page has been made up, a proof should also be pulled. This should receive the O.K. of the page editor as well as the person in charge of advertising make-up. Standard proof-reading marks should be used in advertising as well as copy.

Shoppers' columns. The shoppers' column devoted to a description of merchandise which may be obtained at the various places of business that regularly advertise in the paper is prominent in many school papers (see Example 220). Usually conducted as a service to the advertiser, such columns are rarely charged for. The column may be devoted to either a single firm each week or to a number of firms. The success of such a column depends upon its readability; it has much in common with the personals column.

CAMPUS CORNER

S & Q STYLE
CENTER

by Carroll Pearson

EXAMPLE
220

● **Seven more** months of school left, my friends. Does anyone know how many days and hours left? From the looks of our report cards next week some of us will probably wish time were shorter. . . . Did you know that we have several best-dressed boys in **FSHS?** Or at least we must have because look at all the boys who buy their clothes at the **S & Q. ERNIE SMITHSON,** for one. He bought a jacket and some shirts just recently. . . . I know that we have several art enthusiasts in school, but how many of you have painted sailboats on your bathroom walls? **BARBARA KETCHUM, FSHS** senior, did. She also painted pictures on her bedroom wall. . . . Two of the many boys who shopped at the **S & Q** in the past few weeks are **BARRY HON,** who bought some shirts and socks, and **PRINCE WILMON,** who bought a jacket. . . . When **BUDDY SPRUELL'S** parents were mentioned, **MRS. HELEN McCARTY** exclaimed, "Parents? Why, I thought he came out of a cracker-jack box!" . . . Boys, **S & Q** has just received some new **REVERE COTTON KNIT** shirts. They can be worn three different ways, collars partly open, completely open, and turtle neck. In tan, gray, and navy, the shirt costs only $4.95.

The Grizzly
Ft. Smith High School
Ft. Smith, Arkansas

Similar in nature but in the "paid space" category is the ad in which the firm purchases the space but one or more staff members provide the copy styled in a personal fashion (see Examples 221 and 222).

Special pages and special issues. Throughout the year the alert advertising staff will find opportunities for special ads, special issues,

388

EXAMPLE
221

Memories?

Below is a review of records which have made the Big "T", plus records which may bring back memories.

TOP SELLERS ARE RISING

Coming up fast to the Big "T" is Jimmy Elledges "Funny How Time Slips Away" and Steve Berry's "The Story of the Ring."

Taking a glance at the top selling albums of the day you'd find Elvis Presley's "Blue Hawaii" at the top followed by Harry Belafonte's "Jump Up Calypso". On the light side you'd find Bob Newhart's "Behind the Button Down Mind" a real laugh getter.

Oldies But Goodies

"Oldies but Goodies" is the name given to records that never die, but live on in the memories of teens who danced and sang to these records. Among the top of the "Oldies but Goodies" are "Tonight, Tonight" by the Mellow-Kings, "In the Still of the Night" by the Five Satins, "Twilight Time" by the Platters, and "Your Tender Lips" by the Clovers. Just for laughs try to remember some of the parties you went to and who you were going out with when these songs were popular.

Big Ten Records

This is the Jordan High "Big Ten" survey. Jordan's independent and most dependable compilation of record popularity. Here are the "Big Ten" sounds around Jordan High.

1) Big Bad John   Jimmy Dean--Columbia
2) Sometime   Gene Thomas--U.A.
3) Runaround Sue   Dion--Laurie
4) Goodbye Cruel World   James Darren--Col Pix
5) Please Mr. Postman   The Marvelettes--Tamla
6) It Will Stand   The Showman--Minit
7) Bristol Stomp   The Dovells--Parkway
8) Fool No. 1   Brenda Lee--Decca
9) Moon River   Henry Mancini--RCA Victor
10) Let's Go Trippin'   Dick Dale--Deltone

Without A Photography Teacher, Could The School Paper Come Out?

All of the teachers at Jordan are essential. One of the most essential ones, however, is Mr. Mellencamp. Without his advice and supervision the Cat's Purr wouldn't have any pictures to add color and interest to its pages.

Mr. Mellencamp is the photography advisor for the Jordan paper. He teaches five periods of photography each day and has been at Jordan for six years. Jordan is the only school at which he has taught.

Columbus, Indiana, was Mr. Mellencamp's birthplace. He went to college for five years and has a Bachelor of Arts degree. He majored in sociology. Before becoming a teacher, Mr. Mellencamp

was a professional photographer.

Every picture in the Cat's Purr has a lot of work behind it and a lot of people who do the work as well. Each picture starts with a picture assignment. This is a special blank filled out by the person who edits the page on which the picture will appear.

KEEP JORDAN'S CAMPUS CLEAN

Are you a T.D. (trash dropper)? There seems to be a large number of Trash Droppers around the Jordan campus.

Dirty grounds have been a big problem at Jordan. For this reason, nutrition has been taken away from Jordan's student body until the grounds are cleaned up and kept clean.

Dirty grounds is not the only thing that will keep Jordan from having nutrition. Not only are there T.D.'s around campus, but there are fire bugs as well. These little bugs are constantly lighting fires in the trash cans.

The trash can fires cost money. It costs money to buy new trash cans or paint old ones. It also costs the school about $50.00 each day Jordan doesn't have nutrition.

Keeping the grounds clean and stopping the trash-can fires can give the student body many things. First, if the campus is kept fairly clean, Jordan will continue to have nutrition. Second, if the grounds are exceptionally clean, school will be dismissed at 3 on Friday.

All Jordan students are urged to make an individual effort to see that all trash goes in the trash cans and no more fires are started.

Nutrition means more money for Jordan. More money for Jordan means more money for the student body. This money provides for dances, assemblies, and athletic equipment. So be sure not to be a T.D. or a firebug.

BEING DEPENDABLE IS VERY IMPORTANT

There are many traits that are admirable in people, and dependability is certainly one of them.

Being dependable will help you now, while in high school, and later on in life when you're out on your own.

It can help you now by giving you respect a student wants from teachers. It can also help gain the things in life each person surely wants, and it can give responsibility to those who earn it.

IMPORTANCE OF COLLEGE

College and the teen-ager is always a good subject. Why should teen-agers go to college?

First and foremost in the specialized age in which we live a college education is almost a necessity.

As the saying goes, "Behind every successful man you will find an intelligent woman." Therefore, it is necessary for girls as well as boys to have the background of an education.

If you have a college education it will not only help you to get a better job but will also give you more self confidence in your social life.

Jarman Shoes

THEY ARE HERE

See the new

"TITAN"

and the new

"POLARIS"

at

Bunday - Fox SHOES

4442 Atlantic Avenue
Long Beach
Phone Ga. 35945

REPLIES ON 25 HR. DAY

Recently, teachers and students on the Jordan Campus were asked the question. "If you had one day that consisted of 25 hours, what would you do during that extra hour?" Here are some of their replies.

MRS. KRAMER - go to the mountains
MR. P. DAVIS - read the Bible
MR. DIBS - relax
MR. EDMUNDS - sleep
BOB ASCH - go surfing
ANN CAMFIELD - go to Northridge
RON CHOUINARD - go to the Canteen
EUGENE WISE - play football
KEN CRUMP - have fun

RODGER ELLIOT - go out with Sue
JOHN SUTTIE - go surfing
JACK TYLER - laugh
KATHY VAUGHN - sleep
DAN WASSON - go sailing
LARRY STREETZ - read a magazine
SUE WILLIAMS - do Miss Druschel's homework with Sandy Bernard
MYRNA WILLISTON - go surfing

Don't Make Fun of Others

The words "rank" and "chop" are widely misused. The real meaning for the word "rank" is; a social division or class; stratum of society; a high position in society; high degree. Teens today are partly right. They use the word "rank" to specify a social division or class, a stratum of society. But the stratum of the teens are speaking of is the so-called lower class. Why are they thought of as the lower class? Because maybe they don't dress quite as well as you and your friends. Or maybe they like to study?Or is it because they don't talk exactly as you do?

According to the Webster's New World Dictionary, the definition of the word 'chop' is; to cut into small bits; to cut by blows with an ax or other sharp instrument. That's just what you do to someone's morale when you 'chop' someone. But the sharp instrument you use isn't an ax; instead you use your tounge.

Have you ever been constantly ridiculed? Probably not. It's a fact that everyone wants people to like him. Have you ever put yourself in the position of the person being ranked or 'chopped? If you have, I'm sure you would look upon people who do these things in real disgust.

PRIZE WINNER

in the sportswear department. Bob Dunbar, Jordan's Young Careerist, models the casual look in sportswear from our Varsity Shop, 125 Pine Avenue. His shirt, by Eagle, is in batiste oxford cloth, and over it he wears a classic shetland sweater with crew neck by Lord Jeff. The pants, of course, are A - 1 tapers, in cotton twill. All this goes to prove that for the best looking clothes in town, for the man about town, it's the Varsity Shop.

Buffums VARSITY SHOP

Mondays and Fridays, 9:30 a.m. to 9 p.m. Other days, 9:30 to 5:30

AMERICAN GYM
Courses 1¢ Up
1117 E. ARTESIA

Hippodrome Skating Rink

628 Alamitos Ave.   He. 58233

Use student activity card plus 50 cents for admission on Friday From 7:30 - 10:30 P.M.

Cat's Purr
David Starr Jordan High School
Long Beach, California

EXAMPLE

222

Karen Johnson, Ken Hood, Shirley Bottorff (front row), Betty Villiers, Connie Burchett, Cheryl Lockhart, and Joy Brundige (back row) help spark students and friends to ignite the team to win, just as students after the game hail KING'S FINE FOODS in Bethany for the best food inside or out. It's now enlarged to serve you better!

1515   NORTH   COTNER

Northeastern
Northeast High School
Lincoln, Nebraska

or special pages. Christmas, Thanksgiving, commencement, and Easter all offer the possibility of special campaigns. In addition, such events as the opening of a new neighborhood theater or store provide the opportunity for large cooperative ads.

Just as a paper can make news, so can it make advertising. One paper published a special edition and distributed it free at a sectional basketball tournament. Advertising was secured from restaurants and other establishments that ordinarily were not considered regular prospects. Though effective in securing added income, special editions or pages should not appear too often, or readers and merchants may tire of them.

Some advertising is seasonal, and securing such business calls for staff alertness. For instance, firms seeking to employ high school graduates will want to advertise just before graduation. Some firms will want space in the school paper over a period of time to establish goodwill, even though actual employment comes after graduation.

390

CHAPTER LABORATORY

1. Prepare a list of advertising positions on your school paper, and analyze them. Are they sufficient?
2. Is the advertising rate schedule in your school realistic? Could more revenue be derived through a rise in rates, or would ads lost offset it? Discuss in class.
3. Have a staff representative explain the advertising contract used by your school paper before the class. Is it a good contract?
4. Prepare a list of the types of business firms that could profit by advertising in your paper, and prepare a list of prospects who have not advertised in the paper this year. Make up a master list as a class project.
5. Select one of these prospects, and, during class, outline plans for approaching the firm. Discuss your plans with the class and with the teacher.
6. Devise an ad for this firm and prepare a layout.
7. After familiarizing yourself with your paper's rates, contract, and other advertising procedures, approach the firm (with the layout) to sell an ad for your paper.
8. In class, discuss the quality of the ads carried by your school paper. Compare with good standards of make-up and with advertising in other school papers and the daily press. Suggest improvements.
9. Through one member of the class, make arrangements for an advertising representative from a local daily paper to discuss newspaper advertising before the class.
10. Secure copies of other school papers in your city, and make a list of their advertisers that might be prospects for your paper. Present the assembled list to the advertising department.
11. From a list of the firms now advertising in your school paper, select those that could profit by larger advertisements. Plan a sales approach to effect this.

24 NEWSPAPER CIRCULATION

If the school newspaper is worth publishing, it is worth putting into the hands of the reader. This may be accomplished only through energetic circulation and effective distribution. Both require the attention of especially designated staff members sufficiently interested to go after the necessary results.

SELLING THE PAPER

If approximately 50 per cent of the revenue of the average paper comes from the sale of advertising space, it follows that practically all of the balance must come from the readers. Both the number of subscribers and the amount of money received from the sale are indicated by the significant term *circulation*.

The activity fee. The student activity fee is the simplest of all the sales systems, a plan in which the student buys all of his activities in one package. Behind this general activities fund is a well-planned budget, each activity being supported by its predetermined share of the total. The New York City schools call this the GO—General Organization.

The idea of the combined student fee came to the high schools from the college campus. Unlike the college system, in which the amount may be automatically added into the student's registration fee, the public high school cannot require payment. The appeal must be made through a subscription drive.

The most popular way of budgeting the student fund is to assign each of the participants (football, newspaper, senior play, etc.) a percentage in advance. It is then simple to make the eventual distribution of funds.

The subsidy. In a few instances a school newspaper is subsidized by the school district. An example is *The Broadcaster,* Bloom Township High School, Chicago Heights, Illinois, which secures half its support from the school district. This subsidy does not lessen *The Broadcaster's* efforts to secure advertising revenue, for the other half of its support comes from that source. The paper is given to all students and faculty.

The administration's point is that only a portion of the student body is able to subscribe to the paper. Furthermore, the school board looks upon the paper as an excellent public relations medium, the free distribution providing maximum coverage. The fine quality of this newspaper shows that subsidy need not deter the students' initiative and enterprise.

The Holmespun, Holmes High School, Covington, Kentucky, a five-column, four-page paper, is issued fifteen times a year on a budget of $4225. Revenue is derived from the Board of Education, $2000; advertising, $815; subscriptions, $945; and the remainder from the sale of extra copies of pictures appearing in the paper and the yearbook.

The subscription drive. The general fund is the most popular plan of financing school papers, but it is also common for school newspapers to solicit subscriptions independently. Unless the school paper has a source of income permitting free distribution, some sort of subscription drive or campaign is necessary if the publication is to succeed. Al-

393

though some school papers exist on the sale of single copies, little financial planning is possible unless the staff has a fairly definite estimate of its income from the sale of papers. Campaigns may be staged annually or semiannually. The latter may be preferable because a larger subscription price can be collected twice a year than could be collected in one lump sum. The subscription plan gives the staff a much sounder basis for planning than the single-sales plan.

"High-pressure" tactics. Staff members should learn early that "high-pressure" sales tactics can never substitute for consumer enthusiasm. Forced buying may result in increased income for one or two terms, but the results are usually not permanent and are often detrimental. If the paper is not really wanted, forced subscriptions will result in dropped subscriptions when collections roll around. With regard to the subscription campaign, the function of the circulation department is to make it convenient for all to subscribe. Of course, the campaign may well include an educational program to acquaint newcomers to the school with the nature and merits of the publication.

The campaign assembly program. The campaign assembly program is one of the most effective methods of inaugurating the subscription drive. The possibilities of this kind of promotion are limited only by the ingenuity of those who plan it. Its nature may range from a general consideration of the merits of the paper to a preview of the coming issues. With careful planning, the campaign assembly may help improve the students' attitude toward the paper. One-act plays with the newspaper office as a setting might be effective for this assembly.

At times, competition among homerooms or classes is used as an incentive in a subscription drive. The well-established paper, however, can make its point by a more moderate approach. For instance, the *Washington Scroll* of Milwaukee solicits directly through the homerooms on the positive note that the students want to buy the paper. For the purpose, the *Scroll* provides a simple system of a combined subscription and collection envelope, backed by an explicit list of directions for the homeroom teacher (see Example 223).

394

EXAMPLE
223

		Cashier			

THE WASHINGTON SCROLL

Name ....
       LAST   PRINT   FIRST

   ROOM................ROW.....................SEAT...............

☐   I enclose $.   for (1) Semester

☐   I enclose $.   and agree to pay the balance

   by........**MAR 17**........

☐   I wish to subscribe without a down payment

   and agree to pay the balance by....**MAR 17**....

A Scroll in Every Student's Home

(side column headings: Scroll Partial Payments — Amt. Due — Amt. Pd. — Date)

INSTRUCTIONS TO HOMEROOM TEACHERS

1. Have all students *letter* their names, last name first.
2. Indicate *HOMEROOM — ROW — SEAT*.
3. Have those students subscribing and paying in full at this time, place an "X" in the first square, place their money in the envelope and mark the amount enclosed on the front of the envelope. If the student does not have the correct change, refunds will be made after school tonight in Room 309.
4. Have those students subscribing and making a PARTIAL PAYMENT place an "X" in the second square.
5. Have those students subscribing without a down-payment place an "X" in the third square.
6. If the student is not subscribing, have him write "Not Subscribing" in the upper margin.
7. Payments may be made in the *Scroll* office, Room 309, daily from 8:10 to 8:25 A.M. All payments are due by. . . .

The Washington Scroll
Washington High School
Milwaukee, Wisconsin

MAKING COLLECTIONS AND DELIVERIES

Frequency and method of collection. The circulation department must decide how and when collections will be made, according to local conditions. Some schools accept subscriptions only on a cash basis, thus giving the paper only to those students who are able to make the payment in one lump sum. This is the easiest and least troublesome method. However, most school-paper staffs will find, particularly if they have a higher subscription fee, that a material increase in the number of subscriptions will result if a time or installment method of payment is worked out.

The need for an adequate plan. If the installment method is used, the system must make it convenient to remove the names of those individuals who do not fulfill their obligations from the delivery lists. Laxity in this matter lessens respect for the publication.

Unfortunately there is no one best plan. Two quite different collection and distribution methods are reported here. They are widely different in nature, yet each functions well in the school in which it was developed.

PLAN A*

Job Description for the Positions of Circulation Manager and Assistant Circulation Manager

1. To receive on each collection day money from each of the fifteen captains, count it, record the amount in cash book, investigate any discrepancies, make up the deposit, and take it to the safe in the office.

†2. To check captains' stamp books (count stamps and see if equivalent in money has been turned in) and at least once a month thereafter; notify each captain regarding the status of his book and check it with him if this seems desirable.

3. To check wall cards [see Example 224] from each homeroom on the date of each issue and see if numbers of subscribers have been recorded correctly. Withdrawn students are to be marked off the card.

4. To add names of withdrawn students to the mailing list and to see that copies due them are mailed.

†5. To record on the summary card with every issue the number of copies of each issue ordered by each homeroom, and to total

*The Jeffersonian, Thomas Jefferson High School, Richmond, Virginia.
†Indicates duties performed by the circulation manager. The other duties are delegated to the assistant or performed jointly.

396

JEFFERSONIAN SUBSCRIBERS

EXAMPLE
224

ROOM NO._____   Lieutenant_____

NAME Last Names ONLY. PRINT—using ink.	NUMBER AND DATE OF ISSUES							NAME Last Names ONLY. PRINT—using ink.	NUMBER AND DATE OF ISSUES						
	1	2	3	4	5	6	7		1	2	3	4	5	6	7
TOTAL															

Captain_____ Captain's H.R._____

these so that additional copies may be ordered from the printer if necessary.

6. To keep a record of the number of copies of each issue sold by each captain.

†7. To secure from the office the enrollment of each homeroom on the date of each issue and to compare this with the number of subscriptions sold in that room and in this way determine whether the room merits a quota or 100 per cent card.

†8. To see that each room receives the proper quota or 100 per cent card after each issue.

†9. To present 100 per-cent-for-the-term cards and to award $1.00 prizes for the 100 per-cent-for-the-term subscriptions secured by date of first issue.

10. To prepare these 100 per-cent-for-the-term banners, i.e., cut out numbers and paste them in the proper place for the date. To write lieutenant's name and homeroom number on back.

11. To prepare collection envelopes [see Example 224] for the captains each week, i.e., record captain's name, homeroom number, and collection dates.

12. To count out the number of copies ordered by each homeroom, to put this number and the homeroom number on the top copy.
†13. To load truck and distribute papers to homeroom.
14. To fold 25 copies of each issue for the file and to prepare a few copies for each captain to sell as "extras" on the Monday following date of issue.
15. To prepare these materials for use by captains and lieutenants at the beginning of the term:

    A. 15 stamp books—Check to see that each has proper number of stamps, number pages, and fill in the collection dates and homerooms. Put name and homeroom number of captain on front, also numbers of 2 rooms from which he is to collect.

    B. 58 wall cards—Fill in dates of publication, name and homeroom numbers of captains and lieutenants.

16. To revise, if necessary, mimeographed instructions for captains and lieutenants.
†17. To distribute these in the meeting of each group (captains and lieutenants) called at the beginning of the term and to explain them.
†18. To substitute for a captain whenever necessary and to investigate his own duties.
†19. To give out stamp books and make announcements to captains at the beginning of homeroom period each collection day.
†20. To prepare a list of prospective graduates in each 4H homeroom and ask lieutenants in these rooms to solicit mail subscriptions from these students and turn in his report to the staff room by a designated time.
21. To notify by post card those whose subscriptions have expired and to solicit renewals.
22. To address, check, and stamp wrappers for regular subscribers and those receiving complimentary copies.
23. To fold, wrap, and mail copies.
24. To type for each mail subscriber a card bearing his name and address and the issues he is to receive.

How the plan works. The circulation staff includes the circulation manager, his assistant, 15 captains, and 58 lieutenants, who solicit subscriptions, collect money, and distribute the paper in their respective homerooms. The money collected is passed from lieutenant to captain and on to the circulation manager in collection envelopes (Example 225). Gummed stamps, issued to the captains, who pass them

398

EXAMPLE

225

The Jeffersonian

THOMAS JEFFERSON HIGH SCHOOL
RICHMOND, VIRGINIA

Captain ....

Home Room ....

DATE	AMOUNT

This Envelope Must Be Turned In

to the Staff Room Each Collection Day

on to the lieutenants, are then pasted in the appropriate spaces on the subscription card in each homeroom (Example 224).

PLAN B

Satisfactory tag method. Because they are somewhat inflexible, distribution lists are sometimes considered cumbersome and inadequate. Lists of names that must be checked and rechecked before each issue of the paper is delivered require unnecessary expenditures of time and energy; in addition, such lists are extremely difficult to manipulate without errors. The staff of one paper has overcome this obstacle through the use of delivery tags (see Example 226).

EXAMPLE

226

	SCHOOL SPIRIT SUBSCRIPTION	Locker No.

Dist.

Name ....

Home Room .... Adviser.......................................

6th Period Class..; ....

Subject   Room

○   Check here if Committee of One ☐

8	7	6	5	4	3	2	1	C

Col.

The tag is used as the original subscription card and is filled out by the subscriber at the time of the campaign. Thereafter, it serves as a collection tag and as a delivery tag. It thus serves three purposes. For the benefit of installment subscribers, collectors representing the paper call on each homeroom twice each week with the appropriate tags strung on a flexible chain key ring. If the subscriber pays his installment, the sum is indicated in the square for the particular week; if he does not pay or is absent, an "X" is recorded in the same square. If the subscriber pays the full subscription price, a hole is punched in the square at the lower right corner by the locker number. This removes all paid-up members from the homeroom lists, thus reducing the number of cards each collector has on his ring.

Making the distribution. Of the many distribution methods used, one of the most satisfactory is the individual locker method for schools in which each student is supplied with a hall locker bearing a number. Most standard lockers have "vents" into which the paper can be inserted if it is carefully folded. This makes it completely unnecessary to open the lockers and assures complete distribution. The locker system is particularly effective when used in combination with the tag system. After the second collection of the week, the members of the circulation staff have only to rearrange their tags to correspond to the numbering of the various lockers, group them into moderate-sized routes, place them again on flexible rings, and make their rounds. Two students, one holding the ring and calling the locker numbers and the other inserting the papers, can easily distribute two hundred papers in a forty-minute period.

400

The complaint desk. No distribution system is stronger than the students who operate it. No matter how carefully the system is developed, there will always be a small number of students who do not receive their papers. The circulation department must arrange to take care of these complaints. If the subscriber knows where to go to make his complaint, when the occasional slip occurs, and if he is treated in a courteous manner by the staff members who meet him there, he will go away still a booster for the paper.

On the days when the paper is distributed, certain staff members designated in advance should remain in the newsroom after school to receive complaints. The use of a printed form similar to Example 227 will make it possible to keep a record of complaints. The circulation manager can then make an intelligent effort to improve the service. If the installment-payment method is used, there will usually be a number of students who were absent when collections were made or who for some other reason did not pay and who, consequently, did not receive their papers. To take care of these customers, the staff members delegated to operate the complaint desk should also be provided with small envelopes similar to Example 228. If these are used, no bookkeeping will be necessary at the time. Instead, the staff member may accept the payment, record the necessary information on the envelope, and turn it over to the cashier as soon as possible. This is the type of service that students appreciate.

COMPLAINT CARD

Name ....

Home Room .... Locker No. ....

No. Times Missed .... Amount Paid ....

Paper Torn .... ☐

Paper Ragged .... ☐

Paper Missing .... ☐

Receiver ....

EXAMPLE
227

401

EXAMPLE

228

THE SCHOOL SPIRIT

Home Room Deposit Envelope

(For your convenience in depositing)

Adviser..H. R. ....

Amount Enclosed ....,.....for......... Subscriptions

Date.............................Checked ....

....

Newsroom leaks. If students are able to get a paper without cost in the newsroom after school, they will soon discover there is no point in subscribing, and subscription lists will dwindle. The same is true when staff members make an effort to "take care of" their friends. The student body as a whole will not think any more of the paper than do staff members themselves.

If the paper is worth the price asked of the general student, it deserves a paid-up subscription from the staff member. Staff members have no right to receive their papers free just because of their position. The alert circulation manager will "sell" all staff members before he sends them out to solicit subscriptions from others. Unpaid-for copies will consist only of those on the exchange list and those used in the day-to-day activity of the staff.

Where and when. The most popular time and place for delivery of the school paper seems to be Friday during the first period homeroom or registry room. Second in popularity is the last period of the day, usually in the classrooms. In Spokane, Washington, however, the *Lewis and Clark Journal* is delivered on Wednesday morning. The papers are picked up in the front hallway from the circulation manager by representatives of the homerooms. Each presents an identity card enabling him to collect the papers.

Some papers, such as the *North Central News,* also of Spokane, have a mailbox for each homeroom in the newspaper office. The homeroom number and the list of students eligible for papers are marked on each box. The pickup is on Friday morning, the staff having stuffed the boxes the night before.

MAIL SUBSCRIPTIONS

A fertile field. There is a fertile field of possible subscribers who may be served by mail. Alumni, next year's freshmen, and interested patrons are among those who may be induced to subscribe by an adequate campaign. As with in-school subscriptions, the customer must be given service. If papers are allowed to remain in the newsroom two or three days before they are mailed, an unfavorable attitude will develop toward the publication and a reduction in income ensue. Whoever is delegated to oversee this job should no more think of postponing it than would the editorial department think of getting the paper out a day late.

Recording the mail subscription. Adequate methods of recording the names and addresses of mail subscribers are necessary to insure delivery. A card similar to the one in Example 229 should be used. The main part of the card should be 3 by 5 inches to fit a standard filing box and should be punched so that a rod will fit through, as with library cards, to prevent the loss of cards. The stub serves as the customer's receipt given at the time of payment.

The exchange list. The exchange list should also be handled by the mailing department. A card such as the one in Example 230, similar to the mail subscription card but of a different color, should be used. The two colors make it possible to discard those that are to be used only throughout the year or term and to retain those of a permanent nature such as exchanges.

The School Spirit Mail Subscription

Name ....

Address ....

City and State ....

Subscription for .... first; .... Second Semester, 19 .... -19 ....

Rates: 60 cents per semester; two semesters, $1.10

Received ....

The School Spirit 19 .... -19 ....

Mail Subscription for ....
.... first, ... second semester ....

Change of address must be made two weeks in advance (give old address) to School Spirit Mailing Head, Bosse High School, Evansville 14, Indiana.

EXAMPLE
229

```
Name  . . . . . . . . . . . . . . . . . . . . . . . . . . . . . . . . . . . . . . . . . . . . . . . .

Address . . . . . . . . . . . . . . . . . . . . . . . . . . . . . . . . . . . . . . . . . . . . . .

P.O.  . . . . . . . . . . . . . . . . . . . . . . . . . . . . . . . . . . . . . . . . . . . . . . .

Remarks:




                              ◯
```

MAILING COSTS

Third-class rates. Most school papers are mailed as third-class matter. This means that each paper sent costs two cents provided it weighs no more than two ounces. In the event that it does weigh more, the cost increases at the rate of a cent for each ounce or fraction thereof up to eight ounces.

Second-class rates. Postal authorities have made provision, however, for newspapers and similar publications to be mailed as second-class matter. Every staff should investigate the second-class rates to determine if there is an advantage to be gained. In the case of a paper that carries second-class privileges, there is a minimum fee of not less than one-eighth cent per copy.

Requirements for admission. The following directions, adapted from Part 132.22 of the *Postal Manual,* United States Post Office Department, explain the various qualifications necessary for entering a publication as second-class matter.

Except as otherwise provided by law, the conditions upon which a publication shall be admitted to the second class are as follows:
First, it must regularly be issued at stated intervals, as frequently as four times a year, and bear a date of issue, and be numbered consecutively.

404

Second, it must be issued from a known office of publication.

Third, it must be formed of printed paper sheets, without board, cloth, leather, or other substantial binding, such as distinguish printed books for preservation from periodical publications. *Provided,* that publications produced by the stencil, mimeograph, or hectograph process, or in imitation of typewriting, shall not be regarded as printed within the meaning of this clause.

Fourth, it must be originated and published for the dissemination of information of a public character, or devoted to literature, the sciences, arts, or some special industry, and have a legitimate list of subscribers. Nothing herein contained shall be so construed as to admit to the second-class rate regular publications designed primarily for advertising purposes, or for free circulation, or for circulation at nominal rates.

Procedure and cost. If staff members are reasonably certain that their publication meets the four conditions stated above, the first step in entering the publication as second-class matter is to secure a copy of Form 3501 from the local postmaster. After the form has been carefully filled out and sufficient evidence of a bona fide list of subscribers has been submitted, it should be sent together with a payment of twenty-five dollars to the local postmaster. In the event that the subscription list is in excess of 2,000 and not more than 5,000 the fee is fifty dollars. This fee will be retained by the post office if the application for entry is honored. If the publication is not accepted, half of the fee will be retained and half will be returned.

Advantages. In addition to the financial saving involved in entering a publication as second-class matter, the advantages are twofold: mail subscription rates may be reduced to the same level as other subscriptions, and a great amount of time spent in attaching stamps to each copy is saved. After a publication is entered as second-class matter, the postmaster will ask the staff to make a small postage deposit. Each week as the papers are sent in bundles to the post office, the postmaster will deduct the mailing cost from the balance and notify the staff of the amount deducted.

Addressing copies to be mailed. While some staffs will be fortunate enough to have a machine for the purpose of addressing, the majority will have to rely upon some other system. Typing names or addressing by hand is not satisfactory because of the large amount of time consumed and because of the opportunities for errors and omissions. A very satisfactory plan is that in which the names and addresses are printed on a narrow sheet of gummed paper and quickly cut and applied.

EXAMPLE
231

WEEKLY CIRCULATION DEPARTMENT REPORT

Issue number ....   Date.......................................

Deliveries Route No. 1....   ....

Deliveries Route No. 2....   ....

Deliveries Route No. 3....   ....

Deliveries Route No. 4....   ....

Miscellaneous Deliveries...   ....

Total Route Deliveries ....

Mail Subscribers ....

TOTAL PAID CIRCULATION..................... ....

Exchanges Mailed ....

For Use of Editorial Staff.......... ....

For Use of Business Staff........... ....

Other "Free" papers ....

TOTAL "NOT PAID" CIRCULATION............. ....

Papers on Hand ....

Papers Not Accounted for ....

TOTAL NUMBER OF PAPERS ORDERED PRINTED.... ....

Number of complaints this week: 1........ 2........ 3........ 4........

M........

Number of "drops" this week ....

Circulation Manager ....

Head Mailing Department ....

Business Manager ....

SUMMARY OF THE WEEK'S ACTIVITIES

As a department of the business division, the circulation staff is expected to report on its activities of the week to the whole group. In the staff meeting the business manager will probably call upon the circulation manager to speak for that department. A report form such as that in Example 231 is helpful; it includes total paid circulation, total free circulation, papers not accounted for, number of drops, and number of complaints. The weekly report should also include a summary of the group's special activities such as the mailing of special form letters or the zoning of the city for future circulation campaigns. Such reports will furnish the basis for discussion on how to improve the work of the circulation department and how to overcome staff difficulties.

CHAPTER LABORATORY

1. Find out all you can about how collections are handled in your school. How can the plan be improved?
2. Analyze the distribution system of your school paper, and suggest improvements if they are needed.
3. Make a further study of distribution details in your school to find out whether or not there are "leaks." Are any students obtaining the paper without payment? What do you recommend?
4. If students are not subscribing to the paper in sufficient numbers in your school, try to account for this lack and suggest improvements.
5. Make a study of mail subscriptions in your school. Is there a possibility of increasing the paper's income through a mail subscription drive?
6. How much is your paper spending on postage to distribute the paper each year? Would a second-class permit be economical? Could your paper meet the qualifications set up in the United States Postal Laws and Regulations?
7. If your school supports a student fund with a single activity fee, what portion of the "take" is allocated for the newspaper? What part of the paper's total revenue does this represent?
8. Compare your paper's sales record with other city or neighboring school publications, in both numbers and percentage of students subscribing. Each class member could collect the information from a different school.

PART FIVE

THE
SCHOOL PRESS
FAMILY

"We live under a government of men
—and morning newspapers."
—Wendell Phillips

25 PUBLISHING THE YEARBOOK

The newspaper holds no monopoly in the field of student journalism. It shares its attractions with two other publications, the yearbook and the magazine. In no way are they competitors, for their purposes are distinct and their demands upon the high school journalist entirely different.

THE DISTINCTION OF THE YEARBOOK

The yearbook (sometimes known as the annual) is ordinarily published by the senior class as a review of the year or as a history of the class. It stands as a memory book, a gratification of the moment, a reference for tomorrow. Its purpose establishes its nature—for the most part pictures carry the burden of the story, text material doing the rest. To get an over-all impression of the job to be done, a staff can do no better than to study a few successful yearbooks. The balance of pictures and words speaks for itself. There is always a place for originality and ingenuity in such a publication, but a yearbook without ample photography is not a yearbook.

410

There are some features in photographic treatment common among yearbooks. Seniors, for instance, are presented individually with larger photographs than those of the individual students in the other classes (if other classes are included). Faculty members are often included in individual photographs because of student interest. Space, costs, and the requirements of design and interest make the group photograph a necessity in most other treatments.

At one time it was considered desirable to close the book with a jokes section. This tradition has passed, for there is little distinction and nothing personal in such a section. It is much more important to preserve a face or a fact in a memory book than a joke that was old before the book left the press.

A record of the academic life of the school, the sports program, the social life of the school, and similar significant activities is the backbone of the publication. It requires ingenuity to present classroom activities effectively, but reader interest is its reward. Curriculum is a challenge to good editorship.

PLANNING THE YEARBOOK

The plan of the yearbook has one main purpose—to tell the story of the school year or senior class in a logical and interesting manner.

Tradition invites the staff to use last year's plan—to substitute new pictures and text in the old form. But last year's staff may have followed the same procedure last year, and on and on into the past. Every book issued should reflect the new year, in staff ingenuity as well as in student life.

Basic ingredients. Each yearbook usually has the following sections: a table of contents; a chapter on administration and faculty; a chapter on curriculum and classroom studies; sections on the senior class, underclasses, athletics and other extracurricular activities; advertising; and an index.

The big problem of planning is the sequence of these divisions within the publication. After the table of contents, sometimes forgotten, tradition dictates this order: administration, faculty, seniors, underclasses, sports, and other activities and organizations, advertising, and possibly the index. Within the past few years, however, new ideas have found their way into many yearbooks:

1. The curriculum and classroom programs have developed into an accepted section of the publication. Text and photographs feature honors, new offerings, work in the classroom and laboratory, and the intensified efforts of students in their studies.

2. Directories at the end of the book are now a part of the typical layout. Such features include a general index, an index to advertisers, an index to seniors, and an index to the faculty. The yearbook staff is also usually noted in this end-matter. In a few instances the senior directory includes the home addresses and telephone numbers of each student.

3. An introduction or orientation to the book or the school usually opens the yearbook. It is like a movie short, advertising a coming attraction. Usually eight to sixteen pages, it presents the theme of the book, covers high points of the year, or in some other way tempts the reader to go further.

4. There is a growing attempt to rearrange the contents of the book. The faculty section is often moved to the middle of the volume or is combined with classroom coverage in a section that treats curriculum as well as teachers. At times the underclasses come before the seniors, but naturally in less display.

Balance in content. Since the yearbook is a record, it stresses photographs but depends upon text for continuity and understanding. Balance in emphasis is important. Emphasis should shift from year to year, reflecting the significance of the year's events. For example, an important championship should be played up in contrast to a mediocre athletic season. The occupancy of a new or temporary building, a year of major curriculum change, a new administration, pronounced growth in the student body, a major school anniversary—these deserve unusual treatment.

Reader interest. The book must invite reader interest from its opening page. The theme selected might be featured at the beginning and used throughout to tie the sections together. If an outstanding student artist is available, his talents should be capitalized upon, but student art or photography should not be used unless it is of superior quality.

Ingenuity must devise possibilities to supplement the standard sections of the book, for example:

(1) in a school in which many students commute via school bus— a section treating bus runs and typical experiences on the bus;

(2) where do students go after school—the favorite spots in the community;

(3) informal pictures of teachers, especially in the classrooms as the students remember them;

(4) a book divided into months instead of standard sections, moving from September through June;

(5) informal shots of students' favorite haunts—the hallways, the front steps, loafing places on the campus, the cafeteria;

(6) in the school with good assemblies, the year's assembly schedule might be the theme tying the book together;

(7) front pages of the school paper might be reproduced as full-page section openers throughout the book;

(8) any one photograph might well record two things at the same time—a group of three or four students, such as class officers, might be "shot" in the main office, in the cafeteria, or with the stadium in the background.

THE THEME OF THE YEARBOOK

One of the best considerations of yearbook theme appeared in an issue of *Helps,* the bulletin issued periodically by the National Scholastic Press Association. The discussion is included here with the courtesy of the Association:

Start work in May on developing your theme. One of the more significant areas under general editorial plans which can be initiated and in some cases completed during spring months is the yearbook's basic idea or theme. The new editors can select, shoot pictures, write copy, and decide upon art work, etc., depending upon the type of theme. In general, choice of theme seems to be the most perplexing area for the

413

new editor. After establishing a general idea of what kind of yearbook the new editors want, perhaps the following check list of theme ideas will provide more specific suggestions:

I. The School. A major source of theme ideas is the school—its functions and activities.
    A. Student life may be portrayed in many ways:
        1. As it is lived from day to day.
        2. By using glorified phrases such as Story of the Year, It Seems as Though it Were Only Yesterday, etc.
        3. By using typical students as guides.
        4. By writing about it in letters, postcards, diaries, notebooks, etc.
        5. By expressing youth and the spirit of fun through use of a theme based on a pun, catch phrase, figure of speech, a gala event, games or gaiety in general.
    B. The school itself has many attributes on which to base themes:
        1. Traditions, insignia, seal, or motto.
        2. Name of school (or famous man for whom named), name of the book.
        3. Famous alumni—their lives, accomplishments, and contributions.
        4. Anniversaries.
        5. Outstanding success in a school activity.

II. The Community often offers interesting theme ideas:
    A. Themes may feature the important industry, name of city or community, local color such as special celebrations and festivals, location or special peculiarities of the town.
    B. The history of the town, life of a great citizen, a colorful era, symbols of early days, local myths and characters, anniversaries or historical days may provide a basic idea.
    C. Some books have featured the city itself, civic activities, government.

III. The State. Theme possibilities lie again in the history, customs, traditions, industries, name, state flower, state bird, etc.

IV. The Nation. Many staffs go still farther for excellent themes concerning their schools and yearbooks—patriotic themes, our newest states, our great men, national elections, the census, etc.

414

V. The Wide World furnishes many possibilities:
   A. The color and interest of other lands—Africa, South America, Canada, etc.
   B. News events such as Olympic games, world fairs, expeditions.
   C. Developments in modern science, inventions and transportation, space, the endless sky, etc.
   D. Nature—birds, animals, flowers, rivers, etc.
   E. Arts and crafts such as:
      1. Music—symphonies, Broadway shows, popular songs, etc.
      2. Literature—characters from well-known books or myths.
      3. Publications—frequently yearbooks appear in the form and style of a special type of publication (magazine, newspaper, dictionary, etc.)
   F. History—lives of great men, anniversaries.

VI. Ideals, goals, and intangibles provide many worthwhile theme ideas:
   A. Hope for world peace and understanding among all the nations.
   B. Specifically religious goals and ideals.
   C. Friendship, personal development, cooperation among individuals.
   D. Work, achievement, challenges.

Plan your theme carefully—and early—for it is probably the greatest unifier you will have.*

FINANCING THE BOOK

The first rule of yearbook management is to set a reasonable budget and live within it. "Reasonable" means an expenditure figure that can be matched by equivalent revenue. Increased costs of publication demand that high schools plan carefully to avoid a deficit at the time of publication. High costs do not mean that the publication is losing out in its large market. Instead, they mean that the staff must give extra time, thought, and imagination to carrying out the assignment. Al-

*This section has been carried by permission of the National Scholastic Press Association.

415

though membership on the staff may be taken as an honor, it is first a responsibility.

As is true of the newspaper, the two main sources of revenue for the yearbook are advertising and circulation. With a budget in mind, the staff plans a book modest enough to come within the budget. To reverse the procedure may mean financial embarrassment. Past yearbooks provide a comfortable point with which to begin planning. If it is the school's first venture in yearbooks, schools of similar size and circumstances in communities of similar size and circumstances invite investigation. Furthermore, the school press associations are a rich source of help. Printing and engraving companies that publish yearbooks are ready to supply bulletins and company representatives to schools producing such books.

A list of suggestions by which revenue has been added by some yearbook staffs follows:

1. Charge each senior a nominal fee to help finance the engraving of his individual picture.

2. Secure the seniors' prints free from the photographer in exchange for awarding him the contract to photograph the seniors, his revenue coming from the extra portraits sold to the student.

3. Charge clubs and organizations a reasonable fee for the inclusion of their group photographs.

4. Avoid expensive professional art work.

5. Avoid expensive color layouts.

6. Use an inexpensive yet attractive cover.

The staff must always try to sell the maximum number of copies, since the more books printed, the less the average cost of producing each copy. Running extra copies after the minimum figure contracted represents only the cost of paper, binding, and printing.

Advertising. Much that applies to the sale of advertising for school papers (see Chapter 23) is applicable to the sale of advertising for the yearbook. Rates, however, are set not by the inch but by the page, the half page, the quarter page, and the eighth or sixth of a page. Page rates vary from fifty to one hundred dollars.

Yearbook production costs. It is an advantage to a yearbook staff to be able to compare tentative budget estimates with the experiences of other schools. Credit for a valuable survey of this kind, reported here, goes to the Columbia Scholastic Press Association and the trade magazine *Book Production.*

Each year the schools entering yearbooks in the Columbia Critique and Contest submit with their yearbooks an entry form containing information on the number of copies issued, costs of publication, and related data. These forms have been studied for some years by the news editor of *Book Production,* and the data summarized and published.*

The combined run-down of one annual Critique of the yearbooks submitted was as follows:

No. of Entries	Average Books per School	Total Books	Average Cost per Book	Average Cost per School	Total Production Costs
1,312	769	1,009,297	$5.53	$4,253	$5,580,994

A sampling of costs for representative schools of different sizes is given in Example 232. It includes printing by both letterpress and offset.

The study estimates that the annual production cost of high school yearbooks in the nation reaches 60 million dollars. Since it is big business, some publishing houses specialize in school yearbooks; one such firm publishes the books of over 8000 schools and colleges each year.

CARE IN ORGANIZATION

Planning for publication must begin a year ahead, and the work must progress systematically week by week. The book published in May requires a staff the previous May. The staff prepares a tentative layout of the entire book, called a dummy, which approximates the completed product, page for page. As the dummy is developed, the proportions

---

*The information given here (covering the 1959 Columbia Critique) is reprinted with permission from *Book Production* Magazine, 404 Park Avenue South, New York 16, New York.

EXAMPLE

232

SAMPLING OF SCHOOL EXPENDITURES FOR YEARBOOKS

Book "A" (letterpress)...250 copies

Printing & Binding	$1,797	53%
Covers	189	5%
Engraving	1,200	35%
Photography	200	7%
	$3,386	100%

Average cost of book...$13.54

Book "B" (offset).......250 copies

Printing & Binding	$1,414	80%
Covers	77	4%
Photography	239	13%
Miscellany	45	3%
	$1,775	100%

Average cost of book...$7.09

Book "C" (letterpress)...805 copies

Printing, Binding, Covers	$3,351	59%
Engraving	1,800	33%
Photography	335	6%
Miscellany	165	2%
	$5,651	100%

Average cost of book...$7.03

Book "D" (offset).......800 copies

Printing & Binding	$2,797	81%
Covers	312	9%
Miscellany	324	10%
	$3,433	100%

Average cost of book...$4.29

Book "E" (letterpress)..2,325 copies

Printing	$4,111	45%
Binding	1,395	16%
Covers	698	7%
Engraving	2,290	25%
Photography	475	5%
Miscellany	225	2%
	$9,194	100%

Average cost of book...$3.95

Book "F" (offset)......2,200 copies

Printing, Binding, Covers	$8,930	97%
Photography	238	3%
	$9,168	100%

Average cost of book...$4.16

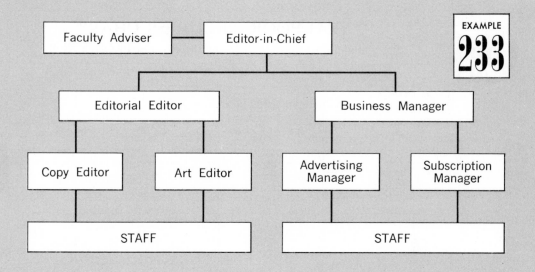

EXAMPLE

233

Faculty Adviser	Editor-in-Chief
Editorial Editor	Business Manager
Copy Editor	Art Editor	Advertising Manager	Subscription Manager
STAFF	STAFF

of text material and pictures are indicated on each page. The dummy is planned within the limits of the budget. The book should be a multiple of thirty-two pages in length, such as 128 or 160 pages. Since large sheets of paper fold into thirty-two-page forms for printing, the costs will be lower and there will be no blank pages.

Behind this planning there must be a well-balanced staff representing the two important phases of publication work—editorial and business. Working under a faculty adviser is the top editor, usually called the editor-in-chief. Example 233 outlines a framework which can be filled in with the number of positions necessary for the project in question. The 240-page book will call for a more elaborate staff than a book of ninety-six pages. The editor-in-chief must be good enough to manage a budget as well as to plan the content of the book creatively. Staff members should be selected for competence, not because of popularity or patronage.

Progress chart. The editor-in-chief must know the state of progress of every aspect of the yearbook at any moment. A detailed record or running account such as the one pictured in Example 234 is essential.

EXAMPLE

234

A YEARBOOK PROGRESS CHART

that editors find helpful in checking the work of PRODUCTION

PAGE NO.	PAGE DESCRIPTION	COPY ASSIGNED TO	COPY DUE	COPY SENT TO PRINTER	DRAWING OR PHOTO ASSIGNED TO	DRAWING OR PHOTO DUE	DRAWING OR PHOTO SENT TO ENGRAVER	PAGE COMPLETED
37	Blank							✓
38	Achievement - Copy	J. H. W.	12/15	12/25				✓
39								
40	Faculty	H. Q. B.	1/20	1/21	E. R.	12/31	1/6	✓
41	Section							
42								
43	Classes–Sub-divisional	J. H. W.	12/15	12/25				✓
44	Classes - Divisional				E. S. L.	12/18	1/3	✓
45	Senior – Sub-title				E. S. L.	12/18	1/3	✓
46	Senior - Title				E. S. L.	12/18	1/3	✓
47	Senior Class Officers	H. Q. B.	2/1					
48	Senior Memorial Com.	H. Q. B.	2/1					
49								
50	Senior Class	R. E. S.	1/20	1/21	E. R.	1/10		
51	Section							
52								

This example is taken from the *Warren Yearbook Progress Chart*, developed by the S. D. Warren Company, 89 Broad Street, Boston, Mass., and reproduced here by permission of the publishers.

Fundamentals of yearbook planning. The ingenuity and resourcefulness that go into the publication of a yearbook represent something over and beyond the fundamental structure. Through its experience in the judging of student publications, the Columbia Scholastic Press Association office has reviewed some of the vital details of this planning. The following suggestions are included by permission of CSPA and represent the efforts of that office to do everything possible to raise the standards of school journalism.*

1. The first, most important detail in planning is to number all pages.

2. Every yearbook requires a title page, which must contain the following data: (a) the name of the book; (b) the year; (c) the school

*These suggestions have been supplied by the Columbia Scholastic Press Association, and are carried here with their permission. The pointers appear in the CSPA manual, *Yearbook Fundamentals*.

which publishes the book; and (d) the city and state in which the school is located.

3. There is no requirement that end pages be made up of pictures. Plain paper costs less and may be just as effective.

4. Section pages should be placed on the right hand, if possible, to introduce each of the divisions into which the content generally falls. It is far better to place on these section pages pictures of local people or sights than to purchase them from the publisher.

5. Since balance is necessary on pages which face each other, the layout should be made on two pages at a time: left and right. Margins, headings, pictures, and copy should all balance to a reasonable extent.

6. When the layout is in progress, bottom, top, left, and right margins should be laid out as the adviser and staff think best. These details must not vary anywhere in the book. Copy or headings must never step outside the margins, but bleed pictures may extend to the edges of the page.

7. Many effective headings are only captions, but the outstanding books generally use "running titles"—full statements extending in balance across every page. These statement-headings should answer as many of the five W's as possible: Who? When? Where? Why? What? —and be as closely connected with the copy as possible.

8. Good photography is valuable in a yearbook, but it cannot stand alone. Copy is necessary to explain the details of every story that a picture suggests. The editorial staff is the historian of the year. If the history is to have value, it must be detailed and complete, recording the activities of every class, club, organization, and team in the school. Writers must not make the error of explaining what a club was organized for; they must tell what the club did during the year, who did it, where, why, how, to what effect. As many names of students as possible should be included.

9. Pictures without captions are meaningless. What are the people doing? Who are they? Identification of all people in group pictures, by name, should be included—unless the group is very large. Groups of more than eighteen or twenty people are too large; they should be broken up into smaller sections, large enough so that all faces can be recognized.

10. Type used for write-ups should be large enough so that the reader's eyes will not be strained. Years of experience have shown that a 10-point, light-faced type is best, because it is easily read and is ornamental on any page. This copy type should not be changed anywhere in the book. When copy is written, or when page proofs are read, copy must be edited—added to or subtracted from—so that write-ups will fill the allotted spaces. This is generally to the bottom margin of each page.

11. Photographs should generally show people or groups in action, that is, informally. Faculty members may be pictured at their desks, reading, talking, even cooking. Senior portraits are always formal. Underclassmen, when the groups are large, should be broken up into smaller sections. Above all, sports pictures should be action shots, and should be large enough so that the details of the action are apparent. It is always better to have one large clear picture than ten small, dull ones.

12. There is nothing in the book more important than photographs and copy showing classroom work. If possible, every subject taught in the school should be pictured and discussed. Yearbooks have been severely criticized by readers for omitting this vital information.

13. Vague headings, such as *Senior Play,* are bad. Name the play. In the copy, write a review of the production, giving names. Caption photographs with information that describes exactly what is occurring.

14. The Class Will, Class Prophecy, and Class History have sunk into disuse. If the editors wish to include them, however, pages of solid type should be broken up with drawings, candid pictures, or cartoons. If a will is included, it might well be printed in legalistic English, witnessed, and sealed. Do not use a heading such as *Class Prophecy* or the like. A definite heading is needed, such as *It Could Happen Then.*

15. Photographs with large useless backgrounds should be cropped before they are used. In a yearbook, as much as anywhere else, the people count most. Cut away unnecessary backgrounds and foregrounds. Do not pay money for useless space.

16. In selecting an idea or theme for the book, great care must be used. This idea must be apparent on every page, in every write-up, all through the book. Nothing is of greater help in carrying out a theme

than statement headings on every page connecting the theme with the copy. No intangible theme should be pictured, for it might become ludicrous.

17. The dedication of the book should be simple and formal. Dedications, however, are not vital to a good book.

18. A hard cover is generally preferable to a padded one, for it holds its shape and firmness better.

19. Members of the staff and the adviser should "see" the book as often as possible while it is being printed and bound. Every photograph, every engraving, every word on every page of type should be rigidly inspected before the final printing. If photography is blurred, if there are splotches of white space, if type fades out because of poor printing, if copy does not reach—and stop at—bottom margins, if there are misspellings or errors in composition, all this is the fault of adviser and staff, for they have the right to insist upon their orders being carried out.

EXAMPLE
235

EXAMPLE
236

Valley Administration, Honor Societ

"IT SEEMS LIKE YESTERDAY!" Lucille Rosenow, superintendent, reminisces as she and Dewey Breisch, principal, discuss graduation with Seniors, Lane Reynolds, Mike Flanagan, and Jan Latsha. Miss Rosenow has been with the class of '61 since First Grade and was graduated with them.

First Lady of District 275, Miss Lucille Rosenow, deemed planning for the new middle school as the highlight of her last year as superintendent. Responsibility for the whole system included duties so complicated and varied that a complete book is devoted to defining them. However, out of the maze of budgets, bus routes, and lunch programs, she found most pleasurable her work with people —the total staff and students.

Seeing that there is an educational atmosphere and an air of cooperation for students and faculty alike, is one of the duties of Principal Dewey Breisch. Working along with the student council, he supervises and expedites major student activities.

Counselor Frank Farrell has everyone's number—that is, every grade achieved by each student in Golden Valley since kindergarten. Although the majority of his time was devoted to assisting the college-bound seniors, Mr. Farrell also conducted a Seventh Grade guidance class, "How to Study."

Exemplifying, coordinating, and guiding, these three lead Valley's... proper channels to a meritorious edu... form the backbone of the stu...

Balanced above the trophy case, the Honor Society plaque adds new style and luster to the front foyer. But beauty and sparkle cost many pretty pennies—ten of them for each of the 478 engraved letters. This, reduced to a specific effort in the matter of fund raising, required the sale of 1 4/5 fruitcakes per name in bronze.

Another NHS project found A and B honor roll students combing the Golden Valley hills in search of Wendell Wilkie campaign buttons. This occasion was an invitational scavenger hunt and dinner, one of three honor roll parties initiated by the Society to promote and honor scholarship.

Maximum national membership of 15 per cent of the Seniors, 10 per cent of the Juniors, and 5 per cent of the Sophomores was filled by adding eight students to the Society in 1961 for a total membership of 17.

As nature welcomed spring, the National Honor Society ushered in its members at the formal induction March 21. The qualities of scholarship, leadership, character, and service prevailed at the candlelight ceremony. President Beth Schwartz invited the members, their parents, the administration, faculty, Board of Education, and students of the A and B honor roll to the reception following the induction.

18

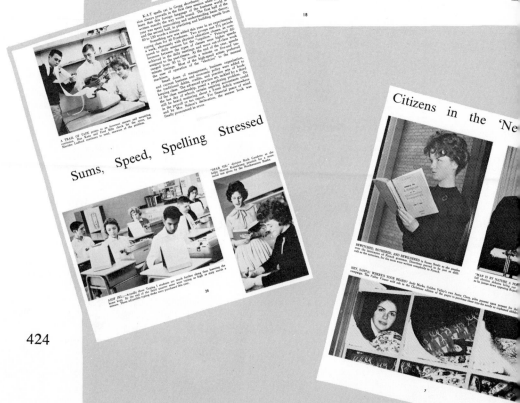

K-A-T spells cat in Gregg shorthand. Amused confusion always prevails in the first class session when students learn that this foreign language of the business world is not exactly the way words sound. The first basic of the year was concentrating in perfecting and understanding theory, and the words a minute...

...to 120 within a minute...

Teaching new was added this year in an experimental typing class run by Freshmen. Two groups met 2½ periods a week alternately upon for the "regular..." Principal difficulty between the meeting of classes were higher work achieved in the daily meetings. At the most of the class, words assigned to the participants... from 30 to 70 words a minute on the year, minute timings. Most of the high-speed artists preferred machine... ease of operation of the "electrics" to the manual...

Small doses of management, business organization, and current business economics... policy were asked to and traditional debits, credits, and practice. A bit of bookkeeping... the class membership create a perplexing problem. On the last day of school, certain subjects and instants in the... heard on every... about a "trial deficit somewhere and by Mrs. Nelson's declaration, the answer book was finally pronounced in error.

A TRAIL OF TAPE points to an innocent stream and mounting confusion. Don Katz and Carol Billa cheer for the error, but Merridee Lindford continues in total, unaware of the problem.

Sums, Speed, Spelling Stressed

"DEAR SIR," dictates Ruth Gardner as she helps Sharon Kolenkamp interpret to a secretarial test given by the Northwestern Banks.

ASDF JKL.... Actually these Typing I students are work harder doing than learning the home keys. By the end of the third summer time typing as high as sixty cents a minute. These adjustable typing desks were purchased this year.

25

Citizens in the 'Ne

BEWITCHED, BOTHERED, AND BEWILDERED is Susan Steele as she puzzles over the intricacies of French grammar. Directions proved to be just as difficult as the exercises, for the texts were written completely in French.

HEY, SANTA! WHERE'S YOUR BEARD Andy Meeks, Golden Valley's own Santa Claus, piles present upon present for the campaign. The Valley Times sold ads in the Christmas edition of the paper to purchase these toys for needy or orphaned child...

"MAN IS BY NATURE A PO... left. Bettina debates bitter as he jumps down opposing Stan...

NA'
Flan
ing
Mik

424

EXAMPLE

237

Encourage Scholarship

HELPING STUDENTS PLAN FOR THE FUTURE is the job of Counselor Frank Farrell. Here he and Senior Jay Gibbons pore over Jay's file, which contains records ranging from a First Grade IQ Test to his College Boards. The average Senior visited Mr. Farrell four times during the year.

SOCIETY membership was increased to 17 w... ..., Margie Hoines, Kathy Felt, Jan Lar... ... Doug McNeil, Jay Gibbons, J... La...

JANICE KAYE NICHOLS
(Jan)
Pep Club 2; GAA 1, 2, 3, 4; Valleyettes 3; Choir 3, 4; Red Cross 3, 4.

SARAH PARTRIDGE NOBLE
(Sally)
Sophomore Class Secretary; Valley Flower Page Editor 4; Pep Club 3; GAA 1, 2, 3, 4; Choir 3; Spanish Club 3.

CORNERED by Golden Valley's persuasive treasboard members, Pat Johnson doesn't know which style show to attend. The treasboard members and their respective sponsors are: Barb Brown, Daytona, Sally Noble, Penney; and Avis Peterson, Donaldsons. Each of the girls modeled in her sponsor's show as part of her duties.

WELL DRESSED Valleyette Sally Noble models the "Rrrr Stratosphere" for Pawlyn's slight from her 1920 Model A Ford.

AVIS MARIE PETERSON
Valley Advertising Co-Editor 4; Valley Flower Page Editor 3, 4; Junior Prom Editor 3; Pep Club 4; GAA 1, 2, 3, 4; Pom Pom Girl 4; Red Cross 3, 4; Vice Chair 4; Speech Contest 3, 4; Varsity Debate 3, 4; Homecoming Queen 4; Attendant 3; Triple Trio 4.

WILLIAM EMORY PROFFITT III
(Bill)
Football 1, 2, 3, Co-Captain 4; January Thaw 3; Lettermen's Club 3, 4.

PHILIP JOSEPH RAABE
(Phil)
Valley Flower 4; Choir 4.

James Jones, Jr.
Anne Knickerbocker
Leslie Korok
Robert Larson
Peggy Lindberg

Bruce Lindsey
Marider Ludford
Erland Maki
Jay Martin
Daniel McAuliffe

Charles McCann
Linda O'Dell
Patricia Patlin
Christine Petersen
Stephen Sahly

Juniors Author 100,000 Words

HUCKLEBERRY HOUND announces Homecoming to admirer Ellen Chester. Huck's subtle humor appealed to Valley.

GRINNING MISCHIEVOUSLY, Steve Sahly antagonizes Sophomore Leslie Mitchell with the age-old water stunt.

425

EXAMPLE
238

Franco

With the final "bang" of school lockers on June 9, and with gulps of dismay or elation, Valleyites turned over another leaf and plodded homeward.

The typical Valley student managed a variety of pastimes during the leisurely summer months. The booming labor force of previous years dwindled, as shown by an increase in applications and a decrease in jobs. Summer-type work obtained varied from day camp assistant counselor to daddy's helpers.

Sleep, a full eight hours, took up a great amount of time during these lazy months, but for the more active personality, swimming rated high.

Steve Pawlcyn's plans included learning the art of skin diving, while Sally Noble hoped to end "right side up" on a trampoline.

Other leisure activities included trips to the lake, miniature golfing, and, for some, six grueling weeks at West High summer school. These lucky few voted for English as their favorite summer-time subject, while others advanced their knowledge in math and languages.

After a full day of work or play, many familiar faces were seen at McDonald's for a quick order of fries and cokes.

The slow, yet eventful march into the future continues for the typical Valley sun-burned girl and muscled boy as fall rolls into Valley High.

MISS GOLDEN VALLEY, Dianne Borchert, was chosen at the 14th annual Lilac Ball and will be the community's representative in the Aquatennial Queen of Lakes Contest. Barb Anderson, Kathy Felt, Pat Johnson, and Beth Schwartz also vied for the crown.

...teen Franco demonstrates finesse with a ...McNeil. Gus also found time for tennis, ...lub, Senior Class Play, track, and choir.

Vikings Swing to Summer Fun

MAY 19, 1961, CEDAR LAKE: Icy waters greeted Seniors when they took the season's first quick dip in 50-degree weather. Making a quicker exit are Dan Kane, Barb Anderson, Bill Kuhlmann, Dianne Borchert, Wade Turner, Kathy Felt, Jack Rosholt, Lane Reynolds, and Mike Steele.

93

KING AND QUEEN of Hearts ...are crowned by 1960 royalty, ...and three balloons, 40 inches in...

Hillbill

AMIDST STREAMERS and ...Neil anticipate an enchanted ...formal dance.

CASEY AT THE BAT, Bill Kuhlmann tensely and a time for first-baseman in the squad's line. 384 limm batting average.

VARSITY BASEBALL SQUAD—Front row: Don McNeil, Judd Nelson, Jeff McLeod, Morgan Nelson, Dick ...Jay Martens, Ron P. Row 2: ...Terry R. ...

Errors Plague Hot-Hitting Nine

EVER WONDERED WHAT it's like to hit against Golden Valley's fast-balling righthander, Rick Carlson? Well, here's your chance.

Golden Valley labored at inopportune moments and plunged to sixth place in the MVC baseball standings.

Opening the season in defeat, U-High twice carried a 3-2 lead into the bottom of the seventh. Errors threw the ball away twice and U-High scored the winning runs. GV enjoyed a twice away from the scene...

SAFE OR OUT? Third baseman Terry Rosengren tries to stymie Bob Bass' attempted advance in a Viking practice session.

VARSITY BASEBALL SCORES			
Opponent	GV	Opponent	GV
Glen Lake	5-4	Eden Prairie	
Hutto	2-4		
Hopkins	0-16	Minnetonka	1-2
U-High	3-2	Wayzata	1-3
Burnsville	8-4	Chanhassen	3-2
	2-6	Chaska	5-2
		West	1-3

106

EXAMPLE
239

Golf, Tennis Fill Leisure Time

Spurred by newly-built tennis courts right next to the school building and an abundance of public and private golf courses in the area, many Valleyites discovered the fun and challenge of golf and tennis.

The newly-built tennis courts on the east side of the high school became, when it opened in the fall one spring morning. Principal Dewey Britsch became such a fan that even cold weather couldn't stop him. Almost every Saturday during the winter he and two or three other men would be found in the gym playing a match. The GAA and Miss Maria Leona Darraine's girls' Phy. Ed. classes also frequent visitors to the courts. Both with their school and village lands. Do to outdoor courts are reserved for student play until 5 p.m.

Golf was also high on the list of student's recreational favorites. With the challenging Theodore Wirth Public Golf Course right in Golden Valley and a second public course only 15 minutes away, any Valleyite had an opportunity to try his skill against a small golf ball and 18 long holes. With seven private courses within five miles or the school, many were lucky enough to play some of the tough-est courses in the Upper Midwest.

While Golden Valley had no regular golf team competing in meets with other schools, four Sophomore did compete the Vikings at the District Golf Tournament held on May 22 at Minnetonka Country Club. Name of the McLeod, Dave Wigren, Pete Statt, Doug McNeil, and Jim Marks qualified for the Regional tournament, the only other Valley Conference school who entered a full team. They also beat Richfield, a Lake Conference school.

Dave Wigren led the Tourname with an 88, despite six double bogies, Doug McNeil followed with a 94; Pete Statt had a 100 and Jim McLeod a 112. Jerry Holewa acted as the boy's coach for the tournament.

TEEING OFF in the District Tournament is Viking Dave Wigren, who paced Golden Valley entrants with an 88.

PETE STATT DISHES up a mighty serve as he shows off his tennis form on the courts beside the school.

DIGGING DIVOTS AND DRIBBLING DRIVES, this "gruesome foursome," Doug McNeil, Dave Wigren, Jim McLeod, and Pete Statt, represented Golden Valley on May 22, at the District 18 Golf Meet.

107

Dianne Borchert, elected by the student body, ... Miller. Traditional red and white streamers ... hearts and arrows motif.

"I CAN COOK TOO!" Determined to being Maury Christensen and Little Zack to Marry'n' Sam's altar, Andy Marks resorts to feminine pleading. The world of hay bales and "hitchin'" bells was left behind at the magic hour of midnight.

THREE HOBOS AND A RELUCTANT DEBUTANTE arrive at the annual Sadie Hawkins dance in their hitch-biker's special. Charlene Wente, left, has just about won the battle with Mike Flanagan, but Bill Kuhlmann still needs a bit of encouragement from Marilyn Smith to make his appearance at the Dogpatch Doin's.

Exchange Burlap for

and Doug Mc-
...inspired semi-

3:25 p.m., work began; 4:00 p.m., work continued; 5:00 p.m., the class was working harder; 6:00 p.m., the last balloons were half-heartedly hung; 7:35 p.m., the crew rode home for a quick change; 7:55 p.m., they were back to greet guests, determined to enjoy themselves at Golden Valley's third annual Sophomore-sponsored Valentine Dance.

Anticipating few difficulties in their first attempt at organizing a dance, the Sophomores let the days slip by. As Class President Jim Miller wryly admitted, "Most of the actual decorating was done just one hour before the dance was scheduled to begin."

But pride replaced fatigue with one look at the faces of the couples as they stepped into the dreamy atmosphere, perfect for any cupid's arrow.

Climaxing the evening was the coronation of Wade Turner and Dianne Borchert as King and Queen of Hearts by last year's reigning couple, Jan Bouley and Denny Miller. Dianne, radiant in yellow chiffon, demurely tilted her head to receive the crown, a wreath of red and white carnations.

Adding to the atmosphere of the red-and-white wonderland was the music of Jim Rhodes and his "golden sax." Balloons tied on the girls' wrists brightly complemented the festive decorations.

Trying a new approach, the Sophomores dimly lit the teachers' lounge off the cafetorium in an enchanting pink. Here guests and royalty enjoyed cookies and punch in a misty atmosphere.

82

Valentine Lace

Gunny sack dresses, blue jeans, patch-covered shirts, and ragged overalls were sanctioned only once in the 1960-61 school year——on Sadie Hawkins Day! Dogpatch-inspired costumes spiced the annual dance.

Before the hay dance Sue Ostroot opened her home for a feed of hot corn bread and tangy cider.

Back at school, the cafetorium became a new world. Hay bales and corn stalks supported a red privy which caught the eye of many a "Cornhusker."

A new addition to the traditional Sadie Hawkins motif was an original mist created by hay-bale dust. This irregularity combined with sneezes, red eyes, and giggles, added a new twist to the Senior-sponsored dance. Music for dancing was recorded, but the listening variety was live, via the Triple Trio's medley of mountain ditties.

Corsages fashioned of radishes and celery entwined in turnip tips were popular because of their appropriateness of style and cost.

Voted as wearing the most original costumes at the hoedown, King Bill Kuhlmann and Queen Marilyn Smith literally walked away with all honors——a corn cob pipe and pair of rubber lips.

Marry'n' Sam, in the persons of Pete Statt and Jim McLeod, was on hand to issue the wedding licenses. With only a ring and a kiss, the couples were "hitched" until the bewitching hour of midnight. After the dance the majority of "Dogpatchers" and their "trips" roared out of the parking lot and headed for Mac's Pizza Place.

MODELING THE LATEST gunny-sack formality are Gregg Parmelee, Jean DeVilliers, Dianne Borchert, Kristi Prestegaard, Gus Franco, and Bill Borchert. Hay bales and corn stalks held up the rickety outhouse for the unorthodox setting of the mountain portrait.

83

427

EXAMPLE
240

Richard Kooseman
Stephen Lang
Barbara Lang
Joanne Lenske
Linda Martin

James McCabe
Marilyn McManus
Julie Mikucki
Bruce Mixer
Mark Molianen

Eileen Murphy
Barry Nelson
Katherine Norby
Gerald Nordley
Roger Noren

8th   Graders   Build   Pet   Beasts

IT'S A PET PARADE, featuring beastly charmers constructed in eighth grade art classes by Jeff Farnam, Mark Hinshaw, Joanne Lenske, Eileen Murphy, and Julie Mikucki. The vividly-colored animals are of papier mache.

72

Freshmen   See   Law   in   Action

"Do you swear to tell the truth, the whole truth, and nothing but the truth, so help you God?" The Ninth Grade, in their first experience at traffic court, in conjunction with their study of Minnesota's government, heard this oath many times.

Adding even more to the diversity of their civics class was an excursion to the historic and beautiful Capitol of the "Gopher State."

Here members of the class were able to see lawmakers in action and to tour the domed structure constructed almost entirely of building products from Minnesota.

Money was raised by the Freshmen, under the leadership of class advisers Mrs. Eleonora Conrad, Harold Plofld, and William Cardinier, through class dues at $1.50 a semester and class parties.

Class parties ranging from "romantic" to "thrill-filled" proved to students that variety can be exciting. After the annual dunking at Taylor's Falls on May 27, during the dunking Sophomore Class excursion. Only regrets Mrs. Sheehy had about Dary's dip was that he didn't have a hat coming from Excelsior's roller coaster.

The all-important step from Junior to Senior High posed an exciting challenge. Members of the class added many extracurricular activities to their schedule and were able to get a sneak preview of hectic coming years.

The class had the distinction of being first in experimenting with a new program. In addition to the required six subjects, they were able to choose between health and typing as alternate to physical education.

John Addams
William Adelfson
Henry Albert
Roger Anderson
Lois Bills

Janet Beuchee
Darrell Brown
Paul Byrda
Eileen Carlson
Michael Carroll

Alison Coutts
Steven Dzenski
David Dennison
Jean DeVilliers
Donald Dickey

Lester Erickson
Timothy Ewald
Harold Fahrendorff
Marilyn Falkers
Timothy Flanagan

66

Sophs'   Spring   Splash   at   Falls

One . . . . two . . . . three . . . . . SPLASH! And Dary Sheehy was suddenly dumped in the lake! His unexpected bath occurred at Taylor's Falls on May 27, during the annual Sophomore Class excursion. Only regrets Mrs. Sheehy had about Dary's dip was that he didn't have a bar of soap in his pocket.

A bus was chartered to take the group to the area, where they played softball, canoed, drained 144 bottles of pop within the first hour, and had a lively squirt-gun fight, before returning that evening for dancing and ping-pong at Margie Flanders' home. This, the second Sophomore Class party, was even more enthusiastically received than the first one, a hayride at Ding's Ranch followed by a party at school.

The Sophomores began to find out what it is like to work together through these parties and their varied money-making efforts. Besides sponsoring the Valentine's dance, they sold refreshments at two basketball games this winter and had two successful bake sales this spring. Their remaining money will be used for next year's prom.

Officers reported that advisers, Robert Lockwood and Mrs. Jo Ann Herring, had been a big help to them.

Last fall the newly-elected class president, Marnie Mollberg, left Golden Valley for the "Sunny South" of Jacksonville, Florida, and Jim Miller, as vice-president, took over her duties. A National Honor Society position will be vacated when member Margie Flanders moves to Lansing, Michigan, this summer.

Irene Balfanz
Lynn Ballak
Dean Besley
JoAnne Brueckelmyer
Jinx Bryant
Gregory Cohn

Gayle Coughlin
Judith Cummer
Karen Engbusser
Paul Engbusser
Jeffery Esau
Margaret Flanders

Theresa Gomsrud
Edgar Hall
Barbara Hansen
Frederick Hase
Judith Hedland
Thorwald Johnson

Judith Koch
Kathleen Larsen
Claude McLeod
Jeffery McLeod
James Miller
Leslie Mitchell

64

CHAPTER LABORATORY

1. Select one of the chapter's suggestions for a yearbook theme and develop it for your school in one or two pages.
2. Create a table of contents for a ninety-six-page yearbook; indicate sections, number of pages, etc.
3. Lay out three double pages (two facing pages) for the book, indicating the sections from which each set is taken.
4. Discuss your yearbook's budget in class; compare it with the examples in Example 232, making suggestions for its improvement.
5. Lay out a page showing three advertisements for your yearbook. Choose firms from your community.
6. Devise an index that you think desirable for the book. What types of divisions should it include?
7. Write a 300-word essay analyzing the differences between a school newspaper and a school yearbook.
8. Examine your school's last three yearbooks; analyze their content and layout, and discuss in class.
9. Analyze the organization of your yearbook staff in diagram form. Discuss its practical aspects in class, and suggest improvements.
10. Of the yearbook examples included in the chapter, select three that you think are excellent. What principles do they follow that can be applied to all books? Discuss in class.

26 PUBLISHING THE MAGAZINE

"Last night the evening fell too quickly, so someone scooped out a piece of the sun and dropped it into my next-door valley."

But this account of dusk was not carried in a school newspaper, where imagination is held captive by facts, and sentence structure is simple and direct. Instead, this story as recorded by one Randy Watson, then a student at the Oceanside, New York, High School, found shelter in the school magazine, *The Lens*.

And unlike the photographic approach of newspaper art, the drawing that illustrated Randy's story of dusk was also of the imagination. (See Example 241.)

And in the same issue of *The Lens*, a thirty-two-page, 9- by-12 inch magazine, Charles Jurrist told what he had to say in Example 242.

THE THIRD MEMBER OF THE SCHOOL-PRESS FAMILY

The third member of the school-press family, and the eldest of the group, is the school magazine. Since its beginnings early in the nineteenth century, it has remained devoted to its original purpose—providing an outlet for creative ability. Its pages present a collection of

EXAMPLE
241

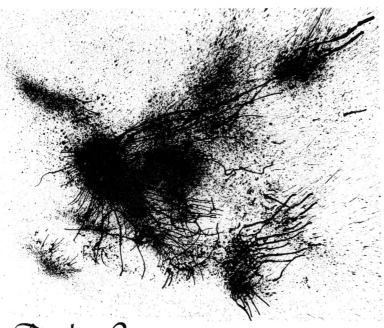

Dusk Landing

Last night the evening fell too quickly, so someone scooped out a piece of the sun and dropped it into my next-door valley. He buttered the dough-puffed clouds, floating like dumplings in the red hot baking dish of the sky, and sifted the sunshine 'till it rose, a powdered gold dust, gently up and out and around every hill but mine as I stood in the soft blackness of my kingdom. The molten liquid chunk of a star bubbled and frothed in the earth-rounded bowl, and shone the temptation of hot beauty ever-lasting.

Then someone gathered all the people of the earth on His lumpy sky landings, and each took a turn to glide down, down into the warmth of eternity. Someone stayed, waiting till the very last. He could not hold back while the man before him basked into death's solitude on the long ride down. He jumped before his time, and Dame Justice of the old west wind blew him a bit. Missing the mark, he dropped just this side of heaven.

The Lens
Oceanside High School
Oceanside, New York

Credo

EXAMPLE
242

CHARLES JURRIST

We are all so witty, so urbane, polished and wise.
We hurl our fragile banalities
    onto the polished parquet floor of sterile conversation
    where we expect them to glitter—our cynical truths.
And all our brilliant young society
    gasps with delight at our profundity.
These brittle crystals which mirror some true light
    will endure as we whirl about them
    in our gossamer dancing slippers.
But they will be pulverized
    by the first touch of the peasant's sturdy shoe.
And after we have gone—our thin rays of reflected light dispersed
    the timeless peasants and their abiding faith
    will still people the earth.

There is no God say we
    and in our suburban, philosophical dissertations
    this may begin to seem quite logical.
But science—that godless craft
    which supposedly destroys all faith
    is a great restorer within me.
Open your eyes for once—
Drop your glossy sheath of trite affected wisdom—
Look with unclouded vision
    at nature or—Yourself—
The human mind—this gray mass
    not too unlike other mortal tissue
    which produces feelings, love, hate
Thoughts
    and an infinite variety of subtle sensations.
Did this arise from carbon atoms
    warmed by the sun in some primordial ocean?
I think not—I know not
But there is a God!

the best literary and art effort of the students. Its very existence represents not only a selection of such work but also a stimulus to such effort.

The newspaper reports the school's events; the yearbook records its history; the magazine says, "Here is a story—a poem—you should read, a drawing you should see."

At times a school is careless in distinguishing the characteristics of the three publications and will issue from time to time a publication that bears features of all three. It may carry class photographs as would a yearbook, record the accounts of sports events as would a newspaper, and contain students' creative writing as would a magazine. In make-up, such a hybrid is more apt to resemble the magazine than its other two parents. It is preferable for student journalists to know exactly the purpose of their efforts, and to choose the proper publication to achieve it.

There are three general types of high school magazines, (1) literary, (2) news, and (3) hodge-podge.

The literary magazine. The literary magazine is by far the most common and the most distinctive. Distinct in character from both the newspaper and the yearbook, it stands as an outlet for literary and artistic creativity. Its contents are the highest quality work produced by the students in the school; every student is a potential source of supply. Consequently, its production must be organized to cover the entire school.

The art work in the literary magazine is an integral part of the copy and is planned into the make-up; it is of two types, that which is used to illustrate an article or a poem, and that which stands alone as a distinctive piece of work. The various media include wash drawings, line drawings, photographs, and block prints. Now and then an etching from an advanced art class appears.

The news magazine. The news magazine is issued in the school that does not or cannot publish a newspaper; consequently it fulfills the functions of the paper as well as of the literary magazine. It is an extremely difficult journalistic form to master, for it has no commercial models to follow, and due to infrequency of publication, news coverage is difficult.

The news magazine therefore leans toward the recording of events, moving close to the function of the yearbook. Published under a cover, it is more likely to be saved by the student than is the newspaper and often stands as the year's record of the school.

The hodge-podge magazines. There is no standardized term to describe those magazines that follow no well-formulated editorial policy. Generally, they do not limit themselves in their field of coverage; they are also generally unartistic in appearance, and they lack balance in art work and written copy.

Such a magazine is usually the only publication in the school, which permits the staff to throw into the journalistic hopper anything that happens to strike the vision or the fancy of the editors. Make-up immediately becomes a problem, for copy is more abundant than space, and there are no distinct editorial purposes to assist the staff in selection. Such a publication is obviously not desirable, if anything else can be managed.

EXAMPLE
243

WAITIN' FOR THE CHILDREN

TO COME

HOME

Tired old Mama, rockin' in the door,
Rockin' in the door
Rockin' in the door
Waitin' for the children to come home
To come home
From the war.

See her there, rockin' in the door,
Tired hair, black no more.
Milky eyes oft gaze upon
Muddy waters, tired hot sun.
Rock away, now, rock away.
Pass the day, Mama, pass the day.
Sighin', heavin', barely breathin',
Back inside, Mama, no deceivin'.

Tears don't come so easy now,
Do they, Mama, do they now?
Salt-stained tired hands still hold
Some treasures of her children bold,
Her children bold who went to win
A war, it seems
And left some old chipped warriors tin,
And childhood dreams.

Mama, Mama, home we've come,
Twelve dead Yankees is our sum.
Stop that rockin', do ya hear?
End your waitin', Mama dear.
Close your tired eyes and sleep,
Just join us in that peaceful sleep.

by tom kavelin

Council
Manhasset High School
Manhasset, New York

38

Artistic standards in make-up. It is somewhat futile for a magazine staff to select the outstanding literary and art work of the students, and then publish it in a manner that violates the artistic sentiment or purpose that underlies the magazine's very existence. As a whole, the magazine itself must stand as a creative production. The first impression of its cover, and the first reaction to any page, must be pleasing. Otherwise, the pieces of student work within would be blemished before they were ever read or seen. Layout and planning require the best artistic talent in the school. (See Examples 243 through 248.)

The magazine, like the yearbook, is a publication in which a single page cannot be planned or envisioned alone. A page is only half of the whole; the other half is the facing page. (See Examples 243 through 245.) The examples from high school magazines that practice this basic principle of magazine planning stand out in effectiveness. The appealing appearance of any single page could easily have been lost had the editors failed to arrange the facing page in good taste and balance.

Having acquainted herself with the passengers, Malathi turned to look out of the windows at the panorama of scenery that rolled by the rocking, noisy train. She watched as a field hard as rock, where a lone farmer tried vainly to make his bullock break the sod, yielded to green fields of rice fed by tiny streams. Rows of shops heralded the approach of a city and people young and old alike stopped their work to wave to the train as it rattled past "tongas" and factory funnels blowing smoke everywhere. The peace of a village well where the citizens met to draw water and discuss the news was shattered as the train rumbled through. They, too, had stopped and turned to wave. Towards dusk came the scene that stood out most in Malathi's mind. The luminous hue of a glorious sunset silhouetted a farmer and his oxen plodding home after a hard day's work, when in the city a factory funnel blew soot out of its chimney disfiguring the simple beauty of a lovely scene.

She fancied she smelled the ugly soot and awakened to find herself gliding past a geometrically planned New Jersey housing area, sitting beside the same silent passengers, and as she sighed, she yearned for the simple charm and variety of a rattling Indian train and Indian landscape! But who would understand her? Such sights must be seen to be understood, and missed to be enjoyed.

Bonnie Farmer

ON THE PLAYGROUND

By Margaret Neisser

I had seen Penny's mother at our annual school fairs. Each year she and Penny's older brother and sister came to sing folksongs at our school fair. They always wore pretty outfits that my mother said they got in Switzerland, the place with all the mountains that we studied in school. Mummy said Penny's mother was a good folksinger and sang all over the world.

But I didn't know her very well. I knew Penny better, because she was in my grade, Mrs. Irwin's third grade. I never went to Penny's house, but I liked to play with her. I thought she was the prettiest girl in our class. Her hair was so long that when she took the rubber band off and let the pony tail down she could sit on it. Penny was always having fun, especially during recess when we played kickball and jump rope. She was good at jump rope but even better at kickball. Her brother who was almost twenty had taught her how to kick the ball right down the foul lines so people would think it was out of bounds and let it go too long before picking it up. She always got at least to second base.

When Mrs. Irwin told us that Penny would not be in school for a while because her mother had died, I felt very sorry for Penny. I asked my mother where she was going to live, if she had to live in an orphanage, but Mommy said Penny's older brother and sister would take care of her. I thought that was very nice because I didn't think orphanages would be fun to live in.

The day before Penny came back, Mrs. Irwin told us to be very nice to her and remember not to say anything about mothers because that might remind Penny that her mother was dead.

Penny came back on a real spring kind of day that feels as if recess should be for all day. She wore one of her Switzerland dresses, the one that had blue sewing and a tight little jacket, and she didn't look any different. When we went out to recess, I wondered if she was going to play. But when I got out the jump rope, she got out a kickball. "It's a perfect day for kickball," she said.

Soon the kickball game started. It was an awfully close game so I put down my jump rope to watch. The team Penny was on was behind by just one run and Sally was on second base and Penny was up. I saw her screw up her face like she did when she was angry and go way back to the backstop for a good running kick. The ball went right

nine

435

EXAMPLE
244

Leaves of Lemure

SWAYING trees and leaves. Leaves in piles lining the streets, not pretty leaves with vibrant colors, but ordinary brown leaves. A rusty colored Irish Setter running out of a yard chasing a rolling garbage can, his red coat contrasting with the brown of the day. And the dog plowing through a pile of leaves and rolling in his crisp bed. But he got up and scratched himself, shaking the leaves out of his fur, and ran to the corner where the crowd stood, his ears and tail flying as he ran. And I saw him run up to them, and they threw rocks and he ran into the yard.

"Get outta here ya mutt!" the grey-faced boy muttered. He grabbed the girl and spoke roughly. She laughed and pulled away slightly.

And more leaves fell.

Do you mind standing here in the rain with me? I'm lonely and a walk would be so nice. You used to take walks with me every day. It's funny, now I spend all my time pretending you're with me. Will you ever leave me for good? I'm trying so hard to keep whatever I have, even if it's only memories. Why should I go so soon when the wind is playing tricks for me? And the drops are on my lashes and the cold is in my hair. I want to walk through a street and see nothing! No white picket fences, no red geraniums in plaster pots; no silly inflated globe all lit up in a window, each country colored pink, yellow, green; no address sign hanging on a hinge; no cracks in sidewalks or holes in the streets filled with pebbles; no someone else to take your place.

But leaves in October are so nice. Even if they're not pretty. All right, we'll go; it's late anyway. The buses will be leaving. Do you have your guitar? Oh, you don't play. Well, don't worry, you can sing. The red dog will be here when we return. They are leaving now, too. Only they're going in to eat. Probably coffee and french fries and ketchup. They wouldn't think of being near the school on the weekend. But they have so much fun standing on the corner.

There's Howie running to get a good seat with Barbara. That orange sweater he's wearing is for her. Do you like this red bow in my hair? He stayed up all night once, walking in the park with the boys, shouting his love for all to hear, climbing benches, running wildly, singing until the sun rose; and then he went home and saw his father getting up for work. The he felt sick from being up all night. The coffee churned in his stomach as he was singing his love for her. Oh, were you there that time? That's right, you told me about it.

I don't want to sit near them, in the back, where the juniors sit. School buses always look so different from other buses. I'll just sit and look out the window and no one will notice I'm here. Can't we go for a walk in the rain instead? Guitars and singing. I don't know that song. I'm sucking on a

20

"charm" and pretending I can't sing with it in my mouth. In the front of the bus a radio is blaring. Drown out that music! Sing!

Why doesn't the bus leave already?

Do you remember the last time we took this trip? Early spring: warm hues, whirling miles. I knew that you'd never come with me again. Do you think about me the way I think about you? I don't suppose you do.

Overstuffed seats and springs creaking to the music. Oh, I don't want that boy from chemistry, Gregory, to sit next to me.

"Really, the seat is very uncomfortable. No, it's not taken."

What could I do? He's taken your seat and now in silence we sit. Howie has a chess game and he's teaching Barbara. They sing, too, with the guitars while they're playing chess. He wants to put his arm around her. She giggles and pushes him away. When I see them together, I feel so jealous because I want to be with you.

The wheels crush the leaves. The cracks in the road swallow them as they press together.

Are you still with me? And the rain, always rain to veil the leaves. I'll write you a poem. His peering eyes searching scientifically over my shoulder.

"What are you writing?"

An open window. Fluttering white, a gust grabbing and gone.

"Gregory, do you always carry the Sunday Times with you?" Well, yes,

(Continued on Page 42)

21

The Misfittings

"ANNIE, do you think he may like me . . . really, I mean?"

"Yes, Maddie, he's crazy about you," I answered, yawning. If she had lit her fangs into Tony Curtis, then the whole idea might have been somewhat possible. But no, Curtis would be too easy for Maddie. She had to have that All-American schnook, Ken Darrel. He sounds it, doesn't he? All-American, that is. Well, if you like that tall blond Aryan look attached rather comfortably to a body that reads "A nickel a touch" on each bicep, then I suppose you might call Ken Darrel All-American.

I worriedly glanced at Maddie, sprawled out on my bed, chewing on the tip of her long straggly red braid. She was small for her age and very sensitive about it. However, being four-feet-ten with a figure correctly developed for her 16 years was something that could hardly escape notice. I thought of Ken's giraffish height of six-feet-four. Maddie would have to stand on tiptoes to reach his bellybutton. I realized, miserably, that this Ken Darrel stage might leave permanent, damaging effects on her sensitivity.

Maddie was swooning over a crinkled picture of Ken, his cocky arrogant smile undiminished by the defeat he had just suffered as captain of the football team. The group of deflated egotists, who were his teammates, gallantly held their captain above the reproach that the frustrated sports editor of the Winthrop Herald was at last able to fire at this inviolable hero. But any one of the six or seven loyal Winthropians who had trudged through the drizzling rain to see their school lose again to their ancient enemy, Linton High, would have to agree with the school newspaper; it was King Ken himself who messed up in the last quarter, enabling the city championship to go to Linton for the thirty-ninth year in a row. I just couldn't see Maddie flipping over the captain of a losing team.

"If Kenny's so nuts about me," Maddie was sighing, "then how come Elizabeth Anne Hydride has him wrapped around her little toe?"

"How should I know?" I was getting quite exasperated. "Maybe he has some great affinity for athlete's foot or ringworm!"

"I don't believe it!" said Maddie, her eyeballs rolling in disgust. "You have the most emetic sense of humor of anyone I know!" I purred and got off the floor, unwinding my backbone.

"Seriously," I said, "what are you going to do about Elizabeth?" Maddie's shoulders dejectedly swallowed her head, for Ken's girlfriend, Elizabeth Anne Hydride, had a shapely figure that was Winthrop's answer to Marilyn Monroe. Of course, Winthrop has more than that.

Well, if there is one thing that Winthrop does have, it's school spirit. Like the time the principal liquidated the swimming team because the guys

4

5

EXAMPLE
245

From the portfolio of

Judy Blum

artist-laureate
of the class of '61

26

ber.

The city pavement was warm and
hard after the grass in the park. My
teacher had kept me after school that
day, and the buildings made long shadows against the streets. It was easy to
walk home slowly on a warm day and
think about Kenneth who was my friend,
and the gods and goddesses who had
lives of their own and forced real people
to perform for them.

I saw Kenneth yesterday, for the first
time in many years. It was one o'clock, and a wind blew
the brittle leaves across the grass. I had
two hours to spend before my next class,
and with three notebooks resting against
my arm, I came to the park. I chose a
bench that faced the street, because I
wanted to see the traffic and the people
who hurried through the November
wind.

Very few people come to the park on
windy autumn days. I was quite alone
on the wooden bench with the crisp,
fragile leaves at my feet. The apartment
house across the street was large and
new. Its walls were clean white brick,
and I could see a small part of the lobby
through the enormous glass entrance. I
looked at the glass doorway and at the
two bushes on either side, so different
from the gentle green of the park. Traffic noises rose from the street before me,
and the wind blew scraps of paper
against the stone buildings. Suddenly I
found myself rushing across the street
toward a young man who waited at the
corner.

Kenneth did not recognize me at once.
After several seconds he spoke my name
slowly, and then he introduced me to
the tall blond woman who held his arm.
She was his wife, and she

Postea
by ROBERT SHAPLEY

The street lights outline shadows.
Off across the sky, the crescent
Cups the pool of liquid stillness.
Rhythmic clapping of the brittle leaves
Accompanies the swift thrusts of wind
That grasps and unfolds with cold fingers.

Chill darkness cleanses the walks:
Only here and there the lights
Stretch into night.
Newspapers cartwheel past yellowed buildings.
An insane green is cast on the ground
From hunched streetlamps.

Only in the mind are colors left;
The vapor of a rose
And the touch of a russet leaf
Are fragile shadows of something gone.
Some intense dream that has transpired
Now is fled to this dark awakening.
Avenues are empty,
The lighted houses locked,
Muting other melodies of sensation;
The night envelops and bathes like the surf.
The willow with her arched body
Breathes out a sigh. Swollen silver bells
Ring out lost remembered tones.

Le Sacre
by BARRY LOEWER

Gusts of autumn wind
pile leaves against the summer's ruin.
The trees rage with color
and toss sardonic acorns
on the eager earth.

The door swings open!
It groans an invitation
that entertains our boldest dreams.
'Oh do not hesitate,' it cries.
We ride its wave downward,
turning, turning in the tide of lies.
We cannot hold its breaking fury,
and winter greets our dream's demise.

Design by PHYLLIS KATZ

3 by Jane Dobak
Spring '60

Here are some small reproductions
of original block prints which have
appeared in "Soundings" over the
past twenty-five years.

Block Prints

Sandy Allik   Spring '59

David Fradin   Spring '60   Pat Byrne   Spring '57

layout by Phyllis Katz

The staff. There is greater variety in staff positions on magazines than on papers and yearbooks. This variety may reflect a greater diversity in this field. Responsibility, however, must be designated and the number and nature of positions reflect the size and nature of the magazine. There must be an editor-in-chief, and also a business manager if funds must be raised.

The good editor of the school newspaper is likely to be a good writer, but this is not necessarily true of the magazine editor who is more likely to be collector than producer. The magazine's possible reporters include all the students, and vary from issue to issue.

Staff positions are needed in both literary and art work, and students with interest and talent in these fields are likely to participate. Consequently, it is natural for many staff members to draw upon themselves for content. Good leadership by the faculty advisers is needed to guard against the danger of students outside the project looking upon it as a closed corporation, unsympathetic to their own creative efforts. The success of the magazine depends upon all possible sources of material in the school, for school magazines include essays, short stories, articles, features, poems, sketches, and art work. Some magazines even include original musical compositions.

There is no one best staff organization. Each school must organize its magazine staff according to the demands of its situation. In general, however, there should be an editor-in-chief, a literary editor, a business manager, an art editor, and sufficient staff in each department, including typists. Faculty advisers should be drawn from the English, art, and business departments of the school.

The size of the magazine. A representative sampling of student magazines indicates that the number of pages they contain ranges from a low of thirty-two to a high of eighty, with the typical size being forty-eight pages. The dimensions range from 6 by 8½ inches to 9 by 12 inches, and include every intermediate variation.

Artistic and make-up possibilities are greater in magazines in which page sizes do not exceed 7 by 10 or 7½ by 10½ inches. It becomes difficult in the larger publication to balance art and copy. Furthermore, the balance of facing pages is simpler with smaller pages.

438

Financial support. The limited issue of most magazines yearly reflects lack of financial support rather than lack of good copy. As is true of the newspaper, however, support can be derived from both the sale of the publication and the sale of advertising.

The magazine is better sold by individual copy due to the limited number of issues. Collections should be made before publication date. Some schools, however, find it practical to sell subscriptions for the three or four issues per year at the beginning of the year. Advertising is usually limited to two or three pages at the back of the publication. However, owing to the longer life of the magazine as compared with the paper, higher rates may be charged per column inch.

One more detail. The magazine must include sufficient information about the school and the publication, including the names of the city, the school, the staff, and the frequency of issue. Much that appears in the newspaper mast belongs in the magazine.

Some miscellaneous pointers. The following are a few of the many details that students must consider in the publication of a magazine:

1. All contributions must carry the names of the authors and artists.

2. The standard of work selected for print must be kept at the desired level. It is better to issue an excellent smaller magazine than an inferior larger one.

3. The magazine must interest the students as well as the contributors.

4. There is no preferred number of issues a year. Three or four a year are common, but in the beginning, one or two well done would be better than three or four poorly prepared. Quality always comes before quantity. If the school has a good newspaper, two magazines might satisfy the literary need. If no paper exists, four or six magazines with a broader editorial base would be preferable. This is a matter for each school, depending upon its local conditions, to decide.

5. The material must be well edited and well proofread. Good grammar, punctuation, and spelling are required, for the publication is the school's best effort in educational attainment. (See pages 204 through 220.)

6. Good taste in the selection of material is essential at all times.

7. There must be a good working relationship between the art staff and the literary staff. One type of work balances and contributes to the other.

8. Utmost care should be taken in the title page. Among other things, the reader should be able to find the name of the school and its address, the volume and number, the frequency of publication, the price, and the staff and advisers. The table of contents is an essential feature.

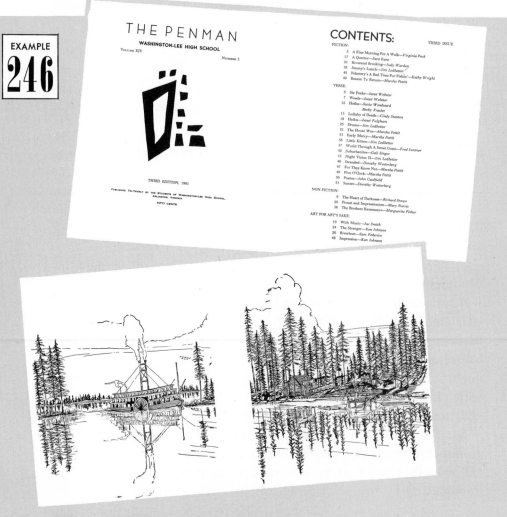

9. The magazine should open with some of the outstanding literary and art work—putting the magazine's "best foot forward."

10. Advertisements, in layout and typography, must maintain the magazine's artistic standards. Neglect in the proper presentation of advertisements will nullify the publication's other accomplishments.

In school magazine work, just as in other publication endeavor, one of the best helps is the study of good examples. There are two sources: the magazines on the newsstand and those that are being issued by schools.

EXAMPLE
247

The Penman
Washington-Lee High School
Arlington, Virginia

EXAMPLE
248

442

The Musician

Eyes? Yes, they are really eyes, not merely seeing, but seeing through and through; they're dark and discerning and soft and angry and loving. They see life, those velvet black probes peering from behind the blackrimmed, pendantic glasses. They can grow hard with anger or tender with love, and all behind the black-rimmed glasses.

The cheeks, so gaunt, are covered with the bristly stubble of black beard. High cheekbones protrude from the sunken skin—rugged and defiant. The thick black mane of hair is uncut and wild—defiance, defiance, always defiance.

The hands of a musician—long, thin, tapering fingers ending in hard, long nails grown from long, delicate hands. These are purposeful hands, musical hands, expressive, emotional hands. They evoke music from the strings of the guitar, wringing from the steel all the emotions of the player. The fingers vibrate with the strings to the sad sounds of Flamenco; they whip across the strings in savage fury to the tunes of social protest; they caress the strings with tender songs of love. These hands express love, anger, sadness and joy all through the music.

The mouth is the outlet for the thoughts which whirl furiously in the turbulent brain. The thin, tight lips grow tighter to scream anger with society or to argue. They smile with happiness to sing or joke; they tremble with emotion or sad music. They laugh—oh, that laugh—deep throated, of the cynic, but these are lips which must not always show cynicism—they need to show hope and love and laughter and music.

This is the musician, sensitive to the very nerves in his fingertips. Aweful and beautiful and emotional and deep. This musician—so much a part of his music—the music he loves.

SUSAN GORDON

After This—What?

Disenchanted
he floated
by his childhood
in great slowmotion strides,
past
empty names
with cobwebbed corners
where ghosts of ideals
mocked
so softly
through dusty panes
showing dimly, dirty rooms.

RANDY WATSON

9

Ye Who Enter...

FRANCINE BRECHER

"The whole world's a farce," Mark thought with overpowering disdain, as he trudged along the straight, narrow path. Bare and bitterly frigid mountains surrounded him. "Just like life," he thought, "destitute of everything. Where is that Garden of Eden Bible talks about, or is it a fake like everything else?"

The path rounded into a curve, then branched off abruptly into a fork. After a moment's deliberation he turned left, shrugging to indicate the irrelevance of his course. He cared not where he went. Following the path for a while, soon he realized he was approaching the end. Suddenly Mark stopped, transfixed by the sight laying before him. Between the mountains, as if from nowhere, appeared a valley. Everywhere trees were laden with every variety of fruit. The omnipresent sun shone brighty, revealing a velvet-like carpet of grass adorned with splendid delicacies.

Mark leaped into the air, let out a whoop of ecstasy, and then bolted toward the entrance. Then he saw a gate blocking passage to this coveted land. Observing a huge lock secured to the gate, he made an attempt to jump over it. As he jumped, the barrier seemed to become an unconquerable being, ascending just beyond his reach. It was almost as though some unseen being were trying to warn him against entering.

He was not going to be deterred so easily. While contemplating his next plan of action, Mark noticed a sign tacked on the gate. "ABANDON ALL HOPE YE WHO ENTER HERE".

"Ha," he thought. "This is just another ruse to prevent my happiness. This time they're not going to do it. I'm too intelligent to be deceived. Couldn't they think of something less preposterous?" As he thought this, the lock fell from the gate. He entered.

For a moment he was spellbound by what lay before him; but as Mark was not one to be overwhelmed by anything, he dispensed with this attitude at once.

"All alone in a valley," he thought triumphantly, "which leaves nothing to be desired." And with that in mind, he began to indulge in all this paradise offered. As he walked along the path, he came upon a lavish banquet prepared for one. "Why, this must have been intended for me," he gloated. About to partake of his entree, he saw a hostel of the most beautiful, alluring women he had ever seen, offering him champagne, sparkling burgundy, and exquisite liqueurs.

Mark basked in luxury, drinking and consuming until he could hold no more. Then, with one girl on each knee, he complacently watched the dancing girls perform for him. He was a king.

Every day Mark wandered further into this bewitching land, following the path and indulging in the splendor of his Utopia. One day Mark was overcome by the sensation that the farther he travelled the smaller the valley got. At first consoled himself with the fact that it was an illusion, but soon he was no longer able to deny to himself that the walls of the valley were closing in. One wall was time, the other retribution.

Finally Mark was enclosed in a space no larger than a closet. Then he saw another gate, his means of escape! "I outsmarted everyone," he thought. The next moment his exultance changed to fear. So big and fat was he, that he could not squeeze his bulk through the small space. He swung around to run back, but alas, there were too many people behind him!

◆

Art's free expression of feeling,
Often leaves some people reeling.
But who is to say
that the paints of today
Should have been put on the ceiling.

DIANE SOVIK

21

CHAPTER LABORATORY

1. If your school issues a magazine, analyze a typical issue by determining the amount allocated to prose, poetry, art, advertising, and other material. Suggest improvements, if any are needed.

2. Study the magazine's budget and suggest improvements in financing and expenditure.

3. Analyze the artistic appearance of the publication, pointing out weaknesses, strengths, and possible changes.

4. Make a preliminary plan for a thirty-six-page school magazine; consider the type of magazine, the format, types of copy, amount of advertising, etc.

5. If your school has a magazine, discuss its staff plan in class. If not, plan a staff organization for a magazine to serve your school.

6. Analyze in class a collection of magazines from other schools.

7. From the examples in this chapter, select the best-appearing pages and explain their merits.

8. Write a story or a poem or draw something suitable for your school magazine. Do your very best work.

9. Examine an issue of your magazine, analyze the advertising, and suggest improvements.

10. How many publications should a school the size of yours be able to support? If your school is not up to this standard, explain why in class discussion. Each student should prepare his notes in advance.

27 THE SCHOOL PRESS ASSOCIATIONS

Behind every good high school publication is a competent faculty adviser, and behind every good faculty adviser is the leadership and support of a least one national school press association. The vast network of student publications, extending from coast to coast, is serviced by four such professional power plants. They are, by date of establishment: The National Scholastic Press Association, 1921, University of Minnesota; The Columbia Scholastic Press Association, 1924, Columbia University; Quill and Scroll, 1926, State University of Iowa; and the Catholic School Press Association, 1931, Marquette University.

These school press associations publish four press magazines that are subscribed to by over thirty thousand and read by at least ten times that many student editors and reporters. The four associations claim ten thousand member schools and are buttressed by two active national associations of faculty advisers. Thus these four organizations move ahead as a continuous influence for better student journalism. They have served in this capacity for years, and much of the progress of the school press must be attributed to them. Beginning on a modest scale, their offices have expanded with the phenomenal expansion of student publications. Their services are so rich and varied that only direct contact with their respective headquarters can produce a complete picture, and thus only the high points of their history and service will be touched upon in this chapter, in order of their foundation.

THE NATIONAL SCHOLASTIC PRESS ASSOCIATION

History. The National Scholastic Press Association was founded on April 22, 1921, at the University of Wisconsin by 126 editors and faculty advisers of school publications. At its fall meeting it adopted the name Central Inter-Scholastic Press Association. When Professor E. Marion Johnson, instrumental in its founding, moved to the University of Minnesota as head of the department of journalism in the fall of 1926, the Association's headquarters were also moved, and have remained there since.

In March 1928, the name was changed to National Scholastic Press Association because of the national expansion of membership. In 1933 it was decided to conduct all college-newspaper activities independently of the high school group. Accordingly, the Associated Collegiate Press was formed. College yearbooks and magazines, however, remained under the jurisdiction of the parent organization; The director of NSPA is also the director of ACP.

Services. The purpose of the Association is to promote cooperative effort by scholastic editors to improve school publications, to better serve the cause of education and the individual institutions they represent. To make this possible it offers the following among its varied services:

1. A semi-annual critical analysis of school newspapers and an annual critical analysis of yearbooks and magazines are offered to member publications. With the aid of competent judges and comprehensive guidebooks, each member publication receives constructive criticism based on writing, editing, content, and make-up. This activity is called the All-American Critical Service. Deadlines for these services are December 15 and May 15 for high school newspapers;

445

January 15 and June 1 for college newspapers; June 15 for all magazines, and June 15 for spring yearbooks. Summer and fall yearbooks are judged as late entries.

For judging, publications are grouped according to size of school and frequency and method of publication. Since the Association was founded, more than 85,000 publications have received this critical analysis. Ratings are given to all publications entered. Scorebooks and certificates for framing are sent to every entry after judging is completed. Ratings are: All American, First Class, Second Class, Third Class, and Fourth Class (no honor certificate).

2. A mimeographed or printed bulletin of publication suggestions called *Helps* is sent periodically to member publications. Separate editions are published for newspapers, magazines, and yearbooks. College newspapers do not receive this service but instead are furnished the Feature Service, a semi-monthly news-feature release, and the Business Review, an idea exchange for business managers which is published six times during the school year.

3. A loan service of outstanding student publications is available at NSPA headquarters.

4. Two publications conferences and short courses, one for NSPA and one for ACP, are held each year in the fall. These meetings bring publication experts to the school press through round-table discussions and lectures.

5. Publications may submit their individual problems to the Association staff for consideration.

6. Help is extended to state and regional scholastic press associations as well as to other groups interested in the advancement of scholastic journalism.

7. Research studies into scholastic publishing are conducted.

8. Guide books covering the basic steps in scholastic publishing are provided all member publications.

9. A continuous service is provided for those newspaper and magazine staffs who wish to receive immediate, issue-by-issue criticism of their publications.

10. The Association serves as an outlet for some textbooks, awards, and other specialized material for scholastic publications.

Membership. All high school or college publications are eligible for membership in NSPA and ACP. Membership is by publication, not by school. Dues payable annually are as follows: high school newspapers, $9.50; college newspapers, $13.00; high school yearbooks, $10.00; college yearbooks, $11.00; magazines (all) $7.50. Newspapers are judged twice a year. Continuous service and loan service are on a membership-plus-extra-fee basis. Continuous service fees for newspapers are as follows: criticism of one issue, $2.50; three issues, $6.00; five issues, $10.00; each additional issue, $2.00 each.

The Scholastic Editor. This magazine is the official organ of NSPA. It is published at NSPA headquarters monthly from October to June inclusive. Subscription rates are $4.00 for one year, $7.00 for two years. Individual copies may be purchased for 50 cents. The magazine was founded in 1921; it now has a circulation of 4,000 with an estimated readership of 40,000 student journalists. (See Example 249.)

Scholastic Roto is a rotogravure picture supplement published for high school student newspapers monthly from September through May (except for January). Information about it may be obtained by writing to NSPA. (See Example 250.)

Collegiate Digest is a monthly rotogravure picture supplement for college newspapers published from October through June. Information about it may be obtained by writing to ACP.

National Association of Journalism Directors. This is an organization of "publication directors of journalism—editorial, business, printing, and art, in public, private, and parochial secondary schools; in junior colleges and in teachers colleges." It is an affiliate of NSPA, National Education Association, and the National Council of Teachers of English. The purposes of NAJD are to function in joint operation with NSPA; to offer a forum for the interchange of plans pertaining to school publications; to present a pattern for the ideals of student journalism in America; to encourage student publications to develop a sense of responsibility and moral obligation not only to the school but also to the community, in both school and civic affairs; to spread information on the professional status of advisers through summer courses, through actual work on commercial publications, or through

EXAMPLE
249

The SCHOOL
PRESS REVIEW ★

DECEMBER, 1960

THE NATIONAL MAGAZINE FOR ALL STUDENT PUBLICATIONS

SCHOLASTIC EDITOR

41st Year of Publication

OFFICIAL ORGAN OF THE N.S.F.A. AND N.A.J.D.

NOVEMBER 1961

**All American
Newspaper
Ratings**

**Pros and Cons
Of Critical
Services**

**How to Keep
Your Readers
Reading**

THE
CATHOLIC
SCHOOL

EDITOR

VOLUME XXX   NUMBER TWO   JANUARY, 1961

Quill and Scroll

INTERNATIONAL HONORARY SOCIETY FOR HIGH SCHOOL JOURNALISTS

LESLIE G. MOELLER
Directs Education for Journalism
(Story on Page 8)

APRIL-MAY, 1960

PRICE THIRTY-FIVE CENTS

writing for publications; and to further the understanding of school administrators and the community with the work, plans, and hopes of the students.

Annual dues are $2.00 and may be sent to NSPA.

Address. National Scholastic Press Association or Associated Collegiate Press, 18 Journalism Building, University of Minnesota, Minneapolis 14, Minnesota.

THE COLUMBIA SCHOLASTIC PRESS ASSOCIATION

History. The Columbia Scholastic Press Association was organized at Columbia University in the fall of 1924, as an outgrowth of several annual gatherings of the editors of secondary-school publications in the New York metropolitan area.

Dr. Joseph M. Murphy has served as director from its inception, with time out for military service from 1942 to 1946 and again from 1951 to 1953. The Association is sponsored by the University, and the Board of Governors includes the president and other administrative officials.

The first contest for newspapers was held in 1925 with 179 entries, and the first convention held that year attracted 308 delegates. Today the convention, held each March, draws approximately 5000 delegates, and over 1700 publications are entered for rating. The Judging of yearbooks was added in 1935 with 105 entries. Today over 1500 books are served each year, and an October conference draws over 1300 participants.

There are "divisions" which have been organized to serve special groups, such as private schools, junior high schools, and others, in addition to the basic program which is built around the high school. Each division is headed by an adviser chosen by the member schools. These chairmen, the officers of the Advisers Association, and the Director together determine the policies and handle the business of the Association.

There are score books covering newspapers, magazines, duplicated publications, and yearbooks. Score sheets have been issued for ele-

449

mentary newspapers and magazines and for foreign language publications. Rating is based on a 1000-point scoring system.

Services. Among the services that CSPA offers are the following:

1. An annual contest or rating of newspapers, magazines, and yearbooks that are members of the Association. A recent contest included publications from 49 states, the District of Columbia, Puerto Rico, Okinawa, Canada, the Philippines, Thailand, and American dependents' schools in Japan, France, Germany, and Spain.

Newspapers are entered in December, magazines in January, and yearbooks in July. Publications are grouped according to school types and sizes for judging. "Medalist" honors go to the publications of "distinction" selected in limited numbers from those making first place. Ratings, according to scores, are first, second, third, and fourth place. "All-Columbian" honors are given to one outstanding newspaper in each of the following fields: heads, news stories, sports, editorials, features, creative literary work, and advertising. The honors for magazines are for typography, general layout, stories and essays, editorials, verse, features, creative work, and art and illustrations. In all classes but fourth, certificates bearing embossed gold, silver, and bronze seals are awarded.

2. In addition to the ratings just mentioned, additional critical service can be secured at any time upon payment of a special fee.

3. The Association issues from time to time publication aids, such as a style book, proofreaders' cards, humor hints, and sports writing hints, as well as the series of score books that serve the rating program.

4. The annual convention is set up as a short course in journalism for the delegates. Well-known journalists and publishers deliver talks and give advice to the delegates, supplemented by leading advisers in the school publication field.

5. Other awards are made from time to time. For instance, in cooperation with the Writer's Club of Columbia University, three medals are awarded annually for the best poem, story, and article published in a member publication during the year. In other such programs CSPA works with associations to advance publication work and to develop the civic consciousness of the editors.

EXAMPLE
250

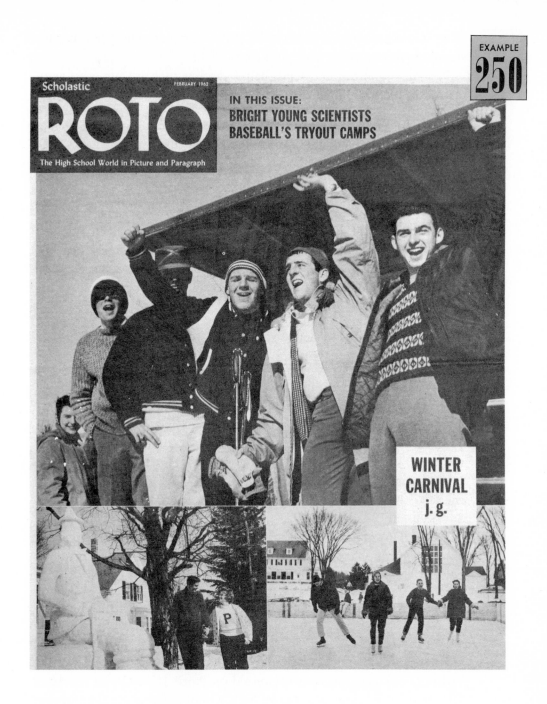

Scholastic
FEBRUARY 1962

ROTO

The High School World in Picture and Paragraph

IN THIS ISSUE:
BRIGHT YOUNG SCIENTISTS
BASEBALL'S TRYOUT CAMPS

WINTER
CARNIVAL
j. g.

451

6. Gold keys are awarded each year to advisers who perform outstanding work in the school publication field.

7. The organization extends help to groups such as state press associations interested in student journalism.

Publication. The 1925 convention voted to establish *The School Press Review* as the official organ. Individual subscriptions are $2.50, which is included in the membership fee of the publications. The *Review* is issued monthly, October to May inclusive, its circulation exceeding 3,400.

Membership. Membership is by publication, not by school. Each pays $8.00 as it enters the annual contest, $2.50 of which goes for the magazine subscription. Since the Association is maintained through the sale of publications, convention fees, and membership fees, the latter are adjusted from time to time.

Address. Columbia Scholastic Press Association, Columbia University, Box 11, Low Memorial Library, New York City.

Advisers Association. The CSPA Advisers Association is an autonomous organization of teacher-advisers, holding its annual meeting in the spring at the New York convention. The dues of $1.50 may be paid with the publication fee. The organization, with over 2000 members, is centered in CSPA headquarters, but its funds are maintained separately. Officers are elected biennially, a quarterly bulletin is issued, and most recently a study guide, *Springboard to Journalism,* has been published.

The Advisers Association strives to keep school publication work strictly educational, free from entanglements, amateur in spirit and content, and avocational in nature.

QUILL AND SCROLL

History. Quill and Scroll, the international honorary society for high school journalists, was organized on April 10, 1926, at the State University of Iowa by a group of high school advisers for the purpose of encouraging and rewarding *individual* achievement in journalism, creative writing, and school publications.

Since that time, charters have been granted to more than 8,000 high schools in every state of the Union and in more than a score of countries on every continent. Approximately 500,000 high school journalists have been admitted to membership. Because of the size of the organization, national conventions have not been held since the early years of the Society's history. Many state and regional press conventions provide special sessions for Quill and Scroll members.

Membership. Charters are granted to schools rather than to publications, and individual membership in the Society is obtained only through these local chapters. When a charter is granted, the advisers to publications automatically become members of Quill and Scroll.

A student journalist may become a member if he meets the following requirements:

1. He must be a junior or senior.
2. He must be in the upper third of his class in general scholastic standing.
3. He must have done superior work in some phase of journalism or school publication work, such as writing, editing, business management, or production.
4. He must be recommended by his adviser and approved by the executive secretary of the Society.

Students doing creditable work in poetry, essays, or other forms of creative writing are eligible for membership, as well as the regular staff members of all publications of the school.

Each school establishing a chapter is sent a copy of the chapter manual, which contains the constitution and bylaws, suggestions for chapter programs, and activities and suggested initiation services. Initiations may be held at any time of the year. Many schools conduct initiations several times during the year, whenever a new group of candidates becomes eligible for membership. No particular number of students is required to organize a chapter, and there is no limit to the number that may be admitted in any one year. Membership is restricted only by the membership requirements.

To be eligible for a Quill and Scroll charter, a high school must publish a newspaper, a yearbook, or a magazine considered of sufficient merit by the executive council. Schools where students gather and write news under supervision for regular town or city newspapers are also eligible to join, as are those having mimeographed papers.

There are no annual dues, either for the chapter or for the individual members. A school pays a charter fee of $5.00 when it is granted a charter. When a candidate is accepted for membership, he pays a basic initiation fee of $2.50. The Society provides each new member with a gold badge and a year's subscription to *Quill and Scroll* magazine.

Services. The Society offers an annual critical service for newspapers, evaluating the publications for schools throughout the country. Ratings are given on the basis of points earned through a comprehensive analysis of all phases of the newspaper. The highest rating "The Gallup Award" (named for George H. Gallup, one of the society's founders), is an honor coveted by any school.

Quill and Scroll conducts various contests in which national winners are selected and awarded national-award gold keys. The Society is also active in promoting observance of National Newspaper Week in high schools.

Through the Quill and Scroll Foundation, a number of Edward J. Nell (for twenty-five years executive secretary of the Society) Memorial Scholarships in Journalism, valued at $500 each, are awarded each year. The Foundation also sponsors research and special studies in scholastic journalism and publishes a number of booklets dealing with school publications.

Quill and Scroll magazine is issued four times a year and has a circulation in excess of 25,000. It is devoted entirely to scholastic journalism, school publications, and information concerning the program and the various activities of the Society. The subscription costs $1.25 per year.

Quill and Scroll works closely with state high school press associations as well as with professional journalism organizations in a continuing program to improve scholastic journalism.

454

Address. Quill and Scroll Society, School of Journalism, State University of Iowa, Iowa City, Iowa.

CATHOLIC SCHOOL PRESS ASSOCIATION

History. Since 1931 the Catholic School Press Association, with headquarters at Marquette University, has provided services to publication staffs in Catholic high schools and colleges. More than a thousand members now avail themselves of the benefits furnished by the Association.

Services. The Association offers the following services to members:

1. Each member newspaper and magazine receives a criticism once each semester on its editorial content, typography, headlines, art work, and style.

2. Magazines, newspapers, and yearbooks are judged in an annual survey and rating. "All Catholic," "First Honors," and "Publications of Distinction" certificates are awarded. A rating sheet indicating the weak and strong points of the publication is sent to the adviser.

3. The Catholic School Editor is published in November, January, March, and June. In it are printed contest results, survey and rating results, and notes on member press activities, as well as articles on journalism.

4. Each year prizes are awarded for the best student writing printed in member publications in the fields of reporting, editorial, article, feature, short story, and poetry in high school and college divisions. Prizes also are awarded for the best photograph by a student published during the previous year and for the best published student art work.

5. A style book is available at 25 cents per copy.

6. A distinctive insignia printing plate for its masthead is sent to each member publication upon request.

7. Pins or keys are available for students who do outstanding work on publications while maintaining high scholastic averages.

8. National conventions are held in Milwaukee every other year. Sectional meetings are held on alternate years.

The membership fee of $5.00 for each publication includes all services listed above.

Address. Catholic School Press Association, 552 N. 13 Street, Milwaukee, Wisconsin.

OTHER SOURCES OF LEADERSHIP

Throughout the country, state school press associations take part in the progress of student journalism. Since a permanent office staff is usually impossible, they are often centered in college or university departments of journalism. A few energetic faculty sponsors who teach high school journalism as a profession can make the difference between an effective state organization and one that exists in name only.

In some of the larger metropolitan areas, a local newspaper sponsors an annual weekend clinic for student editors. The cooperation of a few schools with an interested daily newspaper can build such a clinic into a real journalistic asset.

Although some schools are too small to provide such a course in journalism, the publication of a good school paper is best assured when journalism is included as a regular subject. The daily period permits instruction in the basic principles of newswriting often neglected when the paper is an exclusively after-school activity.

More and more, summer-study opportunities are being provided on campus for high school editors and faculty advisers.

Teacher-study programs. A few years ago the *Wall Street Journal* established the Newspaper Fund to promote journalism by means of teacher fellowships. The Fund recognizes (1) the importance of good high school publications in promoting journalism as a career, and (2) the teacher as the key to quality student journalism.

At its inception in 1959, summer study fellowships were granted to 131 teachers from 42 states. The second year the Fund made similar grants to 316 teachers from 49 states, and gave more limited assistance to 100 others. The program keeps growing in popularity. Stipends cover room, board, tuition, incidental expenses, and in many instances travel.

456

Summer study for students. The significance of high school journalism is also recognized by colleges and universities across the nation. The continuous improvement in the student press reflects the summer study opportunities offered to student editors as well as to faculty advisers. Such workshops, ranging from one to five weeks, are now offered annually on more than thirty campuses.

The pioneer program, the National Institute for High School Journalists, was held in 1930 by the Medill School of Journalism of Northwestern University. It has drawn its participants from the high schools of every state in the Union. Ohio University at Athens, Ohio, draws as many as 1400 students to its intensive, one-week publication workshop.

Among the other institutions providing these annual institutions or workshops are Texas Technological College, the State University of Iowa, Syracuse University, Michigan State University, the University of Michigan, the University of Wisconsin, the University of Southern California, and Brigham Young University.

All aspects of student publication work are covered. Besides professional journalism teachers, leadership is provided by prominent editors and stimulating lecturers on current affairs. State press associations, local newspapers, and similar agencies cooperate with the colleges in sponsoring these programs. Lester G. Benz, editor of *Quill and Scroll,* says of the value of such workshops:

(1) They stimulate enthusiasm and help build high morale on the publication staff;

(2) they serve to popularize journalism and publications work, thereby attracting more capable students to serve on the staffs;

(3) they improve the quality of student publications; and

(4) they help stimulate student interest in journalism as a career.

The interest of the management of *Quill and Scroll* in these summer study programs for teachers and students marks that society as a good source of continued information on this subject.

ATTITUDE TOWARD CONTESTS

National press associations have contributed heavily to the constant progress of student journalism. However, a question still remains— What is to be gained by entering a particular contest?

457

Publication staffs should have a definite reason for entering contests; the winning of honors is not sufficient in itself. The paper that wins high honors should determine why it wins them; the paper that does not win high honors should study its weaknesses. The contest, although it has led many a paper to improvement, must not be the sole motivation for a better school publication. Each school's situation, reader interest, and service to school and community should be the primary incentives in publishing a school paper, and the contest should be a means to this end. Only then, through the ratings and other services of worthy press associations, is it time to evaluate the publication in respect to good student journalism the country over.

Andrew Carnegie is quoted as having said that he knew nothing about making profits, he only knew how to make steel. The school newspaper staff should not be concerned about the winning of contests; it need only know how to edit a good school paper.

Student press associations are service organizations; the rating of papers is one of their most valuable services. The paper that can obtain membership in the large national associations enlists invaluable help. The staff can even base its study of the publication upon the rating books used in the contests.

The staff that wants to move ahead should—
1. hold membership in at least two national press associations.
2. submit its publications for annual rating.
3. read the magazines and other bulletins of the associations as they arrive, and use them as the basis of discussions on how to improve the local publications.
4. actively participate in state or regional school press associations if they exist.
5. send representatives annually to a national press convention if at all possible. A local daily paper might sponsor such a project, or money can be raised by special events.
6. secure the help of professional journalists on the local daily papers, in speaking to the staff, judging the quality of stories, and giving other types of advice.

Help is at hand in any school locality, but the staff must take time to make an inventory of the sources.

458

CHAPTER LABORATORY

1. Have the editor of your paper explain to the class your school's membership in press associations, costs, services secured, etc.
2. If a staff member has ever attended a national convention of student journalists, have him discuss the experience with your group.
3. As a class, study the last score books received by your school paper from the critical services to which it subscribed. Discuss the paper's strong and weak points as revealed in the ratings.
4. As an individual project, present a proposal for the improvement of the paper based on one of the foregoing criticisms.
5. Does your paper hold membership in a state press association? If so, what are the services of this organization? How do they compare with those of the national groups?
6. Four class members should present a panel discussion of the advisability of holding membership in national and state associations at the same time.
7. What are the leading differences among the national press magazines? How does your school make use of these magazines?
8. Select a topic for an article that you might write for one of these magazines, and prepare an outline of the article. Discuss these ideas in class.
9. In class discussion, consider the possibility of a local newspaper sponsoring an annual student-press clinic for a day.
10. Consider ways in which your local paper might be induced to send delegates to a national convention? Discuss in class.

Newspaper Glossary

Ad: abbreviation for *advertisement*

Add: additional material for a story already written or in type

Advance: a story of an event written before it takes place

Assignment: a specific story allotted to a reporter to be covered

Bank: one section of a headline; often called *deck*

Banner: a headline extending across the top of the page; streamer

Beat: usually called *scoop*—a story published in one paper ahead of the others

Beat: a particular territory to which a reporter is assigned to cover the news regularly; also *run*

B.f.: boldface or black-face type

Box: story enclosed by rules or other border; heads are also sometimes boxed

Break (v.): News is said to break when it is made known for publication

Break (n.): The break in a story is the point at which it is continued to another column or page

Bulletin: a brief telegraphic news item giving the bare essentials with no details

Bulldog or *bullpup:* the early edition of the Sunday paper mailed to distant points

By-line: a line at the beginning of a story giving the name of the person by whom it was written

Caps: indicates type to be set in capital letters, also known as "upper case" letters. THIS LINE IS SET IN CAPS.

Caps and l.c.: Capitals and lower case, indicates the main words of the head to be capitalized, all other letters to be small (lower case). This Line Is Set Caps and Lower Case.

Caps and small caps: capitals and small capitals. THIS LINE IS SET CAPS AND SMALL CAPS.

Caption: the heading printed over or under a cut

Case: a partitioned shallow box that holds type

Chase: a metal frame into which type and cuts are placed and locked for printing or stereotyping

City room: This phrase once meant the room of a newspaper office where just the city news was handled, but now it usually refers to the complete editorial room or newsroom.

Color: To put color into a story is to enliven it with atmosphere to create reader interest. To exaggerate the facts is to color the news.

460

Column: a vertical division of a page set off by rules. Most daily papers are eight columns wide

Column: a regular feature of a paper written regularly by one writer and carrying his name.

Column rule: a rule used to separate columns

Combination head: blanket, spread, or canopy head. A head, the first deck of which extends over related stories, and possibly a cut

Composing room: the room in which the type is set in preparation for printing

Composite story: a story having many related incidents, each of which might be handled by a different reporter

Condensed type: a type face thin compared with its height, once popular in headlines but now criticized because of difficulty in reading it

Copy: manuscript prepared by the reporter for publication

Copy desk: the table at which copy is read and headlines prepared

Copyreader: one who works at a copy desk

Correspondent: a reporter working outside the city in which his paper is published

Cover: To cover a story is to collect all available information about the event and then to write the story

Credit line: a line on a story or picture acknowledging the courtesy of another publication for its use

Cropping: to mark for reproduction only the central essential features of a photograph

Crossline: a deck of a head made up of a single line

Crusade: a campaign conducted by a newspaper to further a particular cause, such as a safety campaign

Cub: a beginning reporter

Cut (n.): an engraving, etching, or wood block from which a picture is printed. A newspaper picture itself is often called a cut.

Cut (v.): To cut a story is to shorten it by eliminating unnecessary words or lines.

Cut-line: the explanation under a cut; as the person's name

Cutoff rule: a metal rule used to separate stories, ads, cuts, and stories, or other composition units

Cutoff test: A news story that "stands the cutoff test" is one written with the least significant events at the end so that they may be cut without spoiling the effect.

Dash: a horizontal rule used between decks of a head and between stories

Datebook: an assignment editor's book in which are recorded future news events; future book

Dateline: the line at the beginning of a story giving the town and the date

Dead: said of type or copy that is of no further use

Deadline: the time after which no copy can be received for a particular edition

Deck: a division of a headline; also called *bank*

Dingbats: small metal ornaments occasionally used for decorative purposes, as below the streamer

Display type: type faces that are bolder than ordinary type, used especially in advertisements

Distribute: to separate and return type to the proper cases after use in a particular job

Dogwatch: The dogwatch or *lobster trick* refers to the small group left in a news office for emergency after the regular editions have all gone to press and the regular staff has gone home.

Dope: information concerning a coming event

Down style: a newspaper style calling for a minimum use of capital letters; opposite of *up style*

Dress: the make-up of a newspaper, especially the style of type and heads

Drop-line: a headline deck in which all lines are of equal length, each being stepped in a little farther than the previous one; sometimes called *stagger-head*

Dummy: a rough layout of a page, showing approximate location of all copy, head, and cuts. See *Layout.*

Dupe: a story that by mistake appears twice in a paper

Ears: boxes, either ruled or unruled, at the upper corners of the front page, giving weather news, name of edition, or other short announcements

Edition: A newspaper has so many runs of the presses during a day, the papers of a run being an edition, as "home" or "final" edition.

Editorialize: to inject opinion into a news story

Em: a common unit of measurement in typography; a space the width of which is equivalent to the type height

En: a measure of type one half an em

End mark (#): used on copy to indicate end of a story

Exchanges: copies of papers exchanged regularly among schools

Extra: a special edition issued by a newspaper because of important news breaking

Family: A family of type is composed of all the type of a certain design. Goudy, Bodoni, and Cloister are some of the many families.

Feature (n.): A feature story is not written from a news angle, but from a human interest point of view. The feature of a story is the main fact.

Feature (v.): A story or a fact in a story is featured by giving it prominence.

Filler: stories or items of various lengths, with more than news value, kept on hand to fill space

462

Flag: the heading, usually in the upper corner of the editorial page, that gives the name of the publisher, subscription rates, and other information about the paper; also called *masthead*

Flash: an important news item that comes over the press wire

Flush: type set without being indented

Flush left head: a headline, each line of which starts flush with the left side of the column

Fold: the point at which a newspaper page is folded in half

Folio: the page, page number

Follow-up: a story giving new developments or facts about an event, at least one account of which has appeared previously

Font: a complete assortment of type of one size and face

Form: a printing job, such as a newspaper page, completely assembled and locked in a chase ready for printing

Format: the design or arrangement of a publication. See *dummy* and *layout.*

Fourth Estate: refers to the newspaper profession, the press

Future book: an assignment editor's book in which are recorded future news events; also *datebook*

Galley: a tray on which type is placed once it is set

Galley proof: an impression on paper of a galley of type

Ghost writer: a professional writer who writes stories that appear under another's name

Grapevine: a term given to copy on hand that can be used at an indefinite time for filler

Guideline: a keyword placed by a copyreader at the top of each page of a story to aid the compositor

Halftone: a metal plate made from a photograph, ready for printing

Handout: copy prepared for publication, furthering some specific interest, and given to a paper

Hanging indention: a deck of a head the first line of which is set flush on both sides, while all the remaining lines are indented the same distance

Head: headline

Hell box: a box in which dead type is thrown

Hold: an instruction on a piece of copy showing it is to be held for further notice

Hole: a space on a page still to be filled

Human interest: a story appealing to the emotions

Indent: to set copy in a distance from the column margin

Insert: additional copy to be inserted at a specific point in a story

Interview (n.): a story secured by conversing with someone

Interview (v.): to engage someone in conversation for the purpose of securing news

Inverted pyramid: a deck of a head, formed like a pyramid upside down

Italics: type that slants, resembling script. The newspaper terms in this list are set in italics.

Jim dash: a very short dash used between decks of a head

Jump: To continue a story to another page is to jump it.

Jump head: the head on the continuation of a story to another page

Kill: to destroy a story or part of one before it is published

Layout: the plan of a page, an ad, or other item of printing, drawn roughly as a guide

l.c.: abbreviation for lower case, the small letters in a printer's case

Lead (led): a thin strip of metal for spacing out lines of type

Lead (leed): the first paragraph of a newspaper story

Leader: the editorial given first position

Leaders: dots or dashes used to lead the eye across the page, as . . . .

Legend: the explanation that accompanies a cut

Legman: the reporter who gathers the facts for a story

Libel: an untruth published in a paper

Linotype: a typesetting machine that sets solid lines from molten metal

Lower case: the smaller letters in a font

Make-ready: the preparation of a form by the pressman for printing

Make-up: the arrangement of stories, cuts, and heads on a page

Masthead: See *Flag.*

Mat or matrix: a papier-mâché impression of a type form, from which stereotypes are cast

Morgue: collection of cuts and stories in newspaper office kept for possible future use

Must: copy that the head of the paper has ordered must be published

Nameplate: the heading at the top of the front page bearing the paper's name

News-feature: a cross between a straight news and a feature story

No-count head: a headline in which no definite number of units is required and each line of which usually begins flush with the left side of the column

Overbanner: banner printed above the nameplate

Overline: the headline above a picture

Pad: to lengthen a story by elaboration, when the facts at hand don't merit it

Personals: short items about individuals, usually handled as a society-page column

Photo: photograph

Pi: a jumbled mass of type

Play-up: to feature a certain point in a story

Point: the unit of measurement denoting the height of type. 10-point type is two points higher than 8-point type.

Policy: the paper's accepted attitude concerning public questions

Position: A story or cut is said to have a certain position on the page.

Proof: an inked impression taken from composed type for the purpose of determining errors

Proofreader: one who reads proof and marks errors

Puff: an item disguised as a news story that really furthers the business of some firm

Q and A: question and answer style of writing, used in stories having many questions and answers. Quotation marks are eliminated.

Quads: pieces of metal used for spacing in composing type

Quoins: wedges of metal used to fasten type in chases

Quotes: quotation marks. A quote story is one in which a person is frequently quoted.

Railroad: to hasten a story through to the press at the last moment without careful editing

Release: to permit a story to be published at a certain date

Reporter: one who gathers and writes up news for a paper

Review: a summary of a book, dramatic production, etc., written for a newspaper

Rewrite: a story rewritten from another published story. The one doing this work is a *rewrite man.*

Rule: a strip of metal with a line as its face used in composition

Run: a specified route a reporter must take daily for gathering news

Run-around: the continuation of a story around a cut that is narrow enough to permit type to be set beside it.

Scoop: a story appearing in one paper before the others get it

Sig cut: cut of signature or name of firm

Slug: a line of type set on a linotype machine

Small caps: capital letters the size of lower case letters. THIS LINE IS SET CAPS AND SMALL CAPS.

Sob story: a story that appeals to the reader's sympathy

Solid: Type set without leading is set solid.

Spacing: the amount of white space between letters or lines of type

Spot news: stories that break unexpectedly

Staff: the personnel that gets out a paper

Standing: refers to type that is left standing to be used again

Stet: written on copy that has been marked for change to indicate that it is to be left as it originally was

Stick: a small hand tray used for setting type

Stone: a steel- or stone-top table on which a printer makes up the pages of a paper

Streamer: See *Banner.*

Stylebook: the printed set of grammatical and typographical rules that a paper has adopted for the sake of uniformity

Subhead: one-line inserts, frequently boldface, used to break up a long story

Suspended interest: A story is said to have suspended interest when the writer intentionally does not satisfy the reader's curiosity until late in the lead or the story.

Take: the portion of a story given to the compositor at one time

Thirty (30): used at the end of a news story to indicate completion. The origin of the term is uncertain.

Tie-in: the section of a follow-up story that tells the reader what has gone before

Time copy: copy that can be used later, sometimes marked A.O.T.—any old time

Tombstone heads: also called *bumped heads;* heads of the same style and type placed side by side, and thus confusing to read

Upper case: capital letters

Up style: a style calling for an extensive use of capitals: opposite of *down style*

W.f.: a proofreader's mark to indicate wrong font, style, or size of letter used

Widow: a line containing less than a full line of type, continuing a story and appearing at the top of a column or page—considered bad typography

Yellow journalism: the practice of coloring the news to make a sensational appeal to public interest

466

Index

467

469